T0214101

Communications
in Computer and Information Science 1247

Commenced Publication in 2007
Founding and Former Series Editors:
Simone Diniz Junqueira Barbosa, Phoebe Chen, Alfredo Cuzzocrea,
Xiaoyong Du, Orhun Kara, Ting Liu, Krishna M. Sivalingam,
Dominik Ślęzak, Takashi Washio, Xiaokang Yang, and Junsong Yuan

More information about this series at http://www.springer.com/series/7899

Mohammad S. Obaidat (Ed.)

E-Business
and Telecommunications

16th International Conference, ICETE 2019
Prague, Czech Republic, July 26–28, 2019
Revised Selected Papers

 Springer

Editor
Mohammad S. Obaidat
Fellow of IEEE, Dean of College
of Computing & Informatics
University of Sharjah
Sharjah, UAE

University of Jordan
Amman, Jordan

University of Science
and Technology Beijing
Beijing, China

ISSN 1865-0929   ISSN 1865-0937 (electronic)
Communications in Computer and Information Science
ISBN 978-3-030-52685-6   ISBN 978-3-030-52686-3 (eBook)
https://doi.org/10.1007/978-3-030-52686-3

This Springer imprint is published by the registered company Springer Nature Switzerland AG
The registered company address is: Gewerbestrasse 11, 6330 Cham, Switzerland

Preface

The present book includes extended and revised versions of a set of selected papers from the 16th International Joint Conference on e-Business and Telecommunications (ICETE 2019), held in Prague, Czech Republic, in the period July 26–28, 2019.

ICETE 2019 received 166 paper submissions from 41 countries, of which 6% were included in this book. The papers were selected by the event chairs and their selection is based on a number of criteria that includes the reviews and suggested comments provided by the Program Committee members, the session chairs' assessments, and also the program chairs' global view of all papers included in the technical program. The authors of selected papers were then invited to submit a revised and extended version of their papers having at least 30% new material.

ICETE 2019 is a joint conference aimed at bringing together researchers, engineers, and practitioners interested in information and communication technologies, including data communication networking, e-business, optical communication systems, security and cryptography, signal processing and multimedia applications, and wireless networks and mobile systems. These are the main knowledge areas that define the six component conferences, namely: DCNET, ICE-B, OPTICS, SECRYPT, SIGMAP, and WINSYS, which together form the ICETE joint conference.

The papers selected and included in this book contribute to the understanding of relevant trends of current research in "Secure and Efficient Matrix Multiplication with MapReduce," "Evaluation of Floating-Point Arithmetic Protocols Based on Shamir Secret Sharing," "Polyphonic Recordings Applied to Single-Channel Audio Source Separation," "Automatic Sleep Scoring Toolbox and Its Application in Sleep Apnea," "Copyright Protection Method for Vector Map Data," "Ways in which Classification and Typification Contribute to Comprehensibility," "Dynamic Taint Tracking Simulation," "Invisible Hybrid 3D Video Watermarking Robust against Malicious Attacks," "Reconfigurable Implementation of Elliptic Curve Cryptography over GF (2^n)," and "Application of Error Detection in Networks by Protocol Behavior Model." They basically cover the areas of ICETE 2019.

We would like to thank all the authors for their contributions and also to the reviewers who helped ensure the quality of this publication.

July 2019   Mohammad S. Obaidat

Organization

Conference Chair

Mohammad S. Obaidat — University of Sharjah, UAE, University of Jordan, Jordan, and University of Science and Technology Beijing, China

Program Co-chairs

DCNET

Christian Callegari — Dip Ing Informaz, Italy

ICE-B

Marten van Sinderen — University of Twente, The Netherlands
Paulo Novais — Universidade do Minho, Portugal

OPTICS

Panagiotis Sarigiannidis — University of Western Macedonia, Greece

SECRYPT

Pierangela Samarati — Università degli Studi di Milano, Italy

SIGMAP

Sebastiano Battiato — University of Catania, Italy
Ángel Serrano Sánchez de León — Universidad Rey Juan Carlos, Spain

WINSYS

Pascal Lorenz — University of Upper Alsace, France
Franco Davoli — University of Genoa, Italy

DCNET Program Committee

Gianni Antichi — Queen Mary University of London, UK
Pablo Belzarena — UdelaR, Uruguay
Valentín Carela-Español — Auvik Networks Inc., Spain
Paolo Castagno — University of Torino, Italy
Zesheng Chen — Purdue University Fort Wayne, USA
Luca Deri — Ntop, Italy
Hiroaki Fukuda — Shibaura Institute of Technology, Japan
Francesco Gringoli — University of Brescia, Italy

Pascal Lorenz	University of Upper Alsace, France
Eliane Martins	Universidade Estadual de Campinas, Brazil
Matteo Sereno	University of Torino, Italy
Giovanni Stea	University of Pisa, Italy
Tatsuya Suda	University Netgroup Inc., USA

DCNET Additional Reviewers

| Gabriel Gomez Sena | Universidad de la República, Uruguay |
| Federico Larroca | Universidad de la República, Uruguay |

ICE-B Program Committee

Andreas Ahrens	Hochschule Wismar, University of Technology, Business and Design, Germany
Dimitris Apostolou	University of Piraeus, Greece
Ana Azevedo	CEOS, ISCAP, PPORTO, Portugal
Efthimios Bothos	Institute of Communication and Computer Systems, Greece
Alexandros Bousdekis	Information Management Unit, National Technical University of Athens, Greece
Rebecca Bulander	Pforzheim University of Applied Science, Germany
Christoph Bussler	Google, Inc., USA
Wojciech Cellary	Poznan University of Economics and Business, Poland
Chun-Liang Chen	National Taiwan University of Arts, Taiwan, China
Dickson Chiu	The University of Hong Kong, Hong Kong
Ritesh Chugh	Central Queensland University, Australia
Michele Colajanni	University of Modena and Reggio Emilia, Italy
Rafael Corchuelo	University of Sevilla, Spain
Mariana Curado Malta	CEOS, Polytechnic of Porto, Portugal
Ioanna Dionysiou	University of Nicosia, Cyprus
Peter Dolog	Aalborg University, Denmark
Inma Hernández	Universidad de Sevilla, Spain
Abderrahmane Leshob	University of Quebec at Montreal, Canada
Olga Levina	FZI Research Center for Information Technology, Germany
Yung-Ming Li	National Chiao Tung University, Taiwan, China
Rungtai Lin	National Taiwan University of Arts, Taiwan, China
Liping Liu	University of Akron, USA
Peter Loos	German Research Center for Artificial Intelligence, Germany
Babis Magoutas	Information Management Unit, National Technical University of Athens, Greece
Wilma Penzo	University of Bologna, Italy
Ruben Pereira	ISCTE, Portugal
Krassie Petrova	Auckland University of Technology, New Zealand

Agostinho Pinto	CEOS, ISCAP, PPORTO, Portugal
Charmaine Plessis	University of South Africa, South Africa
Pak-Lok Poon	Central Queensland University, Australia
Ela Pustulka-Hunt	FHNW Olten, Switzerland
Manuel Resinas	Universidad de Sevilla, Spain
Fernando Romero	University of Minho, Portugal
Jarogniew Rykowski	Poznan University of Economics and Business, Poland
Ahm Shamsuzzoha	University of Vaasa, Finland
Hassan Sleiman	Renault Group, France
Riccardo Spinelli	Università degli Studi di Genova, Italy
Zhaohao Sun	PNG University of Technology, Papua New Guinea, and Federation University Australia, Australia
James Thong	Hong Kong University of Science and Technology, Hong Kong
Ben van Lier	Centric, The Netherlands
Alfredo Vellido	Universitat Politècnica de Catalunya (UPC), Spain
Yiannis Verginadis	ICCS, National Technical University of Athens, Greece

ICE-B Additional Reviewers

Patrick Lübbecke	German Research Center for Artificial Intelligence GmbH, Germany

OPTICS Program Committee

Siti Barirah Ahmad Anas	Universiti Putra Malaysia, Malaysia
Tiago Alves	Instituto Superior Técnico, Instituto de Telecomunicações, Portugal
Nicola Andriolli	Scuola Superiore Sant'Anna, Italy
Gaetano Assanto	Università degli Studi Roma Tre, Italy
Hercules Avramopoulos	National Technical University of Athens, Greece
Adolfo Cartaxo	Instituto de Telecomunicações, ISCTE - Instituto Universitário de Lisboa, Portugal
C. Chow	National Chiao Tung University, Taiwan, China
Giampiero Contestabile	Scuola Superiore Sant'Anna, Italy
Bernard Cousin	University of Rennes 1, France
Fred Daneshgaran	California State University, Los Angeles, USA
Marija Furdek	Chalmers University of Technology, Sweden
Marco Genovese	INRIM, Italy
Habib Hamam	Université de Moncton, Canada
Sang-Kook Han	Yonsei University, South Korea
Nicholas Ioannides	London Metropolitan University, UK
Miroslaw Klinkowski	National Institute of Telecommunications, Poland
Koteswararao Kondepu	Scuola Superiore Sant'Anna, Italy
Guo-Wei Lu	Tokai University, Japan
Lenin Mehedy	IBM Research, Australia

Tetsuya Miyazaki	National Institute of Information and Communications, Japan
Maria Morant	Universitat Politècnica de València, Spain
John Moscholios	University of Peloponnese, Greece
Masayuki Murata	Osaka University, Japan
Syed Murshid	Florida Institute of Technology, USA
Scott Newman	Optiwave, Canada
Yasutake Ohishi	Research Center for Advanced Photon Technology, Japan
Satoru Okamoto	Keio University, Japan
Albert Pagès	Universitat Politècnica de Catalunya (UPC), Spain
Jordi Perelló	Universitat Politècnica de Catalunya (UPC), Spain
João Rebola	Instituto de Telecomunicações, ISCTE-IUL, Portugal
Shaymaa Riyadh Tahhan	Al-Nahrain University, Iraq
Enrique Rodriguez-Colina	Universidad Autónoma Metropolitana, Mexico
Mehdi Shadaram	The University of Texas at San Antonio, USA
Salvatore Spadaro	Universitat Politecnica de Catalunya (UPC), Spain
Ripalta Stabile	Eindhoven University of Technology, The Netherlands
Takuo Tanaka	RIKEN, Japan
Bal Virdee	London Metropolitan University, UK
Hui Yang	Beijing University of Posts and Telecommunications, China
Alessandro Zavatta	CNR, Italy

SECRYPT Program Committee

Ehab Al-Shaer	University of North Carolina at Charlotte, USA
Muhammad Asghar	The University of Auckland, New Zealand
Francesco Buccafurri	University of Reggio Calabria, Italy
Cagri Cetin	USF, USA
Frederic Cuppens	Télécom Bretagne, France
Nora Cuppens	IMT Atlantique, France
Sabrina De Capitani di Vimercati	Università degli Studi di Milano, Italy
Roberto Di Pietro	Hamad Bin Khalifa University, Qatar
Mario Di Raimondo	Università of Catania, Italy
Josep Domingo-Ferrer	Rovira i Virgili University, Spain
Ruggero Donida Labati	Università degli Studi di Milano, Italy
Alberto Ferrante	Università della Svizzera Italiana, Switzerland
Josep-Lluis Ferrer-Gomila	Balearic Islands University, Spain
Sara Foresti	Università degli Studi di Milano, Italy
Steven Furnell	University of Plymouth, UK
Joaquin Garcia-Alfaro	Télécom SudParis, France
Angelo Genovese	Università degli Studi di Milano, Italy
Dimitris Gritzalis	AUEB, Greece
Stefanos Gritzalis	University of Piraeus, Greece

Jinguang Han	Queen's University Belfast, UK
Xinyi Huang	Fujian Normal University, China
Vasilis Katos	Bournemouth University, UK
Sokratis Katsikas	Norwegian University of Science and Technology, Norway
Shinsaku Kiyomoto	KDDI Research Inc., Japan
Albert Levi	Sabanci University, Turkey
Kaitai Liang	University of Surrey, UK
Jay Ligatti	University of South Florida, USA
Giovanni Livraga	Universita degli Studi di Milano, Italy
Javier Lopez	University of Malaga, Spain
Masahiro Mambo	Kanazawa University, Japan
Yunlong Mao	Nanjing University, China
Evangelos Markatos	ICS, Forth, Greece
Fabio Martinelli	CNR, Italy
Ahmed Meddahi	IMT Lille Douai, France
David Megias	Universitat Oberta de Catalunya, Spain
Alessio Merlo	University of Genoa, Italy
Haralambos Mouratidis	University of Brighton, UK
Farid Naït-Abdesselam	Paris Descartes University, France
Rolf Oppliger	eSECURITY Technologies, Switzerland
Stefano Paraboschi	University of Bergamo, Italy
Joon Park	Syracuse University, USA
Gerardo Pelosi	Politecnico di Milano, Italy
Günther Pernul	University of Regensburg, Germany
Silvio Ranise	Fondazione Bruno Kessler, Italy
Indrakshi Ray	Colorado State University, USA
Pierangela Samarati	Università degli Studi di Milano, Italy
Nuno Santos	INESC, Portugal
Andreas Schaad	University of Applied Sciences Offenburg, Germany
Fabio Scotti	Università degli Studi di Milano, Italy
Cristina Serban	AT&T, USA
Daniele Sgandurra	Royal Holloway, University of London, UK
Basit Shafiq	Lahore University of Management Sciences (LUMS), Pakistan
Vicenc Torra	University of Skövde, Sweden
Juan Ramon Troncoso-Pastoriza	EPFL, Switzerland
Corrado Visaggio	Università degli Studi del Sannio, Italy
Haining Wang	University of Delaware, USA
Lingyu Wang	Concordia University, Canada
Xinyuan Wang	George Mason University, USA
Edgar Weippl	University of Vienna, SBA Research, Austria
Zheng Yan	Xidian University, China
Meng Yu	The University of Texas at San Antonio, USA
Mo Yu	Google, USA

Jiawei Yuan	University of Massachusetts Dartmouth, USA
Qiang Zeng	University of South Carolina, USA
Lei Zhang	Refinitiv, USA
Shengzhi Zhang	Boston University, Metropolitan College, USA
Yongjun Zhao	The Chinese University of Hong Kong, Hong Kong

SECRYPT Additional Reviewers

Giada Sciarretta	Fondazione Bruno Kessler, Italy
Bruhadeshwar Bezawada	Colorado State University, USA
Roberto Carbone	Fondazione Bruno Kessler, Italy
Cagri Cetin	University of South Florida, USA
Vasiliki Diamantopoulou	University of the Aegean, Greece
Giacomo Giorgi	CNR-IIT, Italy
Qinwen Hu	The University of Auckland, New Zealand
Christos Kalloniatis	University of the Aegean, Greece
Diptendu Kar	Colorado State University, USA
Elisavet Konstantinou	University of the Aegean, Greece
Chao Lin	Wuhan University, China
Chengjun Lin	The Chinese Academy of Sciences, China
Salvatore Manfredi	Fondazione Bruno Kessler, Italy
Lorenzo Musarella	University of Reggio Calabria, Italy
Manos Panaousis	University of Greenwich, UK
Ivan Pryvalov	CISPA, Germany
Athanasios Rizos	CNR, Italy
Antonia Russo	University of Reggio Calabria, Italy
Neetesh Saxena	Bournemouth University, UK
Stavros Shiaeles	Plymouth University, UK
Yifan Tian	Embry-Riddle Aeronautical University, USA
Xu Yang	RMIT University, Australia
Yuexin Zhang	Swinburne University of Technology, Australia

SIGMAP Program Committee

Harry Agius	Brunel University London, UK
Rajeev Agrawal	North Carolina Agricultural and Technical State University, USA
Fadoua Ataa Allah	Royal Institute of Amazigh Culture (IRCAM), Morocco
Arvind Bansal	Kent State University, USA
Adrian Bors	University of York, UK
Kaushik Das Sharma	University of Calcutta, India
Carl Debono	University of Malta, Malta
Zongming Fei	University of Kentucky, USA
Jakub Galka	University of Science and Technology, Poland
Jerry Gibson	University of California, Santa Barbara, USA

Seiichi Gohshi	Kogakuin University, Japan
William Grosky	University of Michigan, USA
Amarnath Gupta	University of California, San Diego, USA
Haci Ilhan	Yildiz Technical University, Turkey
Razib Iqbal	Missouri State University, USA
Li-Wei Kang	National Yunlin University of Science and Technology, Taiwan, China
Sokratis Katsikas	Norwegian University of Science and Technology, Norway
Constantine Kotropoulos	Aristotle University of Thessaloniki, Greece
Choong-Soo Lee	St. Lawrence University, USA
Chengqing Li	Xiangtan University, China
Martin Lopez-Nores	University of Vigo, Spain
Ilias Maglogiannis	University of Piraeus, Greece
Hong Man	Stevens Institute of Technology, USA
Daniela Moctezuma	Conacyt (CentroGEO), Mexico
Chamin Morikawa	Morpho, Inc., Japan
Alejandro Murua	University of Montreal, Canada
Hiroshi Nagahashi	Japan Women's University, Japan
Ioannis Paliokas	Centre for Research and Technology - Hellas, Greece
Joao Paulo da Costa	University of Brasília, Brazil
Yiming Qian	Simon Fraser University, Canada
Peter Quax	Hasselt University, Belgium
Paula Queluz	Instituto Superior Técnico, Instituto de Telecomunicações, Portugal
Simone Santini	Universidad Autónoma de Madrid, Spain
Ángel Serrano Sánchez de León	Universidad Rey Juan Carlos, Spain
Andreas Uhl	University of Salzburg, Austria
Sudanthi Wijewickrema	The University of Melbourne, Australia

WINSYS Program Committee

Ali Abu-El Humos	Jackson State University, USA
Fatemeh Afghah	Northern Arizona University, USA
Andreas Ahrens	Hochschule Wismar, University of Technology, Business and Design, Germany
Aydin Akan	Istanbul University, Turkey
Vicente Alarcon-Aquino	Universidad de las Americas Puebla, Mexico
Jose Barcelo-Ordinas	Universitat Politècnica de Catalunya (UPC), Spain
Marko Beko	Universidade Lusófona de Humanidades e Tecnologias, Portugal
Luis Bernardo	Universidade Nova de Lisboa, Portugal
Llorenç Cerdà-Alabern	Universitat Politècnica de Catalunya (UPC), Spain
Gerard Chalhoub	Universté Clermont Auvergne, France
Sungrae Cho	Chung-Ang University, South Korea

Carl Debono	University of Malta, Malta
Panagiotis Fouliras	University of Macedonia, Greece
Janusz Gozdecki	AGH University of Science and Technology, Poland
Fabrizio Granelli	Università degli Studi di Trento, Italy
Stefanos Gritzalis	University of Piraeus, Greece
Aaron Gulliver	University of Victoria, Canada
David Haccoun	École Polytechnique de Montréal, Canada
Chih-Lin Hu	National Central University, Taiwan, China
A. R. Hurson	Missouri S&T, USA
Georgios Kambourakis	University of the Aegean, Greece
Majid Khabbazian	University of Alberta, Canada
Charalampos Konstantopoulos	University of Piraeus, Greece
Gurhan Kucuk	Yeditepe University, Turkey
Wookwon Lee	Gannon University, USA
David Lin	National Chiao Tung University, Taiwan, China
Ju Liu	Shandong University, China
Elsa Macias López	University of Las Palmas de G.C., Spain
Koosha Marashi	Romeo Power Technology, USA
Sarandis Mitropoulos	Ionio University, Greece
Marek Natkaniec	AGH University of Science and Technology, Poland
Amiya Nayak	University of Ottawa, Canada
Gregory O'Hare	University College Dublin (UCD), Ireland
Cristiano Panazio	Escola Politécnica of São Paulo University, Brazil
Grammati Pantziou	University of West Attica, Greece
Jordi Pérez-Romero	Universitat Politècnica de Catalunya (UPC), Spain
Dennis Pfisterer	University of Lübeck, Germany
Symon Podvalny	Voronezh State Technical University, Russia
Jorge Portilla	Universidad Politécnica de Madrid, Spain
Neeli Prasad	International Technological University, USA
Julian Reichwald	Cooperative State University Mannheim, Germany
Heverson B. Ribeiro	IRT b<>com (Institute of Research and Technology), France
Jörg Roth	University of Applied Sciences Nuremberg, Germany
Angelos Rouskas	University of Piraeus, Greece
Farag Sallabi	United Arab Emirates University, UAE
Manuel García Sánchez	Universidade de Vigo, Spain
Altair Santin	Pontifical Catholic University of Paraná (PUCPR), Brazil
Nicola Santoro	Carleton University, Canada
Christian Schindelhauer	University of Freiburg, Germany
Winston Seah	Victoria University of Wellington, New Zealand
Christopher Silva	The Aerospace Corporation, USA
Alvaro Suárez-Sarmiento	University of Las Palmas de Gran Canaria, Spain
Bishal Thapa	Raytheon BBN Technology, USA
César Vargas Rosales	Tecnológico de Monterrey, Mexico

Shibing Zhang   Nantong University, China
Zhenyun zhuang   Facebook, USA

Invited Speakers

Jalel Ben-Othman   University of Paris 13, France
Adlen Ksentini   Eurecom, France
Soon Xin Ng   University of Southampton, UK
Sebastiano Battiato   University of Catania, Italy

Contents

Signal Processing and Multimedia Applications

Data Communication Networking

Application Error Detection in Networks by Protocol Behavior Model

Martin Holkovič[1](✉), Libor Polčák[2], and Ondřej Ryšavý[2]

[1] Faculty of Information Technology, NES@FIT, Brno University of Technology,
Bozetechova 1/2, 612 66 Brno, Czech Republic
`iholkovic@fit.vutbr.cz`
[2] Faculty of Information Technology, Centre of Excellence IT4Innovations,
Brno University of Technology, Bozetechova 1/2, 612 66 Brno, Czech Republic
`{polcak,rysavy}@fit.vutbr.cz`

Abstract. The identification of causes of errors in network systems is difficult due to their inherent complexity. Network administrators usually rely on available information sources to analyze the current situation and identify possible problems. Even though they are able to identify the symptoms seen in the past and thus can apply their experience gathered from the solved cases the time needed to identify and correct the errors is considerable. The automation of the troubleshooting process is a way to reduce the time spent on individual cases. In this paper, the model that can be used to automate the diagnostic process of network communication is presented. The model is based on building the finite automaton to describe protocol behavior in various situations. The unknown communication is checked against the model to identify error states and associated descriptions of causes. The tool prototype was implemented in order to demonstrate the proposed method via a set of experiments.

Keywords: Network diagnostics · Automatic diagnostics · Timed automata · Protocol model from traces · Encrypted data diagnostics · Application behavior model

1 Introduction

Computer networks are complex systems equipped with different network devices and hosts that provide and consume application services. Various types of errors, such as misconfiguration, device failures, network application crashes, or even user misbehavior can cause that expected network functions are not available. Users perceive network problems by the inaccessibility of web services, the degraded performance of network applications, etc. Usually, it is the role of network administrators to identify the cause of problems and to apply corrective activities in order to restore the network functions again.

The network troubleshooting process is often described as a systematic approach to identify, diagnose and resolve problems and issues within a computer

© Springer Nature Switzerland AG 2020
M. S. Obaidat (Ed.): ICETE 2019, CCIS 1247, pp. 3–28, 2020.
https://doi.org/10.1007/978-3-030-52686-3_1

network. Despite the published procedures, methods and techniques, and tool support, the network diagnostics is a largely manual and time-consuming process. Troubleshooting often requires expert technical knowledge of network technologies, communication protocols, and network applications. Another complication is that the administrator often needs to check the number of possible sources to find the real source of the problem. It amounts to check log files in network devices or network applications, the current content of various tables, traces of network communication, etc. Although an experienced administrator usually has advanced skills in network troubleshooting that helps the administrator to quickly identify problems there may be situations that are hard to solve and not evident until the detailed network communication analysis is carried out.

The need for advanced tools that support network diagnostics is expressed by most network professionals surveyed in the report presented by Zeng et al. [31]. Existing tools can provide various information about the network, such as service status and performance characteristics, which is useful for problem detection but they often do not provide enough information for the cause identification. In computer networks, there can happen a lot of different problems. Many of them can be identified by using a network traffic analyzer. The traffic analyzer is a software to intercept the data packet flow that in the hand of an experienced administrator enables to check for the latency issues and other networking problems which help to reveal the root cause. However, using a traffic analyzer requires an understanding of different communication protocols. Also, the number of flows that need to be analyzed can be large making the analysis long and tedious task.

In order to improve the network troubleshooting process, we propose to develop a tool that automatically generates a protocol behavior model from the provided examples (traces) of the protocol conversations. In particular, a network administrator is required to provide two groups of files. The first group contains traces of normal (expected) behavior, while the second group consists of known, previously identified error traces. Based on these distinct groups, the tool is able to construct a protocol model that can be later used for detection and diagnosis of issues in the observed network communication. Once the model is created, additional traces may be used to improve the model gradually.

When designing the system, we assumed some practical considerations:

- It should not need to be required to implement custom application protocol dissectors to understand the communication.
- Application error diagnostics cannot be affected by lower protocols, e.g., version of IP protocol, data tunneling protocol.
- The model should be easily interpretable and also useful for other activities too, e.g., security analysis, performance analysis.

The main benefit of this work is a new automatic diagnostic method for the detection of errors observable from the application protocol communication. The method is based on the construction of a protocol behavior model that contains both correct and error communication patterns. An administrator can also use the created model for documentation purposes and as part of a more detailed analysis, e.g., performance or security analysis.

This paper is an extended version of the paper *"Using Network Traces to Generate Models for Automatic Network Application Protocols Diagnostics"* [13]. We have added and improved several parts that extend the original paper, in particular: i) models of protocols are better described, ii) the processing of ungeneralizable requests (and states) have been completely reworked, iii) the diagnostics engine can now include time information, iv) and preliminary evaluation of encrypted traffic analysis was realized.

The focus of the previous contribution was only on detecting application layer errors in enterprise networks. We did not consider errors occurred on other layers and domains, e.g., wireless communication [24], routing errors [10], or performance issues [19]. However, in this extended version, we are also able to cope with performance problems. Because we are focusing on enterprise networks, we have made some assumptions on the accessibility of data sources. For instance, we expect that administrators using this approach have full access to network traffic in the network. Even if the communication outside the company's network is encrypted, the traffic between the company's servers and inside the network can be sometimes available unencrypted, or the data can be decrypted by providing server's private key or logging the session keys[1]. However, because the encrypted traffic forms the majority of all communication on the Internet, we also preliminary evaluated whether the presented approach (generating models from traces) is applicable to encrypted traffic.

The paper is organized as follows: Sect. 2 describes existing work comparable to the presented approach. Section 3 defines model used for diagnostics. Section 4 overviews the system architecture. Section 5 provides details on the method, including algorithms used to create and use a protocol model. Section 6 presents the evaluation of the tool implementing the proposed system. Section 7 discusses some problems related to our approach. Finally, Sect. 8 summarizes the paper and identifies possible future work.

2 Related Work

Traditionally, error detection in network systems was mostly a manual process performed by network administrators as a reaction to the user reported or detected service unavailability or connectivity loss. As it is a tedious task various tools and automated methods were developed. A survey by [26] classifies the errors to network systems as either *application-related* or *network-related* problems. The most popular tool for manual network traffic analysis and troubleshooting is Wireshark [20]. It is equipped with a rich set of protocol dissectors that enables to view details on the communication at different network layers. However, an administrator has to manually analyze the traffic and decide which communication is abnormal, possibly contributing to the observed

---

[1] http://www.root9.net/2012/11/ssl-decryption-with-wireshark-private.html.

problem. Though Wireshark offers advanced filtering mechanism, it lacks any automation [12].

Network troubleshooting can be done using active, passive, or hybrid methods [27]. Active methods rely on the tools that generate probing packets to locate network issues [2]. Specialized tools using generated diagnostic communication were also developed for testing network devices [23]. The advantage of active methods is that it is possible to detect a certain class of errors quickly and precisely identify the problem. On the other hand, generating diagnostic traffic may be unwanted in some situations. Passive detection methods rely on information that can be observed in network traffic or obtained from log files, dumps, etc.

During the course of research on passive network diagnostic methods, several approaches were proposed utilizing a variety of techniques. In the rest of this section, we present the different existing approaches to network diagnostics closely that relates to the presented contribution.

Rule-Based Methods. Rule-based systems represent the application of artificial intelligence (reasoning) to the problem of system diagnosis. While this approach was mainly popular for automated fault detection of industrial systems, some authors applied this principle to develop network troubleshooting systems. [15] introduced rule-based reasoning (RBR) expert system for network fault and security diagnosis. The system uses a set of agents that provide facts to the diagnostics engine. [9] proposed distributed multi-agent architecture for network management. The implemented logical inference system enables automated isolation, diagnosis, and repairing network anomalies through the use of agents running on network devices. [11] employed assumption-based argumentation to create an open framework of the diagnosis procedures able to identify the typical errors in home networks. Rule-based systems often do not directly learn from experience. They are also unable to deal with new previously unseen situations, and it is hard to maintain the represented knowledge consistently [25].

Protocol Analysis. Automatic protocol analysis attempts to infer a model of normal communication from data samples. Often, the model has the form of a finite automaton representing the valid protocol communication. An automatic protocol reverse engineering that stores the communication patterns into regular expressions was suggested in [30]. Tool *ReverX* [3] automatically infers a specification of a protocol from network traces and generates corresponding automaton. Recently, reverse engineering of protocol specification only from recorded network traffic was proposed to infer protocol message formats as well as certain field semantics for binary protocols [17]. The automated inference of protocol specification (message format or even protocol behavior model) from traffic samples was considered by several authors. [8] presented *Discover*, a tool for automatic protocol reverse engineering of protocol message formats from network traces. The tool works for both binary and text protocols providing accuracy about 90%. The different approach to solve a similar goal was proposed by [29]. They instrumented network applications to observe the operation of processing network messages. Based on this information their method is able to recreate a message format, which is used to generate protocol parser. This work was extended by the same authors in [7] with an algorithm for extracting the state machine for the analyzed protocol. [16] developed a method based on Markov models called *PRISMA*, which infers a functional state machine and message format of a protocol from network traffic alone. While focused on malware analysis, the tool is capable to identify communication behavior of arbitrary services using binary or textual protocols. Generating application-level specification from network traffic is addressed by [28]. They developed a system called *Veritas* that using the statistical analysis on the protocol formats is able to generate a probabilistic protocol state machine to represent the protocol flows.

Statistical and Machine Learning Methods. Statistical and machine learning methods were considered for troubleshooting misconfigurations in the home networks by [1] and diagnosis of failures in the large networks by [6]. *Tranalyzer* [4] is a flow-based traffic analyzer that performs traffic mining and statistical analysis enabling troubleshooting and anomaly detection for large-scale networks. *Big-DAMA* [5] is a framework for scalable online and offline data mining and machine learning supposed to monitor and characterize extremely large network traffic datasets.

Automata-Based Analysis. Timed automaton is one of the natural representations of the behavior models for communication protocols. For example, [14] uses timed automata to model parallel systems and to detect errors by verifying the satisfaction of given properties. However, they do not assume to learn the model automatically. Another work [21] proposes a heuristic state-merging algorithm that learns the model automatically. They are using NetFlow records and time windows to create models that are later used to detect malware and infected hosts. [18] uses a model described by timed automata to diagnose errors. The system monitors several sensors which values are converted into timed sequences to be accepted by the timed automata, which are able to detect violations of the measured values to the predefined model.

3   Model Representation

Diagnosed protocols are described using models that define the protocols' communications as pair sequences. Each pair consists of a request and a reply message, as shown in Fig. 1. These requests and replies are pre-specified message types specific for each protocol. In addition to the original paper, models will take the form of a timed finite automaton, which, in addition to the message order, will also contain timestamp - time since the last reply was received. The finite automaton will process the input sequence and will traverse through the model states. The result of the traverse process will be the result of diagnostics.

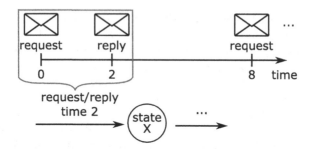

Fig. 1. An illustration of a protocol messages conversion into a finite state automaton. Requests and replies are paired together with the time of their arrival since the last pair.

Each model processes a message sequence that is distinguished by a 6-tuple: source and destination IP address, source and destination port, L4 protocol, and session ID. The session ID is an optional parameter specified for each protocol to distinguish multiple conversations that are transmitted within a single connection. When transferring multiple conversations over a single connection, the model does not describe the entire connection, but only individual conversations.

The finite automaton works with the input alphabet, which is a pair of request and reply values. Both the request and the reply values are composed of packet fields, such as the value of the *"ftp.request.command"* attribute for the FTP request and value of the *"ftp.response.code"* attribute for its reply. If the input symbol (request/reply pair) is repeated (which might mean periodic reports), the model will contain a transition to the same state.

For each request/reply pair, the time since the last reply message or the beginning of the communication is calculated. Using this time, the interval at which the message must arrive for the finite automaton to transition through the state is calculated. Before calculating the interval range, it is necessary to calculate a minimum, a maximum, and a square root of standard deviation from the time values. The interval is calculated in the range from *"minimum − $\sqrt{std\ deviation}$"* to *"maximum + $\sqrt{std\ deviation}$"*, including extreme values. If the number of values is less than 5, the interval is from zero to infinity (all pairs will match this interval).

A model has a form of a timed finite automaton [22, Def. 6.4]—a 6-tuple $(S, S_0, \Sigma, \Lambda, C, \delta)$, where:

- S is a finite set of states,
- $S_0 \in S$ is an initial state,
- Σ is a finite input alphabet ($\Sigma \cap S = \emptyset$, $\epsilon \notin \Sigma$), where $\Sigma =$ (request, reply) and ϵ is an empty value,
- Λ is a finite output alphabet ($\Lambda \cap S = \emptyset$, $\epsilon \notin \Lambda$), where $\Lambda =$ error description and ϵ is an empty value,
- C is a finite state of clocks,

- $\delta \colon S \times (\varSigma \cup \epsilon) \times \varPhi(C) \to S \times \varLambda^* \times 2^C$ is a transition function mapping a triplet of a state, an input symbol (or empty string), and a clock constraint over C to a triplet of a new state, an output sequence, and a set of clocks to be reset. It means, given a specific input symbol, δ shifts the timed transducer from one state to another while it produces an output if and only if the specified clock constraint hold.

4   System Architecture

This section describes the architecture of the proposed system which learns from communication examples and diagnoses unknown communications. In this extended version, the architecture now works with timed information inside automata's transitions, and a new concept of model generalization is described. The system takes PCAP files as input data, where one PCAP file contains only one complete protocol communication. An administrator marks PCAP files as correct or faulty communication examples before model training. The administrator marks faulty PCAP files with error description and a hint on how to fix the problem. The system output is a model describing the protocol behavior and providing an interface for using this model for the diagnostic process. The diagnostic process takes a PCAP file with unknown communication and checks whether this communication contains an error and if yes, returns a list of possible errors and fixes.

The architecture, shown in Fig. 2, consists of multiple components, each implementing a stage in the processing pipeline. The processing is staged as follows:

- **Input Data Processing** - Preprocessing is responsible for converting PCAP files into a format suitable for the next stages. Within this stage, the input packets are decoded using protocol parser. Next, the filter is applied to select only relevant packets. Finally, the packets are grouped to pair request to their corresponding responses.
- **Model Training** - The training processes several PCAP files and creates a model characterizing the behavior of the analyzed protocol. The output of this phase is a protocol model.
- **Diagnostics** - In the diagnostic component, an unknown communication is analyzed and compared to available protocol models. The result is a report listing detected errors and possible hints on how to correct them.

In the rest of the section, the individual components are described in detail. Illustrative examples are provided for the sake of better understanding.

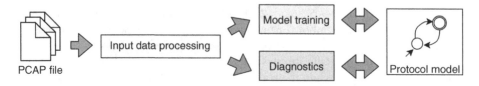

Fig. 2. After the system processes the input PCAP files (the first yellow stage), it uses the data to create the protocol behavior model (the second green stage) or to diagnose an unknown protocol communication using the created protocol model (the-third purple stage) [13]. (Color figure online)

4.1 Input Data Processing

This stage works directly with PCAP files provided by the administrator. Each file is parsed by *TShark*[2] which exports decoded packets to JSON format. The system further processes the JSON data by filtering irrelevant records and pairs request packets with their replies. The output of this stage is a list of tuples representing atomic transactions.

We have improved the data pairing process in this extended paper to support timed transitions in the model. The system calculates time between the arrival time of the current and the last reply message. For the first reply message within the communication, the time since the beginning of the communication is used. In the case requests do not have corresponding replies, the system uses the requests arrival times. The result of the pairing process is a sequence of pairs

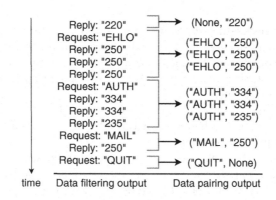

Fig. 3. An SMTP communication in which the client authenticates, sends an email and quits. The left part of the example shows a list of requests and replies together with the time of their arrival in the protocol-independent format. The right part shows a sequence of paired queries with replies, which are the output of the *Input Data Porcessing* stage. For each pair, time since the last pair is also saved. The system pairs one request and one reply with the special *None* value.

---

[2] https://www.wireshark.org/docs/man-pages/tshark.html.

with time information, where each pair consists of one request and one reply. The Fig. 3 shows an example of this pairing process.

4.2   Model Training

After the *Input Data Processing* stage transformed input PCAP files into a list of request-response pairs, the *Model Training* phase creates a protocol model. For example, we can consider regular communication traces that represent typical POP3 protocol operations with the server: the client is checking a mail-box, downloading a message or deleting a message. The model is first created for regular communication and later extended with error behavior.

Learning from Traces with Expected Behavior. The model creation process begins by learning the protocol behavior from input data representing regular communication. The result of this training phase is a description of the protocol that represents a subset of correct behavior. The model is created from a collection of individual communication traces. When a new trace is to be added, the tool identifies the longest prefix of the trace that is accepted by the current model. The remaining of the trace is then used to enrich the model.

During a traverse within the model, the time attribute of each request-reply pair is added to transitions (each transition has an auxiliary variable containing a list of time attributes). If the number of saved time values within a transition is greater than 5, the time interval of the model transition is recalculated as described in Sect. 3.

Model Generalization. Unfortunately, *TShark* marks some unpredictable data (e.g., authentication data) in some protocols as regular requests and does not clearly distinguish between them. These values are a problem in later processing because these unpredictable values create ungeneralizable states during the model learning phase. Therefore, all transitions that contain requests with unpredictable values are removed from the model and replaced by new transitions.

An unpredictable request value is a request value which is contained inside only one transition - no matter the previous state, the next state, and the reply value. The wildcard value will replace these request values. The time interval of the transition is kept at value from zero to infinity. Which requests contain unpredictable values is determined during the learning process of the model. During this process, the amount of times a request value is being used (no matter the current automata state) is counted (count 1 = unpredictable).

Multiple transitions with unpredictable requests and an identical reply value may originate from a single finite automata state. In this case, all these transitions with the next finite automata states are merged. The merging idea is displayed in Fig. 4. After all input traces are used for the model to learn, there is a state from which four transitions are originating. The gray dashed lines are transitions that occurred only once within the input. These two transitions contain various request values, but the same reply value ("OK"). After generalizing these three transitions, a new transition containing the request wildcard value and the "OK" reply value will be added to the model.

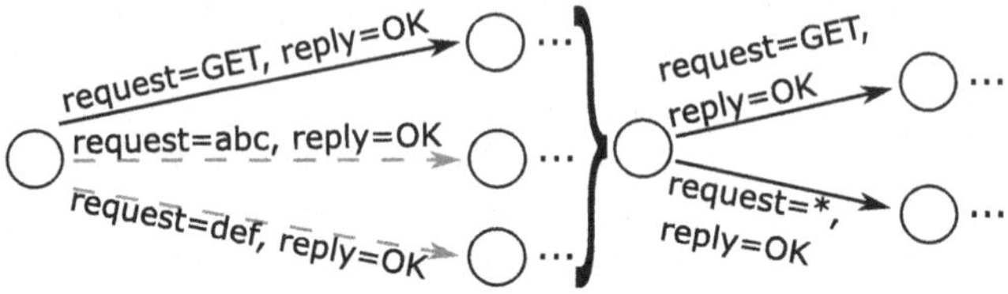

Fig. 4. Illustration of replacing unpredictable requests by a wildcard value (*). The replaced transitions are merged into one generic transition.

When traversing through an automaton, in each state, transitions with explicit commands are checked as first. When no match is found, the model checks if there is a wildcard command value and a reply value for the current state.

Learning the Errors. After the system learns the protocol from regular communication, the model can be extended with error traces. The system expects that the administrator prepares that error trace as the result of previous (manual) troubleshooting activities. The administrator should also provide error description and information about how to fix the error.

When extending the model with error traces, the procedure is similar to when processing correct traces. Automaton attempts to consume as long prefix of input trace as possible ending in state s. The following cases are possible:

- *Remaining input trace is not empty:* The system creates a new state s' and links it with from state s. It marks the new state as an "error" state and labels it with a provided error description.
- *Remaining input trace is empty:*
  - State s is error state: The system adds the new error description to existing labeling of an existing state s.
  - State s is correct state: The system marks the state as *possible error* and adds the error description.

4.3 Diagnostics

After the system creates a behavioral model that is extended by error states, it is possible to use the model to diagnose unknown communication tracks. The system runs diagnostics by processing a PCAP file in the same way as in the learning process and checks the request-reply sequence with their time attributes against the automaton. Diagnostics distinguishes between these classes:

– **Normal:** The automaton accepts the input trace and ends in the correct state.
– **Error:** The automaton accepts the input trace and ends in the error state.
– **Possible error:** The automaton accepts the input trace and ends in the possible error state. In this case, the system cannot distinguish if the communication is correct or not. Therefore, the system reports an error description from the state and leaves the final decision on the user.
– **Unknown:** The automaton does not accept entire the input trace, which may indicate that the trace represents a behavior not fully recognized by the underlying automaton.

It is important to notice that during the traverse within the automaton, the time attribute of each request-reply pair is compared with time constraints. In case the time attribute does not fulfill the constraint, the model generates a warning message. However, the diagnostic process does not stop, and the traverse process continues to the next state in the same way as if the time constraint was fulfilled.

5 Algorithms

This section provides algorithms for (i) creating a model from normal traces, (ii) generalization of the model, (iii) updating the model from error traces and (iv) evaluating a trace if it contains an error. The algorithms are based on algorithms from the original paper. The difference is that in this version, they need to work with timed transitions. All presented algorithms work with a model that uses a deterministic timed finite automaton (DTFA) as its representation.

To simplify algorithms' codes, we have defined time interval $\langle 0; \infty \rangle$ as the default interval. If the interval is not specified, the model uses this value which has less priority when traversing throw the model states. Only when there is no match with a specific interval, the system checks default values.

5.1 Adding Correct Traces

Algorithm 1 takes the input model (DTFA) and adds missing transitions and states based on the input sequence (P). The algorithm starts with the *init_state* and saves it into the *previous_state* variable. The *previous_state* variable is used to create a transition from one state to the next. In each loop of the while section, the algorithm assigns the next pair into the *current_state* variable until there is no next pair. From the *previous_state* and the *current_state*, the *transition* variable is created, and the system checks if the DTFA contains this *transition*. If the DTFA does not contain it, it is added together with the *time_value*. Otherwise, the new *time_value* is added to the *transition*. If at least five time values are saved, the *time_interval* is calculated and applied to the *transition*.

Before continuing with the next loop, the *current_state* variable is assigned to the *previous_state* variable. The updated model will be used as the input for the next input sequence. After processing all the input sequences, which represent normal behavior, the resulting automaton is a model of normal behavior.

Algorithm 1. Updating model from the correct traces.

Inputs: P = query-reply pairs sequence with time value; DTFA = set of the transitions
Output: DTFA = set of the transitions
previous_state = init_state
while *not at end of input P* **do**
    current_state = get next pair from *P*
    transition = previous_state → current_state
    if *DTFA does not contain transition* **then**
       add *transition* to DTFA and save *time_value* to the *transition*
    else
       add *time_value* to the saved times in *transition*
       if *saved times >= 5* **then**
          calculate the *time_interval* constraint and apply it to the *transition*
    previous_state = current_state
end
return DTFA

Algorithm 2. Generalization of the model.

Inputs: DTFA = set of transitions
Output: DTFA = set of transitions
foreach *transition ∈ DTFA* **do**
    if *transition contains only one time* **then**
       new_transition = make copy of *transition*
       remove *transition* from *DTFA*
       replace request in *new_transition* by wildcard
       if *DTFA does not contain new_transition* **then**
          add *new_transition* to DTFA
end
return DTFA

5.2 Model Generalization

The Algorithm 2 takes all transitions from a model one by one (variable *transition*), calculates the number of times each *transition* was used, and checks whether the *transition* was used only once (contains only one time value). Only one time value means that in all of the input traces, the *transition* was used only once. The model creates a new copy of the *transition* (variable *new_transition*) and removes the old one.

The wildcard value replaces the request value in the *new_transition*. The algorithm checks whether the model contains this *new_transition*, and if not, it is inserted into the model. This presence control ensures that a single transition replaces multiple ungeneralizable states with a wildcard request value.

5.3 Adding Error Traces

The Algorithm 3 has one more input (*Error*), which is a text string describing a user-defined error. The start of the algorithm is the same as in the previous case. The difference is in testing whether the automaton contains the *transition*

Algorithm 3. Extending the model with error traces.

Inputs: P = query-reply pairs sequence; DTFA = set of transitions; Error = description of the error
Output: DTFA = set of transitions
previous_state = init_state
while *not at end of input P* **do**
    current_state = get next pair from *P*
    transition = previous_state → current_state
    if *DTFA contains transition* **then**
        if *transition fulfills time_interval* **then**
            if *transition contains error* **then**
                append *error* to *transition* in DTFA
                return DTFA
            previous_state = current_state
        else
            add *transition* to DTFA and mark it with *error*
            return DTFA
    else
        add *transition* to DTFA and mark it with *error*
        return DTFA
end
return DTFA

---

specified in the input sequence. If so, the system checks whether the *transition* fulfills the *time_interval*. This time interval checking is an improvement of the algorithm from the previous paper. Only when the *time_interval* is fulfilled, the system checks to see if the saved *transition* also contains errors. In this case, the algorithm updates the error list by adding a new *error*. Otherwise, the algorithm continues to process the input string to find a suitable place to indicate the error. If the *transition* does not fulfill the *time_interval* restriction or the *transition* does not exist, it is created and marked with the specified *error*.

5.4 Testing Unknown Trace

The Algorithm 4 uses previously created automaton (DTFA variable) to check the input sequence P. According to the input sequence, the algorithm traverses the automaton and checks whether the transitions contain errors. If an error in some transition is found, the system returns an errors description messages (*errors*) to the user. If the *transition* was not found, the algorithm returns an unknown error. In this case, it is up to the user to analyze the situation and possibly extend the automaton for this input.

In this extended paper, the system also verifies if the input sequence fulfills transitions time restrictions. With each *transition*, the time value is compared to the *time_interval*. If the *transition* does not fulfill the *time_interval*, the system creates a warning message to the user. More than one warning message can be generated because the generating of warning messages does not stop the diagnostic process.

Algorithm 4. Checking an unknown trace.

Inputs: P = query-reply pairs sequence; DTFA = set of transitions
Output: Errors = one or more error descriptions
previous_state = init_state
while *not at end of input P* **do**
    current_state = get next pair from *P*
    transition = previous_state → current_state
    if *DTFA contains transition* **then**
        if *transition doesn't fulfill time_interval* **then**
           | create warning that *transition* does not matched the interval and continue
        if *transition contains error* **then**
           | return *errors* from *transition*
        previous_state = current_state
    else
        | return "unknown error"
end
return "no error detected"

---

6 Evaluation

We have implemented a proof-of-concept tool which implements the Algorithm 1, 2, 3, and 4. In this section, we provide the evaluation of our proof-of-concept tool to demonstrate that the proposed solution is suitable for diagnosing application protocols. Another goal of the evaluation is to show how the created model changes by adding new input data to the model. We have chosen four application protocols with different behavioral patterns for evaluation.

The results from the original's Subsects. 5.1, 5.2 and 5.3 are the same and still valid. From this reason the Subsects. 6.1 and 6.3 are the same as in the original paper, and in the Subsect. 6.2 the figure showing the model's complexity during the model training is omitted. The new content is in the following subsections. Section 6.4 tests the benefit of using finite automata as the model by detecting a performance problem inside a communication. The last Sect. 6.5 tries to verify whether the proposed approach is somehow usable for encrypted traffic.

6.1 Reference Set Preparation and Model Creation

Our algorithms create the automata states and transitions based on the sequence of pairs. The implication is that repeating the same input sequence does not modify the learned behavior model. Therefore, it is not important to provide a huge amount of input files (traces) but to provide unique traces (sequences of query-reply pairs). We created our reference datasets by capturing data from the network, removing unrelated communications, and calculating the hash value for each trace to avoid duplicate patterns. Instead of a correlation between the amount of protocols in the network and the amount of saved traces, the amount of files correlates with the complexity of the analyzed protocol. For example, hundreds of DNS query-reply traces captured from the network can be represented by the same query-reply sequence (*A type query, No error*).

After capturing the communication, all the traces were manually checked and divided into two groups: (i) traces representing normal behavior and (ii) traces containing some error. In case the trace contains an error, we also identified the error and added the corresponding description to the trace. We split both groups of traces into the training set and the testing set.

It is important to notice that the tool uses traces to create a model for one specific network configuration and not for all possible configurations. Focus on a single configuration results in a smaller set of unique traces and smaller created models. This allows an administrator to detect situations which may be correct for some network, but not for a diagnosed network, e.g., missing authentication.

6.2   Model Creation

We have chosen the following four request-reply application protocols with different complexity for evaluation:

- **DNS:** Simple stateless protocol with communication pattern - domain name query (type A, AAAA, MX, ...) and reply (no error, no such name, ...).
- **SMTP:** Simple state protocol in which the client has to authenticate, specify email sender and recipients, and transfer the email message. The protocol has a large predefined set of reply codes resulting in many possible states in DTFA created by Algorithm 1 and 2.
- **POP:** In comparison with SMTP, the protocol is more complicated because it allows clients to do more actions with email messages (e.g., download, delete). However, the POP protocol replies only with two possible replies (+OK, −ERR), which reduce the number of possible states.
- **FTP:** Stateful protocol allowing the client to do multiple actions with files and directories on server. The protocol defines many reply codes.

Table 1. For each protocol, the amount of total and training traces is shown. These traces are separated into *proper* (without error) and *failed* (with error) groups. The training traces are used to create two models, the first without errors and the second with errors. The *states* and *transitions* columns show the complexity of the models. [13].

Protocol	Total traces		Training traces		Model without error states		Model with error states	
	Proper	Failed	Proper	Failed	States	Transitions	States	Transitions
DNS	16	8	10	6	18	28	21	34
SMTP	8	4	6	3	11	18	14	21
POP	24	9	18	7	16	44	19	49
FTP	106	20	88	14	33	126	39	137

The proof-of-concept tool took input data of selected application protocols and created models of the behavior without errors and a model with errors. The Table 1 shows the distribution of the input data into a group of correct training traces and a group of traces with errors. Remaining traces will be later used for testing the model. The right part of the table shows the complexity of the generated models in the format of states and transitions count.

Based on the statistics of models, we have made the following conclusions:

– transitions sum depicts the model's complexity better than the state's sum;
– there is no direct correlation between the complexity of the protocol and the complexity of the model. As can be seen with protocols DNS and SMTP, even though the model SMTP is more complicated than DNS model, there were about 50% fewer unique traces resulting in a model with 21 transitions, while the DNS model consists of 34 transitions. The reason is that one DNS connection can contain more than one query-reply and because the protocol is stateless, any query-reply can follow the previous query-reply value.

Part of the original paper is a figure with four charts outlining the same four protocols, as displayed in Table 1. These four charts show the progress of increasing the model size and decreasing the number of diagnostic errors when new traces are added to the model. The model creation process was split into two parts: training from traces without errors and learning the errors.

6.3   Evaluation of Test Traces

Table 2 shows the amount of successful and failed testing traces; the right part of Table 2 shows testing results for these data. All tests check whether:

1. a successful trace is marked as correct (TN);
2. a failed trace is detected as an error trace with correct error description (TP);
3. a failed trace is marked as correct (FN);
4. a successful trace is detected as an error or failed trace is detected as an error but with an incorrect error description (FP);
5. true/false (T/F) ratios which are calculated as $(TN+TP)/(FN+FP)$. T/F ratios represents how many traces the model diagnosed correctly.

As the columns T-F ratio in Table 2 shows, most of the testing data was diagnosed correctly. We have analyzed the incorrect results and made the following conclusions:

– **DNS:** False positive - One application has made a connection with the DNS server and keeps the connection up for a long time. Over time several queries were transferred. Even though the model contains these queries, the order in which they came is new to the model. The model returned an error result even when the communication ended correctly. An incomplete model causes this misbehavior. To correctly diagnose all query combinations, the model has to be created from more unique training traces.

Table 2. The created models have been tested by using testing traces, which are split into *proper* (without error) and *failed* (with error) groups. The correct results are shown in the true negative (*TN*) and true positive (*TP*) columns. The columns false positive (*FP*) and false negative (*FN*) on the other side contain the number of wrong test results. The ratio of correct results is calculated as a true/false ratio (*T-F ratio*). This ratio represents how many testing traces were diagnosed correctly. [13].

Protocol	Testing traces		Testing against model without error states					Testing against model with error states				
	Proper	Failed	TN	TP	FN	FP	T-F ratio	TN	TP	FN	FP	T-F ratio
DNS	6	2	4	2	0	2	75%	4	1	1	2	63%
SMTP	2	1	2	1	0	0	100%	2	1	0	0	100%
POP	6	2	6	2	0	0	100%	6	2	0	0	100%
FTP	18	6	18	6	0	0	100%	18	5	1	0	96%

TN - true negative, TP - true positive, FN - false negative, FP - false positive, T-F ratio - true/false ratio

- **DNS:** False positive - The model received a new SOA update query. Even if the communication did not contain the error by itself, it is an indication of a possible anomaly in the network. Therefore, we consider this as the expected behavior.
- **DNS:** False negative - The situation was the same as with the first DNS False positive mistake - the order of packets was unexpected. Unexpected order resulted in an unknown error instead of an already learned error.
- **FTP:** False negative - The client sent a PASS command before the USER command. This resulted in an unexpected order of commands, and the model detected an unknown error. We are not sure how this situation has happened, but because it is nonstandard behavior, we are interpreting this as an anomaly. Hence, the proof-of-concept tool provided the expected outcome.

All the incorrect results are related to the incomplete model. In the stateless protocols (like DNS), it is necessary to capture traces with all combinations of query-reply states. For example, if the protocol defines 10 types of queries, 3 types of replies, the total amount of possible transitions is $(10 * 3)^2 = 900$. Another challenge is a protocol which defines many error reply codes. To create a complete model, all error codes in all possible states need to be learned from the traces.

We have created the tested tool as a prototype in Python language. Our goal was not to test the performance, but to get at least an idea of how usable our solution is, we gathered basic time statistics. The processing time of converting one PCAP file (one trace) into a sequence of query-replies and adding it to the model took on average 0.4 s. This time had only small deviations because most of the time took initialization of the *TShark*. The total amount of time required to learn a model depends on the amount of PCAPs. At average, to create a model from 100 PCAPs, 30 s was required.

6.4   Timed Transitions

For this test, we took a model of the SMTP protocol from the previous test, and we have extended it with new PCAP files. These new PCAP files contain two problems that could not be detected without a timed finite automata model:

1. **overloaded SMTP server** - all requests from the server have a high delay;
2. **overloaded authentication LDAP server** - the SMTP server responds to requests at an average speed, but user authentication, which uses an external LDAP server takes considerably longer.

Unfortunately, we do not have PCAP files with these errors from a real production network, so we had to create them. We achieved this by manually overloading the SMTP server, LDAP server, or creating a delay for the communication between these two servers.

The part of the extended model that covers authentication problems is displayed in Fig. 5. Red colored transitions cover situations where, regardless of the authentication type and authentication result, a slow response is detected. The model describes two authentication methods: simple authentication (name and password in one message) and login authentication (name and password sent separately). As described in Algorithm 3, these new transitions have a time interval with the value <0; ∞>. Therefore all traces that do not match the original time restrictions are matched by these new transitions.

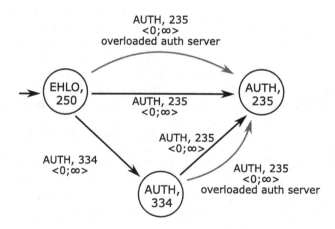

Fig. 5. The segment of the SMTP model which contains new transitions and states related to the high delay from the authentication server. (Color figure online)

We have tested the created model on other captured PCAP files. With overloaded LDAP servers or high communication latency between an SMTP and an LDAP server, the model correctly detected a problem related to the authentication. When the SMTP server was overloaded, the model correctly detected overload at the beginning of the communication.

However, the extended SMTP model was not able to correctly diagnose a situation where the beginning of the communication was OK, and the overload of the SMTP server began during client authentication. Although other delayed responses followed the delayed response for authentication, the system stopped at the first error and erroneously detected an authentication problem.

6.5   Encrypted Data Diagnostics

We have performed another type of evaluation aimed at verifying if the method proposed by us applies to encrypted traffic or not. As described in the previous sections, the diagnostic process uses request-reply values, but we are not able to detect this in encrypted communication. To overcome this limitation, we have proposed a modification to the model in the way that the model uses the size of the encrypted data (TLS record size) instead of the request-reply value.

Because we only consider the size of the application data, which can easily vary even if the request value or the reply value is the same, it is necessary to work with a range of values. We are using an algorithm similar to the one used to calculate the range for time intervals. From the set of values, we calculate the minimum, maximum, and square root of the standard deviation. The range of the interval that will accept messages will have a value ranging from "$minimum - \sqrt{std\ deviation}$" to "$maximum + \sqrt{std\ deviation}$". The difference from the calculation of the time intervals is that with a range of application data sizes, the interval is calculated from even a single value, and it is not required to have at least five values.

With this modified approach of diagnostics, we are not able to diagnose such a range of errors as in unencrypted traffic. However, we are still able to obtain at least basic information about the state of communication. We have based this idea on the fact that protocol communication between endpoints goes through different states. Protocol standards specify these states and their order. Diagnostics of encrypted communication, do not analyze exactly what caused the error but only when (or in which state) the error occurred.

As in the case of unencrypted communications, a model should be created only from traces belonging to one service (on a single server) and applied to the same service. With other configurations, the content of messages can be different, which would cause different sizes of the messages themselves.

To verify the idea of diagnostics based on the size of application data, we have captured ten correct and three error SMTP communication traces. From these communications, a model was created, which is shown in Fig. 6. The Figure shows three detectable errors that also separate the SMTP protocol states - welcoming client, user authentication, and e-mail sending. Based on this test, we have reached the conclusion that the approach is usable. However, to use the model in the real-world, the model should be trained from more traces.

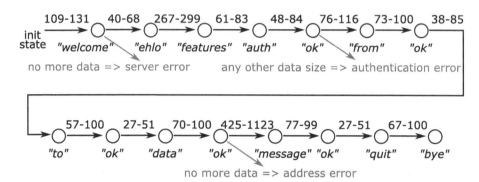

Fig. 6. The segment of the SMTP model which contains new transitions and states related to the high delay from the authentication server.

7   Discussion

This chapter describes some of the topics we have come across when developing and using the tool.

7.1   Fully Trained Model

One of the fundamental questions when using the tool is when the model is fully (or for X%) trained and when it is possible to switch from training mode to diagnostic mode. The simplest way of specifying how much percent the model is trained is by calculating all possible transitions. Transitions are connecting any two states, which are defined by request/reply values. The total number of states is $requests\_count * replies\_count$, and the total number of transitions is $states\_count^2$. Of course, many combinations of requests and replies do not make sense, but the algorithm can never be sure which combinations are valid and which are not. The problem with counting all possible combinations is that without predefined knowledge of the diagnosed protocol, the tool can never be sure if all possible requests and replies have already been seen or not.

One way to determine whether a model is trained without knowing the total number of states is by checking the list of trained states when processing new input data. If the system has not detected a new state for a certain amount of iterations, it will declare that the list is complete, and the model is fully trained. Here comes the problem of determining how long to wait for a new value.

Basically, there are three approaches that can be combined:

A1 amount of new files - waiting for X new files to be processed (e.g., 100);
A2 training duration - waiting for an X lasting interval;
A3 unique amount of clients - waiting for X unique clients (e.g., 10).

Unfortunately, each of these approaches has drawbacks that cannot be eliminated entirely:

ReA1. If most (or all) new files have the same content type (for example, the same client queries the same DNS translation type), then the number of these files is not important. We have partially solved this problem by creating communications fingerprints and ignoring duplicate fingerprint files. This is why the evaluation section describes so few unique communications. As an example, we take the SMTP protocol. Most conversations had an identical pattern - welcoming the client, user authentication, and sending an email. The responses to all commands were without any error. Although the welcome message (timestamp), login information, email addresses, and email content varied from one communication to the next, the fingerprint was the same as all of this data was deleted in the *Input Data Processing* stage. So even though we had dozens of these conversations, we counted them as just one conversation.

ReA2. By taking communications carried during a limited time frame, e.g. 24 h, we may not cover situations that arise less frequently or irregularly. For example, SMTP clients can process requests to send a message even when the client is offline and then send these messages at once when the client is online again. However, the situation, when a client sends multiple messages at once, does not occur often, and a 24-h window might not be enough.

ReA3. This criterion can only be applied if a large number of clients connect to a single server. In the case of a pre-defined server-server communication, this criteria makes no sense. Even with a larger amount of clients, all clients may use the same application, the same settings, and perform the same activity.

In our opinion, the best option is to combine all three mentioned approaches and select parameters so that the data sample used is relevant and that the model is trained within an acceptable time. For example, waiting for 100 unique sequences in the SMTP protocol or 1000 communications if only one communication happens per day is meaningless. However, even in this case, we are not able to capture the following situations:

- Protocol updates can introduce new version of the protocol which may introduce new types of commands or responses.
- Another version (e.g., by an update) of the application or a brand new application will appear on the network. This may cause the client to start to communicate with the server with a different pattern of behavior.
- Some types of errors are associated with less frequently used features, which occur very irregularly. Such errors are hard to catch and get into the model.

From our experience, it is not possible to determine when the model is fully trained or at least trained from X%. Even if the model does not grow for a long time, it can suddenly expand by processing a new trace (new extensions, programs with specific behavior, program updates).

Nevertheless, the model incorporates means to train even in the diagnostic phase (when the tool is deployed). An administrator that encounters a false error can always improve the model. Consequently, as time passes, the model can adapt to handle infrequent communications and protocol/application updates.

7.2   Data Labeling

During model training, an administrator needs to determine if there is an error in conversation manually. If an error is detected, an administrator creates a description of this error. This process is time-consuming and requires knowledge of the modeled protocol and computer networks in general. However, it is important to realize that in the case of manual diagnosis, the administrator has to perform a similar diagnosis. Hence, our approach does not introduce additional requirements for administrators' skills. Therefore, we do not think that the need to manually mark communications is a disadvantage of our method.

Another possible way to label data can be by applying artificial intelligence or machine learning. However, we think that even with machine learning, supervised learning has to be used. Therefore, it is still necessary to analyze the content of the communications manually and instruct the algorithm. Another question is, how easy it is for the network administrator to work with artificial intelligence, and whether network administrators without programming knowledge understand working with machine learning.

7.3   Model of Models

As part of our proposed approach, we do not model relationships between individual communications or between different protocols. Each model describes one particular communication with one protocol. However, there are more complex errors that cannot be detected or diagnosed by analyzing just a single communication. An example is downloading a web page content. This activity can consist of multiple individual communications: user authentication, HTML page download, and download of other elements such as images or scripts. Another example is that during communication with an application server, the server establishes another connection to the RADIUS server to authenticate the user.

To be able to diagnose problems that are spread across multiple communications correctly (even over multiple protocols), it is necessary to create a model which will consist of several models describing individual communications ("model of models"). This high-level model can check one communication and, based on its result, launch another model for the following communication or generate a diagnostic report.

7.4   Another Usage of Models

The proposed models do not apply to network diagnosis only. Another application is the security analysis. The model can be trained to accept only communications which fulfill the security policy. Other communications that are not accepted by the trained model are reported as possibly dangerous. Another type of security analysis is by visualizing the model and employing a manual analysis. Our tool can export models to a format suitable for graphical visualization. From the trained models, an administrator can make some deductions. For example, if some users are not using the recommended authentication or some communications contain outdated commands.

Another possible model usage is related to time transitions within the model. We think it makes sense to investigate whether it is possible to use models for profiling communications. For example, in the case of FTP communication, if the browsing and downloading of files are without delays caused by user interaction, it is possible to associate such communication with a tool that automatically browses and downloads server content.

8   Conclusions

In the presented paper, we have proposed an automatic method for generating automata from network communication traces and their use in the network diagnostic process. The diagnostic system is designed to learn from both normal error-free communication sequences as well as from erroneous traces in order to create an automata-based model for the communication protocol behavior. The states in the automaton can be labeled with additional information that provides diagnostic information for the error detected.

The method requires network traces prepared by an expert to create a good model. The expert is expected to annotate network traces and label the known errors. The current model is only applicable to query-response protocols and those that provides a sufficient amount of information to observe their state. We demonstrated that if the model is created based on the reasonable sample of good and error behavior it can be used in any network environment.

We have implemented the method in a proof-of-concept tool[3] and use it in a set of experiments for demonstration purposes. The tool has been tested on a limited set of application protocols of different types, e.g., e-mail transfer, file download, domain name resolution. Experiments show that the suitability and usability of the model heavily depend on the network protocol. Although the model typically does not cover all possible scenarios, it is useful for diagnosis of repetitive error. As the model can learn errors during deployment, an administrator does not have to deal with errors not encountered during learning phase more than once.

Acknowledgements. This work was supported by The Ministry of Education, Youth and Sports from the National Programme of Sustainability (NPU II) project IT4Innovations excellence in science - LQ1602.

---

[3] https://github.com/marhoSVK/semiauto-diagnostics

References

1. Aggarwal, B., Bhagwan, R., Das, T., Eswaran, S., Padmanabhan, V.N., Voelker, G.M.: NetPrints: diagnosing home network misconfigurations using shared knowledge. In: Proceedings of the 6th USENIX symposium on Networked Systems Design and Implementation, pp. 349–364, July 2009. http://portal.acm.org/citation.cfm?id=1559001

2. Anand, A., Akella, A.: Net-replay: a new network primitive. ACM SIGMETRICS Perform. Eval. Rev. **37**(3), 14–19 (2010). https://doi.org/10.1145/1710115.1710119

3. Antunes, J., Neves, N., Verissimo, P.: ReverX: reverse engineering of protocols. Technical report 2011–01, Department of Informatics, School of Sciences, University of Lisbon (2011). http://hdl.handle.net/10451/14078

4. Burschka, S., Dupasquier, B.: Tranalyzer: versatile high performance network traffic analyser. In: 2016 IEEE Symposium Series on Computational Intelligence (SSCI), pp.1–8 (2017). https://doi.org/10.1109/SSCI.2016.7849909

5. Casas, P., Zseby, T., Mellia, M.: Big-DAMA: big data analytics for network traffic monitoring and analysis. In: Proceedings of the 2016 Workshop on Fostering Latin-American Research in Data Communication Networks (ACM LANCOMM 2016), pp. 1–3 (2016). https://doi.org/10.1145/2940116.2940117

6. Chen, M., Zheng, A., Lloyd, J., Jordan, M., Brewer, E.: Failure diagnosis using decision trees. In: Proceedings of International Conference on Autonomic Computing, pp. 36–43 (2004). https://doi.org/10.1109/ICAC.2004.1301345. http://ieeexplore.ieee.org/document/1301345/

7. Comparetti, P.M., Wondracek, G., Krügel, C., Kirda, E.: Prospex: protocol specification extraction. In: 2009 30th IEEE Symposium on Security and Privacy, pp. 110–125 (2009)

8. Cui, W., Kannan, J., Wang, H.J.: Discoverer: automatic protocol reverse engineering from network traces. In: Proceedings of 16th USENIX Security Symposium on USENIX Security Symposium, SS 2007, p. 14. USENIX Association, Boston (2007). Article no 14. ISBN 1113335555779

9. De Paola, A., et al.: Rule based reasoning for network management. In: 7th International Workshop on Computer Architecture for Machine Perception (CAMP 2005), pp. 25–30, July 2005. https://doi.org/10.1109/CAMP.2005.47

10. Dhamdhere, A., Teixeira, R., Dovrolis, C., Diot, C.: NetDiagnoser: troubleshooting network unreachabilities using end-to-end probes and routing data. In: Proceedings of the 2007 ACM CoNEXT (2007). https://doi.org/10.1145/1364654.1364677

11. Dong, C., Dulay, N.: Argumentation-based fault diagnosis for home networks. In: Proceedings of the 2nd ACM SIGCOMM Workshop on Home Networks, Home Networks 2011, pp. 37–42. Association for Computing Machinery. New York (2011). https://doi.org/10.1145/2018567.2018576

12. El Sheikh, A.Y.: Evaluation of the capabilities of wireshark as network intrusion system. J. Global Res. Comput. Sci. **9**(8), 01–08 (2018)

13. Holkovič, M., Ryšavý, O., Polčák, L.: Using network traces to generate models for automatic network application protocols diagnostics. In: Proceedings of the 16th International Joint Conference on e-Business and Telecommunications Volume 1: DCNET, ICE-B, OPTICS, SIGMAP and WINSYS, pp. 43–53. SciTePress - Science and Technology Publications (2019). https://www.fit.vut.cz/research/publication/12012

14. Ivković, N., Milić, L., Konecki, M.: A timed automata model for systems with gateway-connected controller area networks. In: 2018 IEEE 3rd International Conference on Communication and Information Systems (ICCIS), pp. 97–101. IEEE (2018)

15. Kim, S., et al.: A rule based approach to network fault and security diagnosis with agent collaboration. In: Kim, T.G. (ed.) AIS 2004. LNCS (LNAI), vol. 3397, pp. 597–606. Springer, Heidelberg (2005). https://doi.org/10.1007/978-3-540-30583-5_63

16. Krueger, T., Gascon, H., Krämer, N., Rieck, K.: Learning stateful models for network honeypots. In: Proceedings of the 5th ACM Workshop on Security and Artificial Intelligence, AISec 2012, pp. 37–48. Association for Computing Machinery, New York 2012). https://doi.org/10.1145/2381896.2381904

17. Ladi, G., Buttyon, L., Holczer, T.: Message format and field semantics inference for binary protocols using recorded network traffic. In: 2018 26th International Conference on Software, Telecommunications and Computer Networks (SoftCOM) (2018). https://doi.org/10.23919/SOFTCOM.2018.8555813

18. Lunze, J., Supavatanakul, P.: Diagnosis of discrete-event system described by timed automata. IFAC Proc. Vol. **35**(1), 77–82 (2002)

19. Luo, M., Zhang, D., Phua, G., Chen, L., Wang, D.: An interactive rule based event management system for effective equipment troubleshooting. In: Proceedings of the IEEE Conference on Decision and Control, vol. 8(3), pp. 2329–2334 (2011). https://doi.org/10.1007/s10489-005-4605-0

20. Orzach, Y.: Network Analysis Using Wireshark Cookbook. Packt Publishing Ltd., Birmingham (2013)

21. Pellegrino, G., Lin, Q., Hammerschmidt, C., Verwer, S.: Learning behavioral fingerprints from netflows using timed automata. In: 2017 IFIP/IEEE Symposium on Integrated Network and Service Management (IM), pp. 308–316. IEEE (2017)

22. Polčák, L.: Lawful interception: identity detection. Ph.D. thesis, Brno University of Technology, Faculty of Information Technology (2017). https://www.fit.vut.cz/study/phd-thesis/679/

23. Procházka, M., Macko, D., Jelemenská, K.: IP networks diagnostic communication generator. In: Emerging eLearning Technologies and Applications (ICETA), pp. 1–6 (2017)

24. Samhat, A., Skehill, R., Altman, Z.: Automated troubleshooting in WLAN networks. In: 2007 16th IST Mobile and Wireless Communications Summit (2007). https://doi.org/10.1109/ISTMWC.2007.4299084

25. łgorzata Steinder, M., Sethi, A.S.: A survey of fault localization techniques in computer networks. Sci. Comput. Program. **53**(2), 165–194 (2004)

26. Tong, V., Tran, H.A., Souihi, S., Mellouk, A.: Network troubleshooting: survey, taxonomy and challenges. In: 2018 International Conference on Smart Communications in Network Technologies, SaCoNeT 2018, pp. 165–170 (2018). https://doi.org/10.1109/SaCoNeT.2018.8585610

27. Traverso, S., et al.: Exploiting hybrid measurements for network troubleshooting. In: 2014 16th International Telecommunications Network Strategy and Planning Symposium, Networks (2014). https://doi.org/10.1109/NETWKS.2014.6959212

28. Wang, Y., Zhang, Z., Yao, D.D., Qu, B., Guo, L.: Inferring protocol state machine from network traces: a probabilistic approach. In: Lopez, J., Tsudik, G. (eds.) ACNS 2011. LNCS, vol. 6715, pp. 1–18. Springer, Heidelberg (2011). https://doi.org/10.1007/978-3-642-21554-4_1

29. Wondracek, G., Comparetti, P.M., Kruegel, C., Kirda, E.: Automatic network protocol analysis. In: Proceedings of the 15th Annual Network and Distributed System Security Symposium, NDSS (2008)

30. Xiao, M.M., Yu, S.Z., Wang, Y.: Automatic network protocol automaton extraction. In: NSS 2009 - Network and System Security (2009). https://doi.org/10.1109/NSS.2009.71
31. Zeng, H., Kazemian, P., Varghese, G., McKeown, N.: A survey on network troubleshooting. Technical report Stanford/TR12-HPNG-061012, Stanford University (2012)

Cooperative Communications, Distributed Coding and Machine Learning

Soon Xin Ng[(✉)]

School of Electronics and Computer Science, University of Southampton,
Southampton SO17 1BJ, UK
sxn@ecs.soton.ac.uk
http://www.wireless.ecs.soton.ac.uk

Abstract. In this contribution, we will investigate how cooperative communications using relay nodes can achieve a higher channel capacity, compared to conventional transmissions. Then, a distributed coding scheme is designed for approaching the corresponding channel capacity. More specifically, a virtual Irregular Convolutional Code (IRCC) is designed based on an iterative learning algorithm and the resultant component encoders are distributed to multiple relay nodes. The near-capacity scheme is applied to an Unmanned Aerial Vehicle (UAV) network for improving the transmission rate at the cell-edge or isolated area. Machine learning algorithm is used to find the optimal location for the UAVs, which serve as the relay nodes. It is shown that a high performing next-generation wireless communications scheme can be created by incorporating cooperative communications, distributed coding and machine learning algorithms.

Keywords: Cooperative communications · Cooperative diversity · Distributed coding · Irregular Convolutional Codes · Iterative learning algorithm · Machine learning

1 Introduction

A high-capacity Multiple-Input Multiple-Output (MIMO) channel can be created by employing multiple antennas at both the transmitter and receiver sites [12,33]. MIMO schemes offer reliable transmissions at high data rates and low transmit power. However, the correlation of signals transmitted from a small mobile unit equipped with multiple antennas degrades the attainable performance. As a remedy, a virtual MIMO system can be created based on cooperative communications [4,32] with the aid of user cooperation, where each User Equipment (UE) may be equipped with just a single antenna. More explicitly, user cooperation enables shared antennas from various UEs, which are further apart, without the problem of signal correlations. A Source Node (SN) may be assisted by several Relay Nodes (RNs) for conveying source signals to a Destination Node (DN). Explicitly, the broadcast nature of wireless transmission makes reception at RNs possible at no extra cost. Furthermore, relaying typically benefits from

© Springer Nature Switzerland AG 2020
M. S. Obaidat (Ed.): ICETE 2019, CCIS 1247, pp. 29–58, 2020.
https://doi.org/10.1007/978-3-030-52686-3_2

a reduced path loss, which makes cooperative communications power efficient. Popular cooperative communications protocols are Decode-And-Forward (DAF), Amplify-And-Forward (AAF), Compress-and-Forward (CAF) and coded-cooperation schemes. However, a strong channel code is required for mitigating potential error propagation in the DAF, CAF and coded-cooperation schemes or for mitigating noise enhancement in the AAF scheme.

The history of channel coding dates back to Shannon's pioneering work in 1948 [40], where he showed that it is possible to design a communication system having an infinitesimally low probability of error, whenever the rate of transmission is lower than the capacity of the channel. Classic coding design aims to approach the channel capacity by 'optimal distance' channel codes, which require a huge number of trellis states or code memory, based on a non-iterative decoder. The invention of turbo codes by Berrou et al. in 1993 [9], was a breakthrough in the history of error control coding, although concatenated codes have been proposed by Forney in 1966 [13]. Low-Density Parity-Check (LDPC) codes constitute another family of near-capacity codes, which were invented by Gallager in 1962 [14] but were only revived in 1995 [30]. Further near-capacity codes include Turbo Trellis Coded Modulation (TTCM) [37], Self Concatenated Convolutional Codes (SECCCs) [25], Space-Time Trellis Codes [42] and Polar Codes [5].

Distributed Coding schemes [44], which involve joint coding design between the Source Node (SN) and Relay Nodes (RNs), are promising coding techniques conceived for approaching the achievable capacity of the relay channel with the aid of iterative detection at the Destination Node (DN). More specifically, Distributed Turbo Codes [6, 27,45,48], Distributed Low Density Parity Check Codes [2,3,35], Distributed Turbo Trellis Coded Modulation [38], Distributed Space-Time Codes [18,22,24,43], Distributed Self-Concatenated Convolutional Codes [26], Distributed Rateless Codes [28] and Distributed Soft Coding [46] have been proposed for cooperative communications. On the other hand, Irregular Convolutional Codes (IRCCs) [29,41] constitute a powerful outer code family conceived for assisting serially-concatenated channel coding schemes in approaching the corresponding channel capacity [16,21,23]. More explicitly, $K \geq 1$ out of N component codes are chosen to produce an encoded sequence having a length of N_c bits. The pth subcode produces a sub-sequence having a length of $\alpha_p N_c$ bits, where α_p is the pth IRCC weighting coefficient. The K component codes and their weighting coefficients are chosen in order to create an EXtrinsic Information Transfer (EXIT) [8,29] curve for the IRCC to match that of the inner code. Near-capacity performance can be achieved, when the area between the EXIT curves of the inner and outer codes is minimized. Recently, a near-capacity Distributed IRCC (DIRCC) was proposed and investigate in [34]. Furthermore, selecting beneficial RNs that exhibit high-quality source-to-relay and relay-to-destination links is capable of significantly reducing the overall transmission power of the relay network [1,20].

On the other hand, Artificial Intelligent (AI) and Machine Learning (ML) have been developed over the decades to a state that they are now working really well. ML involves the design and analysis of algorithms, which enable machines or computers to learn and solve problems. The AI/ML based Deep Blue defeated the world's chess champion in 1997, by using a tree search algorithm that evaluates millions of moves at every turn. On the other hand the Go game is a board game originated in China more than 2,500 years ago. It is a game of profound complexity having 10^{170} possible board configurations. Traditional AI/ML, which constructs a search tree over all possible position, would have no chance to win a human professional player in the Go game. However, in 2017, the AI/ML AlphaGo program managed to beat the human Go champion for the first time [7]. More specifically, the AlphaGo program is based on both advanced tree search and deep neural networks. A range of ML algorithms have been developed for assisting the next generation wireless networks [19]. Further research works have constantly been conducted for creating ML based intelligent wireless networks [31].

In this contribution, some popular cooperative communication schemes and distributed coding schemes are reviewed. The design of channel codes based on EXIT charts and iterative learning algorithm are investigated. Then, a near-capacity distributed coding scheme is applied to a Unmanned Aerial Vehicle (UAV) network [47]. The rest of this paper is organised as follows. Some popular cooperative communications models are outlined in Sect. 2, a few distributed coding schemes are reviewed in Sect. 3, while the relay channel capacity is computed in Sect. 4 before the iterative learning based code design is described in Sect. 5. Power allocation and relay selection mechanisms are discussed in Sect. 6. Further applications of the proposed scheme in UAV network are investigated in Sect. 7, while the conclusions are offered in Sect. 8.

2   Cooperative Communications Models

The conventional direct link communications system between a SN (s) and a DN (d) is shown in Fig. 1, where severe pathloss can happen since the pathloss is proportional to the distance. The single relay and multiple relay aided 2-hop cooperative communications systems are depicted in Fig. 2 and Fig. 3, respectively. Half-duplex relaying is considered in this paper due to its practicality. The transmitted frames from the SN and RN are denoted as $\mathbf{x}_s$ and $\mathbf{x}_r$, respectively. Relaying or cooperative communication is the popular technique to reduce the pathloss. More explicitly, the reduced-distance-related pathloss reduction (or geometrical gain) [6, 15, 26] of the SN to the k RN (r_k) link with respect to a direct link having a reference distance d_0 is given by:

$$G_{sr_k} = \left(\frac{d_0}{d_{sr_k}} \right)^{\Phi},$$

(1)

where d_{ab} stands for the distance between node a and node b, while Φ is the pathloss exponent. A free-space pathloss model was considered, which corresponds to $\Phi = 2$.

The two-hop relaying models in Fig. 2 and Fig. 3 require $2L$ symbol periods to transmit L source symbols to the DN, because half-duplex RNs are invoked. By contrast, the successive relaying model of Fig. 4 requires only $L + 1$ symbol periods for the same transmission because the SN transmits continuously for L symbol period and there is always one RN listens to the SN while another RN transmits to the DN. Furthermore, a two-way relaying model seen in Fig. 5 can convey L symbols using only L symbol periods. More explicitly, the RN can detect both symbols from SN and DN during the first $L/2$ symbol period, before combining both symbols (e.g. using network coding) and broadcasting them simultaneously to both SN and DN during the second $L/2$ symbol periods. If the receive SNR is too low for the RN to detect both symbols from SN

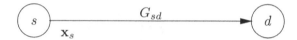

Fig. 1. Direct link communications system.

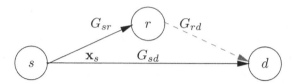

Fig. 2. Single relay model.

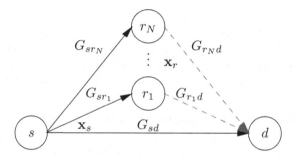

Fig. 3. Multiple relays model.

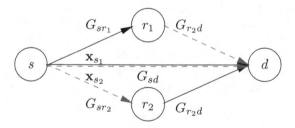

Fig. 4. Successive relaying model.

and DN simultaneously, then the RN can detect symbols from SN during the first one-third period and from DN during the second one-third period, before broadcasting the combined symbols during the third one-third period. The later method would require $3L$ symbol periods to transmit $2L$ symbols, i.e. $2L/3$ symbols for L symbol periods.

The two-way relaying model can be further extended to a butterfly relaying model shown in Fig. 6. More specifically, the RN in a butterfly relaying model can jointly detects $L/2$ symbols from each of the two SNs during the first $L/2$ period, then broadcasts the combined symbols to both DNs during the second $L/2$ period. This results in a transmission of L symbols during L symbol periods.

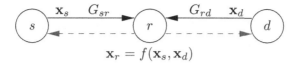

Fig. 5. Two-way relaying model.

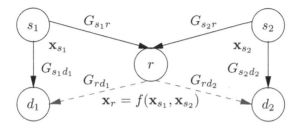

Fig. 6. Butterfly relaying model.

3 Distributed Coding Schemes

In this section, a few distributed coding schemes proposed for the two-hop half-duplex relaying system will be reviewed. More explicitly, Distributed Turbo Coding (DTC) was proposed in [6], under the idealistic assumption that a perfect link exists between the SN and RN. However, as seen in Fig. 7, the DTC employs only a single component code at the SN, where iterative decoding at the RN is not possible. Hence, the SN-RN link performance is far from the achievable channel capacity. A three-component Distributed TTCM (DTTCM) scheme was proposed in [38], where the SN employs a two component TTCM encoder for enabling a near-capacity SN-RN link, where an iterative TTCM decoder is used at the RN together with a single component encoder, as seen in Fig. 8. The DTTCM decoder is shown in Fig. 9, where iterative decoding across three component decoders is invoked. Another near-capacity distributed code known as Distributed SECCC (DSECCC) was proposed in [26], where a single-component self-concatenated encoder was used at the SN, where iterative decoding can be performed as the RN using the SECCC decoder, as seen in Fig. 10. Furthermore, Fig. 11 depicts the DSECCC decoder at the DN. These distributed codes are based on a single-relay model seen in Fig. 2.

A near-capacity Distributed IRCC (DIRCC) scheme was investigated in [26], where an IRCC was designed for the Unity-Rate Code (URC) [11] assisted SN for enabling near-capacity SN-RN link as seen in Fig. 12. A few RNs are selected for creating another IRCC encoder at the RNs based on the multiple relay model of Fig. 3. Iterative decoding across two IRCC decoders and a URC decoder as depicted in Fig. 13, was capable of approaching the corresponding relay channel capacity. More specifically, as seen in Fig. 3 the SN s broadcasts a frame of coded symbols $\mathbf{x}_s$ during the first transmission phase T_1, which is received by the DN d and all the RNs. The carefully selected K out of N RNs decode $\mathbf{x}_s$ and re-encode a portion of the decoded bits to form the virtual IRCC coded symbols $\mathbf{x}_r = [\mathbf{x}_{r_1} \ \mathbf{x}_{r_2} \ \dots \ \mathbf{x}_{r_k} \dots \ \mathbf{x}_{r_K}]$, where the sub-sequence $\mathbf{x}_{r_k}$ is transmitted by the kth RN, r_k, during the kth timeslot of the second transmission phase T_2. Each selected RN transmits its encoded symbol sequence in different timeslots to the DN.

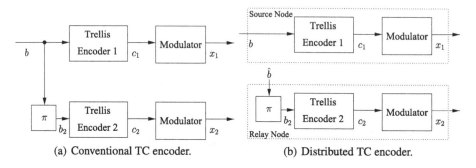

(a) Conventional TC encoder.   (b) Distributed TC encoder.

Fig. 7. The schematic of a two-component Distributed Turbo Coding Scheme, where $\{\hat{b}\}$ is the decoded bit sequence from the decoder at the RN.

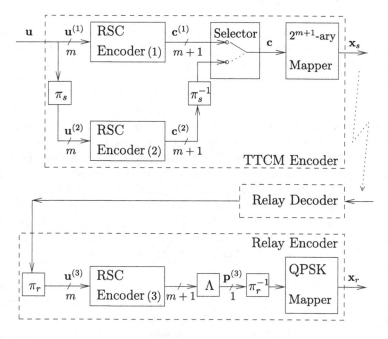

Fig. 8. The schematic of a three-component Distributed TTCM encoder [38] ©IEEE, 2009.

For the DIRCC scheme, the jth signal received at the kth RN during T_1, when N_s symbols are transmitted from the SN, can be written as:

$$y_{r_k,j}^{(T_1)} = \sqrt{G_{sr_k}}\, h_{sr_k,j}^{(T_1)}\, x_{s,j} + n_{r_k,j}^{(T_1)}, \tag{2}$$

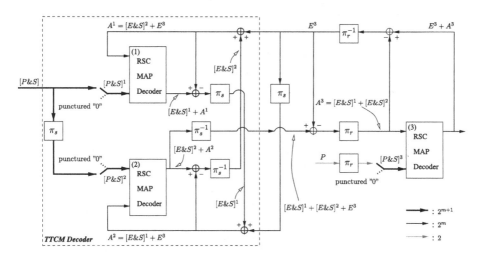

Fig. 9. The schematic of the DTTCM decoder [38] ©IEEE, 2009.

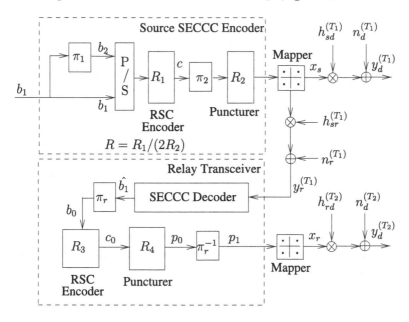

Fig. 10. The schematic of the two-component Distributed Self-Concatenated Convolutional Coding encoder [26] ©IEEE, 2010.

where $j \in \{1, \ldots, N_s\}$ and $h_{ab,j}^{(T_l)}$ is the complex-valued fast Rayleigh fading channel coefficient between node a and node b at instant j during the lth transmission phase T_l, while $n_{b,j}^{(T_l)}$ is zero-mean complex AWGN at node b having a variance of $N_0/2$ per dimension during T_l. Without loss of generality, a free-space pathloss model having a

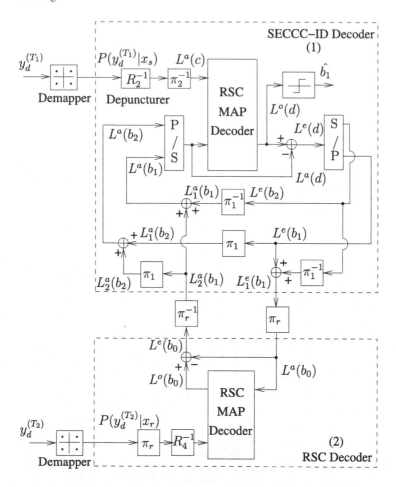

Fig. 11. The schematic of the DSECCC decoder [26] ©IEEE, 2010.

pathloss exponent of 2 was considered. Hence, the reduced-distance-related pathloss reduction of the SN-to-RN link with respect to the SN-to-DN link can be computed as:

$$G_{sr_k} = \left(\frac{d_{sd}}{d_{sr_k}}\right)^2,\qquad(3)$$

where the reference distance is given by $d_0 = d_{sd}$, while d_{ab} stands for the distance between node a and node b. Similarly, the jth signal received at the DN during T_1 can be expressed as:

$$y_{d,j}^{(T_1)} = \sqrt{G_{sd}}\, h_{sd,j}^{(T_1)}\, x_{s,j} + n_{d,j}^{(T_1)},\qquad(4)$$

where $G_{sd} = 1$ since $d_0 = d_{sd}$. Each RN decodes the received signal for retrieving the original information sequence. Only a portion of the re-encoded sequence at each RN is transmitted to the DN.

The jth symbol from the kth RN received at the DN during the second transmission phase T_2, can be written as:

$$y^{(T_2)}_{r_k d,j} = \sqrt{G_{r_k d}}\, h^{(T_2)}_{r_k d,j}\, x_{r_k,j} + n^{(T_2)}_{d,j},\tag{5}$$

where the modulated symbol sequence of the k RN is given by $\mathbf{x}_{r_k} = [x_{r_k,1} \cdots x_{r_k,j} \cdots x_{r_k,L_k}]$, while L_k is the number of modulated symbols and the geometrical gain of the RN-to-DN link with respect to the SN-to-DN link is given by:

$$G_{r_k d} = \left(\frac{d_{sd}}{d_{r_k d}}\right)^2.\tag{6}$$

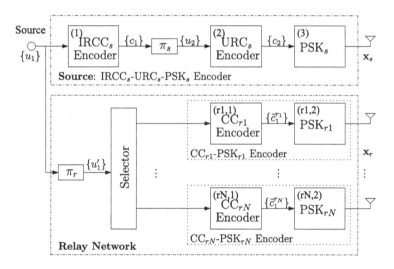

Fig. 12. Schematic of the DIRCC encoder when perfect decoding is achieved at RNs [39] ©IEEE, 2015.

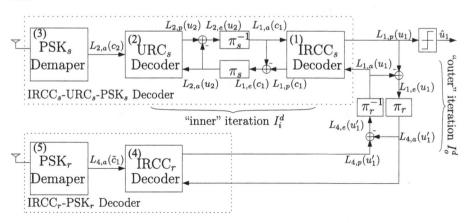

Fig. 13. Schematic of the DIRCC decoder at the DN [39] ©IEEE, 2015.

The total number of coded symbols of the virtual IRCC formed by the K RNs is given by:

$$N_r = \sum_{k=1}^{K} L_k. \tag{7}$$

In general, each RN may transmit a different number of coded and modulated symbols, i.e. $L_k \neq L_p$ for $k \neq p$, according to the designed $IRCC_r$.

If $x_{a,j}$ is the jth symbol transmitted from node a, the average receive Signal to Noise power Ratio (SNR) at node b is given by:

$$\Gamma_r = \frac{E\{G_{ab}\}E\{|h_{ab,j}|^2\}E\{|x_{a,j}|^2\}}{N_0} = \frac{G_{ab}}{N_0}, \tag{8}$$

where $E\{|h_{ab,j}|^2\} = 1$ when communicating over fast Rayleigh fading channels and $E\{|x_{a,j}|^2\} = 1$. For convenience, the average *transmit SNR* is defined as the ratio of the average power transmitted from node a to the noise power encountered at the receiver of node b[1] as:

$$\Gamma_t = \frac{E\{|x_{a,j}|^2\}}{N_0} = \frac{1}{N_0}. \tag{9}$$

Hence, we have:

$$\Gamma_r = \Gamma_t \, G_{ab},$$
$$\gamma_r = \gamma_t + g_{ab} \, [\text{dB}], \tag{10}$$

where $\gamma_r = 10\log_{10}(\Gamma_r)$, $\gamma_t = 10\log_{10}(\Gamma_t)$ and the geometrical gain in decibels is given by $g_{ab} = 10\log_{10}(G_{ab})$. Hence, we can achieve the desired receive SNR by simply changing the transmit power (which governs γ_t) or by selecting a RN at an appropriate geographical location (which defines g_{ab}). In other words, the Channel State Information (CSI) is not required for computing the average receive SNR at each transmission symbol period.

4   Relay Channel Capacity

The two-hop half-duplex relay channel capacity can be calculated by modifying the full-duplex relay channel capacity computation derived in [10]. More specifically, the upper bound C^U and lower bound C^L of our half-duplex relay channel capacity can be computed by considering the capacity of the channel between the SN, RNs and DN as follows:

$$C^U = \min\left\{\lambda C_{(s \to r,d)}, \ \lambda C_{(s \to d)} + (1-\lambda)C_{(r \to d)}\right\} \tag{11}$$
$$C^L = \min\left\{\lambda C_{(s \to r)}, \ \lambda C_{(s \to d)} + (1-\lambda)C_{(r \to d)}\right\} \tag{12}$$

---

[1] This definition is in line with [6,15], but it is unconventional, because it relates the transmit power to the receiver noise measured at two distinct locations.

where $C_{(a \to b,c)}$ is the capacity of the channel between the transmitter at node a and the receivers at both node b and node c. Similarly, $C_{(a \to b)}$ is the capacity of the channel between the transmitter at node a and the receiver at node b. Note that the capacity term $C_{(a \to b,c)}$ or $C_{(a \to b)}$ can be either Continuous-Input Continuous-Output Memoryless Channel (CCMC) capacity or modulation-dependent Discrete-Input Continuous-Output

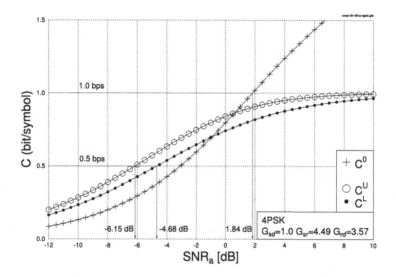

Fig. 14. 4PSK-based DCMC capacity curves of the relay channel when $d_{sr_k} = 0.47d_0$, $d_{r_k d} = 0.53d_0$ and $d_{sd} = d_0$ [39] ©IEEE, 2015.

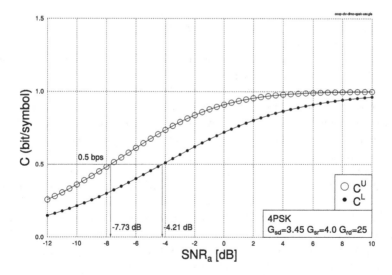

Fig. 15. 4PSK-based DCMC capacity curves of the relay channel when $d_{sr_k} = 0.5d_0$, $d_{r_k d} = 0.2d_0$ and $d_{sd} = 0.5385d_0$.

Memoryless Channel (DCMC) capacity [33,36]. The DCMC capacity is also referred to as the constrained information rate. The ratio of the first transmission period to the total transmission period is given by $\lambda = N_s/(N_s + N_r)$. In this contribution, $N_s = N_r$ is considered, where N_r is given by Eq. (7). This gives $\lambda = 1/2$. Note furthermore that the term $C_{(s \to r,d)}$ considered in the upper bound of Eq. (11) assumes that the RN and DN are capable of perfectly sharing their received signals for joint detection, which is not possible when the RN and DN are not co-located or linked. By contrast, the lower bound is a more practical measure, since it treats the signals received at the RN and DN independently.

The upper and lower bounds of the relay channel capacity curves, which are based on 4PSK DCMC, are shown in Fig. 14 for $\lambda = 0.5$, $G_{sr_k} = 4.50$ and $G_{r_k d} = 3.57$, where SNR_a is the average transmit SNR defined in Eq. (9). The geometrical gains G_{sr_k} and $G_{r_k d}$ can be chosen based on the relay selection mechanism explained in Sect. 6. The 4PSK-based DCMC capacity C^0 of the direct link is also shown in Fig. 14 for comparison. As seen from Fig. 14, a half-rate 4PSK-based scheme has an SNR limit of 1.84 dB, where an error-free throughput of 1 Bit Per Symbol (BPS) is achieved. By contrast, the relay channel capacity of the half-duplex 4PSK-based scheme has SNR limits of -4.68 dB and -6.15 dB for its lower and upper bounds, respectively, when aiming for a throughput of 0.5 BPS. Note that the capacity of the relay channel (both C^U and C^L) is higher than that of the direct link (C^0), when $SNR_a \leq -1$ dB due to the reduced path loss introduced by the RNs. However, the asymptotic capacity of the relay channel is lower than that of the direct link due to the half-duplex constraint.

Figure 15 shows the upper and lower bounds of the relay channel capacity for another scenario when the reference distance is longer than the SN-DN distance, i.e. $d_{sr_k} = 0.5d_0$, $d_{r_k d} = 0.2d_0$ and $d_{sd} = \sqrt{d_{sr_k}^2 + d_{r_k d}^2} = 0.5385d_0$.

5   Iterative Learning Based Code Design

As seen in Fig. 16, the dataword and codeword of Encoder k are denoted as u_k and c_k, respectively. Encoder 1 is normally referred to as the outer encoder, while Encoder 2 is conventionally addressed as the inner encoder. Iterative decoding exchanging mutual information happens at the decoder site. Note that $I_{A(b)}$ and $I_{E(b)}$ denote the *a priori* and *extrinsic* information, respectively, of $b \in \{c_1, u_2\}$ which is either the outer encoder's output bit c_1 or the inner encoder's input bit u_2. The extrinsic information $I_E(u_2)$ becomes the a priori information $I_A(c_1)$ after the deinterleaver, while the extrinsic information $I_E(c_1)$ becomes the a priori information $I_A(u_2)$ after the interleaver.

According to the so-called area property of the EXIT chart [29,41], it can be shown that the area under the normalized EXIT curve of an inner decoder/demapper is related to the achievable DCMC capacity. On the other hand, the area under the inverted EXIT curve of an outer decoder is equal to its coding rate R. Based on these EXIT chart properties, a near capacity concatenated-coding scheme can be designed by matching the corresponding inner and outer decoder EXIT curves, so that a narrow but marginally open EXIT chart tunnel exists between them all the way to the $(x, y) = (1, y)$ point, where $x = I_{E(u_2)} = I_{A(c_1)}$ and $y = I_{A(u_2)} = I_{E(c_1)} \in \{0, 1\}$ as depicted in the EXIT chart of Fig. 20. The design of the IRCC is normally carried out offline, especially

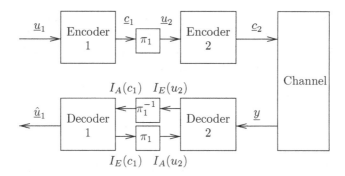

Fig. 16. Two-stage serially-concatenated channel encoder and its iterative decoder.

when communicating over fast Rayleigh fading channels. However, when transmitting over slow fading channels, it may be more beneficial to design the IRCC in real time, by adapting the IRCC coefficients to the prevalent channel conditions. For simplicity, transmissions over fast Rayleigh fading channels was considered in this contribution.

5.1 Code Design for SN

For the IRCC$_s$ design at the SN, an IRCC that consists of $P = 17$ memory-four Convolutional Codes (CCs) given by [29,41] was considered. A total encoded sequence length of $N_c = 120,000$ bits and an effective coding rate of $R = 0.5$ are considered. The pth subcode has a coding rate of R_p and it encodes a fraction of $\alpha_p R_p N_c$ information bits to $\alpha_p N_c$ encoded bits. More specifically, α_p is the pth IRCC weighting coefficient satisfying the following constraints [29,41]:

$$\sum_{p=1}^{P} \alpha_p = 1, \; R = \sum_{p=1}^{P} \alpha_p R_p, \; \alpha_p \in [0,1] \; \forall p, \tag{13}$$

which can be conveniently represented in the following matrix form:

$$\begin{bmatrix} 1 & 1 & \dots & 1 \\ R_1 & R_2 & \dots & R_P \end{bmatrix} \begin{bmatrix} \alpha_1 & \alpha_2 & \dots & \alpha_P \end{bmatrix}^T = \begin{bmatrix} 1 \\ R \end{bmatrix}$$
$$\mathbf{C}\,\boldsymbol{\alpha} = \mathbf{d}. \tag{14}$$

The EXIT function of the IRCC is given by:

$$I_{E(c_1)} = T_{c_1}\left[I_{A(c_1)}\right] = \sum_{p=1}^{P} \alpha_p\, T_{c_1,p}\left[I_{A(c_1)}\right], \tag{15}$$

where $T_{c_1,p}\left[I_{A(c_1)}\right] = I_{E(c_1),p}$ is the EXIT function of the pth subcode. More explicitly, the inverted EXIT curves of the $P = 17$ subcodes having different coding rates ranging from 0.1 to 0.9 are shown in Fig. 17.

Figure 18 shows the EXIT curves of the 17 potential subcodes considered for the *outer decoder* together with a target EXIT curve given by the URC$_8$-4PSK *inner decoder*. The horizontal difference between the inner and outer code's EXIT curves at a given $I_{in} = I_{A(c_1)} = I_{E(u_2)}$ value is given by:

$$e(I_{A(c_1)}) = I_{E(c_1)} - I_{A(u_2)} \tag{16}$$

$$e(I_{in}) = \sum_{p=1}^{P} \alpha_p T_{c_1,p}(I_{in}) - T_{u_2}^{-1}[I_{in}, C_*] \tag{17}$$

where the EXIT function of the inner decoder depends on both $I_{A(u_2)}$ and the DCMC capacity C_*, i.e $I_{E(u_2)} = T_{u_2}[I_{A(u_2)}, C_*]$ and $T^{-1}(.)$ is the inverse function of $T(.)$. There are Q number of sample points $I_{in} \in \{i_1, i_2, \ldots, i_Q\}$ and let $e_q = e(i_q)$ denote the qth error of the Q-sample curve, which has a constraint of $e_q \geq 0 \;\; \forall q$. The error vector $\mathbf{e} = [e_1 \; e_2 \; \ldots \; e_Q]^T$ can be rewritten as:

$$\mathbf{e} = \mathbf{A}\boldsymbol{\alpha} - \mathbf{b}, \tag{18}$$

where $\boldsymbol{\alpha} = [\alpha_1 \; \alpha_2 \; \ldots \; \alpha_P]^T$, while the transfer function matrix $\mathbf{A}$ is given by:

$$\mathbf{A} = \begin{bmatrix} T_{c_1,1}(i_1) & T_{c_1,2}(i_1) & \cdots & T_{c_1,P}(i_1) \\ T_{c_1,1}(i_2) & T_{c_1,2}(i_2) & \cdots & T_{c_1,P}(i_2) \\ \vdots & \vdots & \ddots & \vdots \\ T_{c_1,1}(i_Q) & T_{c_1,2}(i_Q) & \cdots & T_{c_1,P}(i_Q) \end{bmatrix} \tag{19}$$

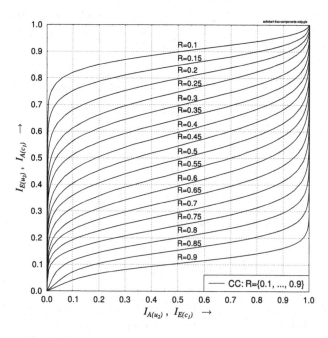

Fig. 17. The inverted EXIT curves of the $P = 17$ subcodes.

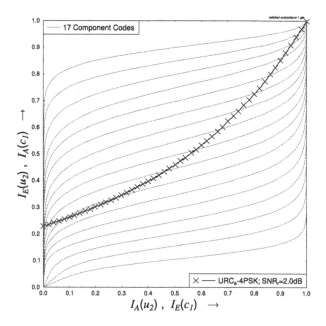

Fig. 18. The EXIT chart of the IRCC$_s$-URC$_s$-4PSK decoder at each RN.

and the vector **b** can be represented as:

$$\mathbf{b} = \begin{bmatrix} T_{u_2}(i_1) \\ T_{u_2}(i_2) \\ \dots \\ T_{u_2}(i_Q) \end{bmatrix}. \tag{20}$$

Let $\mathcal{C}$ be the set of all $\boldsymbol{\alpha}$ satisfying $\mathbf{C}\boldsymbol{\alpha} = \mathbf{d}$, $\mathcal{A}$ be the set of all $\boldsymbol{\alpha}$ satifying $\alpha_p \in [0,1]\ \forall p$ and $\mathcal{E}$ be the set of all $\boldsymbol{\alpha}$ satifying $e_q \geq 0\ \forall q$. The aim of the code design is to find the optimum $\boldsymbol{\alpha}^*$ that minimizes the objective function

$$J(\boldsymbol{\alpha}) = \mathbf{e}^T \mathbf{e} = ||\mathbf{e}||_2^2 \tag{21}$$

with the above three constraints. This can be formulated as:

$$\begin{aligned}
\underset{\alpha}{\text{minimize}} \quad & J(\boldsymbol{\alpha}) = \mathbf{e}^T\mathbf{e} = ||\mathbf{e}||_2^2 \\
\text{subject to} \quad & 1)\ \mathbf{C}\boldsymbol{\alpha} = \mathbf{d}, \\
& 2)\ \alpha_p \in [0,1] && \forall p, \\
& 3)\ e_q \geq 0 && \forall q.
\end{aligned} \tag{22}$$

An iterative learning algorithm can be used to find the solution for Eq. (22). More specifically, a steepest decent based approach was proposed in [29].

Figure 20 shows that it is possible to design an IRCC$_s$ for the SN to have an EXIT curve that matches the EXIT curve of the URC$_s$-4PSK inner encoder at a receive SNR of 2 dB. Here, c_1 is the coded bit of the $IRCC_s$ outer encoder and u_2 denotes the interleaved version of c_1, which is fed to the URC_s-4PSK inner encoder. It was found that $IRCC_s$ only requires seven out of the 17 available component codes, i.e., there are only seven non-zero IRCC weights. The corresponding IRCC weight vector is given by:

$$\widetilde{\boldsymbol{\alpha}}_s = [0.2356z^5_{0.30} \ 0.2052z^6_{0.35} \ 0.0859z^7_{0.40} \ 0.2114z^{10}_{0.55}$$
$$0.1284z^{13}_{0.70} \ 0.0630z^{16}_{0.85} \ 0.0705z^{17}_{0.90}], \tag{23}$$

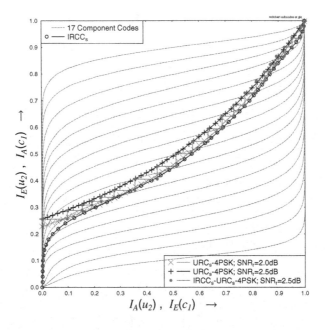

Fig. 19. EXIT chart of the $IRCC_s$-URC-4PSK decoder at the DN.

where the exponent and subscript of the dummy variable z denote the component code index p and its coding rate R_p, respectively, while the pth IRCC weight α_p is the value in front of $z^p_{R_p}$.

According to the capacity curve C^0 of Fig. 14, the corresponding transmit SNR at a capacity of 1 BPS is 1.84 dB. Hence, the $IRCC_s$-URC_s-4PSK scheme is capable of operating within $(2 - 1.84) = 0.16$ dB from the SNR limit of the source-to-relay channel. However, the narrow gap between the two EXIT curves shown in Fig. 20 would require an impractically high number of decoding iterations at the RN. Hence, we should aim for attaining a receive SNR of $\gamma^{sr}_r = 2.5$ dB instead of 2 dB at the RN, in order to achieve a wider gap between these EXIT curves for attaining a lower decoding complexity. Note that these two EXIT curves are generated semi-analytically to predict the actual performance of the $IRCC_s$-URC_s-4PSK scheme. A Monte-Carlo simulation based stair-case-shaped decoding trajectory of the $IRCC_s$-URC_s-4PSK scheme at $\gamma^{sr}_r = 2.5$ dB is shown in Fig. 20 to satisfy the EXIT chart prediction, where it traverses within the gap between the two EXIT curves up to the top right corner.

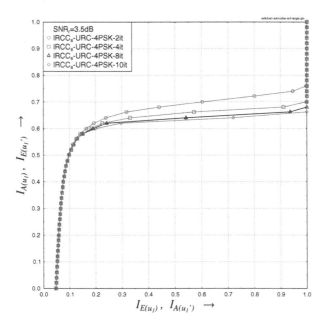

Fig. 20. The EXIT chart of the $IRCC_s$-URC_s-4PSK decoder at each RN [39] ©IEEE, 2015.

5.2   Code Design for RNs

The design of DIRCC involves the $IRCC_s$-URC_s-4PSK scheme as the upper decoder and the $IRCC_r$-4PSK scheme as the lower decoder of Fig. 13. Once the $IRCC_s$ has been designed for the source-to-relay channel, the next task is to design the $IRCC_r$. However, the design of $IRCC_r$ for the relay network is more challenging, because the EXIT curves of both the upper and lower decoders are SNR-dependent. Firstly, we need to find the target EXIT curve based on the $IRCC_s$-URC_s-4PSK decoder. Iterative decoding by exchanging extrinsic information between the amalgamated "PSK_s-URC_s" decoder and the $IRCC_s$ decoder during *Phase I* is performed at the DN, based on a receive SNR of $\gamma_r^{sd} = -3.5\,\text{dB}^2$. The "inner" iterative decoding process can be stopped when further increase of the area A_E above the EXIT curve of the amalgamated "PSK_s-URC_s-$IRCC_s$" decoder becomes marginal. As seen from Fig. 19, eight iterations is a good choice because having more than 8 inner iterations will only marginally increase the area above the EXIT curve of the $IRCC_s$-URC_s-4PSK decoder. The EXIT curve of the 8-iteration based $IRCC_s$-URC_s-4PSK upper decoder at the DN when the receive SNR is $\gamma_r^{sd} = -3.5\,\text{dB}$ is selected as the target EXIT curve, as seen in Fig. 21. Next, an $IRCC_r$ is designed to have an EXIT curve that can closely match the target EXIT curve of the $IRCC_s$-URC_s-4PSK decoder.

The memory-four 17-component IRCC of [29] fails to ensure a good match to the steep $IRCC_s$-URC_s-4PSK EXIT curve shown in Fig. 21. On the other hand, a simple Repetition Code (RC) would give a horrizontal EXIT curve that can match the horr-

---

[2] The rational of considering $\gamma_r^{sd} = -3.5\,\text{dB}$ is explained in Sect. 6.

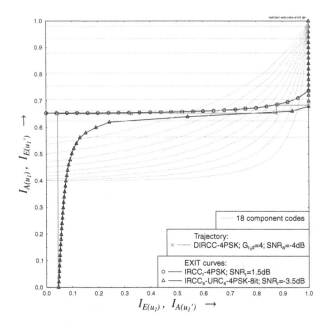

Fig. 21. EXIT chart of the DIRCC-4PSK decoder at the DN [39].

izontal part of the IRCC_s-URC_s-4PSK EXIT curve. Hence, nine RCs having coding rates ranging from 0.1 to 0.5 with a step size of 0.05 were created. Their EXIT curves are shown by the nine horrizontal dashed lines in Fig. 21, where the right-most vertical curve has the lowest coding rate of 0.1 and the left-most vertical curve has the highest coding rate of 0.5. In order to match the gradually sloping part of the IRCC_s-URC_s-4PSK EXIT curve, another nine component Convolutional Codes (CCs), having coding rates ranging from 0.5 to 0.9 with a step size of 0.05 were created. The mother code of these CCs is a half-rate unit-memory CC having a generator polynomial of $[2\ 1]$ in octal format. The same puncturing patterns of the 17-component IRCC in [29] are used for creating CCs having coding rates higher than 0.5. The corresponding nine EXIT curves are shown by the gradually sloping EXIT curves in Fig. 21, where the top-most curve has the lowest coding rate of 0.5 and the bottom-most curve has the highest coding rate of 0.9. Based on these 18 component codes, an IRCC_r-4PSK lower encoder can be designed based on the iterative learning algorithm described in Sect. 5.1. Its EXIT curve is also shown in Fig. 21. The corresponding IRCC weight vector is given by:

$$\widetilde{\boldsymbol{\alpha}}_r = [0.60z_{0.60}^8\ 0.30z_{0.50}^9\ 0.10z_{0.85}^{17}], \tag{24}$$

where the 8th and 9th subcodes are from the RC family while the 17th subcode is from the unit-memory CC family. Hence, only three RNs are needed for the proposed system, where a low-complexity RC or a unit-memory CC are invoked as the RN encoder.

6 Power Allocation and Relay Selection

This section is based on [34], its inclusion in this paper is for completeness. Interested readers are encouraged to find out further details from [34]. More explicitly, the receive SNR required at the RN during T_1 is given by $\gamma_r^{sr} = 2.5\,\text{dB}$ as shown in Fig. 20, while the receive SNR needed at the DN during T_2 is given by $\gamma_r^{rd} = 1.5\,\text{dB}$, as shown in Fig. 21. The idea of the design is to simultaneously achieve these two receive SNRs at the RN and DN, respectively, in order to achieve a BER lower than 10^{-6} at all RNs and DN, at the same time. When this is achieved, there will be minimal error propagation from the DAF-based RNs. Relay selection and/or power allocation can be used to achieve this objective.

6.1 Power Allocation

The receive SNR depends on the transmit SNR according to Eq. (10), we may calculate the minimum required transmission power and then appropriately share it between the SN and RNs. The CSI knowledge is not required[3] for the power allocation mechanism when transmitting over fast Rayleigh fading channels. We can assume that a base station or a central node carries out the RN selection and/or power allocation, followed by broadcasting this information to the participating nodes.

When the number of available RNs is limited and their locations are fixed, power allocation/control can be used for improving power efficiency. Assuming for simplicity that all RNs are located mid-way between the SN and DN, we have geometrical gains of $G_{sr_k} = G_{r_k d} = 4$. In order to achieve $\gamma_r^{sr} = 2.5\,\text{dB}$ at the RN, the corresponding transmit SNR at the SN is given by $\gamma_t^s = 2.5 - 10\log_{10}(G_{sr_k}) = -3.5\,\text{dB}$ according to Eq. (10). Since, we have $G_{sd} = 1$, the corresponding receive SNR at the DN during T_1 is given by $\gamma_r^{sd} = \gamma_t^s = -3.5\,\text{dB}$. The EXIT curve of the IRCC$_s$-URC$_s$-4PSK scheme at $\gamma_r^{sd} = \gamma_t^s = -3.5\,\text{dB}$ is shown in Fig. 21. Furthermore, the required receive SNR at the DN during T_2 is given by $\gamma_r^{rd} = 1.5\,\text{dB}$ and the corresponding transmit SNR at the RN is given by $\gamma_t^r = 1.5 - 10\log_{10}(G_{r_k d}) = -4.5\,\text{dB}$ when $G_{r_k d} = 4$. Hence, the transmit power at the SN has to be $\gamma_t^s - \gamma_t^r = 1\,\text{dB}$ higher than that of the RN, in order to simultaneously achieve an infinitesimally low BER at all RNs and the DN. The average transmit SNR of the power allocation based DIRCC scheme is given by:

$$\tilde{\gamma}_t = 10\log_{10}\left(\lambda 10^{\gamma_t^s/10} + (1-\lambda)10^{\gamma_t^r/10}\right), \tag{25}$$

which equals $\tilde{\gamma}_t = -4\,\text{dB}$ for $\gamma_t^s = -3.5\,\text{dB}$ and $\gamma_t^r = -4.5\,\text{dB}$, where $\lambda = 0.5$, as discussed in Sect. 4. The simulation-based decoding trajectory of the DIRCC-4PSK scheme is shown to verify the EXIT chart predictions of Fig. 21, when $\tilde{\gamma}_t = -4\,\text{dB}$.

6.2 Relay Selection

Furthermore, the receive SNR also depends on the geometrical gain as shown in Eq. (10), we may achieve the required receive SNR with the aid of relay selection, which

---

[3] The CSI knowledge is only needed at the receiver for decoding purposes, where each RN only has to know the CSI between the SN and itself, while the DN only has to know the CSI between the corresponding RNs/SN and itself.

determines the geometrical gains based on the location of the RN according to Eq. (3) and Eq. (6). When communicating over fast Rayleigh fading channels, RN selection can be predetermined based on the RN locations, without the need for the CSI knowledge at each transmission symbol period, because the average power of the fast Rayleigh channel coefficients is unity. By contrast, when transmitting over slow fading channels, RN selection becomes a dynamic process depending on the instantaneous channel variations. Only fast Rayleigh fading channels are considered in this contribution.

In other words, if the transmit powers of the SN and of all the RNs are fixed to a constant value of $\gamma_t^r = \gamma_t^s$, we may select RNs at appropriate geographical locations for achieving different G_{sr_k} and $G_{r_k d}$ values, in order to simultaneously maintain $\gamma_r^{sr} = 2.5\,\text{dB}$ and $\gamma_r^{rd} = 1.5\,\text{dB}$. Assuming that all RNs are relatively close to each other and they are located in the direct SN-to-DN path, where we have $d_{sd} = d_{sr_k} + d_{r_k d}$, it can be shown that the geometrical gains are related to each other as follows:

$$G_{r_k d} = \left(\frac{1}{1 - 1/\sqrt{G_{sr_k}}} \right)^2. \tag{26}$$

Furthermore, since we have $\gamma_t^s = \gamma_t^r$, it can be shown based on Eq. (10) that:

$$\frac{G_{r_k d}}{G_{sr_k}} = 10^{(\gamma_r^{rd} - \gamma_r^{sr})/10}, \tag{27}$$

where we have $\gamma_r^{rd} - \gamma_r^{sr} = 1.5 - 2.5 = -1\,\text{dB}$ in our example. Based on Eq. (26) and Eq. (27), we have the following relationship:

$$G_{sr_k} = \left(1 + 10^{-(\gamma_r^{rd} - \gamma_r^{sr})/20} \right)^2, \tag{28}$$

which gives $G_{sr_k} = 4.50$ for our case and from Eq. (26) we have $G_{r_k d} = 3.58$. Once G_{sr_k} and $G_{r_k d}$ are identified, we may find the corresponding relay distances from Eq. (3) and Eq. (6), which are given by $d_{sr_k} = 0.47 d_{sd}$ and $d_{r_k d} = 0.53 d_{sd}$, respectively. The average transmit SNR of the relay selection based DIRCC scheme is given by:

$$\tilde{\gamma}_t = \gamma_t^r = \gamma_t^s = \gamma_r^{sr} - 10 \log_{10}(G_{sr_k}), \tag{29}$$

where we have $\tilde{\gamma}_t = -4\,\text{dB}$ for our example, which is the same value as that of the power allocation based scenario.

7   Application in UAV Network

Let us now look at the application of the DIRCC scheme for an UAV network. Assumming that the SN is a BS and RNs are the UAVs, e.g. drones, while DN is the mobile user. The top-view of the UAV network is shown in Fig. 22, where drones located within a particular radius from the SN would satisfy a certain SN-RN SNR condition $\gamma_r^{sr} \geq \gamma_{r,\min}^{sr}$. In the case when the drones are located in the direct SN-to-DN path, the side view the UAV network may be depicted in Fig. 23. This arrangement is denoted

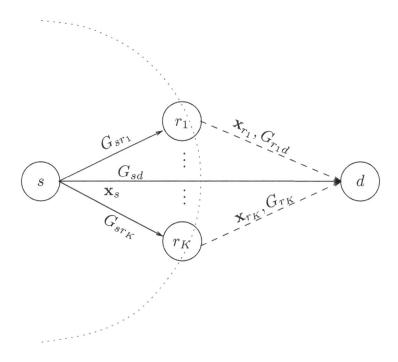

Fig. 22. Top-view of the UAV network.

as Scheme 1, where the drones are located at approximately $d_{sr_k} = 0.47d_0$ and the corresponding geometrical gains are given at the caption of Fig. 22.

By contrast, Fig. 24 shows the corresponding UAV network when the receiving user is located under the drones, where the drones are on the same level as the SN. Note that, the SN-to-DN link may cease to exist when it is blocked by tall buildings, as exemplified by the scenario on the left of Fig. 24. The scenario on the right of Fig. 24 is denoted as Scheme 2, where the drones are located approximately at $d_{sr_k} = 0.4d_0$. The corresponding geometrical gains are given at the caption of Fig. 24.

Based on the DIRCC code design detailed in Sect. 5, the EXIT charts of the DIRCC-4PSK decoder at the DN for both Scheme 1 and Scheme 2 are given in Fig. 25. As seen in Fig. 25, each of the EXIT charts exhibits a narrow tunnel, which predicts a decoding convergence to low BER at average SNRs of -4 dB and -6.5 dB, for Scheme 1 and Scheme 2, respectively.

Monte-carlo simulations are conducted based on simulation parameters given in Table 1. The BER versus average transmit SNR performance of the proposed DIRCC-4PSK scheme is compared to both that of perfect DIRCC-4PSK and to that of the non-cooperative IRCC-URC-4PSK schemes in Fig. 26. Note that the perfect DIRCC-4PSK scheme assumes that there is no decoding errors at each RN, while the proposed DIRCC-4PSK scheme considers a realistic SN-to-RN transmission and actual decoding with potential decoding errors at each RN. The non-cooperative IRCC-URC-4PSK scheme has 30 decoding iterations at the DN. It operates approximately 0.65 dB away

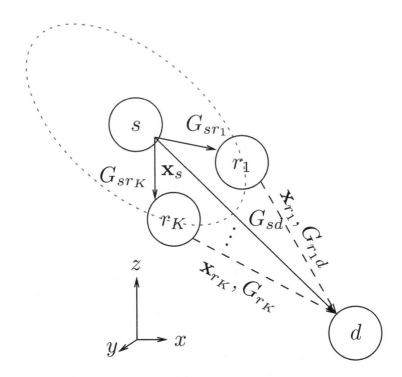

Fig. 23. Side-view of the UAV network, when the RNs are in the direct SN-to-DN path. **Scheme 1:** $G_{sd} = 1$, $G_{sr_k} = 4.50$ and $G_{r_kd} = 3.58$; $d_{sd} = d_0$, $d_{sr_k} = 0.47d_0$ and $d_{r_kd} = 0.53d_0$.

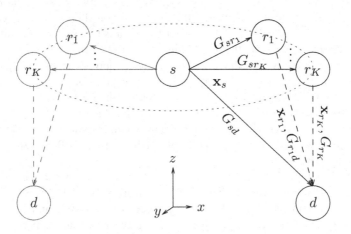

Fig. 24. Side-view of the UAV network, when the RNs are not in the direct SN-to-DN path. **Scheme 2** (right): $G_{sd} = 3.45$, $G_{sr_k} = 4.00$ and $G_{r_kd} = 25$; $d_{sd} = 0.5385d_0$, $d_{sr_k} = 0.5d_0$ and $d_{r_kd} = 0.2d_0$.

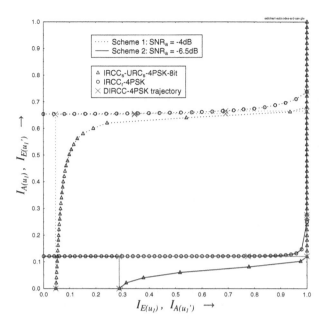

Fig. 25. EXIT charts of the DIRCC-4PSK decoder at the DN for both Scheme 1 and Scheme 2 of the UAV network.

Table 1. Simulation parameters.

Modulation	4PSK
Number of modulated symbols/frame	60,000
Interleaver	Random and bit-based
IRCC weights, $\widetilde{\alpha}_s$	See Eq. (23)
DIRCC weights, $\widetilde{\alpha}_r$	See Eq. (24)
Coding rate of IRCC	0.5
Coding rate of DIRCC	0.5
Number of IRCC-URC-4PSK iterations	30
Number of DIRCC inner iterations	8
Number of DIRCC outer iterations	4
Decoding algorithm	Approximated Log-MAP [21]
Channel type	Fast Rayleigh fading

from its channel capacity at BER $= 10^{-6}$. Both DIRCC-4PSK schemes have 8 inner iterations and 4 outer iterations at the DN. As seen from Fig. 26, the proposed DIRCC-4PSK scheme has negligible performance difference to that of the perfect DIRCC-4PSK scheme for BER $< 10^{-2}$ and it is capable of operating within 0.68 dB from the lower bound of its channel capacity. The BER performance of this scheme, namely

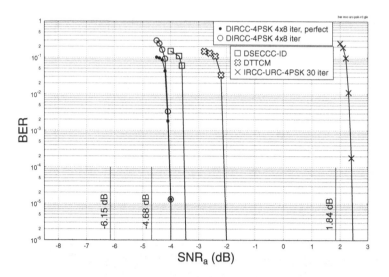

Fig. 26. BER versus SNR_a performance of the proposed DIRCC-4PSK scheme in comparison to perfect DIRCC-4PSK, IRCC-URC-4PSK, DSECCC-ID and DTTCM schemes, when communicating over fast Rayleigh fading channels using a frame length of 60,000 4PSK symbols.

Scheme 1, shows a sharp BER drop at an average SNR of -4 dB, which was predicted in Fig. 25 This near-capacity performance is achieved with the advent of an effective system design, as detailed in Sect. 5 with the aid of powerful iterative decoding at all of the RNs and at the DN.

The performance of the Distributed TTCM (DTTCM) [38] and Distributed Self-Concatenated Convolutional Coding relying on Iterative-Detection (SECCC-ID) [26] schemes are considered as benchmark schemes for the DIRCC scheme. All schemes employ a frame length of 60,000 4PSK symbols for transmission over fast Rayleigh fading channels. The throughput of the 4PSK-based SECCC-ID scheme is 0.5 BPS, which is exactly identical to that of the proposed 4PSK-based DIRCC scheme. However, the throughput of the 4PSK-based DTTCM[4] scheme is 0.667 BPS, because it only transmits parity bits from the RN to the DN. As seen from Fig. 26, the DIRCC scheme outperforms the DSECCC-ID and DTTCM schemes by approximately 0.5 dB and 2.0 dB[5], respectively, at a BER of 10^{-6}. It was found that the proposed DIRCC scheme performs the closest to the relay channel's capacity, when aiming for a throughput of 0.5 BPS, compared to existing DAF-based distributed coding schemes found in

---

[4] The original DTTCM scheme of [38] employed 2/3-rate TTCM-8PSK at the SN and uncoded-4PSK at the RN. The DTTCM scheme considered here uses 1/2-rate TTCM-4PSK at the SN and uncoded-4PSK at the RN, in order to make its throughput as close as possible to the proposed DIRCC scheme for a fair comparison.

[5] In terms of SNR per information bit, the gain of DIRCC over DTTCM is given by 2.0 dB $+10\log_{10}(0.667) - 10\log_{10}(0.50) = 0.76$ dB.

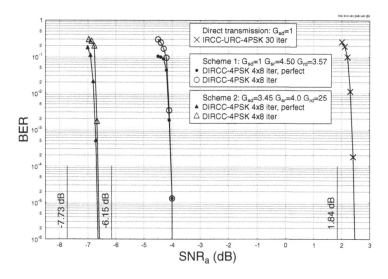

Fig. 27. BER versus SNR$_a$ performance of the proposed DIRCC-4PSK scheme in comparison to perfect DIRCC-4PSK and IRCC-URC-4PSK schemes, when communicating over fast Rayleigh fading channels using a frame length of 60,000 4PSK symbols.

the literature, when communicating over fast Rayleigh fading channels using a single-antenna at each node.

Figure 27 shows the BER performance of both Scheme 1 and Scheme 2, in comparison to the perfect scheme and to the non-cooperative scheme. As seen from Fig. 27, the DIRCC-4PSK Scheme 2 also has negligible performance difference to that of the perfect DIRCC-4PSK scheme, especially for BER $< 10^{-4}$. The BER curve of Scheme 2 has a sharp BER drop at an average SNR of -6.5 dB, which agrees with the prediction given in Fig. 25. This performance is only approximately 1.2 dB away from the corresponding upper BER bound of -7.73 dB.

Another scenario, referred to as Scheme 3, is considered where the ratio of the number of drones to the number of mobile users is very low and the SN (or base station) is far away. Figure 28 shows the top-down view of Scheme 3, where there are only 4 drones serving 100 mobile users. When there is only a RN serving a user, the RN will perform the whole IRCC$_r$ encoding and transmit all codewords of the used subcodes. In Scheme 3, the SN-to-DN link is not available, which is similar to the left section of Fig. 24. Since, the geometrical gain depends mainly on the distance when communicating over fast Rayleigh fading channels, we can assign the drone to a group of mobile users who are closer to it. The K-means learning algorithm is ideal for this assignment task. More specifically, the K-means algorithm is an unsupervised learning algorithm that takes a set of data that contains only inputs and find structure in the data. It can be used to reduce the data dimension by finding suitable representatives (or centroids)

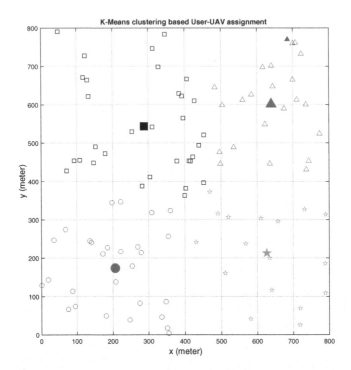

Fig. 28. Scheme 3: K-means based RN selection in a UAV network. The four filled markers are the four drones serving the mobile users on the ground. The 100 mobile users depicted by 100 empty markers are partitioned into four clusters. The cluster membership and drone locations are computed based on the K-means algorithm.

for clusters of data points. More explicitly, we can find the cluster centroids $\mathbf{C}$ and assignment matrix $\mathbf{W}$ such that $\mathbf{CW} \approx \mathbf{X}$ [17]:

$$
\begin{aligned}
\underset{\mathbf{C},\mathbf{W}}{\text{minimize}} \quad & ||\mathbf{CW} - \mathbf{X}||_F^2 \\
\text{subject to} \quad & \mathbf{w}_p \in \{\mathbf{e}_k\}_{k=1}^{K} \quad \forall p = 1 \dots P.
\end{aligned}
\tag{30}
$$

where $\mathbf{e}_k$ is the kth *standard basis vector* and $\mathbf{w}_p$ is the pth column of $\mathbf{W}$, while $||(.)||_F$ is the Frobenius norm of $(.)$. The relationship between the data points and the cluster centroids $\mathbf{C}$ and assignment matrix $\mathbf{W}$ is illustrated in Fig. 29. The objective function of Eq. (30) is non-convex and hence it cannot be minimized over both $\mathbf{C}$ and $\mathbf{W}$ simultaneously. However, it can be solved via *alternating minimization*, i.e. alternatingly minimizing the objective function over one of the variables ($\mathbf{C}$ or $\mathbf{W}$), while keeping the other variable fixed.

In our application, the K-means algorithm can be used for finding the optimal drone locations in a UAV network, and then the drones can be directed to these locations. In this case, the base station as the SN will perform the IRCC$_s$ encoding, while the drone as the RN would relay the IRCC$_r$-encoded source message to the assigned mobile user serving as the DN. As seen in Fig. 28, each of the four drones are directed to the best

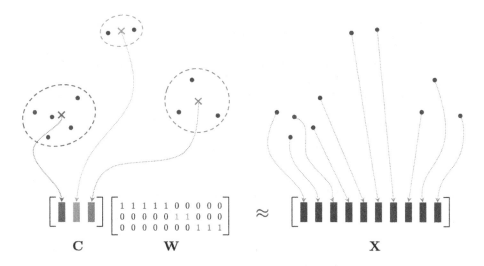

Fig. 29. Illustration of the K-means algorithm [17] ©2016.

locations to serve the mobile users in four clusters. The best locations would change as the mobile users move on the ground. The drone can serve multiple users in a particular cluster based on orthogonal frequency bands or timeslots.

8   Conclusions

In this contribution, it was shown that cooperative communications can create a high-capacity virtual MIMO channel. Then, the Distributed Irregular Convolutional Code (DIRCC) was introduced and investigated for approaching the virtual MIMO channel capacity. EXIT charts based iterative learning algorithm was invoked for creating near-capacity DIRCC schemes. Additionally, machine learning algorithms can be used for code design and for drone location assignment in the UAV network. Three applications were investigated in the UAV network. It was found that cooperative communications, distributed coding and machine learning constitute the important enabling technologies for the next generation wireless systems.

References

1. Bletsas, A., Khisti, A., Reed, D.P., Lippman, A.: A simple cooperative diversity method based on network path selection. IEEE J. Sel. Areas Commun. **24**(3), 659–672 (2006). https://doi.org/10.1109/JSAC.2005.862417
2. Chakrabarti, A., Baynast, A., Sabharwal, A., Aazhang, B.: Low density parity check codes for the relay channel. IEEE J. Sel. Areas Commun. **25**(2), 280–291 (2007)
3. Chakrabarti, A., Baynast, A., Sabharwal, A., Aazhang, B.: Low density parity check codes over wireless relay channels. IEEE Trans. Wireless Commun. **6**(9), 3384–3394 (2007)

4. Sendonaris, A., Erkip, E., Aazhang, B.: User cooperation diversity Part I: system description. IEEE Trans. Commun. **51**(11), 1927–1938 (2003)
5. Arikan, E.: Channel polarization: a method for constructing capacity-achieving codes for symmetric binary-input memoryless channels. IEEE Trans. Inf. Theory **55**(7), 3051–3073 (2009). https://doi.org/10.1109/TIT.2009.2021379
6. Zhao, B., Valenti, M.C.: Distributed turbo coded diversity for relay channel. IEE Electron. Lett. **39**, 786–787 (2003)
7. BBC: Google AI defeats human Go champion. BBC News, 25 May 2017. https://www.bbc.co.uk/news/technology-40042581
8. ten Brink, S.: Convergence behaviour of iteratively decoded parallel concatenated codes. IEEE Trans. Commun. **49**(10), 1727–1737 (2001)
9. Berrou, C., Glavieux, A., Thitimajshima, P.: Near Shannon limit error-correcting coding and decoding: turbo codes. In: Proceedings of the International Conference on Communications, Geneva, Switzerland, pp. 1064–1070 (1993)
10. Cover, T., Gamal, A.E.: Capacity theorems for the relay channel. IEEE Trans. Inf. Theory **25**(5), 572–584 (1979)
11. Divsalar, D., Dolinar, S., Pollara, F.: Serial turbo trellis coded modulation with rate-1 inner code. In: ISIT, Sorrento, Italy, p. 194 (2000)
12. Telatar, E.: Capacity of multi-antenna Gaussian channels. Eur. Trans. Telecommun. **10**(6), 585–595 (1999)
13. Forney, G.: Concatenated Codes. MIT Press, Cambridge (1966)
14. Gallager, R.: Low-density parity-check codes. IEEE Trans. Inf. Theory **8**(1), 21–28 (1962)
15. Ochiai, H., Mitran, P., Tarokh, V.: Design and analysis of collaborative diversity protocols for wireless sensor networks. In: Proceedings of IEEE VTC Fall, Los Angeles, USA, pp. 4645–4649 (2004)
16. Nguyen, H.V., Ng, S.X., Hanzo, L.: Irregular convolution and unity-rate coded network-coding for cooperative multi-user communications. IEEE Trans. Wirel. Commun. **12**(3), 1231–1243 (2013)
17. Watt, J., Borhani, R., Katsaggelos, A.K.: Machine Learning Refined: Foundations, Algorithms, and Applications. Cambridge University Press, New York (2016)
18. Yuan, J., Chen, Z., Li, Y., Chu, L.: Distributed space-time trellis codes for a cooperative system. IEEE Trans. Wirel. Commun. **8**, 4897–4905 (2009)
19. Jiang, C., Zhang, H., Ren, Y., Han, Z., Chen, K., Hanzo, L.: Machine learning paradigms for next-generation wireless networks. IEEE Wirel. Commun. **24**(2), 98–105 (2017). https://doi.org/10.1109/MWC.2016.1500356WC
20. Ju, M., Kim, I.M.: Relay selection with ANC and TDBC protocols in bidirectional relay networks. IEEE Trans. Commun. **58**(12), 3500–3511 (2010). https://doi.org/10.1109/TCOMM.2010.101210.090585
21. Hanzo, L., Liew, T.H., Yeap, B.L., Tee, R.Y.S., Ng, S.X.: Turbo Coding, Turbo Equalisation and Space-time Coding: EXIT-Chart-aided Near-Capacity Designs for Wireless Channels, 2nd edn. Wiley-IEEE Press, New York (2011)
22. Kong, L., Ng, S.X., Maunder, R.G., Hanzo, L.: Maximum-throughput irregular distributed space-time code for near-capacity cooperative communications. IEEE Trans. Veh. Technol. **59**(3), 1511–1517 (2010)
23. Kong, L., Ng, S.X., Tee, R.Y.S., Maunder, R.G., Hanzo, L.: Reduced-complexity near-capacity downlink iteratively decoded generalized multi-layer space-time coding using irregular conv olutional codes. IEEE Trans. Wirel. Commun. **9**(2), 684–695 (2010)
24. Lampe, L., Schober, R., Yiu, S.: Distributed space-time coding for multihop transmission in power line communication networks. IEEE J. Sel. Areas Commun. **24**(7), 1389–1400 (2006)
25. Loeliger, H.: New turbo-like codes. In: Proceedings of IEEE International Symposium on Information Theory, June 1997. https://doi.org/10.1109/ISIT.1997.613024

26. Butt, M.F.U., Riaz, R.A., Ng, S.X., Hanzo, L.: Distributed self-concatenated coding for cooperative communication. IEEE Trans. Veh. Technol. **59**(6), 3097–3104 (2010)
27. Janani, M., Hedayat, A., Hunter, T., Nosratinia, A.: Coded cooperation in wireless communications: space-time transmission and iterative decoding. IEEE Trans. Signal Process. **52**, 362–371 (2004)
28. Shirvanimoghaddam, M., Li, Y., Vucetic, B.: Distributed raptor coding for erasure channels: partially and fully coded cooperation. IEEE Trans. Commun. **61**(9), 3576–3589 (2013)
29. Tüchler, M., Hagenauer, J.: EXIT charts of irregular codes. In: Proceedings of Conference on Information Science and Systems, pp. 465–490. Princeton University (2002)
30. MacKay, D.J.C., Neal, R.M.: Good codes based on very sparse matrices. In: Boyd, C. (ed.) Cryptography and Coding 1995. LNCS, vol. 1025, pp. 100–111. Springer, Heidelberg (1995). https://doi.org/10.1007/3-540-60693-9_13
31. Mao, Q., Hu, F., Hao, Q.: Deep learning for intelligent wireless networks: a comprehensive survey. IEEE Commun. Surv. Tutor. **20**(4), 2595–2621 (2018). https://doi.org/10.1109/COMST.2018.2846401
32. Laneman, N., Tse, D.N.C., Wornell, G.W.: Cooperative diversity in wireless networks: efficient protocols and outage behavior. IEEE Trans. Inf. Theory **50**(12), 3062–3080 (2004)
33. Ng, S.X., Hanzo, L.: On the MIMO channel capacity of multi-dimensional signal sets. IEEE Trans. Veh. Technol. **55**(2), 528–536 (2006)
34. Ng, S.X., Li, Y., Vucetic, B., Hanzo, L.: Distributed irregular codes relying on decode-and-forward relays as code components. IEEE Trans. Veh. Technol. **64**(10), 4579–4588 (2015). https://doi.org/10.1109/TVT.2014.2370737
35. Razaghi, P., Yu, W.: Bilayer low-density parity-check codes for decode-and-forward in relay channels. IEEE Trans. Inf. Theory **53**(10), 3723–3739 (2007)
36. Proakis, J.G.: Digital Communications, 4th edn. Mc-Graw Hill International Editions, New York (2001)
37. Robertson, P., Wörz, T.: Coded modulation scheme employing turbo codes. IET Electron. Lett. **31**(18), 1546–1547 (1995)
38. Ng, S.X., Li, Y., Hanzo, L.: Distributed turbo trellis coded modulation for cooperative communications. In: Proceedings of International Conference on Communications (ICC), Dresden, Germany, pp. 1–5 (2009)
39. Ng, S.X., Li, Y., Vucetic, B., Hanzo, L.: Distributed irregular codes relying on decode-and-forward relays as code components. IEEE Trans. Veh. Technol. **64**(10), 4579–4588 (2015)
40. Shannon, C.E.: A mathematical theory of communication. Bell Syst. Tech. J. **27**, 379–427 (1948)
41. Tüchler, M.: Design of serially concatenated systems depending on the block length. IEEE Trans. Commun. **52**(2), 209–218 (2004)
42. Tarokh, V., Seshadri, N., Calderbank, A.: Space-time codes for high data rate wireless communications: performance criterion and code construction. In: Proceeding IEEE International Conference on Communications 1997, Montreal, Canada, pp. 299–303 (1997)
43. Jing, Y., Hassibi, B.: Distributed space-time coding in wireless relay networks. IEEE Trans. Wirel. Commun. **5**, 3524–3536 (2006)
44. Li, Y.: Distributed coding for cooperative wireless networks: an overview and recent advances. IEEE Commun. Mag. **47**(8), 71–77 (2009)
45. Li, Y., Vucetic, B., Yuan, J.: Distributed turbo coding with hybrid relaying protocols. In: IEEE PIMRC, French Riviera, France (2008)
46. Li, Y., Rahman, M.S., Ng, S.X., Vucetic, B.: Distributed soft coding with a soft input soft output (SISO) relay encoder in parallel relay channels. IEEE Trans. Commun. **61**(9), 3660–3672 (2013)

47. Zhang, Q., Jiang, M., Feng, Z., Li, W., Zhang, W., Pan, M.: IoT enabled UAV: network architecture and routing algorithm. IEEE Internet Things J. **6**(2), 3727–3742 (2019). https://doi.org/10.1109/JIOT.2018.2890428
48. Zhang, Z., Duman, T.: Capacity-approaching turbo coding for half-duplex relaying. IEEE Trans. Commun. **55**(10), 1895–1906 (2007)

e-Business

Product-Service Systems at a Glance

How Classification and Typification Contribute to Comprehensibility

Lukas Waidelich[✉], Alexander Richter, Rebecca Bulander, Bernhard Kölmel,
and Patrice Glaser

IoS - Institute of Smart Systems and Services, Pforzheim University, Tiefenbronner Str. 65,
7175 Pforzheim, Germany
Lukas.Waidelich@hs-pforzheim.de

Abstract. This article intends to provide the reader a comprehensive overview of the Product-Service System (PSS) topic. Besides the historical background and a comparison of definitions, the contribution focuses on the challenging task of classifying and typing PSS. For this purpose, a particularly broad scientific and systematic literature review was carried out, comprising 125 publications. Thereby, the research was focused on the crucial question how PSS can be classified and typed. Widely used PSS classifications and types in literature and their differences were identified. The conclusion describes and compares the six identified PSS classifications. Based on this, different PSS types were analyzed and extracted from PSS classifications and were finally compared for the first time in literature. In addition, the characteristics of the different types of PSS are presented and examined. This research contributes scientifically to the field of PSS classification. The article closes with an outlook on the future role of digital PSS in the context of digitization. In summary, this paper represents a consistent further development of the paper "A Systematic Literature Review on Product-Service Systems Classifications and Types".

Keywords: Product-Service System (PSS) · PSS classification · PSS types · PSS definitions · Servitization

1 Introduction of Product-Service Systems (PSS)

PSS represent an important element for long-term economic success. For this reason, it is essential to understand their essence of PSS. Therefore, this work has the claim to provide a profound overview. Based on the paper "A Systematic Literature Review on Product-Service Systems Classifications and Types" [1] this publication has been enriched with several elements that provide the reader with further information regarding PSS: First, the historical background of PSS is added in the first section. Furthermore, the research design is explained in detail in the second chapter and supplemented with valuable illustrations. Completely revised, the third section contains a comprehensive comparison of PSS definition approaches. The contribution focuses on the PSS classifications and types in section four, which has also been extended by a valuable contribution. The

© Springer Nature Switzerland AG 2020
M. S. Obaidat (Ed.): ICETE 2019, CCIS 1247, pp. 61–84, 2020.
https://doi.org/10.1007/978-3-030-52686-3_3

conclusion of the research concerning the six classifications and associated types is the subject of the fifth section. The sixth section finally contains an outlook on future research.

1.1 Motivation

The current period is strongly marked by uncertainties, both political and economic. Nonetheless, it is astonishing that former big players from the manufacturing sector such as AEG, Grundig, Kodak and Nokia are disappearing from the market or are no longer dominant, even though these companies have been distinguished for many years by excellent product and process innovation [2–4].

The underlying reasons are very multifaceted, for example globalization not only offers opportunities but also poses numerous risks. On the one hand, manufacturing companies are operating on global markets and thus are in direct competition regarding quality, technology and costs. This results in strong international price pressure, stagnant sales and profit margins as well as the decreasing possibility of differentiation in technology and quality due to the increasing equivalence of competing products of competitors [5–7]. These challenges are approached at the level of product and process innovation. In the past, it was sufficient for the company's success to master these two levels. In order to be successful in the long term, the business model must be adapted, because on the other hand established companies are challenged by business model innovations. Driven and empowered by digitization, new, disruptive business models are emerging that replace existing value chains in large parts or even completely. These business model innovations usually hit established providers unprepared and can lead to a complete displacement of the market, as mentioned above in the case of the company examples. Thus, the development of innovative business models is a basic necessity for long-term competitiveness in the economy [4, 7, 8].

A potential and at the same time very promising approach to meet these challenges are the so-called PSS. These are understood to be an offered solution that contains at least one service element in addition to a product [9]. These offers can be seen as a holistic innovation strategy that serves the product, process and business model innovation levels simultaneously. Companies are undergoing a change: they are no longer limiting themselves to the development and sales of products, instead they are supplementing their portfolio with the provision of a system of products and services tailored to specific customer requirements [1, 10–13]. This paradigm shift responds to the changed demand behavior by providing flexibly adaptable product and service components tailored to customer needs. Customer benefit is in the center of attention, a sustainable customer relationship is established, which leads to a long-term competitive advantage [7, 8]. The strategy that targets to complement products with related services is called servitization. This can lead to a constant increase in sales [14, 15].

Nowadays there are many different forms of PSS in daily practice across different industries. These PSS are highly complex, not easy to understand and difficult to categorize. The clear objective of this Article is to identify and compare the different classifications and types of PSS in order to give the reader an overview of the existing literature. Before doing so, the historical development of PSS will be examined within the context of business models.

1.2 History of PSS

As already mentioned in the motivation, innovative business models are the key to long-term competitiveness. Gassmann et al. discovered through their research in the area of business model innovations that 90% of innovations are the result of recombining existing business models. As a result, the business models that have existed since the 18th century are the foundation for today's success. These have usually been accompanied by technological evolution [4]. This evolution will be illustrated by means of researched examples (see Fig. 1).

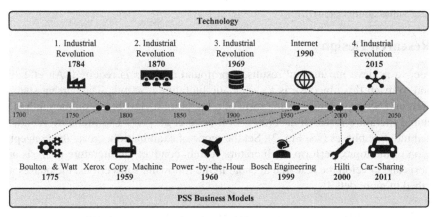

Fig. 1. Evolution of business models and PSS [4, 6, 16].

One of the most widely known business models from this period was developed by Boulton & Watt, who intensified the sale of greatly improved steam engines. The unique aspect of the business model was that the steam engines were not sold, but were rather made available in return for a use-related fee, which was a revolution at the time. This pattern occurs repeatedly with new technologies or product innovations. Two other investigated examples confirm this. The Xerox company developed the photocopier technologically further, so that it had an increased performance range compared to conventional devices of this type. This was also reflected in the price, which was seven times more expensive than technologically inferior competing products. In order to be able to compete in the market, Xerox offered customers the device at a fixed monthly price for a certain number of copies. This gave the company the commercial success it was seeking. The power-by-the-hour business model has long been an established approach for many aircraft engine manufacturers. This can be traced back to the former British manufacturer Bristol Siddley Engines, which guaranteed the customer a faultless use of the engine. In return, the customer paid a fixed amount per operating hour to the manufacturer [6]. Around the turn of the millennium, PSS business models increasingly established themselves in Germany. In 1999, the Bosch company founded the subsidiary Bosch Engineering, which specializes in customized software solutions as an additional service to standardized Bosch hardware solutions, in order to meet increased and individual customer needs. With the introduction of the Hilti Fleet Management business model, the Hilti company offers its customers the availability of high-quality equipment such as hammer drills or similar tools for a monthly fee, thus minimizing its customers' downtime costs. Another business model that focuses on use rather than ownership is car sharing. The company Share Now (formerly Car2Go), which was founded in 2011 and has established itself as a mobility service provider, has achieved widespread success in this area [4, 6].

These business model innovations were accompanied by industrial revolutions and the emergence of the Internet in the 1990 s, which enabled and drove innovation. The fourth industrial revolution, the linking of real objects with virtual processes, is currently in progress. It will create new digital PSS business model opportunities and change existing value chains [4, 16].

2   Research Design

In order to achieve meaningful results, a profound analysis is required. An effective method to reach this objective is a systematic literature research. The current state of research on PSS is presented in the form of a literature review based on the method of structured literature research according to Brocke et al. [17]. The literature review is divided into five phases (see Fig. 2): Set the scope of examination, create the conceptualization of the topic, perform the literature search, conduct the literature analysis and synthesis and develop the research agenda. In the following subsections, the phases are described in more detail.

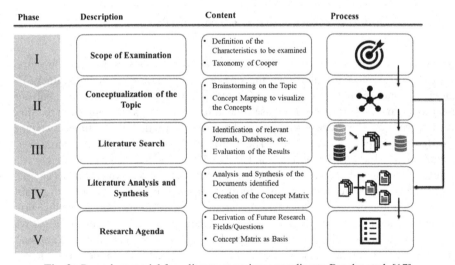

Phase	Description	Content	Process
I	Scope of Examination	• Definition of the Characteristics to be examined • Taxonomy of Cooper	
II	Conceptualization of the Topic	• Brainstorming on the Topic • Concept Mapping to visualize the Concepts	
III	Literature Search	• Identification of relevant Journals, Databases, etc. • Evaluation of the Results	
IV	Literature Analysis and Synthesis	• Analysis and Synthesis of the Documents identified • Creation of the Concept Matrix	
V	Research Agenda	• Derivation of Future Research Fields/Questions • Concept Matrix as Basis	

Fig. 2. Procedure model for a literature review according to Brocke et al. [17].

2.1   Set the Scope of Examination

The scope of the examination was determined at the very beginning of the literature review. For this purpose, the taxonomy of Cooper [18] was applied as envisaged by

Brocke et al. [17]. The prioritization of each category (1) Focus, (2) Objective, (3) Organization, (4) Perspective, (5) Audience and (6) Coverage are marked in grey in Table 1. The focus was on the discovery of existing PSS theories and on the identification of research concepts for PSS classification, typology and definition. The second criterion concerned the research goal, which focuses on the central issues of existing PSS classification patterns. The next characteristic describes the organization of the research, which was conducted from a conceptual point of view. The literature was examined and presented for different concepts. The literature review was conducted from a neutral perspective. The fifth characteristic refers to the audience, which has a scientific character on the one hand and a practical value on the other. Finally, a selective literature research was carried out. This was based on a complete literature research, but only relevant works are discussed in greater detail.

Table 1. Applied taxonomy of Cooper [1, 18].

Characteristics	Categories			
(1) Focus	Research outcomes	Research methods	Theories	Applications
(2) Goal	Integration	Criticism		Central Issues
(3) Organization	Historical	Conceptual		Methodological
(4) Perspective	Neutral representation		Espousal of position	
(5) Audience	Specialised scholars	General scholars	Practitioners	General public
(6) Coverage	Exhaustive	Exhaustive and selective	Representative	Central/pivotal

2.2 Create the Conceptualization of the Topic

The conceptualization phase describes the topic-related documentation of existing knowledge such as keywords, approaches and concepts using the creativity methods of brainstorming. In the next step, a concept mapping was carried out, whereby the contents from the brainstorming were put into a logical context. With growing knowledge this step was iteratively repeated to cover as many concepts as possible.

2.3 Perform the Literature Search

The third phase of the literature review is primarily concerned with identifying and evaluating the relevant literature. The search process is highlighted by an illustration (see Fig. 3) and can be seen as a completion to the sections below, which are divided into journal search, online databases as well as forward and backward search.

The search first concentrated on journal contributions. The Academic Journal Guide (AJG) Ranking 2015 was used to identify high-quality journals [19]. The broad range of PSS topics was addressed with a cross-divisional search for economic, technical and strategic aspects. Journals belonging to category 4 or 4* of the AJG2015 evaluation, which rank among the most renowned journals of the relevant research fields, were considered. The AJG helped to identify 16 relevant journals, which were then systematically searched according to the following pattern: The search process for the following search parameters was standardized for the purpose of achieving comparability and for general application. The examination covered the period from January 1995 to January 2018. The publications were searched using the English search String "Product-Service System" or "PSS" in combination with the term "Classification" in the title, keywords and abstract. The search results were sorted by relevance and the first 100 results were analyzed. The search results were evaluated by a subsequent review of the abstracts regarding the PSS topic focusing on PSS classification, type and definition. Only publications that meet these criteria were considered for the literature analysis. The literature search of the 16 identified AJG journals generated 114 results, of which 13 articles were relevant and considered for the literature analysis.

The prior research in the field of renowned journals led to the identification of four appropriate online databases in which a keyword search was performed. These include "Springer", "ScienceDirect", "Emerald Insight" and "Web of Science". The search parameters and the search process were adopted from the standardized journal search, expanded by the concepts from the previous subsection and searched in English and German form in the four databases: First PSS as a permanent keyword, then in conjunction with the terms "Classification", "Synonym", "Concept", "Relevance" and "Definition". Due to the duplication of previous searches in the field of journals and within the four databases, only new literature was taken into account. The online database search facilitated the identification of 80 additional publications, consisting of journal and conference papers as well as textbooks.

The literature search has also been enriched with a forward and backward search. This search was carried out via ResearchGate, a social network for scientists, and Google Scholar, a specially developed search engine for scientific documents. This enabled the literature search to be extended by a further 32 to a total of 125 relevant publications.

2.4   Conduct the Literature Analysis and Synthesis

This section is divided into two main areas: First, the 125 identified publications from the literature search are examined in detail. Second, the identified concepts from the conceptualization section are compared with the identified articles from the previous section of the literature search.

The completed literature search resulted in 125 literature publications in the field of PSS. The majority of the works (97) were published in English, 28 in German. The largest number of papers were found in the ScienceDirect database (36), followed by Springer (27), Emerald Insight (21), Google Scholar (18), ResearchGate (14) and Web of Science (9). From 1999 to 2017 at least one work was continuously taken into consideration. With 25 included publications from the year 2017, the relevance of the topic is also underlined. In quantitative terms, the works of the author Baines are most frequently represented with five publications. The authors Lightfoot, Nüttgens and Thomas are each represented with four publications. In the area of media types, 79 of the 125 works are papers in journals, 14 in conference papers, 25 in textbooks (mon-ographs), four in individual sections in

Field		Name	AJG 2015	Results	Relevance
Renowned Journals	Economics, Econometrics and Statistics	American Economic Review	4*	0	0
		Annals of Statistics	4*	22	0
		Econometrica	4*	1	0
		Journal of Political Economy	4*	6	0
		Quarterly Journal of Economics	4*	0	0
		Review of Economic Studies	4*	0	0
	General Management, Ethics and Social Responsibility	Academy of Management Journal	4*	0	0
		Academy of Management Review	4*	0	0
		Administrative Science Quarterly	4*	0	0
		Journal of Management	4*	4	0
	OR&MANSCI[1]	Management Science	4*	8	0
		Operations Research	4*	16	0
	Operations and Technology Management	Journal of Operations Management	4*	10	1
		International Journal of Operations and Production Management	4	16	12
		Production and Operations Management	4	29	0
	Strategy	Strategic Management Journal	4*	2	0
		Overall		**114**	**13**

[1]Operations Research and Management Science

Keywords	Springer		ScienceDirect		Emerald Insight		Web of Science	
PSS +	Results	New	Results	New	Results	New	Results	New
	107	12	248	16	93	2	409	3
Relevanz/ Relevance	1	1	5	1	8	0	6	0
Definition / Definition	2	2	3	2	87	0	23	2
Synonym/ Synonym	3	1	4	2	15	1	0	0
Klassifikation/ Classification	1	1	3	3	64	3	22	0
Konzept/ Concept	71	10	31	11	268	3	216	4
Total New	27		35		9		9	
Overall new	80							

(Online Databases)

Keywords	ResearchGate		Google Scholar	
PSS +	Results	New	Results	New
	>200	3	9610	3
Relevanz/ Relevance	4	1	~2.700	2
Definition / Definition	34	3	~7.700	1
Synonym/ Synonym	2	1	~3.200	1
Klassifikation/ Classification	19	3	~4.500	5
Konzept/ Concept	185	3	~6.000	6
Total new	14		18	
Overall new	32			

(Forward & Backward Search)

13 Renowned Journals

80 Online Databases

32 Forward & Backward Search

Overall: 125 Publications

Fig. 3. Literature search process in detail.

textbooks (anthologies) and three in doctoral theses. The publications were evaluated in detail both by publishing house and by journal magazines. A total of eleven monographs and anthologies have been published by Springer Gabler Publishing, eight others by Springer Publishing and five by Springer Vieweg Publishing. The remaining five works have been published by other publishing houses. In the field of journal magazines, 19 papers were published in the renowned Journal of Cleaner Production and 13 papers in the International Journal of Operations & Production Management. The remaining publications are distributed among other magazines.

In the second area, the concept matrix method was used as proposed by Brocke et al. and Webster and Watson [17, 20]. In this regard, the researched literature was analyzed in detail and assigned to the different PSS concepts in the concept matrix. This very comprehensive overview was of major importance for the further procedure, as in this way important publications could be identified, and different aspects of the concepts made visible.

2.5 Develop the Research Agenda

The literature review is completed with the definition of the research agenda. This includes an assessment of the topics which can adequately be found in literature and which require concrete research.

In summary, no literature could be found that comprehensively covers the manifold PSS concepts in sufficient depth. Rather, the concepts are only discussed in isolation or very superficially. In addition, diverse concepts were identified by a number of authors in the field of classification. Compared to other concepts such as synonyms or relevance, this topic is still strongly underrepresented. This reveals a gap in research, which will be investigated in this article. According to the findings mentioned above, the literature review leads to further potential research fields, which will be deepened in form of research questions (RQ) in the following research:

- RQ1: How does the literature define PSS?
- RQ2: Which PSS classifications are in use and how are they designed?
- RQ3: Derived from RQ2 what PSS types exist and how are they described?
- RQ4: Is it possible to summarize PSS types and compare them by characteristics?

3 PSS Definition

Several sources describe PSS as an interdisciplinary field in which different terms are used depending on the scientific discipline. For example, the term servitization is used in the field of business management, while hybrid products and hybrid service bundles are common in the field of information systems. The key term PSS is grouped in the research field of engineering and design, which includes the technical terms functional sales or industrial product-service system [21, 22]. The different designations usually refer to a similar concept [21].

From this point of view, it seems reasonable to define the term of PSS. Therefore, the definition approaches identified in the literature review are listed in Table 2 according to year of publication.

The current state of research shows clearly that even within the PSS field, PSS definitions are characterized by a high degree of heterogeneity. Based on Mont, a number of authors have established concepts with different foci over the past few years [24, 28]. Some authors only focus on market and competition aspects [9, 13], others include sustainability aspects because they argue that PSS inherently have a more positive impact on the environment than traditional business models [24]. Other scientists refer exclusively to the potential to deliver sustainable improvements [23, 26].

Table 2. Overview of the PSS definitions identified by the literature review.

Author/s	Year of publication	PSS definition
Goedkoop et al.	1999	"A Product Service system (PS system) is a marketable set of products and services capable of jointly fulfilling a user's need" [23]
Mont	2001	"[…] a system of products, services, supporting networks and infrastructure that is designed to be: competitive, satisfy customer needs and have a lower environmental impact than traditional business models" [24]
Manzini and Velozzi	2002	"[…] an innovation strategy, shifting the business focus from designing (and selling) physical products only, to designing (and selling) a system of products and services which are jointly capable of fulfilling specific client demands" [13]
Wong	2004	"Product Service Systems (PSS) may be defined as a solution offered for sale that involves both a product and a service element, to deliver the required functionality" [9]
Tukker and Tischner	2006	"Product-service system (PSS): the product-service including the (value) network, (technological) infrastructure and governance structure (or revenue model) that 'produces' a product-service" [25]
Baines et al.	2007	"A PSS is an integrated product and service offering that delivers value in use. A PSS offers the opportunity to decouple economic success from material consumption and hence reduce the environmental impact of economic activity" [26]
van Ostaeyen	2014	"A Product-Service System is an integrated offering of products and services with a revenue mechanism that is based on selling availability, usage or performance" [27]

Based on current knowledge, there is no established PSS definition at present. The most common definition used in the literature originates by the Swedish scientist Mont, who is a pioneer of the PSS concept [22, 29], but to explain the basic principles of PSS, the definition of Wong is useful.

4 PSS Classifications and Types

As already mentioned, PSS are a complex subject. To gain a better understanding of the PSS topic, different classification approaches have evolved over the last decades. In the sections below, the six PSS classifications of the respective authors identified during the literature review process are presented in chronological order. There is at least one PSS type in each classification. These types are also described below.

4.1 Mont

In 2002, Mont published the work "Clarifying the concept of product-service system" [28] and counts among the pioneers of the PSS research area. This work is the basis for further scientific work in the PSS field. One of the main components of the above-mentioned work is the classification of PSS. The classification comprises five elements from which the first PSS types are derived (see Fig. 4) [28].

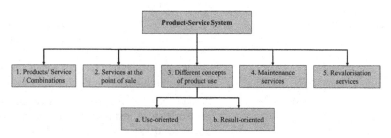

Fig. 4. PSS classification according to Mont [1, 28].

A PSS consists of products, services or a variable combination of both elements. Services at the time of sale include, for example, personal consultation in the salesroom, financing offers for the customer, as well as the product's explanation to the customer. There are two concepts for the use of the products: On the one hand, there is the (a) use-oriented concept, in which the customer derives the product benefit from the product. On the other hand, there is the (b) result-oriented concept, in which the product benefit is made accessible for the customer by the product through the provider. Maintenance services ensure that the product is maintained and that its functions are properly retained. In addition, it is possible to enhance the product through function upgrades and thus extend the product life cycle. The fifth element contains services that are based on the concept of sustainability and close the product-material lifecycle. These include the withdrawal of products, the reuse of functional parts or recycling if the complete reuse is not possible [28].

With the focus on the classification of PSS types, the third is especially interesting. For the first time, the two types of use- and results-oriented PSS are discussed there. In the context of her research Mont does not give detailed definitions of the two types mentioned. However, she establishes the basis for the PSS types, which will be developed in the following years.

The classification of Tukker from the year 2004 presented in the following already draws on the preparatory work of Mont from the year 2002.

4.2 Tukker

Dutch researcher Tukker published the paper "Eight types of product-service system: Eight ways to sustainability? Experiences From SusProNet" [30] in 2004, which is based on research by Mont. The typology included (see Fig. 5) is a special form of classification that is also the most common PSS research classification [30–32].

Tukker positions PSS between pure product and pure service and defines three types of PSS. In addition to the use- and result-oriented PSS already mentioned by Mont, Tukker is presenting the product-oriented PSS type for the first time. Tukker also divides the three PSS types into a total of eight different subtypes, which he classifies as eight archetypal models. The product-oriented PSS is divided into the subtypes product related, advice and consultancy. The use-oriented PSS type is subdivided into the three archetypal models product lease, product renting/sharing and product pooling, while the result-oriented PSS type is divided into the three models activity management/outsourcing, pay per service unit and functional result. Here, it has to be mentioned that the product share from the product-oriented to the use-oriented up to the result-oriented PSS types successively decreases and the service share increases in return [30].

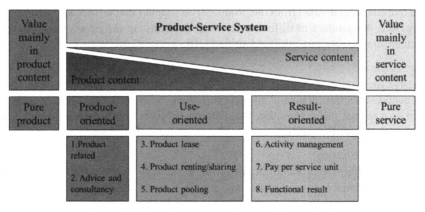

Fig. 5. PSS classification according to Tukker [1, 30].

Described below are the three types of PSS and the eight archetypal models:

Product-Oriented PSS
Concentrates on the sale of products, which are additionally extended by individual services. Two archetypal models can be identified [30]:

Product Related Services
In addition to the sale of a product, the customer is offered additional services that are tailored to the product and serve to ensure usage. These services range from maintenance contracts over the delivery of consumables to the return of the product at the end of its life cycle [30].

Advice and Consultancy Services
In addition to the sale of the product, the supplier offers consulting services to enable the customer the most efficient use of the product. Examples of consulting services in this regard are activities to improve the organizational structure or to optimize logistical processes [30].

Product Related Services

In addition to the sale of a product, the customer is offered additional services that are tailored to the product and serve to ensure usage. These services range from maintenance contracts over the delivery of consumables to the return of the product at the end of its life cycle [30].

Advice and Consultancy Services

In addition to the sale of the product, the supplier offers consulting services to enable the customer the most efficient use of the product. Examples of consulting services in this regard are activities to improve the organizational structure or to optimize logistical processes [30].

Use-Oriented PSS

According to Tukker, the product still plays an important role in the use-oriented PSS, but the business model is no longer focused exclusively on selling the product, but on the use that can be generated from the product. The supplier retains the ownership rights and provides the product to different customer segments in different offering forms. Altogether three archetypes can be identified [30]:

Product Lease

During use, the product remains in the ownership of the provider, who is also in charge of maintenance, servicing, repair and inspection. The customer is charged a fee for using the product on a regular basis. In return, the customer receives an unlimited and individual product usage opportunity [30].

Product Renting/Sharing

Like the lease offer, the product remains in the ownership of the provider during use, who is also accountable for maintenance, servicing, repair and inspection. In the same manner, the customer pays a fee to use the product. The main difference to leasing is the scope of use. In this case the use is limited in terms of time and not restricted to a single individual. In other words, different users may use the same product at different times [30].

Product Pooling

This fifth archetype has identical characteristics to the rental and sharing offer. The only difference is the time of use. The product can be used equally and at the same time by different numbers of users [30].

Result-Oriented PSS

With result-oriented PSS, the customer is not offered a product for sale, but is offered a certain result as a service, which the provider must fulfil. The provider is responsible for the way the service is fulfilled. Three archetypes can be determined:

Activity Management/Outsourcing

In this context, parts of activities are outsourced to third parties. In order to ensure a certain quality, performance indicators are defined, which in many cases are contractual components. This type can be found, for example, in the cleaning or catering industry [30].

Pay per Service Unit

The product is the base that the customer does not have to buy. Together with the customer, a predefined performance is described, which must be paid for according to the extent of use. The provider is responsible for all activities required to provide the performance. Charging is based on the service unit being used [30].

Functional Result

The provider commits to delivering a predefined result to the customer. The focus is exclusively on achieving the result. How the provider achieves the result plays a minor role [30].

As already stated at the start, Tukkers classification is widely accepted in literature and thus represents the reference point for further classifications in the field of PSS research [31].

4.3 Meier et al.

The German researchers Meier et al. developed a similar understanding of PSS nearly at the same time as Tukker. Their paper "Hybride Leistungsbündel" [33] was published in 2005, providing a further classification approach. This approach is aimed exclusively at the B2B market and captures the perspective of a manufacturing company. Meier et al. define a total of three PSS types that can be positioned between a pure product and a pure service (see Fig. 6) [33].

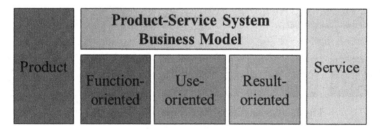

Fig. 6. PSS classification according to Meier et al. [1, 33].

This section describes the three types of PSS according to the authors. In addition to use and result oriented-PSS, which have already been mentioned by Mont and described by Tukker, Meier et al. coin the term function-oriented PSS [28, 30, 33]:

Function-Oriented PSS

In addition to the sale of a product, services are also provided in order to guarantee the functionality of the product over a certain period of time. A meaningful example is a maintenance contract for a production machine [33].

Use/Availability-Oriented PSS

This type guarantees the customer a certain availability of the product. The provider is involved in the customer's business processes for the first time and thus partially bears the production risk. This includes all processes, such as maintenance or repair, in order to guarantee availability. In a further publication, Meier et al. rename this PSS type to availability-oriented PSS [7, 33].

Results-Oriented PSS
The supplier commits to the customer to assume production responsibility for a certain result. Ultimately, only fault-free parts are in-voiced between the supplier and the customer [33].

The classification approach of Meier et al. has parallels to Tukker's concept. However, one major difference is the focus on the B2B market.

4.4 Neely

Three years after Meier et al. released their work on classification, Neely, a renowned researcher at the University of Cambridge, published the paper "Exploring the financial consequences of the servitization of manufacturing" [34]. This work focuses on the empirical investigation of the practical implementation of the servitization concept of manufacturing companies by means of practice-oriented company data. Thereby, Neely provides a classification of PSS. The three already known PSS types product-, use- and result-oriented PSS are discussed and two new PSS types are introduced. Neely thus elicits five different PSS types in a comprehensive way (see Fig. 7) [34].

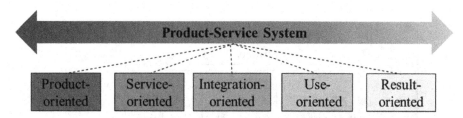

Fig. 7. PSS classification according to Neely [1, 34].

The five PSS types are located between pure product and pure service and are presented one after the other as shown in the diagram:

Product-Oriented PSS
The customer is the owner of the product by purchasing the product. In addition, services are offered that are specifically tailored to the product. This includes, for example, design and development services, installation and maintenance services as well as material procurement services. Compared to integration-oriented PSS, the product is supplemented by all services that contribute to the use of the product [34].

Service-Oriented PSS
As in the previous case, the customer owns the product by purchasing it. A characteristic feature of this PSS type is the inherent service component contained in each product. This means that value adding additional services are included as an integral part of

the performance offer. Neely cites the two examples of health monitoring systems and intelligent vehicle health management. Compared to product-oriented PSS, the service-oriented PSS type includes the integrated combination of product and service for the first time [34].

Integration-Oriented PSS

Product acquisition grants the customer ownership of the product. In addition to the product, services with vertical integration are offered. Consequently, the services offered are not directly related to the product, which makes it possible to distinguish them from product-oriented PSS. Examples are sales and distribution strategies, financial or consulting services and logistics services [34].

Use-Oriented PSS

This PSS type has already been described by Tukker. The focus is increasingly on the use generated by the product. As a result, the provider usually retains ownership of the product and only sells the use of the product to the customer through various forms of offering such as rental, pooling or lease offers [34].

Results-Oriented PSS

The product is increasingly being replaced by a service. In this context, no product is sold to the customer, but a certain result is offered as a service, which the provider must fulfil. When the result is achieved, the customer pays a fixed monetary amount in advance [34].

Neely's research continues Tukker's work and adds two more types of PSS, which allow a more specific differentiation of product related PSS (in the sense of close to pure products).

4.5 Van Ostaeyen et al.

Van Ostaeyen et al. published a publication in 2013 entitled "A refined typology of product-service systems based on functional hierarchy modeling" [32], creating a new understanding of PSS. This is accompanied by the presentation of a new PSS classification based on the two dimensions integration level of the PSS element and the dominant revenue mechanism, which together form the classification matrix according to van Ostaeyen et al. These two dimensions provide information about how deeply the PSS elements are integrated and when revenues can be generated over the PSS lifecycle from the vendor's perspective. Different PSS types can be classified in this matrix. For better understanding of the ambitious issue, a diagram (see Fig. 8) is provided [32].

Van Ostaeyen et al. define a total of three integration dimensions of PSS, which are considered in relation to the revenues generated over the life cycle by the different PSS elements (products and services). There are three levels: segregated, semi-integrated and fully integrated [32]:

- Segregated PSS: Less than 30% of life cycle revenue is generated by a PSS offering [32].

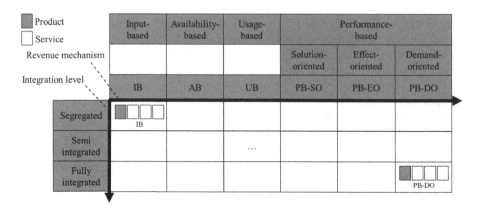

Fig. 8. PSS classification according to van Ostaeyen et al. [27, 32].

- Semi-integrated PSS: At least 30% and up to 80% of life cycle revenue is generated by a PSS offering [32].
- Fully integrated PSS: The life cycle revenue generated by a PSS offering is greater than or equal to 80% [32].

With regard to the dimension of performance orientation, van Ostaeyen identifies a total of four dominant revenue mechanisms, which in some cases can be divided.

Input-Based (IB)
This revenue mechanism is triggered when input is provided, for example, by the functionality of a product or service for a customer. The revenue is transferred from the customer to the provider. In the case of a product or service, ownership of the product or service is transferred to the customer, whereas the revenue of a service is based on the resources (e.g. hours worked) required to provide the service [32].

Availability-Based (AB)
The period in which the product or service is available to the customer plays a decisive role here. The actual usage time of the product or service is not considered. As an example, the payment of a monthly fee to the supplier for the provision of a machine can be mentioned [32].

Usage-Based (UB)
Based on the availability-based revenue mechanism, revenues are only generated by the actual use of the product or service. The usage can be expressed in time units, such as flight hours for an aircraft engine [32].

Performance-Based (PB)
Sales are generated by functional performance of a product or service and defined by performance indicators. This category is divided into three subcategories [32].

Solution-Oriented (PB-SO)
Revenue is generated from the performance of the product or service and measured by solution-oriented performance indicators. External environmental influences are not taken into account [32].

Effect-Oriented (PB-EO)
Revenue is generated on the basis of target-oriented performance parameters of the product or service. These only take into account environmental influences on the system, but not the system used [32].

Demand-Oriented (PB-DO)
Revenues are generated according to the degree to which customer requirements are met. Customer satisfaction is defined by a subjective performance indicator [32].

Through this specific and at the same time more complex differentiation of PSS types using the dimensions of integration level and return mechanisms, van Ostaeyen et al. enable an alternative classification that focuses on monetary value flows.

4.6 Gassmann et al.

As indicated in the introduction, PSS can be considered as a particular form of business models. Therefore, the identifying literature in the area of business model innovation, which has interfaces to PSS, should be considered. Gassmann is a name that was found during the research in this context. As Professor of Innovation Management at the renowned University of St. Gallen and Chairman of the Institute of Technology Management, he concentrates primarily on the empirical research of business models. In 2013, together with his colleagues Frankenberger and Csik, he published his first paper "The Business Model Navigator: 55 Models That Will Revolutionise Your Business" [35]. The second edition of Gassmann et al. contains 55 existing business model concepts, which classify around 90% of all new business models, including PSS business models. This paper describes these business models and assigns them to existing PSS classifications. In contrast to Osterwalder and Pigneur [36], Gassmann et al. describe a business model in four instead of nine dimensions (see Fig. 9).

The four dimensions of Gassmann et al. essentially contain the same contents as those of Osterwalder and Pigneur and are only briefly explained:

Who are our target customers? The customer is the focus of every business model; therefore, the offering company has to identify the relevant customer segments. What do we offer the customer? This dimension describes the promise of benefits and values that is offered to the customer to meet his needs. How do we create value proposition? This includes all processes and activities that a company must carry out in order to fulfil its promise of benefits and values. How is the revenue created? The fourth dimension deals with financial aspects such as the cost structure or turnover [4].

The 55 identified business model patterns of the St. Gallen Business Model Navigator are based on the concretization of the above questions. Each business model pattern has specific characteristics with respect to the four questions. Several types can be identified in the field of PSS business models:

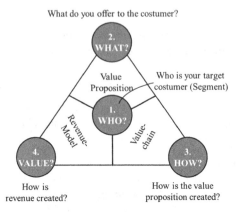

Fig. 9. Business model classification according to Gassmann et al. [1, 35].

Business Model Pattern 20 – Guaranteed Availability

The customer does not obtain any property rights through the purchase of the product, instead receives a guaranteed availability and thus the use of the product. This minimizes downtime costs, as these are covered by the supplier through replacement equipment, as well as repair and maintenance services. By paying a fixed fee to the provider, the customer receives all services necessary for the availability of the product. This pattern has parallels to Tukker's archetype product lease [4, 35].

Business Model Pattern 35 – Pay per Use

This pattern is defined in analogy to Tukker's archetype Pay per service unit. According to this, the customer is only charged for the effective use of a product, i.e. the actually consumed service units. This principle ensures a high level of cost transparency for both the customer and the provider. [4, 35].

Business Model Pattern 38 – Performance-Based Contracting

This pattern is a result-oriented pattern. The customer does not pay for ownership of the product but based on a service measured by a specific result. The supplier receives a fixed monetary amount and in return the supplier bears all cost items such as operating, maintenance and repair costs of the product. In contrast to pattern 35 above, the number of product-uses for the manufacture of a service unit is not crucial. Achieving the pre-agreed result is the objective. A characteristic of this pattern are so-called operator models, in which the product and the operator personnel are to be assigned to the supplier. This pattern can be assigned to Tukker's archetype functional results [4, 35].

Business Model Pattern 40 – Rent Instead of Buy

Instead of purchasing products, the focus here is on product benefits through rental concepts. Due to a more short-term rental price, the customer can gain access to products for which acquisition costs could not be covered. Compared to product acquisition, the provider can access greater sales potential. In terms of ownership rights, it is comparable to model 35, as only temporary ownership is assured. If the parallel to Tukker is drawn, this model belongs to the type product renting/sharing offer [4, 35].

Business Model Pattern 47 – Solution Provider
The supplier provides a customer-specific total solution consisting of product and service. Services include, for example, consulting services or the provision of consumables and spare parts. Tucker's type outsourcing comes close to this model [4, 35].

5 Conclusion

In this section, the results of the literature research on PSS classifications and types are combined and discussed. First, the PSS types are consolidated from the PSS classifications. In the second part, the publication is summarized in general.

5.1 Consolidation of PSS Classification and Types

The PSS classifications identified in the fourth chapter will now be compared. This section contains a consolidation of the PSS types from literature. The work of van Ostaeyen et al. from Sect. 4.5 makes a scientifically valuable contribution, the approach is not used for comparison due to its complexity. However, the business model patterns from Sect. 4.6 are compared as well. The previous PSS classification approaches are consolidated in a visualization (see Fig. 10), which gives an overview of the PSS classification types used in the literature. This clearly shows the relationship between the PSS types and the Gassmann business model patterns. Between pure product and pure service, these business model patterns tend to be characterized by a high service share.

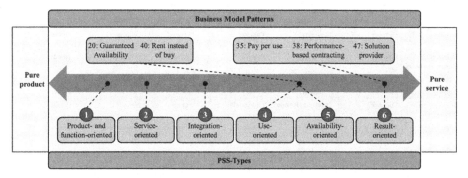

Fig. 10. Consolidation of the identified PSS types the literature [1].

In addition to the consolidation of PSS, a further classification between pure product and pure service is being carried out. This tabulated representation contains a generally applicable definition, a meaningful example and the associated source of the individual PSS types. The elements mentioned are shown in Table 1. This table summarizes all PSS types commonly used in the literature and gives the reader a general overview of the different types.

The differentiation and distinction of the individual PSS types appears to be complex, therefore a more detailed tabular representation should provide assistance. This section is concluded by a comparison of the introduced PSS types listed and analyzed below, under consideration of different PSS characteristics. The comparison is based on the following characteristics: Responsibility for application, affiliation of application employees, ownership, initiation of services, affiliation of service employees and revenue model [37]. The Table 3 should be used for this aim. The PSS type (4) use-oriented has the following characteristics. The customer is responsible for the application and provides the corresponding application personnel. The provider has the rights of ownership, initiates services and provides the corresponding service personnel. Costs are charged for the period used (Table 4).

Table 3. Comparison of the identified PSS types the literature [1].

PSS-type	(1) Product- and function- oriented	(2) Service- oriented	(3) Integration- oriented	(4) Use- oriented	(5) Availability- oriented	(6) Result- oriented
Definition	In addition to the sale of products, services are offered which guarantee and extend the functionality of the product	The sold product contains an inherent service component	In addition to the sale of the product, services are offered that enable vertical integration and do not represent a direct reference to the product	Instead of selling the product, the use of the product is sold over a specific time period	The use of the product is also in the foreground, additionally an agreed availability of the product is guaranteed	Instead of product acquisition, a specific result is offered as a service performance
Example	Maintenance contract for a machine, supply of consumables	Intelligent vehicle health management system	Consulting or logistics services that extend beyond product usage	Leasing or rental offer of a motor vehicle	Guaranteed availability of a machine	Provision of printing equipment, charging based on printed pages
Source	[30, 33, 34]	[34]	[34]	[28, 30, 34]	[7, 33]	[28, 30, 33, 34]

Table 4. Characteristics of the identified PSS types [1].

PSS-type	(1) Product- and function- oriented	(2) Service- oriented	(3) Inte-gration- oriented	(4) Use- oriented	(5) Avail- ability- oriented	(6) Result- oriented
Responsibility for application	Customer	Customer	Customer	Customer	Customer	Provider
Affiliation of application employees	Customer	Customer	Customer	Customer	Customer	Provider
Ownership	Customer	Customer	Customer	Provider	Provider	Provider
Initiation of services	Customer	Customer	Provider	Provider	Provider	Provider
Affiliation of service employees	Customer	Customer/ Provider	Customer/ Provider	Provider	Provider	Provider
Revenue model	By order	By order	By order	By time period	By availability	By result

5.2 Summary of Research

This section summarizes the results of the literature review. This is done on the one hand by answering the RQ, but on the other hand also by recombining the previous results from sections three and four.

This article was preceded by a very detailed literature review, which resulted in 125 identified and evaluated publications. This forms the basis for the contents described, including the seven identified and compared PSS definitions from the third section. Thus, the initial question (RQ1) of how PSS are defined in the literature can be answered positively. It has been shown that there is no universal PSS definition. The definition of Mont is the most common and the one of Wong is the most comprehensible.

The extensive literature research was mainly used to search for PSS classifications. In the end, six different approaches were successfully discovered. This article provides a clear presentation of all six PSS classifications and their design (RQ2). The vast majority of authors classify PSS between pure product and pure service. Mont describes PSS concepts primarily from theory, Neely bases his work on empirical studies with practical relevance, while others relate the PSS classification exclusively to the B2B market. Van Ostaeyen describes PSS at the process level in the most detailed and complex way compared to the other classifications. As with definitions, it can also be said that a generally accepted classification does not exist in this context, but Tucker's work is widely recognized [29, 31]. Furthermore, parallels between PSS and business models were shown.

The classifications described attempt to further group PSS by means of a typification. These types were also identified and described in detail in the research (RQ3). In total, six different types of PSS types were identified by this search, which are described in section four. In addition, specific forms of business model patterns were also examined for PSS content. The result, five business model patterns similar to the PSS types were found and described.

The consolidation and comparison of the PSS types in a next step can be seen as a further success (RQ4). The five business model patterns mentioned were assigned to the PSS types. An overview table is used to compare the six PSS types. The consolidated types are described and illustrated by a practical example. A further table specifies and describes the types in detail using characteristics. This table shows both the similarities and the differences between the six PSS types mentioned.

Altogether, the four research questions presented at the beginning of this paper are answered. Thus, this publication represents a consistent and logical further development of the original work.

6   Outlook of Future Research of PSS

Digitalization continues to advance at a rapid pace and changes existing business models. Currently, PSS are only an intermediary step and will soon be replaced by so-called Digital PSS. In the process, PSS will be enriched with digital elements (services or products). For this reason, it seems to make a considerable amount of sense to carry out further research activities in the field of digital business models with connections to PSS. This publication of the literature research on PSS is a valuable basis. The provided definitions give a first insight and the identified and described PSS classifications and types are very helpful to develop a general understanding of the complex topic PSS. For the future, a perspective change from theory to practice is intended. A PSS classification framework, which is currently under development, will allow to analyze successful companies on the basis of defined characteristics. In this manner, success factors can be derived and an action guideline for a successful transformation to a PSS provider can be developed.

Acknowledgements. The Research Project "Mittelstand 4.0 Kompetenzzentrum Stuttgart" is part of the focal point of support "SMES Digital – Strategies for a Digital Transformation of Business Processes" of the German Ministry of Economics and Energy (BMWi). This support campaign was assigned to push the digitalization of small and medium sized enterprises and craft businesses.

References

1. Waidelich, L., Bulander, R., Richter, A., et al.: A systematic literature review on product-service systems classifications and types. In: Proceedings of the 16th International Joint Conference on e-Business and Telecommunications, pp. 83–94. SCITEPRESS - Science and Technology Publications (2019)
2. Mahler, A., Schiessl, M., Schulz, T., et al.: Unternehmen: schneller, höher, pleite (2013). http://www.spiegel.de/spiegel/print/d-111320095.html. Accessed 30 Apr 2018
3. Gassmann, O., Frankenberger, K., Csik, M.: Geschäftsmodelle aktiv innovieren: Systematischer Weg zur radikalen Geschäftsmodellinnovation. In: Grichnik, D., Gassmann, O. (eds.) Das unternehmerische Unternehmen, pp. 23–43. Springer, Wiesbaden (2013). https://doi.org/10.1007/978-3-658-02059-0_2
4. Gassmann, O., Frankenberger, K., Csik, M: Geschäftsmodelle entwickeln: 55 innovative Konzepte mit dem St. Galler Business Model Navigator, 2. Aufl. Hanser eLibrary. Hanser, München (2017)
5. Kölmel, B., Richter, A., Schoblik, J., et al.: Customer centricity von digitalen produkt-service-systemen. In: Deutscher Dialogmarketing Verband e.V. (ed.) Dialogmarketing Perspektiven 2016/2017, pp. 127–138. Springer, Wiesbaden (2017). https://doi.org/10.1007/978-3-658-16835-3_7
6. Meier, H., Uhlmann, E. (eds.): Industrielle Produkt-Service Systeme: Entwicklung, Betrieb und Management. Springer, Heidelberg (2017). https://doi.org/10.1007/978-3-662-48018-2
7. Meier, H., Uhlmann, E.: Integrierte Industrielle Sach- und Dienstleistungen: Vermarktung, Entwicklung und Erbringung hybrider Leistungsbündel. Springer, Heidelberg (2012). https://doi.org/10.1007/978-3-642-25269-3
8. Vogel-Heuser, B., Lindemann, U.: Innovationsprozesse Zyklenorientiert Managen. Springer, Heidelberg (2014). https://doi.org/10.1007/978-3-662-44932-5
9. Wong, M.T.N.: Implementation of innovative product service-systems in the consumer goods industry. Ph.D. thesis, Cambridge University (2004)
10. Wise, R., Baumgartner, P.: Go Downstream: the new profit imperative in manufacturing. Harv. Bus. Rev. **77**(5), 133–141 (1999)
11. Kowalkowski, C., Gebauer, H., Kamp, B., et al.: Servitization and deservitization: overview, concepts, and definitions. Ind. Mark. Manag. **60**, 4–10 (2017). https://doi.org/10.1016/j.indmarman.2016.12.007
12. Richter, A., Schoblik, J., Kölmel, B., et al.: A review of influential factors for product service system application. Eur. Rev. Serv. Econ. **5**, 65–95 (2018). https://doi.org/10.15122/ISBN.978-2-406-08064-0.P.0065
13. Manzini, E., Vezzoli, C.: A strategic design approach to develop sustainable product service systems: examples taken from the 'environmentally friendly innovation' Italian prize. J. Clean. Prod. **11**(8), 851–857 (2003). https://doi.org/10.1016/S0959-6526(02)00153-1
14. Aurich, J.C., Fuchs, C., Wagenknecht, C.: Life cycle oriented design of technical Product-service systems. J. Clean. Prod. **14**(17), 1480–1494 (2006). https://doi.org/10.1016/j.jclepro.2006.01.019

15. Beuren, F.H., Gomes Ferreira, M.G., Cauchick Miguel, P.A.: Product-service systems: a literature review on integrated products and services. J. Clean. Prod. **47**, 222–231 (2013). https://doi.org/10.1016/j.jclepro.2012.12.028
16. Bosch Hannover Messe 2016 - Alles ist vernetzt: 25.04.2016 Bosch Gruppe Pressemappe (2016). http://www.bosch-presse.de/pressportal/de/de/hannover-messe-2016-alles-ist-vernetzt-43334.html Accessed 20 May 2018
17. Brocke, J., Simons, A., Niehaves, B., et al.: Reconstructing the giant: process on the importance of rigour in documenting the literature search. In: ECIS 2009 Proceedings 161 (2009)
18. Cooper, H.M.: Organizing knowledge syntheses: a taxonomy of literature reviews. Knowl. Soc. **1**(1), 104–126 (1988). https://doi.org/10.1007/BF03177550
19. Chartered Association of Business Schools: Academic journal guide 2015 (2015). https://cha rteredabs.org/academic-journal-guide-2015-view/ Accessed 18 Apr 2018
20. Webster, J., Watson, R.: Analyzing the past to prepare for the future: writing a literature review. MIS Q. **26** (2002). https://doi.org/10.2307/4132319
21. Lifset, R.: Moving from products to services. J. Ind. Ecol. **4**(1), 1–2 (2000). https://doi.org/10.1162/108819800569195
22. Boehm, M., Thomas, O.: Looking beyond the rim of one's teacup: a multidisciplinary literature review of product-service systems. J. Clean. Prod. **51**, 245–260 (2013). https://doi.org/10.1016/j.jclepro.2013.01.019
23. Goedkoop, M., van Halen, C., te Riele, H., et al.: Product service systems ecological and economic basics. Report for Dutch Ministries of Environment (1999)
24. Mont, O.: Introducing and developing a Product-Service System (PSS) concept in Sweden. IIIEE Reports (6) (2001)
25. Tukker, A., Tischner, U.: New Business for Old Europe: Product-Service Development, Competitiveness and Sustainability. Greenleaf Pub., Sheffield (2006)
26. Baines, T., Lightfoot, H.W., Evans, S., et al.: State-of-the-art in product-service systems. Proc. Inst. Mech. Eng. Part B J. Eng. Manuf. **221**(10), 1543–1552 (2007). https://doi.org/10.1243/09544054JEM858
27. van Ostaeyen, J.: Analysis of the business potential of product-service systems for investment goods (2014)
28. Mont, O.: Clarifying the concept of product–service system. J. Clean. Prod. **10**(3), 237–245 (2002). https://doi.org/10.1016/S0959-6526(01)00039-7
29. Haase, R.P., Pigosso, D.C.A., McAloone, T.C.: Product/service-system origins and trajectories: a systematic literature review of PSS definitions and their characteristics. Procedia CIRP **64**, 157–162 (2017). https://doi.org/10.1016/j.procir.2017.03.053
30. Tukker, A.: Eight types of product–service system: eight ways to sustainability? Experiences from SusProNet. Bus. Strat. Environ. **13**(4), 246–260 (2004). https://doi.org/10.1002/bse.414
31. Dimache, A., Roche, T.: A decision methodology to support servitisation of manufacturing. Int. J. Oper. Prod. Manag. **33**(11/12), 1435–1457 (2013). https://doi.org/10.1108/IJOPM-07-2010-0186
32. van Ostaeyen, J., van Horenbeek, A., Pintelon, L., et al.: A refined typology of product–service systems based on functional hierarchy modeling. J. Clean. Prod. **51**, 261–276 (2013). https://doi.org/10.1016/j.jclepro.2013.01.036
33. Meier, H., Uhlmann, E., Kortmann, D.: Hybride Leistungsbündel-Nutzenorientiertes Produktverständnis durch interferierende Sach-und Dienstleistungen. wt Werkstattstechnik online **95**(7/8), 528–532 (2005)
34. Neely, A.: Exploring the financial consequences of the servitization of manufacturing. Oper. Manag. Res. **1**(2), 103–118 (2008). https://doi.org/10.1007/s12063-009-0015-5
35. Gassmann, O., Frankenberger, K., Csik, M.: Geschäftsmodelle entwickeln: 55 innovative Konzepte mit dem St. Galler Business Model Generator, Hanser (2013)

36. Osterwalder, A., Pigneur, Y.: Business Model Generation: A Handbook for Visionaries, Game Changers, and Challengers. Wiley, Hoboken (2010)
37. Leimeister, J.M.: Einführung in die Wirtschaftsinformatik. Springer, Heidelberg (2017). https://doi.org/10.1007/978-3-662-53656-8_9

Security and Cryptography

A Reconfigurable Implementation of Elliptic Curve Cryptography over GF (2^n)

Salah Harb$^{(\boxtimes)}$ [ID], M. Omair Ahmad [ID], and M. N. S. Swamy [ID]

Concordia University, Montreal, QC H3G 1M8, Canada
{s_rb,omair,swamy}@ece.concordia.ca

Abstract. In this chapter, a high-performance area-efficient reconfigurable design for the Elliptic Curve Cryptography (ECC), targeting the area-constrained high-bandwidth embedded applications, is presented. The proposed design is implemented using pipelining architecture. The applied architecture is performed using n-bit data path of the finite field GF (2^n). For the finite field operations, the implementation in the ECC uses the bit-parallel recursive Karatsuba-Ofman algorithm for multiplication and Itoh-Tsuji for inversion. An improved Montgomery ladder algorithm is utilized for the scalar multiplication of a point. Balanced-execution data paths in components of the ECC core are guaranteed by inserting pipelined registers in ideal locations. The proposed design has been implemented using Xilinx Virtex, Kintex and Artix FPGA devices. It can perform a single scalar multiplication in 226 clock cycles within 0.63 μs using 2780 slices and 360 Mhz working frequency on Virtex-7 over GF (2^{163}). In GF (2^{233}) and GF (2^{571}), a scalar multiplication can be computed in 327 and 674 clock cycles within 1.05 μs and 2.32 μs, respectively. Compared with previous works, our reconfigurable design reduces the required number of clock cycles and operates using fewer FPGA resources with competitive high working frequencies. Therefore, the proposed design is well suited in the low-powered resource-constrained real-time cryptosystems such as online banking services, wearable smart devices and network attached storages.

Keywords: Cryptography · Elliptic Curve Cryptography · FPGA · Pipelining architecture · Finite field operations · Field multiplications · Projective coordination · Efficiency

1 Introduction

Elliptic Curve Cryptosystem (ECC) is a public-key cryptosystem, which was first proposed by Neal Koblitz and Victor Miller in the 1980s [15,20]. Since then, many researches have been conducted to explore its robustness levels against other public-key cryptosystems such as El-Gamal, RSA and Digital Signature Algorithm (DSA) [5,27]. These cryptosystems are based on either the integer

© Springer Nature Switzerland AG 2020
M. S. Obaidat (Ed.): ICETE 2019, CCIS 1247, pp. 87–107, 2020.
https://doi.org/10.1007/978-3-030-52686-3_4

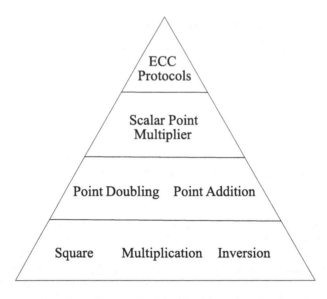

Fig. 1. ECC cryptosystem hierarchy [9].

factorization or discrete logarithm problems [19]. Equivalent security levels with smaller key size, ease of implementation, and resource savings, are among the reasons that make the ECC more appealing and preferable to hardware reconfigurable implementations. Moreover, ECC is well suited to be implemented in such resource-constrained embedded systems, since it provides same security levels as RSA does using small keys. ECC has been standardized by IEEE and the National Institute of Standard and Technology (NIST) as a scheme in digital signature and key agreement protocols [31].

Most public-key algorithms are implemented on software platforms. Performing an algorithm on a general-purpose processor (e.g. CPU) will require most of its resources to produce results due to the large operands used in these very accurate computations. Moreover, their CPU is not suitable for performing such algorithms having, by their nature, a parallel architecture. These issues show that a software implementation of encryption algorithms does not provide the required performance. Due to the diversity in the applications, a trade-off between area, speed and power is required. Some applications, such as RFID cards, sensors in wireless networks and cell phones, demand a small area and low power. Other applications, such as web servers, large bandwidth networks and satellite broadcast require very high throughputs. To address the issues of software implementation and meet trade-offs in numerous applications, efficient hardware platforms were utilized for implementing the cryptographic algorithms, to perform the operations required across multiple applications.

Scalar point multiplication (SPM) is the main point operation in ECC cryptosystems or protocols such as Elliptic Curve Diffie-Hellman (ECDH) [4] for key agreements and Elliptic Curve Digital Signature (ECDS) for digital signatures.

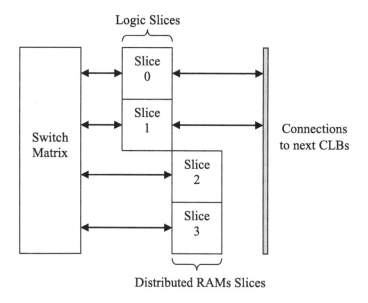

Fig. 2. Structure of CLBs in Xilinx FPGA device.

SPM can be worked over many finite fields (i.e. Galois Fields (GF)) under either prime GF (p) or polynomial fields GF (2^n). SPM has two-point operations, doubling and adding points. Each operation consists of finite field operations such as squaring, addition, and multiplication. Figure 1 presents the hierarchical implementation of the ECC protocol. Polynomial fields are more suited and are efficient to implement on a customizable platform such as FPGAs [33].

1.1 Xilinx FPGA Devices

Field Programmable Gate Array (FPGA) is one of the preferable reconfigurable hardware platforms [34] and offers flexible and more customizable methods for performing and evaluating different hardware implementations. Because of this, and since FPGAs have been employed in the bulk of previous hardware implementations to evaluate their performance, the ECC hardware implementation presented in this chapter has been performed using Xilinx FPGA devices [35]. Current FPGA chips have high-level modules including dedicated block memories (BRAMs), multipliers and accumulator units. These modules are located in reconfigurable logic blocks (CLBs), which are linked via reconfigurable routers and switch matrices. Reconfiguring the FPGA device involves constructing the fundamental operations of the ECC algorithm on CLBs and high-level modules. Each CLB in the FPGA mainly has two types of modules: sequential logic and combination logic. The combinational modules can be implemented to provide output of Boolean functions. Register elements are provided to perform the sequential logic like storing data and passing values among different CLBs. Each CLB contains slices, where each slice contains different components including lookup tables (LUTs), registers, arithmetic logic and multiplexers. In the new 7 series FPGAs, 1 CLB contains 2 slices, each slice consisting of 4 6-input LUTs and 8 Flip Flops (F.Fs). Figure 2 illustrates the structure of logic and memory CLBs. The proposed high-speed ECC core is implemented using the Virtex-5, Virtex-7, Artix-7 and Kintex-7 FPGA devices.

To gain superior performance in today's highly loaded communication networks, utilization of hardware accelerators for physical security continues to create a greater demand for the efficient high-speed implementation of ECC. Based on this, a great number of FPGA implementations of ECC have been published in the literature, where various ranges of latencies and number of clock cycles are achieved targeting applications that require high/low throughputs [9,12,14,16]. Providing high performance, as well as utilizing an efficient area, is a challenge to achieve in FPGA's ECC implementations.

In this chapter, an efficient FPGA hardware implementation of ECC over GF (2^n) using the pipelining architecture is proposed. The main target of our work is to develop a high-performance design that targets systems with constrained resources such as wearable smart devices, processing engines in image steganographic systems [1,3] and network processors. In this chapter, further realizations on software implementation and power consumption for the proposed ECC cores are presented [9]. This chapter is organized as follows. Section 2 describes the arithmetic operations of the ECC, Sect. 3 describes our high-performance hardware implementation core for ECC over GF (2^n), Sect. 4 shows the results, comparisons and software implementation for the adopted design, and finally, Sect. 5 concludes this chapter.

2   Elliptic Curve Cryptography (ECC)

Elliptic Curves (ECs) are formulated by the so called Weiestrass equations, which can be performed on a normal or polynomial basis. In this chapter, we will explore the polynomial basis in GF (2^n) for its efficiency on hardware platforms [33]. The general form of the non-singular curve over GF (2^n) [8] can be represented by

$$y^2 + xy = x^3 + ax^2 + b \tag{1}$$

where a, b $\in$ GF (2^n) and b $\neq$ 0. A set of affine points (x, y) satisfying the curve forms a group [8] with an identity point of that group. There are two fundamental elliptic curve operations, doubling and adding points. Doubling point is denoted as $P_1 = 2P_0$, where P_1 is (x_1, y_1) and P_0 is (x_0, y_0), while point addition is denoted as $P_2 = P_0 + P_1$, where P_2 is (x_2, y_2), and $P_1 \neq P_0$. All points in the selected curve are represented in affine coordinates. Finite field operations are involved in the ECC point operations such as addition, squaring, multiplication and inversion. Dealing with affine coordinates requires an inversion field operation. Due to the complexity in the inversion operation, a projective coordinate is utilized to avoid it by mapping points in affine (x, y) to be represented in (X, Y, Z) form.

Scalar Point Multiplication (SPM) is the main operation that dominates the ECC-based cryptosystems. SPM is the process of adding a point k times, where k is a positive integer and P is a point on the selected curve. SPM is based on the implementation of the underlying point operations, where a series of doubling and adding points is performed by scanning the binary sequence of the scalar k, where $k = k_n k_{n-1} \ldots k_1 k_0$.

There are several methods and techniques to implement $k.P$ efficiently: Binary Add-and-Double Left-Right, Binary Add-and-Double Right-Left as presented in [11], Non-Adjacent-Form (NAF) [22] and Montgomery ladder method [21]. Affine coordinate system is the default representation that some SPM methods use to introduce the points on the elliptic curves, while other SPMs utilize alternative projective coordinate systems for representing the points. The reason for applying different projective systems is to avoid the time/resource consuming inversion field operation. However, it increases the number of field multiplications. Generally, projective systems tend to provide efficient designs of ECC cryptosystem in terms of area/latency.

Lopez-Dahab (LD) [17] projective system is one of the most efficient projective coordinate systems. Points in affine system are mapped to LD projective system, where P at (x, y) coordinate is equal to P at $(X = x, Y = y, Z = 1)$ coordinate. In any SPM, the point multiplication algorithm must be selected first for performing the $k.P$ operation. The next step is to define the projective coordinate operation system for representing the points. The final step is to choose algorithms for the finite field operations, mainly for the multiplication and inversion operations. Figure 3 illustrates the required components for constructing SPM in our ECC cryptosystem. In the present work, Montgomery ladder algorithm is adopted as the point multiplication algorithm and the LD coordinate system to represent the points. For the field multiplication and inversion operations, the Karatsuba-Ofman algorithm and the Itoh-Tsuji algorithm are, respectively, implemented.

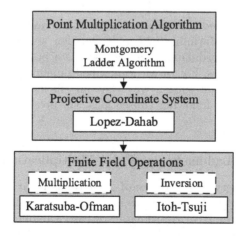

Fig. 3. Main components of SPM [9].

2.1 Finite Fields GF (2^n)

ECC over GF (2^n) is more suitable and efficient for hardware implementation because the arithmetic in the polynomial fields is carry-less. In GF (p), finding points on an elliptic curve requires performing a square root algorithm [10, 33], while the process is much easier over GF (2^n), where the points can be found using generators for polynomials. There are 2n − 1 elements in GF (2^n), which can be represented as binary polynomials. For example, the element in GF (2^n) has a polynomial representation:

$$a_{n-1}x^{n-1} + a_{n-2}x^{n-2} + ... + a_1x^1 + a_0x^0 \tag{2}$$

where x_i is the location of the ith term, and $a_i \in [0, 1]$ is the coefficient of the ith term. Arithmetic operations, such as addition, multiplication, squaring and division (i.e. inversion and multiplication) are applied over these elements. Adding two elements C = A + B is done using the logic XOR. Squaring an element is computed by padding 0s between two adjacent bits of the element. Multiplying two elements C = A · B is a much harder and slower operation than addition and squaring.

The result of squaring an element or multiplying two elements would be out of the field. To reduce it, an irreducible polynomial of degree n ($f(x)$) is used by applying the reduction (modular) step, such as C = (A^2) mod $f(x)$ or C = (A · B) mod $f(x)$. Inversion operation is the most complex operation in terms of time and resources. Obtaining the inverse of an element A is the process of finding another element B that satisfies A · B ≡ 1 mod $f(x)$. Note that $f(x)$ has a major role in the performance of these operations. In this chapter, all curves and irreducible polynomials are chosen based on the recommendation of the NIST [6].

3   High-Speed Core for ECC over GF (2^n)

The proposed architecture of the high-speed ECC core is over GF (2^n) using NIST binary recommended curves. Karatsuba-Ofman and Itoh-Tsuji algorithms are implemented for performing field multiplication and inversion operations, respectively. The LD coordinate system is used as a projective coordinate system to present the points. For SPM, a modified-pipelined Montgomery ladder method is implemented in such a way that an efficient number of pipelined stages are inserted. The following subsections will present more details about these algorithms.

3.1 Montgomery Ladder Scalar Point Multiplication Algorithm

At present, Montgomery ladder is one of the most popular multiplication algorithms used to perform k.P, where k is an integer. It can be implemented in both affine and projective coordinate systems. Doubling and adding point operations are computed in an efficient way for every bit in the sequence of

$k = k_{t-1}k_{t-2}\ldots k_1 k_0$. Algorithm 1 shows the projective coordinate version of Montgomery ladder method [17].

The algorithm is based on performing point operations recursively using the x affine coordinate, which leads to a reduction the number of field multiplications. The y coordinate is used at the post-process affine, which is required to recover the affine coordinates from the LD coordinates. There are many hardware implementations of this algorithm that provide high performance [2,18,28] due to their speed, parallelism capability, resource-constrained systems and power analysis resistance.

3.2   Trade-Off Between Area and High-Performance

Hardware implementations for ECC can be made efficient by adopting some optimization techniques such as determining short-critical path for pipelining, and using minimal resources through resource sharing. Architectural pipelining optimization aims to optimize the long-critical path of the design by breaking

---

Algorithm 1: Montgomery Ladder Scalar Multiplier (k.P) [17].

Input: $k = k_{t-1}k_{t-2}\ldots k_1 k_0$, Point P($x,y$) on Elliptic Curve.
Output: A point Q $= k$P
$\quad X_1 \leftarrow x; Z_1 \leftarrow 1; X_2 \leftarrow x^4 + b; Z_2 \leftarrow x^2;$
$\quad$ **if** $k == 0 \parallel x == 0$ **then**
$\quad\quad$ Q $\leftarrow (0, 0);$
$\quad$ **end if** Stop Loop;
$\quad$ **for** $i = t - 2$ to 0 **do**
$\quad\quad$ **if** $k_i == 1$ **then**
$\quad\quad\quad$ Q $(X_1,Z_1) \leftarrow$ add$(X_1, Z_1, X_2, Z_2); \Rightarrow \{$
$\quad\quad\quad Z_1 \leftarrow X_2 \cdot Z_1; X_1 \leftarrow X_1 \cdot Z_2; T \leftarrow X_1 + Z_1;$
$\quad\quad\quad X_1 \leftarrow X_1 \cdot Z_1; Z_1 \leftarrow T^2; T \leftarrow x \cdot Z_1;$
$\quad\quad\quad X_1 \leftarrow X_1 + T; \}$
$\quad\quad\quad$ Q $(X_2,Z_2) \leftarrow$ double$(X_2, Z_2); \Rightarrow \{$
$\quad\quad\quad Z_2 \leftarrow Z_2^2; T \leftarrow Z_2^2; T \leftarrow b \cdot T;$
$\quad\quad\quad X_2 \leftarrow X_2^2; Z_2 \leftarrow X_2 \cdot Z_2; X_2 \leftarrow X_2 + T; \}$
$\quad\quad$ **else**
$\quad\quad\quad$ Q $(X_2,Z_2) \leftarrow$ add$(X_2, Z_2, X_1, Z_1); \Rightarrow \{$
$\quad\quad\quad Z_2 \leftarrow X_1 \cdot Z_2; X_2 \leftarrow X_2 \cdot Z_1; T \leftarrow X_2 + Z_2;$
$\quad\quad\quad X_2 \leftarrow X_2 \cdot Z_2; Z_2 \leftarrow T^2; T \leftarrow x \cdot Z_2;$
$\quad\quad\quad X_2 \leftarrow X_2 + T; \}$
$\quad\quad\quad$ Q $(X_1,Z_1) \leftarrow$ double$(X_1, Z_1); \Rightarrow \{$
$\quad\quad\quad Z_2 \leftarrow Z_1^2; T \leftarrow Z_1^2; T \leftarrow b \cdot T;$
$\quad\quad\quad X_1 \leftarrow X_1^2; Z_1 \leftarrow X_1 \cdot Z_1; X_1 \leftarrow X_1 + T; \}$
$\quad\quad$ **end if**
$\quad$ **end for**
$\quad$ Return Q $(X_3,Z_3) =$ affine$(X_1, Z_1, X_2, Z_2); \Rightarrow \{$
$\quad x_3 \leftarrow X_1/Z_1;$
$\quad y_3 \leftarrow (x + X_1/Z_1)[(X_1 + x \cdot Z_1)(X_2 + x \cdot Z_2) + (x^2 + y)(Z_1 \cdot Z_2)](x \cdot Z_1 \cdot Z_2^{-1}) + y; \}$

---

it into stages. The number of clock cycles can be improved by adopting parallel field multiplication operations. All these optimization techniques have an impact on the resources required for performing SPM. In pipelining, inserting registers to minimize the critical path delay results in an increase in the number of the clock cycles (latencies) and resources. Obtaining an efficient pipelined design can be achieved by determining the number of stages. More stages yield higher working frequencies, but higher latencies. Balancing this trade-off can be achieved by considering an efficient field multiplier, independency levels among point operations, and finite-state machines that control these operations effectively.

3.3 Proposed High-Speed Area-Efficient ECC Core over GF (2^n)

Algorithm 1 states that a single point multiplication consists of three parts: 1) mapping the affine coordinates to LD coordinates, 2) performing adding and doubling point operations recursively, and 3) obtaining the point from LD coordinates to affine coordinates. In the second part, each iteration consists of the adding and doubling point operations. If k_i is equal to 1, point addition operation is performed on the registers X_1, Z_1, X_2 and Z_2 to obtain the new values for X_1 and Z_1, and at the same time, doubling point operation is performed on the registers X_2 and Z_2 to obtain the new values for the registers X_2 and Z_2. On the other hand, if k_i is 0, the point addition operation is performed on the registers X_2, Z_2, X_1 and Z_1 to obtain the new values for X_2 and Z_2, and the doubling point operation is performed on the registers X_1 and Z_1 to obtain the new values for the registers X_1 and Z_1. Note that registers X_1, Z_1, X_2 and Z_2 hold the LD x-coordinate of the point, once $t - 1$ iterations are completed. In the third part, the LD x-coordinate obtained in part 2 is mapped back to x affine coordinate and then y affine coordinate is determined. The affine coordinates (x_3, y_3) hold the result of kP.

Through this recursive manner, the authors in [18] noticed that the initialization step of Algorithm 1 can be merged into the main loop of the algorithm, where the 4 registers are initialized as follows: $X_1 = 1$, $Z_1 = 0$, $X_2 = x$, $Z_2 = 1$. This eliminates the need of precomputed values to be obtained before starting the main loop. However, it requires extra clock cycles for the merged initialization step. The design in [2] addressed the swapping feature in Algorithm 1 and proposed a merged-improved Montgomery ladder point multiplication algorithm as shown in Algorithm 2.

The proposed high-speed area-efficient hardware design is shown in Fig. 4. The general architecture has three units, an optimized finite-state machine control unit, a GF (2^n) arithmetic unit containing a squarer and a Karatsuba-Ofman multiplier, and a control signal unit. Next, further details are given for these main units in the high-speed ECC core.

Algorithm 2: Merged-Improved Montgomery Ladder Scalar Multiplier (k.P) [2].

Input: $k = k_{t-1}k_{t-2}...k_1k_0$, Point P($x,y$) on Elliptic Curve.
Output: A point Q = kP
  $X_1 \leftarrow 1; Z_1 \leftarrow 0; X_2 \leftarrow x; Z_2 \leftarrow 1$;
  if (**then** $k == 0 \parallel x == 0$) Q $\leftarrow (0, 0)$;
  end if Stop Loop;
  for $i = t - 1$ to 0 **do**
    $T \leftarrow Z_1; Z_1 \leftarrow (X_1 \cdot Z_2 + X_2 \cdot Z_1)^2$;
    $X_1 \leftarrow x \cdot Z_1 + X_1 \cdot X_2 \cdot T \cdot Z_2; T \leftarrow X_1$;
    $X_2 \leftarrow X_2^4 + b \cdot Z_2^4; Z_2 \leftarrow T^2 \cdot Z_2^2$;
    if $(i \neq 0 \ \& \ k_i \neq k_{i-1}) \parallel (i == 0 \ \& \ k_i == 0)$ **then**
      swap(X_1, X_2, Z_1, Z_2); $\Rightarrow$ {
      $T_1 \leftarrow X_1; X_1 \leftarrow X_2$;
      $X_2 \leftarrow T_1$;
      $T_2 \leftarrow Z_1; Z_1 \leftarrow Z_2$;
      $Z_2 \leftarrow T_2$; }
    end if
  end for
  Return Q (X_3,Z_3) = affine(X_1, Z_1, X_2, Z_2); $\Rightarrow$ {
  $x_3 \leftarrow X_1/Z_1$;
  $y_3 \leftarrow (x + X_1/Z_1)[(X_1 + x \cdot Z_1) (X_2 + x \cdot Z_2) + (x^2 + y)(Z_1 \cdot Z_2)] (x \cdot Z_1 \cdot Z_2^{-1}) + y$; }

3.4 Finite-State Machine for the Proposed ECC Core

Finite-State Machine (FSM) is a control model developed to control any hardware design containing multiple components such as registers, addresses and flags. Controlling design includes maintaining proper transitions between these components. Each transition in FSM affects the state (i.e. current values) of the registers and flags. FSM of the proposed high-performance core is implemented in an efficient way, where a minimum number of states are utilized. Figure 5 represents the main FSM of the proposed high-speed core. The main loop of the merged-improved Montgomery ladder SPM starts from state 0 and ends at state 11.

At state 11, the condition (the second if-statement in Algorithm 2) of whether swapping registers must be performed or return state 0 for the next k_i. The swap process is done in a routine that starts from state 53 and ends at state 57. Once i is equal to zero, the results are ready to be mapped back to the affine coordinates. Itoh-Tsuji inversion algorithm is used to achieve this, and it starts from state 12 and ends at state 52. At state 52, a done signal is asserted to indicate that the mapping process is complete, and affine coordinates are obtained.

3.5 Computation Schedule for Montgomery Ladder SPM

In this subsection, we introduce a new efficient scheduling for performing a single scalar point based on the merged-improved version as shown in Algorithm 2. A free-idle cycles schedule is achieved by performing the doubling and adding points in a less-dependent way. This is done by parallelizing the field operations of the point operations, such as squaring and multiplying same or different operands, simultaneously. Figure 6 illustrates our new schedule, where 8 registers are utilized to perform a single loop in Algorithm 2. A and B registers are operands that are connected to the field multiplier, while register C is the operand of the square field operation. Register T is a temporary register, which is used to hold intermediate values. This zero-idle schedule can perform a single SPM iteration in 14 clock cycles using the three pipelined stages Karatsuba-Ofman multiplier, where 3 clock cycles are required to obtain field multiplication results and 1 clock cycle for the square. Four subsequent field multiplications and squares are performed independently and simultaneously from clock number 1 to 4. Each square result is stored in register T.

At 5, results of the first multiplication $(X_1 \cdot Z_2)$ is obtained to multiply with the next multiplication result $(X_2 \cdot Z_1)$ at clock 6 and added at clock 7. The result of the third multiplication $(T^2 \cdot Z_2^2)$ is stored in Z_2 at clock 7. The fourth multiplication $(b \cdot Z_2^4)$ is obtained at clock 8 and added with register T which contains X_2^4. Result of $(X_1 \cdot X_2 \cdot T \cdot Z_2)$ is obtained at clock 10 which is added to the result of $(x \cdot Z_1)$ at clock 13. The total number of clock cycles for performing a single SPM consists of an initialization step, SPM process and LD to affine routine. In our proposed ECC core, there are 9 clock cycles for initialization step, $(\lfloor \log_2(k) + 1 \rfloor) \times 14\text{MUL}$ for SPM process, and $(9 \parallel 10 \parallel 13) \times 3\text{MUL} + (162 \parallel 232 \parallel 570)$ for LD to affine routine.

For example, if the scalar k is 10 and GF (2^{163}), then the total number of clock cycles for performing a single SPM is equal to: $9 + (\lfloor \log_2(10) + 1 \rfloor) \times 14\text{MUL} + 9 \times 3 + 162 = 254$ clock cycles. Note that Itoh-Tsuji algorithm requires $n - 1$ squaring operations and $\lfloor \log_2(n - 1) \rfloor) + HW(n - 1) - 1$ multiplications, where the HW is the Hamming weight of the integer $(n - 1)$. For example, in GF (2^{233}), there are 232 squaring operations and $\lfloor \log_2(232) + 1 \rfloor) + HW(232) - 1 = 7 + 4 - 1 = 10$ multiplications.

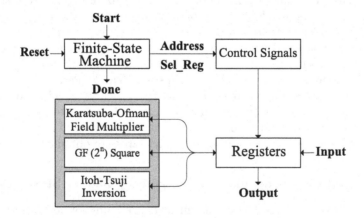

Fig. 4. The proposed high-speed area-efficient hardware design [9].

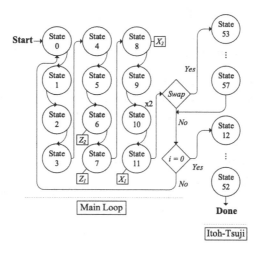

Fig. 5. State machine of the proposed SPM [9].

clk	X_1	X_2	Z_1	Z_2	A	B	C	T
1	1	x	0	1	$X_2 \otimes Z_1$	$\odot Z_2$		
2					$X_1 \otimes Z_2$	$\odot X_2$		SQ
3					$SQ \otimes T$	$\odot T$		SQ
4					$SQ \otimes b$	$\odot T$		
5					ML			SQ
6					$// \otimes ML$			
7			ML		$// \oplus //$	$\odot AD$		
8		SQ			$ML \oplus T$			
9	AD				$x \otimes Z_1$			
10					ML			
11					$//$			
12					$//$			
13					$// \oplus ML$			
14	AD							

AD = Add   SQ = Square   ML = Multplication
$\oplus$ Adder $\odot$ Square $\otimes$ Multiplier

Fig. 6. Computation schedule for the proposed SPM [9].

3.6   Karatsuba-Ofman Field Multiplier

Field multiplication consists of two steps: first, computing $C' = A \cdot B$, and the second, reducing C' by using the mod operation as $C = (C') \bmod f(x)$. This kind of a multiplier is called as the two-step classical field multiplier. The interleaved field multiplier is one of the classical field multipliers [7] that applies the two steps as shift and add operations in iterations. Very few resources are utilized to implement the interleaved multipliers, which makes it a very attractive one to the resource-constrained systems. However, this type of multipliers has a very long critical path due to the dependency between the iterations. The Karatsuba-Ofman field multiplication is a recursive algorithm that performs polynomial GF (2^n) multiplications in large finite fields efficiently [13]. Karatsuba-Ofman algorithm is defined as follows: Let A and B be two arbitrary elements in GF (2^n). Result of $C' = A \cdot B$ is a product of a $2n - 2$ degree polynomial. Both A and B can be represented as two split parts:

$$A = x^{n/2}(x^{n/2-1} \cdot a_{n-1} + \cdots + a_{n/2}) + (x^{n/2-1} \cdot a_{n/2-1} + \cdots + a_0)$$
$$= x^{n/2} \cdot A_H + A_L$$
$$B = x^{n/2}(x^{n/2-1} \cdot b_{n-1} + \cdots + b_{n/2}) + (x^{n/2-1} \cdot b_{n/2-1} + \cdots + b_0)$$
$$= x^{n/2} \cdot B_H + B_L$$

The polynomial of the product C' is:

$$C' = x^n \cdot A_H \cdot B_H + x^{n/2}(A_H \cdot B_L + A_L \cdot B_H) + A_L \cdot B_L$$

The sub-products are defined as the following auxiliary polynomials:

$$C'_0 = A_L \cdot B_L$$
$$C'_1 = (A_L + A_H)(B_L + B_H)$$
$$C'_2 = A_H \cdot B_H$$

Then the product C' can be obtained by:

$$C' = x^n \cdot C'_2 + x^{n/2}(C'_0 + C'_1 + C'_2) + C'_0$$

This field multiplication can be recursive if we split the auxiliary polynomials again with new generated auxiliaries. More recursions result in an increased delay for the Karatsuba-Ofman multiplier [24]. This recursion stops after the threshold q splits, where it ends with a classical field multiplier. Number of splits is optimum when splitting reaches a balance between the utilized area and delay. The work in [38] discusses this trade-off in detail. The optimal splits for the GF (2^{163}), GF (2^{233}) and GF (2^{571}) fields, are shown in Fig. 7. The optimum split is coming from the used FPGA technology in the LUTs [38].

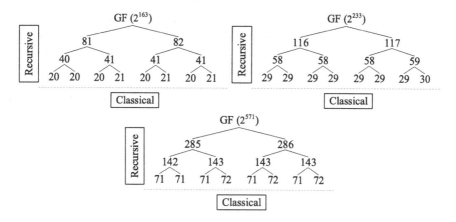

Fig. 7. Recursive splits over different finite fields [9].

FPGA has been fabricated using two technologies: 4-input LUT (i.e. old FPGA devices) and 6-input LUT (i.e. new FPGA devices) [23,30]. For GF (2^{163}), the first recursion results in three auxiliaries: 2 of 82-bit multipliers and 1 of 81-bit multiplier. The second recursion results in 2 of 41-bit and 1 40-bit multipliers for the 81-bit multiplier, and 3 of 41-bit multipliers for the 82-bit multiplier. Finally, the third recursion results in 2 of 21-bit and 1 20-bit multipliers for the 41-bit multiplier, and 3 of 20-bit multipliers for the 40-bit multiplier. The multiplier used after the recursive split is a single-step (no mod operation) classical multiplier which is used for all three fields. Figure 8 shows the logic gate implementation for the classical multiplier. The critical path of the Karatsuba-Ofman multiplier is long due to the recursive nature inherent in its hierarchy. Applying an architectural improvement such as inserting pipelining registers between recursive splits improves the long critical path and provides a higher working frequency.

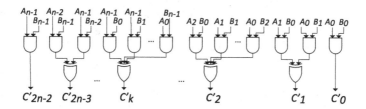

Fig. 8. Logic gate implementation for the classical multiplier [9].

Efficient pipelined Karatsuba-Ofman multiplier can be achieved when the critical path is the shortest. In FPGA, the shortest critical path implies that the delay-to-area ratio is minimum in time and utilized area. To achieve this, different pipelined stages have been inserted in the Karatsuba-Ofman multiplier.

As shown in Fig. 9, an efficient balance in delay-to-area ratio over GF (2^{163}) is achieved by inserting exactly three pipelined stages, where 2121 slices are used and the maximum delay between two registers is 3.4 ns. The first pipelined stage is inserted after the classic multiplier, while the second stage is located after combining all 40-bit, 41-bit, 81-bit, 82-bit recursive splits of the Karatsuba-Ofman multiplier. Note that the FPGA technology that has been used in Fig. 9 is a 6-input LUT.

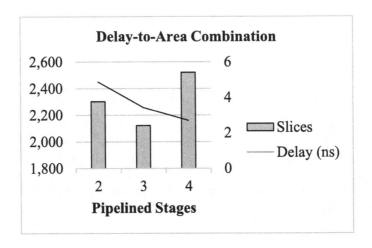

Fig. 9. Delay-to-area ratio using pipelined stages [9].

4   FPGA Implementation: Results and Comparisons

The pipelining architectural approach is applied to the proposed ECC core for higher speed with an efficient utilized area in terms of both the working frequencies and the slices. Elliptic curve doubling and adding point operations are performed using a merged-improved Montgomery ladder scalar point multiplication algorithm. The proposed ECC core does not require any precomputed values or memories for calculations, thus resulting in an efficient design with fewer slices and clock cycles. An effective FSM is developed to control the main ECC components, where a minimum number of states are used for performing the merged-improved Montgomery ladder SPM. To verify the performance of the proposed SPM, our high-speed ECC core is implemented over three finite fields, GF (2^{163}), GF (2^{233}) and GF (2^{571}), using several FPGA devices provided by Xilinx [25]: Virtex-5, Virtex-6, Virtex-7, Kintex-7 and Artix-7. The high-speed core has been synthesized, placed and routed using Xilinx ISE 14.4 design suite [36].

In Xilinx ISE tool, the place and route process reads a netlist of the synthesised design, extracts the components and logic elements, places them on the target FPGA device, and finally interconnects these components and logic elements using CLB routers. For better place and routing process, strategies in placing and interconnecting can be applied such as register balancing and combinational logic optimization. A time constraint is applied for all results to achieve better area-speed ratio with zero timing error. Table 1 presents the place and route results for the proposed high-speed ECC core. Table 2 includes our design compared with other previous ECC hardware implementations. The efficiency is defined as follows:

$$Efficiency = \frac{Number of bits}{Time \cdot Slices} \tag{3}$$

The proposed high-speed core provides higher speed in both Virtex-7 and Kintex-7 FPGA devices, since they are fabricated and optimized at 28 nm technology [25]. The Artix-7 device consumes fewer resources making it well suited for the battery-powered cell phones, automotive, commercial digital cameras and IP cores of SoCs.

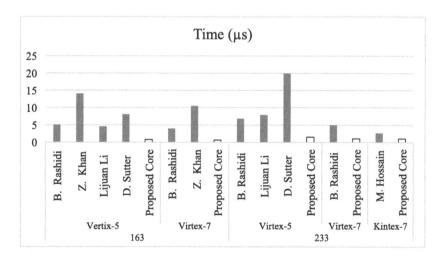

Fig. 10. Time comparison between the proposed high-speed core and the others [9].

The graphical representation in Fig. 10 represents the time comparison between our proposed high-speed core and other designs. As seen from Fig. 10, our design requires the lowest execution time for performing a single successful SPM. As seen from Table 2, our proposed high-speed core outperforms the other ECC hardware implementations in terms of efficiency. The design in [26] provides higher frequencies, but consumes nearly twice the resources of the proposed core over GF (2^{163}), while using the same FPGA device.

The area-efficient hardware implementation in [14] consumes less area than the proposed core, but requires 95% more clock cycles. This large number of

Table 1. FPGA results of the proposed high-speed ECC core: after place and route [9].

GF (2^n)	Device	LUTs	F.Fs	Slices	Clock cycles	Freq (MHz)	Time (μs)	Efficiency
163	Virtex-5	8,900	3,044	2,814	226	291	0.78	74584.42
233		15,672	4,333	4,585	327	217	1.51	33723.19
571		72,259	10,259	21,720	674	198	3.40	7722.93
163	Virtex-7	8,409	3,023	2,780	226	360	0.63	93397.85
233		16,003	4,323	4,762	327	310	1.05	46385.32
571		71,180	10,384	18,178	674	290	2.32	13515.38
163	Artix-7	8,417	3,016	2,693	226	191	1.18	51153.6
233		15,236	4,489	3,977	327	209	1.56	37445.44
163	Kintex-7	8,437	3,023	3,030	226	311	0.73	74028.16
233		15,221	4,483	4,915	327	309	1.06	44796.41
233	Virtex-6	14,402	4,203	4,143	327	239	1.451	38759.1

clock cycles is the result of the increased writing/reading in the distributed RAM-based memory and register shift operations. In [16], a pipelined architecture is applied to SPM, which achieves high performance in terms of the area

Table 2. Comparison between our high-speed ECC core and other works over GF (2^n) [9].

	GF (2^n)	Device	LUTs F.Fs	Slices	Clock cycles	Freq (MHz)	Time (μs)	Efficiency
[26]	163	Vertix-5	- -	5,768	-	343	5.08	5562.87
	233	Virtex-7	- -	10,601	-	359	6.84	3213.32
[14]	163	Virtex-5	3,958 1,522	1,089	4168	296	14.06	10645.71
		Virtex-7	4,721 1,886	1,476	4168	397	10.51	64.47
[16]	163	Virtex-5	9,470 4,526	3,041	1,363	294	4.6	11652.35
	233		15,296 6,559	4,762	1,926	244	7.9	6193.55
[32]	163	Virtex-5	22,039 -	6,059	1,591	200	8.1	3321.26
	233		28,683 -	8,134	2,889	145	19.9	1439.46
	571		32,432 -	11,640	44,047	126	348	140.97
[12]	233	Kintex-7	9,151 9,407	3,016	679776	255.66	2.66	29043.1
Ours	163	Virtex-5	8,900 3,044	2,814	226	291	0.78	74584.42
	233		15,672 4,333	4,585	327	217	1.51	33723.19
	571		72,259 10,259	21,720	674	198	3.40	7722.93
	163	Virtex-7	8,409 3,023	2,780	226	360	0.63	93397.85
	233		16,003 4,323	4,762	327	310	1.05	46385.32
	571		71,180 10,384	18,178	674	290	2.32	13515.38
	163	Kintex-7	8,437 3,023	3,030	226	311	0.73	74028.16
	233		15,221 4,483	4,915	327	309	1.06	44796.41

and working frequencies. However, it requires 84% more clock cycles than that required in our proposed clock cycles, using the same device and field. Our high-speed core achieves greater efficiency than the design presented in [32]. Our design has 88% fewer clock cycles, 33% higher frequency, and 44% fewer slices than that in [32]. Using a Kintex-7 FPGA device, the design in [12] performs on 39% fewer slices than that in the proposed core over GF (2^{233}), but requires large number of clock cycles. In [12], an iterative-based architecture is adopted by all main SPM operations, where the binary (left-to-right) algorithm is used for scalar multiplication, an interleaved field multiplier is implemented for the multiplication operations, and a modified Extended-Euclidian is applied for the inversion operation.

To summarize the comparisons: shift registers, segmented multipliers, or memory-based implementations result in an increased latency (clock cycle) as in [14] and [32]. Iterative architecture is not an efficient way to achieve higher speeds as mentioned in [12]. Pipelining architecture is a more practical way of achieving better performance and maintaining the balance between speed and area, as stated in [26] and [16]. The balance in the speed-area ratio can be achieved when the optimal number of pipelined stages are inserted. Our high-performance ECC core requires fewer slices, and offers decreased latencies with higher working frequencies. This high-speed area-efficient ECC core makes it very suitable for use in different kinds of real-time embedded systems such as cellphone banking services, health-care monitoring using smart watches, and accessing office networks and storage devices while abroad.

4.1   Power Consumption for the Proposed ECC Core

Regarding power consumption, most of the works in Table 2 do not provide a power analysis for their reconfigurable hardware implementations. However, we provide in Table 3 results for the power consumption of our ECC core design. The power analysis was performed using the balanced settings of the Xilinx Power Estimator (XPE) tool [37]. Measuring the power consumption was achieved by running the ECC cores at a maximum running frequency over each finite field based on Table 1. In XPE, the total on-chip power consists of power dissipation of the FPGA device resources such as BRAMs, LUTs, F.Fs and the system clock. In our proposed ECC cores, BRAMs and DSPs are not used, so the total on-chip power relies just on the slice components and the clock. From Table 3, it is seen that the power dissipation increases as the GF (2^n) field is increased. High power consumption in Virtex-5 FPGA devices is related to the older 65 nm design fabrication technology used in these FPGAs. In the newest 28 nm fabrication technology used in the Kintex-7, Artix-7 and Virtex-7, the power consumption is optimized to provide the best levels of power usage. The power consumptions for our proposed ECC cores indicate that they can be used in embedded systems of small devices that operate at low-power levels.

4.2   Software Implementation for the Proposed ECC Core

To ensure the effectiveness of the proposed ECC cores, a software implementation of Algorithm 2 for computing the $k.$P method was developed using the add-on NTL library [29]. It provides a powerful support to the arithmetic modulus over any type of GF. NTL library was built over the C++ programming language, which offers several data structures and algorithms for calculating operations over prime integers and galois fields (GFs) such as multiplication, squaring, inversion, and division [29].

The software implementation is performed using an Intel-7 Quad-Core processor running on 2.8 GHz frequency equipped with a 8 GB RAM. Implementing the merged Montgomery laddar scalar multiplication requires constructing the irreducible polynomials for the three GF (2^{163}), GF (2^{233}) and GF (2^{571}). Once the irreducible polynomials are ready, a point is defined in terms of x and y affine coordinates. This point is the input to the software implementation along with the scalar k. The main loop is defined to scan the bitstream of the scalar k. As a post step, the output points Z_1, Z_2, X_1 and X_1 are used to be mapped to the affine coordinate system, where an inversion field operation is involved. Table 4 shows the elapsed time for computing the SPM over different finite fields. The results are calculated under several trails with different k and P. Comparing Tables 1 and 4, it is clear that the hardware implementation surpasses the software one. For instance, finding $k.$P using Virtex-5 is 7.3 times faster than the software implementation over GF (2^{163}).

Table 3. Power consumptions.

GF (2^n)	Device	Power (Watt)
163	Virtex-5	4.563
233		4.67
571		6.56
163	Kintex-7	0.652
233		0.609
571		1.327
163	Artix-7	0.801
233		1.583
163	Virtex-7	0.87
233		1.014
571		1.434

Table 4. Time elapsed over different GFs.

Trials	GF (2^n)		
	163	233	571
1	0.0106977 s	0.002937 s	0.0120343 s
5	0.084728 s	0.0328966 s	0.0710975 s
10	0.1166 s	0.0621682 s	0.684247 s
20	0.203852 s	0.1271 s	1.67971 s
50	0.378632 s	0.337684 s	1.94468 s

5   Conclusions and Future Work

In this chapter, a efficient pipelined ECC core has been presented over the binary (2^n) NIST recommended curves. Xilinx FPGA devices have been used to evaluate the performance of the proposed ECC core. An efficient Montgomery ladder scalar point method has been developed for performing scalar multiplications (k.P). Karatsuba-Ofman and Itoh-Tsuji algorithms have been used for performing inversion and multiplication finite field operations. A single scalar multiplication over GF (2^{163}) can be done in 0.63 μs at 360 Mhz working frequency in Virtex-7 FPGA devices using 2780 slices, which is the fastest implementation result compared with others. The proposed ECC core is suitable for platforms and applications that require efficiency in terms of area, speed and power consumption such as key exchange agreements in ECDH and signing certificates in ECDS cryptosystems. On other hand, our proposed ECC core can be integrated and embedded with applications that have a security layer in their implementations, such as image steganographic engines. The design of a separable secure image steganographic cryptosystem would be our next step.

References

1. Amirtharajan, R.: Dual cellular automata on FPGA: an image encryptors chip. Res. J. Inf. Technol. **6**(3), 223–236 (2014)
2. Ansari, B., Hasan, M.A.: High-performance architecture of elliptic curve scalar multiplication. IEEE Trans. Comput. **57**(11), 1443–1453 (2008)
3. Dalal, M., Juneja, M.: A robust and imperceptible steganography technique for SD and HD videos. Multimed. Tools Appl. **78**, 5769–5789 (2018)
4. Diffie, W., Hellman, M.: New directions in cryptography. IEEE Trans. Inf. Theory **22**(6), 644–654 (1976)
5. ElGamal, T.: A public key cryptosystem and a signature scheme based on discrete logarithms. IEEE Trans. Inf. Theory **31**(4), 469–472 (1985)
6. Gallagher, P.: Digital signature standard (DSS). Federal Information Processing Standards Publications, volume FIPS, pp. 186–183 (2013)
7. Großschädl, J.: A bit-serial unified multiplier architecture for finite fields GF(p) and GF(2^m). In: Koç, Ç.K., Naccache, D., Paar, C. (eds.) CHES 2001. LNCS, vol. 2162, pp. 202–219. Springer, Heidelberg (2001). https://doi.org/10.1007/3-540-44709-1_18

8. Hankerson, D., Menezes, A.J., Vanstone, S.: Guide to Elliptic Curve Cryptography. Springer, Berlin (2006). https://doi.org/10.1007/b97644

9. Harb, S., Ahmad, M.O., Swamy, M.N.S.: High-performance pipelined FPGA implementation of the elliptic curve cryptography over GF (2n). In: Proceedings of the 16th International Joint Conference on e-Business and Telecommunications, SECRYPT, vol. 2, pp. 15–24. INSTICC, SciTePress (2019). https://doi.org/10.5220/0007772800150024

10. Harb, S., Jarrah, M.: Accelerating square root computations over large GF (2m). In: SECRYPT, pp. 229–236 (2017)

11. Harb, S., Jarrah, M.: FPGA implementation of the ECC over GF (2 m) for small embedded applications. ACM Trans. Embed. Comput. Syst. (TECS) 18(2), 17 (2019)

12. Hossain, M.S., Saeedi, E., Kong, Y.: High-speed, area-efficient, FPGA-based elliptic curve cryptographic processor over NIST binary fields. In: 2015 IEEE International Conference on Data Science and Data Intensive Systems (DSDIS), pp. 175–181. IEEE (2015)

13. Karatsuba, A.A., Ofman, Y.P.: Multiplication of many-digital numbers by automatic computers. In: Doklady Akademii Nauk, vol. 145, pp. 293–294. Russian Academy of Sciences (1962)

14. Khan, Z.U., Benaissa, M.: Throughput/area-efficient ECC processor using montgomery point multiplication on FPGA. IEEE Trans. Circuits Syst. II: Express Briefs 62(11), 1078–1082 (2015)

15. Kocher, P., Jaffe, J., Jun, B.: Differential power analysis. In: Wiener, M. (ed.) CRYPTO 1999. LNCS, vol. 1666, pp. 388–397. Springer, Heidelberg (1999). https://doi.org/10.1007/3-540-48405-1_25

16. Li, L., Li, S.: High-performance pipelined architecture of elliptic curve scalar multiplication over gf (2^m). IEEE Trans. Very Large Scale Integr. (VLSI) Syst. 24(4), 1223–1232 (2016)

17. López, J., Dahab, R.: Improved algorithms for elliptic curve arithmetic in $GF(2^n)$. In: Tavares, S., Meijer, H. (eds.) SAC 1998. LNCS, vol. 1556, pp. 201–212. Springer, Heidelberg (1999). https://doi.org/10.1007/3-540-48892-8_16

18. Mahdizadeh, H., Masoumi, M.: Novel architecture for efficient FPGA implementation of elliptic curve cryptographic processor over gf(2^{163}). IEEE Trans. Very Large Scale Integr. (VLSI) Syst. 21(12), 2330–2333 (2013)

19. McGrew, D., Igoe, K., Salter, M.: Fundamental elliptic curve cryptography algorithms. Tech. rep. 2018, Internet Engineering Task Force (IETF) (2011). http://www.rfc-editor.org/rfc/rfc6090.txt

20. Miller, V.S.: Use of elliptic curves in cryptography. In: Williams, H.C. (ed.) CRYPTO 1985. LNCS, vol. 218, pp. 417–426. Springer, Heidelberg (1986). https://doi.org/10.1007/3-540-39799-X_31

21. Montgomery, P.L.: Speeding the pollard and elliptic curve methods of factorization. Math. Comput. 48(177), 243–264 (1987)

22. Moon, S.: A binary redundant scalar point multiplication in secure elliptic curve cryptosystems. IJ Netw. Secur. 3(2), 132–137 (2006)

23. Percey, A.: Advantages of the Virtex-5 FPGA 6-input LUT architecture (2007)

24. Peter, S., LangendOorfer, P.: An efficient polynomial multiplier in GF (2m) and its application to ECC designs. In: Design, Automation and Test in Europe Conference and Exhibition, 2007, DATE 2007, pp. 1–6. IEEE (2007)

25. Przybus, B.: Xilinx redefines power, performance, and design productivity with three new 28 nm FPGA families: Virtex-7, Kintex-7, and Artix-7 devices. Xilinx White Paper (2010)

26. Rashidi, B., Sayedi, S.M., Farashahi, R.R.: High-speed hardware architecture of scalar multiplication for binary elliptic curve cryptosystems. Microelectron. J. **52**, 49–65 (2016)

27. Rivest, R.L., Shamir, A., Adleman, L.: A method for obtaining digital signatures and public-key cryptosystems. Commun. ACM **21**(2), 120–126 (1978)

28. Roy, S.S., Rebeiro, C., Mukhopadhyay, D.: Theoretical modeling of elliptic curve scalar multiplier on LUT-based fpgas for area and speed. IEEE Trans. Very Large Scale Integr. (VLSI) Syst. **21**(5), 901–909 (2013)

29. Shoup, V.: NTL: a library for doing number theory (2019). https://www.shoup.net/ntl/

30. Product Specification: Virtex-5 family overview (2006)

31. International Organization for Standardization (ISO): Cryptographic techniques based on elliptic curves (2017, August 2000). ISO/IEC 15946–5:2017. https://www.iso.org/standard/69726.html

32. Sutter, G.D., Deschamps, J.P., Imaña, J.L.: Efficient elliptic curve point multiplication using digit-serial binary field operations. IEEE Trans. Ind. Electron. **60**(1), 217–225 (2013)

33. Wenger, E., Hutter, M.: Exploring the design space of prime field vs. binary field ECC-hardware implementations. In: Laud, P. (ed.) NordSec 2011. LNCS, vol. 7161, pp. 256–271. Springer, Heidelberg (2012). https://doi.org/10.1007/978-3-642-29615-4_18

34. Xilinx, I.: Xilinx - adaptive and intelligent (2018). https://www.xilinx.com/

35. Xilinx, I.: Xilinx FPGA devices, Virtex, Kintex, Artix (2018). https://www.xilinx.com/products/silicon-devices.html

36. Xilinx, I.: ISE in-depth tutorial, complete guide (ug695). Tech. rep. 14.1, Xilinx, Inc. (24 April 2012)

37. Xilinx, I.: Xilinx power estimator user guide. Tech. rep. v2019.2, Xilinx, Inc. (30 October 2019). https://www.xilinx.com/support/documentation/sw_manuals/xilinx2019_2/ug440-xilinx-power-estimator.pdf

38. Zhou, G., Michalik, H., Hinsenkamp, L.: Complexity analysis and efficient implementations of bit parallel finite field multipliers based on Karatsuba-Ofman algorithm on FPGAs. IEEE Trans. Very Large Scale Integr. (VLSI) Syst. **18**(7), 1057–1066 (2010)

Evaluation of Floating-Point Arithmetic Protocols Based on Shamir Secret Sharing

Octavian Catrina[(✉)] [iD]

University Politehnica of Bucharest, Bucharest, Romania
octavian.catrina@elcom.pub.ro

Abstract. The development of privacy preserving collaborative applications can be simplified by starting with a collection of protocols that support secure computation with all basic data types and secure and efficient protocol composition. For some tasks, secure computation with real numbers can be efficiently achieved using fixed-point arithmetic. However, many other tasks need the dynamic range and accuracy of floating-point numbers. In this paper, we examine a recently proposed family of floating-point arithmetic protocols, to provide a more comprehensive analysis and evaluation of their construction, complexity, and performance, as well as refined variants and generalizations. The analysis is extended to more general issues: the relations between complexity metrics, protocol performance, and execution environment, as well as their importance for protocol evaluation and optimization.

Keywords: Secure multiparty computation · Secure floating-point arithmetic · Secret sharing · Performance evaluation

1 Introduction

Privacy-preserving collaborative applications enable mutually distrustful parties to carry out joint computations without revealing their private inputs (e.g., data privacy may be required by business or legal reasons). Secure computation is a branch of cryptography that supports these applications by providing cryptographic protocols for computing with private data. Essentially, the parties run a distributed computation with data privacy protected by cryptographic techniques (e.g., linear secret sharing or homomorphic encryption).

Practical applications include statistical analysis, data mining, and optimizations, which require secure computation with real numbers. Fixed-point arithmetic is sufficient for some tasks and the protocols are relatively simple and efficient [3,9,10]. However, more generally, the applications need the dynamic range and accuracy of floating-point numbers [2,4,5,17]. One of the main challenges is to meet the applications' performance requirements, despite the inherent computation and communication overhead of the cryptographic protocols. This motivates ongoing research that explores different secure computation techniques, building blocks, data representations, and tradeoffs [3,6,7,15].

© Springer Nature Switzerland AG 2020
M. S. Obaidat (Ed.): ICETE 2019, CCIS 1247, pp. 108–131, 2020.
https://doi.org/10.1007/978-3-030-52686-3_5

We examine in this paper a recently proposed family of floating-point arithmetic protocols [7], to provide a more comprehensive analysis and evaluation of their construction, complexity, and performance, as well as refined variants and generalizations. These protocols are part of a secure computation framework that supports all basic data types and preserves data privacy using Shamir secret sharing and related cryptographic techniques. The fixed-point and floating-point arithmetic protocols provide the basic functionality and accuracy expected by applications, for practical range and precision settings. For floating-point protocols, priority was given to improving performance and enabling tradeoffs based on application requirements, rather than replicating the format and all the features specified in the IEEE Standard for Floating-Point Arithmetic (IEEE 754).

We evaluate the performance of the protocols for standard single and double precision floating-point numbers and for communication with different data rates and delays (fast LAN and simulated Internet). The results of their complexity analysis and experimental evaluation are combined in a more general analysis of the relations between complexity metrics, protocol performance, and execution environment, as well as their relevance to protocol evaluation and optimization.

Section 2 provides background information about the protocols discussed in the paper: secure computation model, data encoding, building blocks, and complexity and performance issues. Sections 3, 4, 5 and 6 present the family of protocols for secure floating-point arithmetic and their complexity and performance analysis (addition and subtraction, multiplication, division and square root, and comparison). The main results are summarized in Sect. 7.

2 Background on Secure Arithmetic

2.1 Secure Computation Based on Shamir Secret Sharing

The protocols are part of the secure computation framework described in [6–8], based on standard primitives for secure computation using secret sharing [12] and related techniques [11,13,14,19]. We provide a brief overview of this framework.

We assume $n > 2$ parties, $\{P_i\}_{i=1}^n$, that communicate on secure channels and want to run a joint computation where party P_i has private input x_i and expects output y_i. The parties use a linear secret-sharing scheme to create a distributed state of the computation, $\{[\![x_i]\!]\}_{i=1}^n$, where each party has a random share of each secret variable. Then, they run secure computation protocols that compute the shared outputs $\{[\![y_i]\!]\}_{i=1}^n$, preserving data privacy throughout the computation. Finally, they deliver to every party P_i its output y_i using the secret reconstruction protocol of the secret sharing scheme.

The core primitives are based on Shamir secret sharing over a finite field $\mathbb{F}$ and provide secure arithmetic in $\mathbb{F}$ with perfect privacy against a passive threshold adversary able to corrupt t out of n parties. In this model, the parties follow strictly the protocol and any $t + 1$ parties can reconstruct a secret, while t or less parties cannot distinguish it from random values in $\mathbb{F}$. We assume $|\mathbb{F}| > n$, to enable Shamir sharing, and $n > 2t$, for multiplication of secret-shared values. The parties locally compute addition/subtraction of shared field elements by adding/subtracting their own shares, but tasks that involve multiplication require interaction and are computed by dedicated protocols.

The protocols overcome the limitations of secure arithmetic based on Shamir secret sharing by combining it with additive or multiplicative hiding: for a shared variable $[\![x]\!]$ the parties jointly generate a shared random value $[\![r]\!]$, compute $[\![y]\!] = [\![x]\!] + [\![r]\!]$ or $[\![y]\!] = [\![x]\!] \cdot [\![r]\!], x \neq 0$, and reveal y (similar to one-time pad encryption of x with key r). For secret $x \in \mathbb{Z}_q$ and random uniform $r \in \mathbb{Z}_q$ the statistical distance is $\Delta(x + r \bmod q, r) = 0$ and $\Delta(xr \bmod q, r) = 0$, so the protocols offer perfect privacy. For $x \in [0, 2^k - 1]$, random uniform $r \in [0, 2^{k+\kappa} - 1]$, and $q > 2^{k+\kappa+1}$ we obtain $\Delta(x + r \bmod q, r) < 2^{-\kappa}$, hence statistical privacy with security parameter κ [8].

2.2 Data Encoding

Secure computation with Boolean, integer, fixed-point, and floating-point data types is achieved by encoding the values in a finite field $\mathbb{F}$ and using secure arithmetic in $\mathbb{F}$. To distinguish different data representations, we denote $\hat{x}$ a floating-point number, $\tilde{x}$ a fixed-point number, $\bar{x}$ an integer, x a field element, and $[\![x]\!]$ a sharing of x. The data types are defined as follows:

- Binary values are naturally encoded as 0_F and 1_F. This encoding allows efficient secure evaluation of Boolean functions using secure arithmetic in $\mathbb{F}$ [8]. We denote $[\![a]\!] \wedge [\![b]\!] = [\![a]\!][\![b]\!] = [\![a \wedge b]\!]$ (AND), $[\![a]\!] \vee [\![b]\!] = [\![a]\!] + [\![b]\!] - [\![a]\!][\![b]\!] = [\![a \vee b]\!]$ (OR) and $[\![a]\!] \oplus [\![b]\!] = [\![a]\!] + [\![b]\!] - 2[\![a]\!][\![b]\!] = [\![a \oplus b]\!]$ (XOR).
- Integers $\mathbb{Z}_{\langle k \rangle} = \{\bar{x} \in \mathbb{Z} \mid \bar{x} \in [-2^{k-1}, 2^{k-1} - 1]\}$, are encoded in $\mathbb{Z}_q$ by fld : $\mathbb{Z}_{\langle k \rangle} \mapsto \mathbb{Z}_q$, $\mathsf{fld}(\bar{x}) = \bar{x} \bmod q$, for $q > 2^{k+\kappa}$, where κ is the security parameter (negative integers $\bar{x} \in [-2^{k-1}, -1]$ are mapped to $x \in [q - 2^{k-1}, q - 1]$). This enables efficient secure integer arithmetic using secure arithmetic in $\mathbb{Z}_q$: for any $\bar{x}_1, \bar{x}_2 \in \mathbb{Z}_{\langle k \rangle}$ and $\odot \in \{+, -, \cdot\}$, $\bar{x}_1 \odot \bar{x}_2 = \mathsf{fld}^{-1}(\mathsf{fld}(\bar{x}_1) \odot \mathsf{fld}(\bar{x}_2))$; also, if $\bar{x}_2 \mid \bar{x}_1$ then $\bar{x}_1/\bar{x}_2 = \mathsf{fld}^{-1}(\mathsf{fld}(\bar{x}_1) \cdot \mathsf{fld}(\bar{x}_2)^{-1})$.
- Fixed-point numbers, $\mathbb{Q}_{\langle k, f \rangle}^{FX} = \{\tilde{x} \in \mathbb{Q} \mid \tilde{x} = \bar{x}2^{-f}, \bar{x} \in \mathbb{Z}_{\langle k \rangle}, f < k\}$ are first mapped to $\mathbb{Z}_{\langle k \rangle}$ by int : $\mathbb{Q}_{\langle k, f \rangle}^{FX} \mapsto \mathbb{Z}_{\langle k \rangle}$, $\mathsf{int}_f(\tilde{x}) = \tilde{x}2^f$ and then encoded in $\mathbb{Z}_q$. Secure fixed-point multiplication and division require $q > 2^{2k+\kappa}$.
- Floating-point numbers, $\hat{x} \in \mathbb{Q}_{\langle l, g \rangle}^{FL}$, are tuples $\langle \bar{v}, \bar{p}, s, z \rangle$, where $\bar{v} \in [2^{\ell-1}, 2^\ell - 1] \cup \{0\}$ is the unsigned, normalized significand, $\bar{p} \in \mathbb{Z}_{\langle g \rangle}$ is the signed exponent, $s = (\bar{v} < 0)$? $1 : 0$, and $z = (\bar{v} = 0)$? $1 : 0$, encoded in $\mathbb{Z}_q$. The number's value is $\hat{x} = (1 - 2s) \cdot \bar{v} \cdot 2^{\bar{p}}$. If $\hat{x} = 0$ then $\bar{v} = 0$, $z = 1$, and $\bar{p} = -2^{g-1}$ (this simplifies addition, with minimal negative effects on other operations). Secure floating-point multiplication and division require $q > 2^{2\ell+\kappa}$.

The parameters k, f, ℓ and g are not secret. The protocols work for any setting of these parameters that satisfies the type definitions. The applications usually need $k \in [32, 128]$, $k = 2f$, $\ell \in [24, 64]$ and $g \in [8, 15]$, depending on range and accuracy requirements.

2.3   Complexity and Performance

The parties run a synchronized distributed computation that alternates local computation and interactions. They run the same algorithm on their local variables and communicate when they reach an interactive operation: share a secret variable, multiply two shared variables, or reconstruct a shared variable. Figure 1 shows a simple example: a task with two interactive operations executed sequentially or in parallel. The parties run locally until they reach the first interactive operation. Then, for sequential execution, they repeat the following steps:

- P: Prepare the data to be sent during this operation.
- S: Send data to the other parties (same amount).
- R: Receive data from all the other parties.
- F: Process the received data to finish the operation.

The exchanged data depends only on the sender's local state, so sending and receiving can be done in parallel. The computation is synchronized at every interactive operation: each party must receive the expected data from all the others before continuing the execution of the protocol.

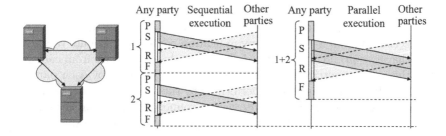

Fig. 1. Interaction rounds during secure computation.

A protocol runs a batch of interactive primitives in "parallel" by executing each step for the entire batch, so the computation is achieved with a single interaction. The messages exchanged by an interactive primitive contain a very small payload: a single field element (10–20 octets for a secret integer encoded in $\mathbb{Z}_q$ or just one octet for a secret bit encoded in $\mathbb{F}_{2^8}$). By parallel execution, these tiny payloads are aggregated in a single message, to reduce packet encapsulation overhead and use more efficient TCP data transfer mechanisms. For large batches, local computation can be allocated to multiple threads, to take advantage of multiple processors and/or cores. Thus, parallel algorithms are essential for fast and efficient secure computation.

The protocols are designed assuming the following general optimizations. Interactive operations that do not depend on each other are executed in parallel, in a single interaction round. Some shared random values are locally generated using the techniques presented in [11,13], while others require inter-action. For any task, all shared random values needed by its building blocks can be precomputed in parallel, with a single interaction.

Table 1. Summary of the main building blocks and their complexity.

Protocol	Task	Rounds	Inter. op.	Precomp.
Div2m($[\![a]\!], k, m$)	$\lfloor \bar{a}/2^m \rfloor; \bar{a} \in \mathbb{Z}_{\langle k \rangle}, m \in [1, k)$	3	$m + 2$	$3m$
Div2mP($[\![a]\!], k, m$)	$\lfloor \bar{a}/2^m \rceil; \bar{a} \in \mathbb{Z}_{\langle k \rangle}, m \in [1, k)$	1	1	m
Div2($[\![a]\!], k$)	$\lfloor \bar{a}/2 \rfloor; \bar{a} \in \mathbb{Z}_{\langle k \rangle}$	1	1	1
PreDiv2m($[\![a]\!], k, m$)	$\{\lfloor \bar{a}/2^i \rfloor\}_{i=1}^m; \bar{a} \in \mathbb{Z}_{\langle k \rangle}, m \in [1, k)$	3	$2m + 1$	$4m$
PreDiv2mP($[\![a]\!], k, m$)	$\{\lfloor \bar{a}/2^i \rceil\}_{i=1}^m; \bar{a} \in \mathbb{Z}_{\langle k \rangle}, m \in [1, k)$	1	1	m
Int2Mask($[\![x]\!], k$)	$\{(\bar{x} = i)? \ 1 : 0\}_{i=0}^{k-1}, \bar{x} \in [0, k)$	1	$k - 1$	$2k - 3$
Pow2Inv($[\![x]\!], m$)	$(y, y^{-1}); \bar{y} = 2^{\bar{x}}, \bar{x} \in [0, 2^m)$	4	$3m$	$6m - 2$
LTZ($[\![a]\!], k$)	$(\bar{a} < 0)? \ 1 : 0; \bar{a} \in \mathbb{Z}_{\langle k \rangle}$	3	$k + 1$	$3k$
EQZ($[\![a]\!], k$)	$(\bar{a} = 0)? \ 1 : 0; \bar{a} \in \mathbb{Z}_{\langle k \rangle}$	3	$\log k + 2$	$k + 3 \log k$
BitDec($[\![a]\!], k, m$)	$\{a_i\}_{i=0}^{m-1}; \bar{a} \in \mathbb{Z}_{\langle k \rangle}, m \in [1, k]$	3	$2m + 1$	$4m - 1$
SufOr($\{[\![a_i]\!]\}_{i=1}^k$)	$\{\bigvee_{j=i}^k a_j\}_{i=1}^k; a_j \in \{0, 1\}$	2	$2k - 1$	$3k$
SufMulInv($\{[\![a_i]\!]\}_{i=1}^k$)	$\{y_i, y_i^{-1}\}_{i=1}^k; y_i = \prod_{j=i}^k a_j \in \mathbb{Z}_q$	1	k	$2k - 1$

The protocols are evaluated using two abstract complexity metrics that focus on interaction. The first metric, communication complexity, counts the invoca-tions of the three primitives discussed above, which send a share from each party to the others. This metric measures the amount of data sent by each party and also reflects the local computation performed by the primitives. The second met-ric, round complexity, counts the interaction rounds, emphasizing the effects of communication delays that are independent of the amount of data.

To facilitate the complexity analysis, the pseudocode that describes the pro-tocols includes annotations that specify the online round and communication complexity for each step that involves interaction between parties.

2.4　Building Blocks

The floating-point arithmetic protocols discussed in this paper are constructed using a subset of the building blocks introduced in [8,10] and extended in [6,7]. These building blocks rely on the secure computation model described in the previous sections for their own security and for secure composition. Table 1 lists their online and precomputation complexity.

Essentially, secure fixed-point and floating-point arithmetic is based on a small set of related protocols that efficiently compute $\bar{b} = \bar{a} \cdot 2^m$ and $\bar{c} \approx \bar{a}/2^m$, for secret $\bar{a}, \bar{b}, \bar{c} \in \mathbb{Z}_{\langle k \rangle}$ and a public or secret integer $m \in [0, k - 1]$. We summarize in the following their functionality and several specific optimizations.

If m is public, $\bar{a} \cdot 2^m$ is a local operation and $\bar{a}/2^m$ is computed by Div2m or Div2mP [8,10]. Div2m rounds to $-\infty$, while Div2mP rounds probabilistically to the nearest integer. Their outputs are denoted $\lfloor \bar{a}/2^m \rfloor$ and $\lfloor \bar{a}/2^m \rceil$, respectively.

For both protocols, the rounding error is $|\delta| < 1$ and $\delta = 0$ if 2^m divides $\bar{a}$. Div2mP is much more efficient and its output is likely more accurate: it returns $\bar{c} = \lfloor \bar{a}/2^m \rfloor + u$, where $u = 1$ with probability $p = \frac{\bar{a} \bmod 2^m}{2^m}$ (e.g., if $\bar{a} = 46$ and $m = 3$ then $\bar{a}/2^m = 5.75$; the output is $\bar{c} = 6$ with probability $p = 0.75$ or $\bar{c} = 5$ with probability $1 - p = 0.25$). However, some applications need Div2m. For example, LTZ uses Div2m to compute $s = (\bar{a} < 0)? \ 1 : 0 = -\lfloor \bar{a}/2^{k-1} \rfloor$. Div2 computes $\lfloor \bar{a}/2 \rfloor$ more efficiently than Div2m.

If m is secret, we can compute $\bar{a} \cdot 2^m$ and $\bar{a}/2^m$ using the protocols PowS2m and DivS2m, respectively, based on the following constructions. Both protocols compute the secret bits $\{x_i\}_{i=0}^{k-1}$, $x_i = (m = i)? \ 1 : 0$. Then, PowS2m computes $\bar{a} \cdot 2^m = \bar{a} \cdot \sum_{i=0}^{k-1} x_i 2^i$ (without interaction), while DivS2m computes the secret integers $\bar{d}_i = \{\lfloor \bar{a}/2^i \rfloor\}_{i=0}^{k-1}$ or $\bar{d}_i = \{\lceil \bar{a}/2^i \rceil\}_{i=0}^{k-1}$ and then $\bar{a}/2^m = \sum_{i=0}^{k-1} x_i \bar{d}_i$ (dot product computed with a single interaction).

Additional building blocks improve the efficiency of these constructions [6,7]:

- Given $m \in [0, k-1]$, Int2Mask computes x_i by Lagrange polynomial interpolation. Remarkably, Int2Mask needs a single online interaction. However, for large k, polynomial evaluation involves a relatively expensive local computation, although the coefficients are public and can be precomputed offline.
- PreDiv2mP generalizes Div2mP to compute $\{\lfloor \bar{a}/2^i \rfloor\}_{i=1}^{m}$ with the same complexity. Similarly, PreDiv2m generalizes Div2m to compute $\{\lfloor \bar{a}/2^i \rfloor\}_{i=1}^{m}$ with the same round complexity and just twice the online communication complexity. More general variants, SelDiv2m and SelDiv2mP, compute a selection of $\{\bar{a}/2^i\}_{i=1}^{m}$ with lower complexity.

Alternatively, we can compute $\bar{a} \cdot 2^m$ and $\bar{a}/2^m$ using the binary encoding of m. Given a secret $\bar{a} \in \mathbb{Z}_{\langle k \rangle}$, BitDec computes the secret bits $\{a_i\}_{i=0}^{k-1}$ so that $\bar{a} = \sum_{i=0}^{k-1} a_i 2^i$. This can be done using binary addition [10] or PreDiv2m [6]. The first variant runs in $\log k + 1$ rounds, with $k \log k$ online interactive operations and k precomputation operations. The second one needs 3 rounds, $2k + 1$ online operations and $4k$ precomputation operations. The second variant reduces the online round and communication complexity, but increases the precomputation complexity. This variant is used in the paper. However, secure binary addition with bits encoded in a small field (and share conversions) can reduce the communication complexity and improve the performance for large batches.

For our integer encoding in $\mathbb{Z}_q$, if $\bar{y}$ divides $\bar{a}$ then $\bar{a}/\bar{y} = \mathsf{fld}^{-1}(\mathsf{fld}(\bar{a}) \cdot \mathsf{fld}(\bar{y})^{-1})$. Therefore, given the secret inputs $\bar{a} \in \mathbb{Z}_{\langle k \rangle}$ and $m \in [0, k-1]$ and a protocol that computes $\bar{y} = 2^m$ and $\mathsf{fld}(\bar{y})^{-1}$, we can compute $\bar{a} \cdot 2^m = \bar{a}\bar{y}$ and $\lfloor \bar{a}/2^m \rfloor = \lfloor \mathsf{fld}^{-1}(\mathsf{fld}(2^k \bar{a}) \mathsf{fld}(\bar{y})^{-1})/2^k \rfloor$. This method uses Protocol 1, Pow2Inv (extended and optimized variant of the protocol Pow2 in [1]).

Protocol 1: Pow2Inv($[\![x]\!], m$).

1   $\{[\![x_i]\!]\}_{i=0}^{m-1} \leftarrow$ BitDec($[\![x]\!], m, m$);   // $3; 2m+1$

2   **foreach** $i \in [0, m-1]$ **do** $[\![c_i]\!] \leftarrow [\![x_i]\!](2^{2^i}-1)+1$;

3   $\{[\![y_i]\!]\}_{i=0}^{1} \leftarrow$ KMulInv($\{[\![c_i]\!]\}_{i=0}^{m-1}$);   // $1; m-1$

4   **return** $\{[\![y_i]\!]\}_{i=0}^{1}$;

Pow2Inv computes $\bar{y} = 2^{\bar{x}}$ and $\mathsf{fld}(\bar{y})^{-1}$, for small $\bar{x} \in [0, 2^m - 1]$, with secret input and output, using the binary encoding of $\bar{x}$. Step 1 computes $\{x_i\}_{i=0}^{m-1}$ so that $\bar{x} = \sum_{i=0}^{m-1} x_i 2^i$ using BitDec. Observe that $\bar{y} = 2^{\bar{x}} = 2^{\sum_{i=0}^{m-1} x_i 2^i} = \prod_{i=0}^{m-1} 2^{x_i 2^i}$. Let $b_i = 2^{2^i}$ and $c_i = b_i^{x_i}$. Step 2 computes $c_i = (x_i = 1)?\ b_i : 1 = x_i(b_i - 1) + 1$. Step 3 computes $y_0 = \prod_{i=0}^{m-1} c_i = 2^{\bar{x}}$ and $y_1 = \mathsf{fld}(\bar{y})^{-1}$ using KMulInv, variant of SufMulInv that returns only $\prod_{i=0}^{m-1} c_i$ and its inverse.

With standard protocols based on Shamir secret sharing, multiplication followed by additive hiding, $c \leftarrow$ Reveal($[\![a]\!][\![b]\!] + [\![r]\!]$), needs 2 interactions and 2 rounds (multiplication and secret reconstruction). We can avoid the first interaction by randomizing the share products using pseudo-random shares of 0 generated with PRZS($2t$) [7,11]. We denote $[\![a]\!] * [\![b]\!]$ this local operation. Now the computation needs a single interaction: $c \leftarrow$ RevealD($[\![a]\!] * [\![b]\!] + [\![r]\!]$), where RevealD is the secret reconstruction protocol for polynomials of degree $2t$. This occurs very often: most of the protocols listed in Table 1 use additive hiding of the input. We add variants of these protocols for input shared with a random polynomial of degree $2t$, and distinguish them by the suffix 'D'.

2.5   Evaluation of the Floating-Point Arithmetic Protocols

Table 2 lists the floating-point protocols and their complexity. All protocols are constructed using the techniques and building blocks discussed in the previous sections, that support secure protocol composition.

The protocols run a distributed computation, with batches of interactive operations executed in parallel. Therefore, the running time is strongly affected by processing and communication resources and by implementation optimizations aimed at using the resources more efficiently. We tested the protocols using our Java implementation of the secure computation framework (an improved version of the implementation used in [7]). The goal of this implementation is to provide early feedback during protocol design: correctness and accuracy tests, verification of complexity metrics, and comparative analysis of protocol variants. Therefore, priority was given to simplicity and modularity, rather than optimizations required for fast parallel processing of large batches of operations. The implementation is essentially single-threaded (except for data sending and receiving), with some performance penalty due to the Java language.

Table 3 shows the measured complexity of the protocol implementations: the number of online rounds (with the theoretical minimum between brackets) and the amount of data sent by party i to party $j \neq i$ during the online and precomputation phases. Small differences between the values in Table 3 and those computed based on Table 2 are due to simplified complexity formulas, optimizations in the precomputation of shared random bits, and tradeoffs between round optimization and modularity. The precomputation can be implemented in 1 round, but currently runs in 2–3 rounds, to preserve modularity and reduce computation and communication for shared random bits in larger fields.

We evaluated the protocols in a configuration with 3 parties, for different floating-point precision and communication settings. The configuration parameters ℓ and g determine the precision and range of the floating-point numbers, and also affect the protocols' communication and computation complexity. We measured the running time for standard single precision, $\ell = 24$, $g = 8$, and double precision, $\ell = 53$, $g = 11$. The testbed consisted of 3 identical computers (each party on its own computer), with 3.6 GHz CPU, running Linux 18.04, and connected to an Ethernet switch. To analyze the relations between protocol running time, complexity metrics, and network bandwidth and delay, we ran the tests for two network settings:

Table 2. Floating-point protocols and their complexity, for $\hat{a}, \hat{a}_i \in \mathbb{Q}^{FL}_{\langle \ell, g \rangle}$.

Protocol	Task	Rounds	Online Inter. Op.	Precomp. Op.	Modulus
AddFL1	$\hat{a}_1 + \hat{a}_2$	16	$6\ell + 3g + 30$	$13\ell + 3g$	$>2^{\ell+2+\kappa}$
AddFL2	$\hat{a}_1 + \hat{a}_2$	18	$5\ell + 3\lceil \log \ell \rceil + 3g + 25$	$10\ell + 6\lceil \log \ell \rceil + 3g$	$>2^{2\ell+1+\kappa}$
MulFL	$\hat{a}_1 \hat{a}_2$	5	$\ell + 7$	$4\ell + 3$	$>2^{2\ell+\kappa}$
DivFL	$\hat{a}_1/\hat{a}_2$	$5 + \theta_1$	$\ell + 2\theta_1 + 6$	$(2\theta_1 + 4)\ell$	$>2^{2\ell+8+\kappa}$
SqrtFL	$\sqrt{\hat{a}}$	$4 + 2\theta_2$	$3\theta_2 + 7$	$(3\theta_2 + 3)\ell$	$>2^{2\ell+8+\kappa}$
LTFL	$\hat{a}_1 <_? \hat{a}_2$	5	$\ell + g + 7$	$3(\ell + g)$	$>2^{\ell+\kappa}$
EQFL	$\hat{a}_1 =_? \hat{a}_2$	3	$\lceil \log(\ell + g) \rceil + 2$	$\ell + g + 3\log(\ell + g)$	$>2^{\ell+\kappa}$

Table 3. Complexity of the implementations of the floating-point protocols.

	$\ell = 24$	$g = 8$	$\log q = 104$	$\ell = 53$	$g = 11$	$\log q = 160$
Protocol	Rounds	Online octets	Precomp. octets	Rounds	Online octets	Precomp. octets
AddFL1	18 (16)	2574	4966	18 (16)	7618	13508
AddFL2	20 (18)	2438	4692	20 (18)	6898	11972
MulFL	5 (5)	402	1236	5 (5)	1200	3432
DivFL	8 (8)	504	3396	9 (9)	1400	9056
SqrtFL	11 (10)	208	3812	13 (12)	380	9684
LTFL	5 (5)	570	1310	5 (5)	1520	3430
EQFL	3 (3)	116	672	3 (3)	200	1198

– LAN communications with high bandwidth and low delay (near-zero): the computers are connected to an Ethernet switch with 1 Gbps data rate (950 Mbps TCP data rate and 0.3 ms round-trip time).
– Internet communications with moderate end-to-end bandwidth and delay: the computers are connected to an Ethernet switch with 100 Mbps data rate and their interfaces simulate using the Linux tool NetEm a 10 ms one-way network path delay (95 Mbps TCP data rate and 20.7 ms round-trip time).

3   Secure Addition and Subtraction

Addition/Subtraction Protocol. Protocol 2, AddFL, computes $\hat{a} \approx \hat{a}_1 + \hat{a}_2$, for secret $\hat{a}_1, \hat{a}_2, \hat{a} \in \mathbb{Q}_{\langle \ell, g \rangle}^{FL}$, $\hat{a}_1 = (1 - 2s_1)\bar{v}_1 2^{\bar{p}_1}$, $\hat{a}_2 = (1 - 2s_2)\bar{v}_2 2^{\bar{p}_2}$, and $\hat{a} = (1 - 2s)\bar{v}2^{\bar{p}}$. AddFL can also compute $\hat{a}_1 - \hat{a}_2$, just by setting $s_2 = 1 - s_2$. It follows the approach proposed in [7], with improvements that reduce round complexity and an alternative radix alignment, with lower communication complexity.

Assume $\bar{p}_1 \geq \bar{p}_2$ and let $\Delta = \bar{p}_1 - \bar{p}_2 \geq 0$ (if $\bar{p}_1 < \bar{p}_2$ we swap the inputs). Let $\bar{v}_1' = (1 - 2s_1)\bar{v}_1$ and $\bar{v}_2' = (1 - 2s_2)\bar{v}_2$. AddFL consists of two main subtasks. The first sub-task computes $\bar{v}_3'$ and $\bar{p}_3'$ so that $\bar{v}_3'2^{\bar{p}_3'} \approx \bar{v}_1'2^{\bar{p}_1} + \bar{v}_2'2^{\bar{p}_2}$. To do this, it aligns the radix point and adds the significands, by computing $\bar{v}_3' = \bar{v}_1' + \lfloor \bar{v}_2'/2^{\Delta} \rceil$ and $\bar{p}_3' = \bar{p}_1$. Since $\bar{v}_1, \bar{v}_2 \in [2^{\ell-1}, 2^{\ell} - 1] \cup \{0\}$, we obtain $\bar{v}_3' \in [-2^{\ell} + 1, 2^{\ell+1} - 2]$. The second sub-task normalizes $\bar{v}_3'$ and $\bar{p}_3'$, to obtain $\hat{a} \in \mathbb{Q}_{\langle \ell, g \rangle}^{FL}$, encoded as described in Sect. 2.2. Both tasks are quite complicated, making secure addition and subtraction the slowest floating-point operations.

When $\Delta > \ell$, we set $\bar{v}_3' = \bar{v}_1'$, since $|\bar{v}_2'/2^{\Delta}| < 1$ and converges rapidly to 0, regardless of sign. Therefore, we actually compute $\bar{v}_2'/2^{\Delta}$ only for $\Delta \leq \ell$. On the other hand, when $\Delta > 0$ and $\bar{v}_2'$ is not divisible by 2^{Δ}, radix point alignment is affected by rounding errors. If $\Delta > 1$ then $|\bar{v}_3'| > 2^{\ell-2}$, so the error is negligible. However, if $\Delta = 1$ and $s_1 \neq s_2$ then $|\bar{v}_3'|$ can be close to the rounding error and accuracy is strongly degraded. To avoid this, AddFL computes $\bar{v}_3' = 2\bar{v}_1' + \lfloor (2\bar{v}_2')/2^{\Delta} \rceil$ and $\bar{p}_3' = \bar{p}_1 - 1$. Thus, for $\Delta = 1$, the division is exact.

The protocol implements the approach described above: aligns the radix point and adds the significands in steps 1–6 and normalizes the result in step 7, using Protocol 5, FX2FL. Steps 1–2 determine the range of $\Delta = \bar{p}_1 - \bar{p}_2$, by computing $c_0 = (\Delta < 0)? \ 1 : 0$, $c_1 = (\Delta \leq \ell)? \ 1 : 0$, and $c_2 = (\Delta \geq -\ell)? \ 1 : 0$ (optimized triple comparison). Steps 3–4 compute the signed values of the significands and obliviously swap the inputs if $\Delta < 0$. Step 5 sets $c_3 = c_1 c_2 = (|\Delta| \leq \ell)? \ 1 : 0$ and $\Delta' = |\Delta|$. The comparisons for c_1 and c_2 in step 2 can be replaced with a comparison for c_3 in step 5 (as in [7]), but this costs 3 additional rounds.

Protocol 2: AddFL$(\{[v_i], [p_i], [s_i]\}_{i=1}^2, \ell, g)$.

1 $[\Delta] \leftarrow [p_1] - [p_2]$;
2 $\{[c_i]\}_{i=0}^2 \leftarrow \mathsf{LTZ}(\{[\Delta], [\Delta] - \ell - 1, -[\Delta] - \ell - 1\}, g+1)$;   // $3; 3(g+2)$
3 $[v_1'] \leftarrow [v_1](1 - 2[s_1])$; $[v_2'] \leftarrow [v_2](1 - 2[s_2])$;   // $0; 2$
4 $\{[v_i'], [p_i']\}_{i=1}^2 \leftarrow \mathsf{Swap}([c_0], \{[v_i'], [p_i]\}_{i=1}^2)$;   // $1; 4$
5 $[c_3] \leftarrow [c_1][c_2]$; $[\Delta'] \leftarrow [p_1'] - [p_2']$;   // $0; 1$
6 $[v_3'] \leftarrow \mathsf{AlignAdd}([v_1'], [v_2'], [\Delta'], [c_3], \ell, g)$;   // $3; \ell + 3$ $(5; 3\lceil \log \ell \rceil + 2)$
7 $([v], [p], [s], [z]) \leftarrow \mathsf{FX2FL}([v_3'], [p_1'] - 1, \ell + 2, 0, \ell, g)$;   // $9; 5\ell + 10$
8 **return** $([v], [p], [s], [z])$;

If $\hat{a}_1 = 0$ or $\hat{a}_2 = 0$, AddFL computes the exact result without having to deal with special cases. Recall we encode $\hat{a} = 0$ as $\bar{v} = 0$ and $\bar{p} = -2^{g-1}$(smallest value). Thus, if $\hat{a}_2 = 0$ then $\bar{p}_1 \geq \bar{p}_2$ and $\bar{v}_2 = 0$, so the protocol sets $\bar{p} = \bar{p}_1$ and $\bar{v} = \bar{v}_1$; if $\hat{a}_2 \neq 0$ and $\hat{a}_1 = 0$ then $\bar{p}_1 < \bar{p}_2$ and the operands are swapped.

We show two solutions for aligning the radix point and adding the significands, with different complexity tradeoffs:

- Protocol 3, AlignAdd1, uses Int2Mask and PreDiv2mP (similar to [7], but simplified). It computes $\{x_i\}_{i=0}^{\ell} = \{(\Delta = i)? \ 1 : 0\}_{i=0}^{\ell}$ in step 1 (for $|\Delta| \leq \ell$), $\bar{v}_2' = (|\Delta| \leq \ell)?\ 2\bar{v}_2 : 0$ in step 2, $\{\bar{d}_i\}_{i=0}^{\ell} = \{\lfloor \bar{v}_2'/2^i \rceil\}_{i=0}^{\ell}$ in step 3, and then $\bar{v}_3 = 2\bar{v}_1 + \sum_{i=0}^{\ell} x_i \bar{d}_i = 2\bar{v}_1 + \lfloor (2\bar{v}_2)/2^{|\Delta|} \rceil$. The online complexity is 3 rounds and $\ell + 3$ interactive operations and the precomputation is 3ℓ operations.
- Protocol 4, AlignAdd2, uses Pow2Inv. Step 1 computes x_1, the multiplicative inverse of $2^{|\Delta|}$ in $\mathbb{Z}_q$. For $|\Delta| \leq 2^\ell$, $2^\ell \bar{v}_2$ is divisible by $2^{|\Delta|}$ so $(2^\ell \bar{v}_2)x_1 = \bar{v}_2 2^{\ell - |\Delta|}$. Steps 2–4 set $\bar{v}_2' = (|\Delta| \leq \ell)?\ 2^\ell \bar{v}_2 : 0$ and then $\bar{v}_3 = 2\bar{v}_1 + \lfloor (\bar{v}_2' x_1)/2^{\ell-1} \rceil = 2\bar{v}_1 + \lfloor (2\bar{v}_2)/2^{|\Delta|} \rceil$, same as for AlignAdd1. The online complexity is 5 rounds and $3\log \ell + 2$ interactive operations and the precomputation is $6\log \ell$ operations. AlignAdd2 trades off 2 additional rounds for lower communication and (especially) lower computation complexity.

Protocol 3: AlignAdd1($[\![v_1]\!], [\![v_2]\!], [\![\Delta]\!], [\![c]\!], \ell, g$).

1 $\{[\![x_i]\!]\}_{i=0}^{\ell} \leftarrow$ Int2Mask($[\![\Delta']\!], \ell + 1$);	// 1; ℓ
2 $[\![v_2']\!] \leftarrow 2[\![v_2]\!][\![c]\!]$;	// 0; 1
3 $[\![d_0]\!] \leftarrow [\![v_2']\!]$; $\{[\![d_i]\!]\}_{i=1}^{\ell} \leftarrow$ PreDiv2mP($[\![v_2']\!], \ell + 1, \ell$);	// 1; 1
4 $[\![v_3]\!] \leftarrow 2[\![v_1]\!] + \sum_{i=0}^{\ell} [\![x_i]\!][\![d_i]\!]$;	// 1; 1
5 **return** $[\![v_3]\!]$;	

Protocol 4: AlignAdd2($[\![v_1]\!], [\![v_2]\!], [\![\Delta]\!], [\![c]\!], \ell, g$).

1 $([\![x_0]\!], [\![x_1]\!]) \leftarrow$ Pow2Inv($[\![\Delta]\!], g + 1, \lceil \log \ell \rceil$);	// 4; 3$\lceil \log \ell \rceil$
2 $[\![v_2']\!] \leftarrow 2^\ell [\![v_2]\!][\![c]\!]$;	// 0; 1
3 $[\![v_2']\!] \leftarrow$ Div2mPD($[\![v_2']\!] * [\![x_1]\!], 2\ell, \ell - 1$);	// 1; 1
4 $[\![v_3]\!] \leftarrow 2[\![v_1]\!] + [\![v_2']\!]$;	
5 **return** $[\![v_3]\!]$;	

Protocol 5: FX2FL($[\![v]\!], [\![p]\!], k, f, \ell, g$).

1 $[\![s']\!] \leftarrow$ LTZ($[\![v]\!], k$); $[\![s]\!] \leftarrow 1 - 2[\![s']\!]$;	// 3; $k + 1$
2 $\{[\![b_i]\!]\}_{i=0}^{k-2} \leftarrow$ PreDiv2mD($[\![v]\!] * [\![s]\!], k, k - 2$);	// 3; $2k - 3$
3 $[\![a_{k-2}]\!] \leftarrow [\![b_{k-2}]\!]$; **foreach** $i \in [0, k - 3]$ **do** $[\![a_i]\!] \leftarrow [\![b_i]\!] - 2[\![b_{i+1}]\!]$;	
4 $\{[\![c_i]\!]\}_{i=0}^{k-2} \leftarrow$ SufOr($\{[\![a_i]\!]\}_{i=0}^{k-2}$);	// 2; $2k - 1$
5 $[\![z']\!] \leftarrow 1 - [\![c_0]\!]$;	
6 $[\![d_{k-2}]\!] \leftarrow [\![c_{k-2}]\!]$; **foreach** $i \in [0, k - 3]$ **do** $[\![d_i]\!] \leftarrow [\![c_i]\!] - [\![c_{i+1}]\!]$;	
7 **if** $(k - 1 > \ell)$ **then**	
8 $\quad [\![v']\!] \leftarrow [\![b_0]\!] \sum_{i=0}^{\ell-1} 2^{\ell-i-1} [\![d_i]\!] + \sum_{i=0}^{k-\ell-2} [\![d_{\ell+i}]\!][\![b_{i+1}]\!]$;	// 1; 1
9 **else** $[\![v']\!] \leftarrow 2^{\ell-k+1} [\![b_0]\!] \sum_{i=0}^{k-2} 2^{k-i-2} [\![d_i]\!]$;	// 1; 1
10 $[\![p']\!] \leftarrow ([\![p]\!] - f - \ell)(1 - [\![z']\!]) + \sum_{i=0}^{k-2} [\![c_i]\!] - [\![z']\!] 2^{g-1}$;	// 0; 1
11 **return** $([\![v']\!], [\![p']\!], [\![s']\!], [\![z']\!])$;	

FX2FL converts integers $\bar{a} \in \mathbb{Z}_{\langle k \rangle}$ or fixed-point numbers $\tilde{a} \in \mathbb{Q}_{\langle k,f \rangle}^{FX}$ to floating-point numbers $\hat{a} \in \mathbb{Q}_{\langle \ell,g \rangle}^{FL}$. Protocol 5 is a general variant that also helps for normalization (adapted from [7]): it takes on input a secret $\bar{v} \in \mathbb{Z}_{\langle k \rangle}$, a public exponent $f \leq k$, and a secret exponent $\bar{p} \in \mathbb{Z}_{\langle g \rangle}$ and returns secret $\langle \bar{v}', \bar{p}', s', z' \rangle$ so that $\hat{a} = (1 - 2s')\bar{v}'2^{\bar{p}'} \in \mathbb{Q}_{\langle \ell,g \rangle}^{FL}$, $\hat{a} \approx \bar{v} \cdot 2^{\bar{p}-f}$ and $z' = (\hat{a} = 0)?\ 1 : 0$.

Recall that $\bar{v} \in [-(2^{k-1} - 1), 2^{k-1} - 1]$ and $\bar{v}' \in [2^{\ell-1}, 2^\ell - 1] \cup \{0\}$. If $\bar{v} = 0$ we set $\bar{v}' = 0$ and $\bar{p}' = -2^{g-1}$. Otherwise, $|\bar{v}| \in [2^{m-1}, 2^m - 1]$ for some secret $m \in [1, k-1]$ and we have to compute $\bar{v}' = |\bar{v}|2^{\ell-m}$ and $\bar{p}' = \bar{p} - f - \ell + m$. When $k - 1 > \ell$ we have 2 cases: if $m \leq \ell$ then $\bar{v}' = |\bar{v}|2^{\ell-m}$ and if $m > \ell$ then $\bar{v}' = \lfloor |\bar{v}|/2^{-\ell+m} \rfloor$. If $k - 1 \leq \ell$ then $m \leq \ell$ and we have only one case: $\bar{v}' = |\bar{v}|2^{\ell-m}$. Therefore, if $m \leq \ell$ the output is $\hat{a} = \bar{v} \cdot 2^{\bar{p}-f}$ (exactly), otherwise $\hat{a} \approx \bar{v} \cdot 2^{\bar{p}-f}$, with relative error $\epsilon < 2^{-(\ell-1)}$ (due to the truncation of $\bar{v}$).

Table 4. Running time of AddFL protocols (milliseconds/operation).

AddFL1	1		10		20		50		100	
LAN	Online	Prec.	Online	Prec.	Online	Prec.	Online	Prec.	Online	Prec.
$\ell = 24$	2.63	3.04	1.59	2.82	1.50	2.78	1.41	2.57	1.40	2.46
$\ell = 53$	5.83	6.67	4.36	6.66	4.19	6.64	4.02	5.91	3.52	5.89
Internet	Online	Prec.	Online	Prec.	Online	Prec.	Online	Prec.	Online	Prec.
$\ell = 24$	193.77	42.41	23.36	9.83	13.68	7.12	7.17	5.16	4.62	4.39
$\ell = 53$	203.84	53.62	30.29	16.36	18.64	13.63	10.79	10.64	7.83	10.49
AddFL2	1		10		20		50		100	
LAN	Online	Prec.	Online	Prec.	Online	Prec.	Online	Prec.	Online	Prec.
$\ell = 24$	2.40	3.16	1.27	2.46	1.19	2.49	1.09	2.29	1.08	2.20
$\ell = 53$	3.84	5.82	2.67	5.66	2.61	5.61	2.48	4.94	2.47	4.95
Internet	Online	Prec.	Online	Prec.	Online	Prec.	Online	Prec.	Online	Prec.
$\ell = 24$	212.10	41.48	24.76	10.28	13.64	6.83	6.69	4.72	4.51	3.93
$\ell = 53$	217.60	50.86	28.34	15.20	16.82	11.99	9.26	9.13	6.93	9.11

Steps 1–5 compute $s' = (\bar{v} < 0)?\ 1 : 0$ and $z' = (\bar{v} = 0)?\ 1 : 0$, together with data used in steps 6–10 for computing $\bar{v}'$ and $\bar{p}'$: $\{\bar{b}_i\}_{i=0}^{k-2} = \{\lfloor |\bar{v}|/2^i \rfloor\}_{i=0}^{k-2}$, $\{a_i\}_{i=0}^{k-2}$, the binary encoding of $|\bar{v}|$, and $\{c_i\}_{i=0}^{k-2} = \{\bigvee_{j=i}^{k-2} a_j\}_{i=0}^{k-2}$. Note that $\bar{b}_0 = \bar{v}(1 - 2s') = |\bar{v}|$ and $c_0 = \bigvee_{j=0}^{k-2} a_j = 1 - z'$. Also, the output of PreDiv2mD serves both for computing the secret index m and for dividing by $2^{m-\ell}$.

Steps 6–9 compute $\bar{v}'$. Step 6 sets $d_i = (i = m - 1)?\ 1 : 0$, for $i \in [0, k-2]$. If $k - 1 > \ell$ we compute $\bar{v}_1 = |\bar{v}|2^{\ell-m}$, if $m \in [1, \ell]$, and $\bar{v}_2 = \lfloor |\bar{v}|/2^{-\ell+m} \rfloor$, if $m \in [\ell+1, k-1]$. At least one of them is 0. Step 8 handles both cases by computing $\bar{v}_1 = \bar{b}_0 \sum_{i=0}^{\ell-1} 2^{\ell-i-1} d_i = |\bar{a}|2^{\ell-m}$, $\bar{v}_2 = \sum_{i=0}^{k-\ell-2} d_{\ell+i}\bar{b}_{i+1} = \bar{b}_{m-\ell} = \lfloor |\bar{v}|/2^{-\ell+m} \rfloor$ and $\bar{v}' = \bar{v}_1 + \bar{v}_2$. If $k \leq \ell + 1$ then $m \leq \ell$ and $\bar{v}' = |\bar{v}|2^{\ell-m}$. This is computed in step 8: $\bar{v}' = 2^{\ell-k+1}\bar{b}_0 \sum_{i=0}^{k-2} 2^{k-i-2}d_i = 2^{\ell-k+1}|\bar{v}|2^{k-m-1} = |\bar{v}|2^{\ell-m}$.

Step 10 computes $\bar{p}'$ in parallel with $\bar{v}'$. If $\bar{v} \neq 0$ then $\sum_{i=0}^{k-2} c_i = m$, since $c_i = 1$ for $i \in [0, m-1]$ and $c_i = 0$ for $i \in [m, k-2]$, Otherwise, $\sum_{i=0}^{k-2} c_i = 0$. Thus, if $\bar{v} \neq 0$, $z' = 0$ and $\bar{p}' = \bar{p} - f - \ell + m$, otherwise $z' = 1$ and $\bar{p}' = -2^{g-1}$.

Complexity and Performance. FX2FL needs 9 rounds, $5k$ online operations, and $10(k-1)$ precomputation operations. If the sign is not secret, we skip step 1 and the complexity is 6 rounds, $4k$ online operations, and $7(k-1)$ precomputation operations. Alternatively [1], we can adapt the normalization used in [6,10] for secure fixed-point division, but this increases the online complexity.

We call AddFL1 and AddFL2 the variants of AddFL that use AlignAdd1 and AlignAdd2, respectively. Their complexity is listed in Table 2. The complexity metrics show that AddFL2 trades off 2 additional rounds for fewer interactive operations. On the other hand, AddFL1 can work in a field $\mathbb{Z}_q$ with modulus of $\ell + \kappa + 2$ bits, while AddFL2 requires $2\ell + \kappa + 1$ bits. The other floating-point arithmetic protocols need a modulus of at least $2\ell + \kappa$ bits, so the applications either use the large modulus for all operations, or extend AddFL1 with share conversions (two more rounds), so that it can run with a smaller modulus.

Both AddFL variants are simpler than the protocol proposed in [1] and reduce the online round and communication complexity roughly by half. This is due to simpler algorithms used in AddFL and FX2FL and new building blocks. However, while reducing the online complexity, some building blocks increase the precomputation (PreDiv2m, BitDec, Int2Mask). This is a valid approach, but the effects depend on implementation optimizations and execution environment.

The complexity of both variants is dominated by normalization. AddFL1 and AddFL2 can be generalized to compute more efficiently secure multi-operand addition, $\sum_{i=1}^{m} \hat{a}_i$: align the radix point to the largest exponent of the m terms and add the significands, by computing $\bar{p}' = \max(\{p_i\}_{i=1}^m)$ and $\sum_{i=1}^{m} \lfloor (2\bar{v}_i')/2^{\bar{p}'-\bar{p}_i} \rceil$, and normalize only the final result. Adding the significands increases the bitlength by up to $\lceil \log m \rceil$ bits, so this optimization scales up well with m.

Table 4 shows the running time per operation for AddFL1 and AddFL2, in LAN and in simulated Internet, for single and double precision, and for batches of 1, 10, 20, 50, and 100 parallel operations. The complexity of the implementations used in these tests is listed in Table 3. The results emphasize the importance of reducing the number of rounds and evaluating secure computation protocols in more realistic network settings. For parties connected to the Internet, with 10 ms one-way delay, the running time is much longer than for parties connected to LANs with delay close to 0. However, the running time per operation decreases quite fast when we compute in parallel larger batches. The gain is stronger for protocols with lower communication complexity and/or larger network delay.

AddFL2 is significantly faster in the LAN, but its advantage almost vanishes in the simulated Internet. Still, it scales up better for larger ℓ and batch size. On the other hand, the tests use the larger modulus required by AddFL2 and other arithmetic operations, while AddFL1 can use a modulus that is ℓ bits shorter.

The complexity metrics in Table 2 and Table 3 suggest similar performance for both variants and some advantage for AddFL2 for large ℓ and large batches (when the benefits of lower communication complexity become more important than those of lower round complexity). However, they take into account only the communication and local computation related to primitive operations. The larger performance difference observed in experiments is due to local computation ignored by these metrics (e.g., Lagrange polynomial interpolation in Int2Mask).

4 Secure Multiplication

Multiplication Protocol. Protocol 6, MulFL, computes $\hat{a} \approx \hat{a}_1\hat{a}_2$, with secret $\hat{a}_1, \hat{a}_2, \hat{a} \in \mathbb{Q}^{FL}_{\langle \ell, g \rangle}$, $\hat{a}_1 = (1 - 2s_1)\bar{v}_1 2^{\bar{p}_1}$, $\hat{a}_2 = (1 - 2s_2)\bar{v}_2 2^{\bar{p}_2}$, and $\hat{a} = (1 - 2s)\bar{v}2^{\bar{p}}$.

MulFL computes $\bar{v}_3 = \bar{v}_1\bar{v}_2$, $\bar{p}_3 = \bar{p}_1 + \bar{p}_2$, $s = s_1 \oplus s_2$, and $z = z_1 \vee z_2$, and then normalizes $\bar{v}_3$. Since $\bar{v}_1, \bar{v}_2 \in [2^{\ell-1}, 2^\ell - 1] \cup \{0\}$, so $\bar{v}_3 \in [2^{2\ell-2}, 2^{2\ell} - 2^{\ell+1} + 1] \cup \{0\}$, normalization is much simpler than for addition: if $\bar{v}_3 < 2^{2\ell-1}$ then $\bar{v} = \lfloor \bar{v}_3/2^{\ell-1} \rceil$ and $\bar{p} = \bar{p}_3 + \ell - 1$, otherwise $\bar{v} = \lfloor \bar{v}_3/2^\ell \rceil$ and $\bar{p} = \bar{p}_3 + \ell$. We adjust $\bar{p}$ for $\bar{v} = 0$ by setting $\bar{p} = \bar{p}(1 - z) - z2^{g-1}$.

There are several ways to efficiently implement this algorithm using the building blocks discussed in Sect. 2.4, with similar complexity. Protocol 6 is a simpler and more compact variant of the protocol presented in [7].

Protocol 6: MulFL($\{[\![v_i]\!], [\![p_i]\!], [\![s_i]\!], [\![z_i]\!]\}_{i=1}^2, \ell, g$).

1 $([\![v']\!], [\![v'']\!]) \leftarrow \mathsf{SelDiv2mPD}([\![v_1]\!] * [\![v_2]\!], \{\ell - 1, \ell\}, 2\ell)$;　　　　// 1; 1
2 $[\![s]\!] \leftarrow [\![s_1]\!] \oplus [\![s_2]\!]$; $[\![z]\!] \leftarrow [\![z_1]\!] \vee [\![z_2]\!]$;　　　　// 0; 2
3 $[\![b]\!] \leftarrow \mathsf{LTZ}([\![v']\!] - 2^\ell, \ell + 1)$;　　　　// 3; $\ell + 2$
4 $[\![v]\!] \leftarrow [\![b]\!]([\![v']\!] - [\![v'']\!]) + [\![v'']\!]$;　　　　// 1; 1
5 $[\![p]\!] \leftarrow ([\![p_1]\!] + [\![p_2]\!] + \ell - [\![b]\!])(1 - [\![z]\!]) - [\![z]\!]2^{g-1}$;　　　　// 0; 1
6 **return** $([\![v]\!], [\![p]\!], [\![s]\!], [\![z]\!])$;

Observe that the output is correctly normalized if we divide with probabilistic rounding to nearest, which is much faster. Moreover, steps 1–2 compute both $\bar{v}' = \lfloor \bar{v}_3/2^{\ell-1} \rceil$ and $\bar{v}'' = \lfloor \bar{v}_3/2^\ell \rceil$ with a single interactive operation, in parallel with s and z. Steps 3–5 normalize the output as follows: if $\bar{v}' < 2^\ell$ then $\bar{v} = \bar{v}'$ and $\bar{p} = \bar{p}_3 + \ell - 1$; otherwise, $\bar{v} = \bar{v}''$ and $\bar{p} = \bar{p}_3 + \ell$. Also, if $z = 1$ then $\bar{v}' = \bar{v}'' = 0$ and we set $\bar{p} = -2^{g-1}$. Step 3 computes $b = (\bar{v}' < 2^\ell)$? 1 : 0 and steps 4–5 obliviously compute $\bar{v} = (b = 1)$? $\bar{v}' : \bar{v}''$ and $\bar{p}' = (b = 1)$? $(\bar{p}_3 + \ell - 1) : (\bar{p}_3 + \ell)$, in parallel, and then $\bar{p} = \bar{p}'(1 - z) - z2^{g-1}$.

Complexity and Performance. MulFL needs 5 rounds, $\ell + 7$ online interactive operations, and $4\ell + 6$ precomputation operations. The complexity is clearly dominated by normalization (steps 3–5). Computing $b = (\bar{v}' < 2^\ell)$? 1 : 0, instead of $b = (\bar{v}_3 < 2^{2\ell-1})$? 1 : 0, adds one round, by preventing parallel computation of SelDiv2mPD and LTZ, but saves ℓ online operations and 3ℓ precomputation operations. The protocol proposed in [1] needs 11 rounds and a total of $8\ell + 10$ operations. The improvement is mainly due to SelDiv2mPD.

The significants can be seen as fixed-point numbers with fractional part of $\ell - 1$ bits, $\tilde{v}_1, \tilde{v}_2 \in [1, 2) \cup \{0\}$, where $\tilde{v}_1 = \bar{v}_1/2^{\ell-1}$ and $\tilde{v}_2 = \bar{v}_2/2^{\ell-1}$. Thus, floating-point multiplication can be described as fixed-point multiplication of the significands, $\tilde{v}_3 = \tilde{v}_1\tilde{v}_2 = \lfloor \bar{v}_1\bar{v}_2/2^{\ell-1} \rfloor$, $\tilde{v}_3 \in [2^{\ell-1}, 2^{\ell+1} - 2^2] \cup \{0\}$, followed by normalization. Based on this interpretation, MulFL can be generalized to compute more efficiently multi-operand multiplication, $\prod_{i=1}^m \hat{a}_i$: multiply all the significands as fixed-point numbers and normalize only the final result. A product of m factors increases the bitlength by $\ell' \in [0, m-1]$ bits. Therefore, although efficient for small m, this optimization does not scale up well with m.

The running time of MulFL is shown in Table 5, for LAN and for simulated Internet. As expected, MulFL is much faster than AddFL, due to its lower round and communication complexity (Table 2 and Table 3). The experiments with MulFL and simulated Internet better emphasize the combined effects of the two complexity metrics: the overall running time for a batch of operations is mainly determined by round complexity and network delay, while lower communication complexity reduces the running time per operation for larger batches.

Table 5. Running time of MulFL protocol (milliseconds/operation).

MulFL	1		10		20		50		100	
LAN	Online	Prec.	Online	Prec.	Online	Prec.	Online	Prec.	Online	Prec.
$\ell = 24$	0.40	0.93	0.17	0.76	0.16	0.75	0.15	0.74	0.15	0.75
$\ell = 53$	0.60	2.00	0.33	1.80	0.32	1.79	0.30	1.86	0.30	1.60
Internet	Online	Prec.	Online	Prec.	Online	Prec.	Online	Prec.	Online	Prec.
$\ell = 24$	51.88	33.21	5.51	5.07	2.94	3.40	1.41	2.35	0.89	1.66
$\ell = 53$	52.28	36.54	5.86	7.09	3.40	5.71	1.82	3.96	1.28	3.03

5   Secure Division and Square Root

Division Protocol. Protocol 7, DivFL, computes $\hat{a} \approx \hat{a}_1/\hat{a}_2$, for secret $\hat{a}_1, \hat{a}_2, \hat{a} \in \mathbb{Q}^{FL}_{\langle \ell, g \rangle}$, $\hat{a}_1 = (1 - 2s_1)\bar{v}_1 2^{\bar{p}_1}$, $\hat{a}_2 = (1 - 2s_2)\bar{v}_2 2^{\bar{p}_2}$, $\hat{a}_2 \neq 0$, and $\hat{a} = (1 - 2s)\bar{v} 2^{\bar{p}}$. It is a streamlined variant of the protocol in [7], with the same complexity.

DivFL uses secure fixed-point arithmetic to divide the significands and then normalizes the result. Let $\tilde{v}_1 = \bar{v}_1 2^{-\ell}$, $\tilde{v}_2 = \bar{v}_2 2^{-\ell}$ and $\tilde{v}_3 = \tilde{v}_1/\tilde{v}_2$. Observe that $\tilde{v}_1, \tilde{v}_2 \in [0.5, 1) \cup \{0\}$, $\tilde{v}_2 \neq 0$ and $\tilde{v}_3 \in (0.5, 2) \cup \{0\}$. Step 1 computes $\tilde{v}_3$ using Protocol 8, DivGS, and then steps 2–6 normalize the result and set $s = s_1 \oplus s_2$ and $z = z_1$. DivGS returns $\bar{v}_3 \in [2^{\ell-1}, 2^{\ell+1} - 1] \cup \{0\}$ and $\bar{v}_3 = \tilde{v}_3 2^\ell$, so DivFL can use the same fast normalization algorithm as MulFL (steps 2–5).

Protocol 7: DivFL($\{[\![v_i]\!], [\![p_i]\!], [\![s_i]\!], [\![z_i]\!]\}_{i=1}^2$).

1 $[\![v_3]\!] \leftarrow \text{DivGS}([\![v_1]\!], [\![v_2]\!], \ell)$;   // $\theta + 1$; $2\theta + 1$
2 $[\![b]\!] \leftarrow \text{LTZ}([\![v_3]\!] - 2^\ell, \ell + 1)$;   // 3; $\ell + 2$
3 $[\![v_3']\!] \leftarrow \text{Div2}([\![v_3]\!], \ell + 1)$;   // 0; 1
4 $[\![v]\!] \leftarrow [\![b]\!]([\![v_3]\!] - [\![v_3']\!]) + [\![v_3']\!]$;   // 1; 1
5 $[\![p]\!] \leftarrow ([\![p_1]\!] - [\![p_2]\!] - \ell + 1 - [\![b]\!])(1 - [\![z]\!]) - [\![z]\!]2^{g-1}$;   // 0; 1
6 $[\![s]\!] \leftarrow [\![s_1]\!] \oplus [\![s_2]\!]$; $[\![z]\!] \leftarrow [\![z_1]\!]$;   // 0; 1
7 **return** $([\![v]\!], [\![p]\!], [\![s]\!], [\![z]\!])$;

The protocol DivGS uses the following variant of Goldschmidt's division algorithm [18]. Let $a, b \in \mathbb{R}$ and $b \neq 0$. The algorithm starts with an initial approximation $w_0 \approx 1/b$, with relative error $\epsilon_0 < 1$, and computes a/b iteratively, as follows: $c_0 = aw_0$, $d_0 = \epsilon_0 = 1 - bw_0$; for $i > 0$ do $c_i = c_{i-1}(1 + d_{i-1})$, $d_i = d_{i-1}^2$. After i iterations we obtain $c_i \approx a/b$ with relative error $\epsilon_0^{2^i}$. For $b \in [0.5, 1)$, the algorithm can start with $w_0 = 2.9142 - 2b$, a linear approximation with relative error $\epsilon_0 < 0.08578$ [16]. The approximation provides about 3.5 exact bits, so for ℓ-bit inputs the algorithm needs $\theta = \lceil \log \frac{\ell}{3.5} \rceil$ iterations. Moreover, the approximation is computed without interaction for secret input and output.

In our setting, the algorithm computes $\tilde{v}_3 \approx \tilde{v}_1/\tilde{v}_2$, for $\tilde{v}_1, \tilde{v}_2 \in [0.5, 1) \cup \{0\}$, $\tilde{v}_2 \neq 0$, and $\tilde{v}_3 \in [0.5, 2) \cup \{0\}$. The inputs and the output are fixed-point numbers with ℓ-bit fractional part, encoded as $\bar{v}_1, \bar{v}_2 \in [2^{\ell-1}, 2^\ell - 1] \cup \{0\}$, $\bar{v}_2 \neq 0$, and $\bar{v}_3 \in [2^{\ell-1}, 2^{\ell+1} - 1] \cup \{0\}$. Fixed-point multiplication is computed as double-precision integer multiplication followed by truncation that cuts off the least significant ℓ bits, with rounding error $\delta_t < 2^{-\ell}$.

Protocol 8: DivGS($[\![v_1]\!], [\![v_2]\!], \ell$).

1   $\theta \leftarrow \lceil \log \frac{\ell}{3.5} \rceil$; $m = 4$; $k \leftarrow \ell + m$;
2   $[\![v_1]\!] \leftarrow 2^m[\![v_1]\!]$; $[\![v_2]\!] \leftarrow 2^m[\![v_2]\!]$;
3   $[\![w]\!] \leftarrow \mathsf{fld}(\mathsf{int}_k(2.9142)) - 2[\![v_2]\!]$;
4   $[\![c]\!] \leftarrow \mathsf{Div2mPD}([\![v_1]\!] * [\![w]\!], 2k+1, k)$;   // 1; 1
5   $[\![d]\!] \leftarrow \mathsf{Div2mPD}([\![v_2]\!] * [\![w]\!], 2k+1, k)$;   // 0; 1
6   $[\![d]\!] \leftarrow \mathsf{fld}(\mathsf{int}_k(1.0)) - [\![d]\!]$;
7   **foreach** $i \in [1, \theta - 1]$ **do**
8      $[\![c]\!] \leftarrow [\![c]\!] + \mathsf{Div2mPD}([\![c]\!] * [\![d]\!], 2k+1, k)$;   // $\theta - 1$; $\theta - 1$
9      $[\![d']\!] \leftarrow \mathsf{Div2mPD}([\![d]\!] * [\![d]\!], 2k+1, k)$; $[\![d]\!] \leftarrow [\![d']\!]$;   // 0; $\theta - 1$
10   $[\![v_3]\!] \leftarrow [\![c]\!] + \mathsf{Div2mPD}([\![c]\!] * [\![d]\!], 2k+1, k+m)$;   // 1; 1
11   **return** $[\![v_3]\!]$;

Goldschmidt's algorithm offers an important advantage: the two multiplications in each iteration can be computed in parallel. However, it also has an important drawback: the iterations are not self-correcting, so the rounding errors accumulate, reducing the accuracy of the result. Moreover, if the error before the last truncation is $|\delta| \geq 2^{-\ell}$, $\bar{v}_3$ may be outside the range $[2^{\ell-1}, 2^{\ell+1} - 1] \cup \{0\}$ required by fast normalization. For instance, if $\bar{v}_1 = 2^{\ell-1}$ and $\bar{v}_2 = 2^\ell - 1$ the output can be $\bar{v}_3 < 2^{\ell-1}$ ($\tilde{v}_1 = 0.5$, $\tilde{v}_2 \approx 1$, $\tilde{v}_3 \approx 0.5$); also, if $\bar{v}_1 = 2^\ell - 1$ and $\bar{v}_2 = 2^{\ell-1}$, the output can be $\bar{v}_3 > 2^{\ell+1} - 1$ ($\tilde{v}_1 \approx 1$, $\tilde{v}_2 = 0.5$, $\tilde{v}_3 \approx 2$).

The output error can be reduced by terminating the algorithm with a modified Newton-Raphson iteration [18], but this requires additional rounds. Alternatively, we can improve the accuracy during the iterations. Let Δ be the accumulated error before the last truncation and suppose $\Delta < \gamma 2^{-\ell}$ for variables with ℓ-bit fractional part. DivGS reduces the error to $\Delta < 2^{-\ell}$ by increasing the fractional part to $\ell + m$ bits, with $m = \lceil \log \gamma \rceil$. For our initial approximation, error analysis shows that we need $m = 4$ for $\ell \in [15, 112]$ ($\theta \in [3, 5]$).

DivGS computes the iterations described above with secret inputs and outputs. Steps 1–3 initialize the algorithm: compute θ and $k = \ell + m$; set $\bar{v}_1 = \tilde{v}_1 2^m$ and $\bar{v}_2 = \tilde{v}_2 2^m$ to obtain fixed-point numbers with fractional part of $k = \ell + m$ bits; compute $\bar{w} = \mathsf{int}_k(2.1942) - 2\bar{v}_2$, the initial approximation of $1/\tilde{v}_2$. Steps

4–6 compute in parallel the initial values of the iteration variables: $\bar{c} = \bar{v}_1 \bar{w}/2^k$ and $\bar{d} = (1 - \bar{v}_2)\bar{w}/2^k$. Steps 7–10 are the θ iterations of the algorithm. An iteration computes in parallel $\bar{c} = \bar{c} + \lfloor(\bar{c}\bar{d})/2^k\rceil$ and $\bar{d}' \leftarrow \lfloor\bar{d}^2/2^k\rceil$ and then sets $\bar{d} = \bar{d}'$.

Square Root Protocol. The square root and its inverse are efficiently computed using the same approach as for division. Protocol 9, SqrtFL, computes $\hat{a} \approx \sqrt{|\hat{a}_1|}$, for secret $\hat{a}_1, \hat{a} \in \mathbb{Q}^{FL}_{\langle\ell,g\rangle}$, $|\hat{a}_1| = \bar{v}_1 2^{\bar{p}_1}$ and $\hat{a} = \bar{v}2^{\bar{p}}$.

SqrtFL uses secure fixed-point arithmetic to compute the square root of the significand and normalizes the result [7]. Let $\tilde{v}_1 \in \mathbb{Q}^{FX}_{\langle\ell,\ell\rangle}$, $\tilde{v}_1 = \bar{v}_1 2^{-\ell} \in [0.5, 1) \cup \{0\}$, $\bar{p}'_1 = \bar{p}_1 + \ell$, $u = \bar{p}'_1 \bmod 2$, and $\bar{p}_2 = \lfloor\bar{p}'_1/2\rfloor$. We want to compute $\hat{a} = \sqrt{\tilde{v}_1 2^\ell 2^{\bar{p}_1}}$, so if $u = 0$ then $\hat{a} = \sqrt{\tilde{v}_1}2^{\bar{p}_2}$, otherwise $\hat{a} = \sqrt{2\tilde{v}_1}2^{\bar{p}_2} = \frac{\sqrt{2}}{2}\sqrt{\tilde{v}_1}2^{\bar{p}_2+1}$. Let $\tilde{v}'_2, \tilde{v}''_2 \in \mathbb{Q}^{FX}_{\langle\ell,\ell\rangle}$, $\tilde{v}'_2 = \sqrt{\tilde{v}_1} \in [\frac{\sqrt{2}}{2}, 1) \cup \{0\}$ and $\tilde{v}''_2 = \frac{\sqrt{2}}{2}\sqrt{\tilde{v}_1} \in [0.5, \frac{\sqrt{2}}{2}) \cup \{0\}$. If $u = 0$ we assign $\bar{v} = \tilde{v}'_2$ and $\bar{p} = \bar{p}_2 - \ell$, otherwise $\bar{v} = \tilde{v}''_2$ and $\bar{p} = \bar{p}_2 + 1 - \ell$.

SqrtFL computes $\sqrt{\tilde{v}_1}$ using Protocol 10, SqrtGS, based on Goldschmidt's square root algorithm and secure fixed-point arithmetic. Rounding errors are handled as in DivGS, by increasing the fractional part of the fixed-point numbers to $k = \ell + m$ bits, $m \geq 4$. Steps 1–2 compute $\tilde{v}_2 \in \mathbb{Q}^{FX}_{\langle k,k\rangle}$, $\tilde{v}_2 \approx \sqrt{\tilde{v}_1} \in [\frac{\sqrt{2}}{2}, 1) \cup \{0\}$ and steps 3–8 normalize $\bar{v}_2 = \tilde{v}_2 2^k$: compute $\bar{v}'_2 = \lfloor\bar{v}_2/2^m\rfloor$, $\bar{v}''_2 = \lfloor\text{int}_k(\frac{\sqrt{2}}{2})\bar{v}_2/2^{k+m}\rceil$, $\bar{p}_2$, and u; obliviously select the correct result by computing $\bar{v} = \bar{v}'_2 + u(\bar{v}''_2 - \bar{v}'_2)$ and $\bar{p} = \bar{p}_2 - \ell + u$; set $\bar{p} = (z_1 = 1)? \bar{p} : -2^{g-1}$.

Protocol 9: SqrtFL($[\![v_1]\!], [\![p_1]\!], [\![z_1]\!]$).

1 $m = 4; k \leftarrow \ell + m;$
2 $[\![v_2]\!] \leftarrow \text{SqrtGS}(2^m[\![v_1]\!], \ell, k);$ // $2\theta + 2; 3\theta + 2;$
3 $[\![v'_2]\!] \leftarrow \text{Div2mP}([\![v_2]\!], k, m);$ // $1; 1$
4 $[\![v''_2]\!] \leftarrow \text{Div2mP}(\text{fld}(\text{int}_k(\sqrt{2}/2))[\![v_2]\!], 2k, k + m);$ // $0; 1$
5 $[\![p_2]\!] \leftarrow \text{Div2}([\![p_1]\!] + \ell, g + 1);$ // $0; 1$
6 $[\![u]\!] \leftarrow [\![p_1]\!] + \ell - 2[\![p_2]\!];$
7 $[\![v]\!] \leftarrow [\![v'_2]\!] + [\![u]\!]([\![v''_2]\!] - [\![v'_2]\!]);$ // $1; 1$
8 $[\![p]\!] \leftarrow ([\![p_2]\!] - \ell + [\![u]\!])(1 - [\![z_1]\!]) - 2^{g-1}[\![z_1]\!];$ // $0; 1$
9 **return** $([\![v]\!], [\![p]\!], [\![z_1]\!]);$

Protocol 10: SqrtGS($[\![v]\!], \ell, k$).

---

1 $\theta \leftarrow \lceil \log \frac{\ell}{5.5} \rceil$; $\alpha \leftarrow$ fld(int$_k$(0.5));

2 $[\![w]\!] \leftarrow$ fld(int$_k$(1.7877)) $-$ Div2mP(fld(int$_k$(0.81))$[\![v]\!], 2k, k$);   // 1; 1

3 $[\![b]\!] \leftarrow$ Div2mPD($[\![v]\!] * [\![w]\!], 2k + 1, k$);   // 1; 1

4 $[\![c]\!] \leftarrow$ Div2($[\![w]\!], k + 1$);   // 0; 1

5 **foreach** $i \in [1, \theta - 1]$ **do**

6       $[\![d]\!] \leftarrow \alpha -$ Div2mPD($[\![b]\!] * [\![c]\!], 2k + 1, k$);   // $\theta - 1$; $\theta - 1$

7       $[\![b]\!] \leftarrow [\![b]\!] +$ Div2mPD($[\![b]\!] * [\![d]\!], 2k + 1, k$);   // $\theta - 1$; $\theta - 1$

8       $[\![c]\!] \leftarrow [\![c]\!] +$ Div2mPD($[\![c]\!] * [\![d]\!], 2k + 1, k$);   // 0; $\theta - 1$

9 $[\![d]\!] \leftarrow \alpha -$ Div2mPD($[\![b]\!] * [\![c]\!], 2k + 1, k$);   // 1; 1

10 $[\![b]\!] \leftarrow [\![b]\!] +$ Div2mPD($[\![b]\!] * [\![d]\!], 2k + 1, k$);   // 1; 1

11 **return** $[\![b]\!]$;

SqrtGS uses a variant of Goldschmidt's square root algorithm [18]. Let $a \in \mathbb{R}$, $a > 0$, and $w_0 \approx \frac{1}{\sqrt{a}}$ such that $aw_0^2 \in [\frac{1}{2}, \frac{3}{2}]$. The algorithm computes both $\sqrt{a}$ and $\frac{1}{2\sqrt{a}}$ iteratively: $b_0 = aw_0$, $c_0 = w_0/2$; for $i > 0$ do $d_{i-1} = 0.5 - b_{i-1}c_{i-1}$, $b_i = b_{i-1}(1 + d_{i-1})$, $c_i = c_{i-1}(1 + d_{i-1})$. After i iterations it obtains $b_i \approx \sqrt{a}$ and $c_i \approx \frac{1}{2\sqrt{a}}$ with relative error $\epsilon_0^{2^i}$. For $a \in [0.5, 1)$, we can take $w_0 = 1.7877 - 0.81a$, a linear approximation of $\frac{1}{\sqrt{a}}$ with relative error $\epsilon_0 < 0.0223$. Since w_0 provides almost 5.5 exact bits, the algorithm needs $\theta = \lceil \log \frac{\ell}{5.5} \rceil$ iterations for ℓ-bit input.

SqrtGS computes $\tilde{b} \in [\frac{\sqrt{2}}{2}, 1) \cup \{0\}$, $\tilde{b} \approx \sqrt{\tilde{v}}$, for $\tilde{v} \in [0.5, 1) \cup \{0\}$, using secure fixed-point arithmetic. Step 2 computes $\tilde{w} = 1.7877 - 0.81\tilde{v}$, the linear approximation of $\frac{1}{\sqrt{\tilde{v}}}$, and steps 3–4 compute the initial values of the variables, $\bar{b} = \lfloor \bar{v}\bar{w}/2^k \rceil$ and $\bar{c} = \lfloor \bar{v}/2 \rfloor$ (in parallel). Steps 5–10 are the θ iterations of the algorithm. An iteration computes $\bar{d} = \text{int}_k(0.5) - \lfloor \bar{b}\bar{c}/2^k \rceil$ and then $\bar{b} = \bar{b} + \lfloor \bar{b}\bar{d}/2^k \rceil$

Table 6. Running time of DivFL and SqrtFL protocols (milliseconds/operation).

DivFL	1		10		20		50		100	
LAN	Online	Prec.	Online	Prec.	Online	Prec.	Online	Prec.	Online	Prec.
$\ell = 24$	0.67	2.66	0.31	2.36	0.29	2.42	0.26	1.91	0.25	1.86
$\ell = 53$	1.03	6.20	0.60	6.22	0.54	4.70	0.51	4.75	0.52	4.71
Internet	Online	Prec.	Online	Prec.	Online	Prec.	Online	Prec.	Online	Prec.
$\ell = 24$	82.84	41.59	8.97	9.35	4.84	6.73	2.27	3.93	1.43	4.04
$\ell = 53$	93.78	48.44	10.72	15.05	5.97	10.14	3.11	9.60	2.15	9.15
SqrtFL	1		10		20		50		100	
LAN	Online	Prec.	Online	Prec.	Online	Prec.	Online	Prec.	Online	Prec.
$\ell = 24$	0.76	2.96	0.27	2.82	0.25	2.42	0.22	2.10	0.19	2.08
$\ell = 53$	0.98	7.16	0.53	6.23	0.46	5.47	0.42	5.38	0.40	5.40
Internet	Online	Prec.	Online	Prec.	Online	Prec.	Online	Prec.	Online	Prec.
$\ell = 24$	113.04	28.86	11.79	8.83	6.17	5.70	2.72	3.89	1.60	4.01
$\ell = 53$	134.17	40.20	14.31	12.79	7.60	9.92	3.59	10.30	2.26	9.86

and $\bar{c} = \bar{c} + \lfloor \bar{c}\bar{d}/2^k \rceil$ (steps 7–8 in parallel). The output preserves the extended precision, so that SqrtFL can accurately compute $\frac{\sqrt{2}}{2}\sqrt{\tilde{v}}$.

Reciprocal of the Square Root. The reciprocal of the square root can be computed using similar protocols, SqrtInvFL and SqrtInvGS, with the same complexity. SqrtInvGS is similar to SqrtGS, but step 10 computes $\tilde{c}$ instead of $\tilde{b}$ and the output is $\tilde{c} = \frac{1}{2\sqrt{\tilde{v}}}$. SqrtInvFL computes $\hat{a}' = \frac{1}{\sqrt{\tilde{v}_1 2^\ell 2^{\bar{p}_1}}}$ using the same method as SqrtFL. If $u = 0$ then $\hat{a}' = \frac{1}{\sqrt{\tilde{v}_1}} 2^{-\bar{p}_2}$, otherwise $\hat{a}' = \frac{1}{\sqrt{2\tilde{v}_1} 2^{\bar{p}_2}} = \frac{\sqrt{2}}{2} \frac{1}{\sqrt{\tilde{v}_1}} 2^{-(\bar{p}_2+1)}$. Let $\tilde{v}_2', \tilde{v}_2'' \in \mathbb{Q}_{\langle \ell, \ell \rangle}^{FX}$, $\tilde{v}_2' = \frac{1}{2\sqrt{\tilde{v}_1}} \in (0.5, \frac{\sqrt{2}}{2}] \cup \{0\}$ and $\tilde{v}_2'' = \frac{\sqrt{2}}{2\sqrt{\tilde{v}_1}} = \sqrt{2}\tilde{v}_2' \in (\frac{\sqrt{2}}{2}, 1] \cup \{0\}$. If $u = 0$ we assign $\bar{v} = \tilde{v}_2'$ and $\bar{p} = -\bar{p}_2 - \ell$, otherwise $\bar{v} = \tilde{v}_2''$ and $\bar{p} = -\bar{p}_2 - 1 - \ell$. Actually, a protocol that computes both the square root and its reciprocal has (roughly) the same online complexity.

Complexity and Performance. The complexity of DivFL is $\theta_1 + 5$ rounds, $\ell + 2\theta_1 + 7$ online operations, and $(2\theta_1 + 4)\ell$ precomputation operations, with $\theta_1 = \lceil \log \frac{\ell}{3.5} \rceil$ ($\theta_1 = 4$ for $\ell \in [29, 56]$). The improvement is due to better initial approximation (less iterations) and more efficient secure fixed-point arithmetic.

An alternative approach to floating-point division with secret inputs and output, suggested in related work, is to first compute the reciprocal $\hat{a}_2' = 1/\hat{a}_2$ and then $\hat{a}_3 = \hat{a}_1 \cdot \hat{a}_2'$. However, DivFL has the same complexity as a protocol that computes $1/\hat{a}_2$ and avoids the additional secure floating-point multiplication. Also, with minor changes, DivFL can compute $\hat{a}_3 = \hat{a}_1/\hat{a}_2$ for public $\hat{a}_1$ and secret $\hat{a}_2$ and $\hat{a}_3$, with slightly lower complexity. Finally, for public $\hat{a}_2$ and secret $\hat{a}_1$ and $\hat{a}_3$, division consists of secure multiplication between $\hat{a}_1$ and public $1/\hat{a}_2$.

Table 6 shows the running time of DivFL for an implementation with the complexity listed in Table 3. MulFL and DivFL use the same components, fast fixed-point multiplication and fast normalization, and have similar online communication complexity. DivFL's additional multiplications make the precomputation more expensive and the larger number of rounds increases the online time for networks with longer delay. However, these rounds are lightweight and their effects are strongly attenuated by large batches or/and low network delay.

The complexity of SqrtFL is $2\theta_2 + 4$ rounds, only $3\theta_2 + 7$ online interactive operations, and $3(\theta_2 + 1)\ell$ precomputation operations, with $\theta_2 = \lceil \log \frac{\ell}{5.5} \rceil$ ($\theta_2 = 3$ for $\ell \in [24, 45]$). SqrtFL is clearly more efficient than protocols that implement similar algorithms using secure floating-point arithmetic (e.g., [1]).

Table 6 shows the running time of SqrtFL for an implementation with the complexity listed in Table 3. SqrtFL and DivFL have similar running time, due to similar protocol structure and complexity (especially for larger batches, that attenuate the effects of the slightly different round complexity).

6   Secure Comparison

Inequality Test. Protocol 11, LTFL, returns $c = (\hat{a}_1 < \hat{a}_2)?\ 1 : 0$ for $\hat{a}_1, \hat{a}_2 \in \mathbb{Q}_{\langle \ell, g \rangle}^{FL}$, $\hat{a}_1 = (1 - s_1)\bar{v}_1 2^{\bar{p}_1}$ and $\hat{a}_2 = (1 - s_2)\bar{v}_2 2^{\bar{p}_2}$, with secret inputs and output [7].

Let $\bar{v}'_1 = (1 - s_1)\bar{v}_1$, $\bar{v}'_2 = (1 - s_2)\bar{v}_2$, $\hat{d} = \hat{a}_1 - \hat{a}_2 = 2^{\bar{p}_2}(\bar{v}'_1 2^{\bar{p}_1 - \bar{p}_2} - \bar{v}'_2)$ and observe that $\hat{d} < 0$ if and only if one of the following mutually exclusive conditions holds: $\bar{p}_1 = \bar{p}_2$ and $\bar{v}'_1 < \bar{v}'_2$; $\bar{p}_1 < \bar{p}_2$ and $s_2 = 0$; $\bar{p}_1 > \bar{p}_2$ and $s_1 = 1$. Let $z_p = (\bar{p}_1 = \bar{p}_2)?\ 1:0$, $c_p^- = (\bar{p}_1 < \bar{p}_2)?\ 1:0$, $c_p^+ = (\bar{p}_1 > \bar{p}_2)?\ 1:0$, and $c_v^- = (\bar{v}'_1 < \bar{v}'_2)?\ 1:0$. LTFL computes $c = (\hat{d} < 0)?\ 1:0 = z_p c_v^- + c_p^-(1 - s_2) + c_p^+ s_1$.

Protocol 11: LTFL($\{[\![v_i]\!], [\![p_i]\!], [\![s_i]\!]\}_{i=1}^{2}$).

1 $[\![c_p^-]\!], [\![c_p^+]\!], [\![z_p]\!] \leftarrow \mathsf{CmpZ}([\![p_1]\!] - [\![p_2]\!], g + 1);$ // $4; g + 6$
2 $[\![d]\!]_{2t} \leftarrow (1 - 2[\![s_1]\!]) * [\![v_1]\!] - (1 - 2[\![s_2]\!]) * [\![v_2]\!];$
3 $[\![c_v^-]\!] \leftarrow \mathsf{LTZD}([\![d]\!]_{2t}, \ell + 1);$ // $0; \ell + 2$
4 $[\![c]\!] \leftarrow [\![z_p]\!][\![c_v^-]\!] + [\![c_p^-]\!](1 - [\![s_2]\!]) + [\![c_p^+]\!][\![s_1]\!];$ // $1; 1$
5 **return** $[\![c]\!];$

The algorithm can be implemented by computing c_p^- and z_p using the protocols LTZ and EQZ [8] and $c_p^+ = (1 - c_p^-)(1 - z_p)$. However, Protocol 12, CmpZ, computes the triple integer comparison more efficiently and offers a simpler solution for LTFL: step 1 computes c_p^-, c_p^+ and z_p using CmpZ, steps 2–3 compute c_v^- using LTZD, and step 4 computes the output.

CmpZ takes on input a secret integer $\bar{a} \in \mathbb{Z}_{\langle k \rangle}$ and outputs the secret bits $c_1 = (\bar{a} < 0)?\ 1:0$, $c_2 = (\bar{a} > 0)?\ 1:0$, and $c_3 = (\bar{a} = 0)?\ 1:0$. Essentially, it extends LTZ to compute the bits c_2 and c_3, besides c_1. Steps 1–5 compute $c_1 = -\lfloor \bar{a}/2^{k-1} \rfloor$ like LTZ, except that step 4 uses Protocol 13, BitCmp, instead of BitLT [8]. Steps 1–3 compute and reveal $b = 2^{k-1} + \bar{a} + r$, where $r = 2^{k-1}r'' + r'$ is a random secret integer that hides $\bar{a}$ with statistical secrecy and $r' = \sum_{i=1}^{k-1} 2^{i-1}r_i$, with $\{r'_i\}_{i=1}^{k-1}$ uniformly random secret bits. Let $b' = b \bmod 2^{k-1}$ and $a' = \bar{a} \bmod 2^{k-1}$. Step 4 computes $u_1 = (b' < r')?\ 1:0$ and $u_2 = (b' = r')?\ 1:0$. Observe that $b' = a' + r' - 2^{k-1}u_1$, so $\lfloor \bar{a}/2^{k-1} \rfloor = (\bar{a} - (b' - r'))2^{-(k-1)} - u_1$. Also, $u_2 = 1$ if $\bar{a} = 0$ or $\bar{a} = -2^{k-1}$, so $c_2 = (1 - c_1)(1 - u_2)$ and $c_3 = (1 - c_1)u_2$.

Protocol 12: CmpZ($[\![a]\!], k$).

1 $([\![r'']\!], [\![r']\!], \{[\![r'_i]\!]\}_{i=1}^{k-1}) \leftarrow \mathsf{PRandM}(k, k - 1);$ // prec: $1; k - 1$
2 $b \leftarrow \mathsf{Reveal}(2^{k-1} + [\![a]\!] + 2^{k-1}[\![r'']\!] + [\![r']\!]);$ // $1; 1$
3 $b' \leftarrow b \bmod 2^{k-1};$
4 $([\![u_1]\!], [\![u_2]\!]) \leftarrow \mathsf{BitCmp}(b', \{[\![r'_i]\!]\}_{i=1}^{k-1});$ // $2; k + 2$
5 $[\![c_1]\!] \leftarrow -(([\![a]\!] - (b' - [\![r']\!]))2^{-(k-1)} - [\![u_1]\!]);$
6 $[\![c_2]\!] \leftarrow (1 - [\![c_1]\!])(1 - [\![u_2]\!]);$ // $1; 1$
7 $[\![c_3]\!] \leftarrow (1 - [\![c_1]\!])[\![u_2]\!];$ // $0; 1$
8 **return** $([\![c_1]\!], [\![c_2]\!], [\![c_3]\!]);$

BitCmp takes on input a public integer $\bar{a} = \sum_{i=1}^{k} 2^{i-1}a_i$ and a bitwise-shared integer $\bar{b} = \sum_{i=1}^{k} 2^{i-1}b_i$, and outputs the secret bits $u_1 = (\bar{a} < \bar{b})?\ 1:0$ and $u_2 = (\bar{a} = \bar{b})?\ 1:0$. BitCmp extends the protocol BitLT [8] so that it returns u_2, besides u_1, with almost the same complexity. Steps 1–5 compute u_1 like BitLT.

Step 3 computes $p_i = \prod_{j=i}^{k}(d_j + 1)$, for $i \in [1, k]$, where $d_j = a_j \oplus b_j$. If $a = b$ then $p_1 = 1$, else p_1 is a power of 2, so $u_2 = p_1 \mod 2$.

Protocol 13: $\mathsf{BitCmp}(a, \{[\![b_i]\!]\}_{i=1}^{k})$.

---

1 **foreach** $i \in [1, k]$ **do** $[\![d_i]\!] \leftarrow a_i \oplus [\![b_i]\!]$;

2 **foreach** $i \in [1, k]$ **do** $c_i \leftarrow 1 - a_i$;

3 $\{[\![p_i]\!]\}_{i=1}^{k} \leftarrow \mathsf{SufMul}(\{[\![d_i + 1]\!]\}_{i=1}^{k})$;   // $1; k$

4 $[\![s_1]\!] \leftarrow c_k[\![d_k]\!] + \sum_{i=1}^{k-1} c_i([\![p_i]\!] - [\![p_{i+1}]\!])$;

5 $[\![u_1]\!] \leftarrow \mathsf{Mod2}([\![s_1]\!], k)$;   // $1; 1$

6 $[\![u_2]\!] \leftarrow \mathsf{Mod2}([\![p_1]\!], k)$;   // $0; 1$

7 **return** $([\![u_1]\!], [\![u_2]\!])$;

LTFL can also be used for the other inequality tests: $c = (\hat{a}_1 < \hat{a}_2)?\ 1 : 0 = (\hat{a}_2 > \hat{a}_1)?\ 1 : 0$ and $1 - c = (\hat{a}_1 \geq \hat{a}_2)?\ 1 : 0 = (\hat{a}_2 \leq \hat{a}_1)?\ 1 : 0$. Moreover, it also works when an operand is public, with the same complexity.

Equality test. Protocol 14, EQFL, computes $c = (\hat{a}_1 = \hat{a}_2)?\ 1 : 0$, for $\hat{a}_1, \hat{a}_2 \in \mathbb{Q}_{\langle \ell, g \rangle}^{FL}$, with secret inputs and output [7].

Protocol 14: $\mathsf{EQFL}(\{[\![v_i]\!], [\![p_i]\!], [\![s_i]\!]\}_{i=1}^{2})$.

---

1 $[\![b_1]\!] \leftarrow 2^{\ell+1}[\![p_1]\!] + 2^{\ell}[\![s_1]\!] + [\![v_1]\!]$;

2 $[\![b_2]\!] \leftarrow 2^{\ell+1}[\![p_2]\!] + 2^{\ell}[\![s_2]\!] + [\![v_2]\!]$;

3 $[\![c]\!] \leftarrow \mathsf{EQZ}([\![b_1]\!] - [\![b_2]\!], \ell + g + 2)$;   // $3; \log(\ell + g + 2) + 1$

4 **return** $[\![c]\!]$;

EQFL is based on the following remark. Let $\hat{a}_1 = (1 - s_1)\bar{v}_1 2^{\bar{p}_1}$, $\hat{a}_2 = (1 - s_2)\bar{v}_2 2^{\bar{p}_2}$, and $c = (\hat{a}_1 = \hat{a}_2)?\ 1 : 0$. Also, let $\Delta = 2^{\ell+1}(\bar{p}_1 - \bar{p}_2) + 2^{\ell}(\bar{s}_1 - \bar{s}_2) + (\bar{v}_1 - \bar{v}_2) = 2^{\ell+1}\bar{d}_p + 2^{\ell}\bar{d}_s + \bar{d}_v$. Observe that $\bar{d}_s \in \{-1, 0, 1\}$ and $|\bar{d}_v| < 2^{\ell}$. If $\bar{d}_s \neq 0$ and $\bar{d}_p \neq 0$ then $0 < |2^{\ell}\bar{d}_s + \bar{d}_v| < |2^{\ell+1}\bar{d}_p|$, hence $\Delta \neq 0$. Thus, $\Delta = 0$ if and only if $\bar{d}_p = 0$, $\bar{d}_s = 0$, and $\bar{d}_v = 0$, hence $c = (\Delta = 0)?\ 1 : 0$.

Complexity and Performance. The complexity of CmpZ is 4 rounds, $k + 5$ online interactive operations, and $3k$ precomputation operations. CmpZ is an interesting integer comparison protocol, that computes a triple comparison with the same communication complexity as LTZ and a single additional round. CmpZ can be used, like LTZ, to compute any integer inequality test [8].

LTFL needs 5 rounds, $\ell + g + 9$ online interactive operations, and $3(\ell + g + 2)$ precomputation operations, similar to the comparison of k-bit fixed-point numbers using LTZ, for $k = \ell + g$. LTFL adds 2 rounds, but usually $\ell + g \leq k$, so the communication complexity is lower. EQFL has the same complexity as EQZ.

Table 7 shows the running time of LTFL and EQFL for implementations with the complexity listed in Table 3. LTFL and MulFL have the same complexity and running time, dominated by a comparison of ℓ-bit integers.

Table 7. Running time of LTFL and EQFL protocols (milliseconds/operation).

LTFL	1		10		20		50		100	
LAN	Online	Prec.	Online	Prec.	Online	Prec.	Online	Prec.	Online	Prec.
$\ell = 24$	0.46	0.91	0.23	0.77	0.21	0.73	0.20	0.74	0.19	0.74
$\ell = 53$	0.68	1.84	0.40	1.60	0.38	1.59	0.37	1.60	0.36	1.54
Internet	Online	Prec.	Online	Prec.	Online	Prec.	Online	Prec.	Online	Prec.
$\ell = 24$	51.89	33.24	5.68	5.09	3.14	3.68	1.54	2.41	0.97	1.72
$\ell = 53$	52.59	35.97	6.25	7.69	3.55	5.70	1.88	3.62	1.40	3.16
EQFL	1		10		20		50		100	
LAN	Online	Prec.	Online	Prec.	Online	Prec.	Online	Prec.	Online	Prec.
$\ell = 24$	0.32	0.68	0.10	0.52	0.08	0.49	0.07	0.47	0.07	0.47
$\ell = 53$	0.38	0.98	0.14	0.81	0.11	0.81	0.11	0.81	0.11	0.69
Internet	Online	Prec.	Online	Prec.	Online	Prec.	Online	Prec.	Online	Prec.
$\ell = 24$	31.24	32.34	3.31	4.55	1.75	2.98	0.82	1.90	0.47	1.33
$\ell = 53$	31.36	33.31	3.39	5.46	1.83	3.86	0.88	2.45	0.55	1.61

7   Conclusions

We examined the family of protocols for secure computation with floating-point numbers proposed in [7], to provide a more comprehensive analysis of their construction, complexity, and running time, as well as several improvements.

The protocols run a synchronized distributed computation structured as a sequence of rounds consisting of local processing and interaction. The complexity analysis uses two metrics: the number of interactive primitives (communication complexity), that accounts for exchanged data and local computation during the execution of these primitives, and the number of rounds, that captures the effects of other communication delays, independent of the amount of data. Both metrics ignore other local computation, although sometimes it cannot be neglected.

The protocols offer arbitrary-precision floating-point arithmetic with the parameters ℓ, the bit-length of the normalized, unsigned integer significand, and g, the bit-length of the signed integer exponent. The precision affects the protocols' complexity in two ways (Table 2):

– Larger significands require larger fields, hence more data to send and more expensive field arithmetic. Supporting all operations requires $q > 2^{2\ell+\kappa+8}$.
– The precomputation and online communication complexity depend on ℓ and g, due to binary computation in some sub-tasks. The number of rounds is constant for AddFL, MulFL, LTFL, and almost constant for DivFL and SqrtFL.

The protocols work accurately for the entire range of practically relevant values of ℓ and g, enabling tradeoffs between accuracy and performance according to application requirements. To evaluate the performance differences, we measured the running time for standard single and double floating-point precision. The results agree (roughly) with the complexity analysis, but the execution environment also has a strong influence.

Secure computation based on secret sharing relies on interactive primitives that exchange tiny amounts of data (each party sends a field element to the others). Therefore, the communication overhead and delays are substantially reduced by executing the primitives in parallel. This optimization achieves higher performance gains for lighter primitives (e.g., smaller field or ring), protocols that trade off higher round complexity for lower communication complexity, and implementations optimized for massive parallel computation.

The tests with batches of floating-point operations show the effects of processing the interactive primitives in parallel: the running time per operation decreases for larger batches and the effects are stronger for longer network delay and protocols with lower communication complexity.

As a side effect of these optimizations, the distribution of workload to rounds is no longer uniform: the work done in a round depends on the number of primitives executed in parallel, which can vary by orders of magnitude. Moreover, the design of the protocols involves tradeoffs between communication and round complexity or precomputation and online complexity: we have to choose between solutions that reduce some metrics at the cost of increasing others.

The relations between complexity metrics and running time are affected to a large extent by the execution environment:

- In LAN tests, high data rates (1 or 10 Gbps) and near-zero network delay strongly attenuate the effects of the amount of exchanged data and the number of rounds, while increasing the contribution of local processing, as well as the effects of implementation optimizations.
- The opposite happens in Internet tests, due to longer delay and lower data rate. The running time for an operation is determined by network delay and the number of rounds, and decreases gradually for larger batches.

The precomputation generates the shared random values for an entire task in 1–3 rounds (depending on implementation) with relatively large computation and communication complexity. This is due to building blocks that trade off larger precomputation complexity for lower round and online communication complexity (Table 1). The execution environment also affects the precomputation. In Internet tests, the precomputation time per operation depends mainly on communication delays and decreases steadily for larger batches. In LAN tests, it hardly changes, since a large part of it is local computation time.

These factors complicate the evaluation of the protocols based on complexity analysis. The complexity metrics offer useful insight and performance predictions, but we need experiments to evaluate the effects of tradeoffs, different execution environments, and computation ignored by the complexity analysis.

The parties can allocate local resources according to their budget and performance requirements, but have little or no control of end-to-end Internet performance. Therefore, using parallel algorithms and precomputation to reduce the communication delays is a valid approach to optimizing secure computation. However, achieving the expected benefits requires implementations that efficiently use the processing and communication resources (distribute the workload on multiple cores, exploit bulk data transfer techniques, and so on).

The different behavior observed in LAN tests and Internet tests shows how important it is to evaluate and optimize the protocols for execution environments that are similar to those of the target deployment scenarios. In practical deployments, with several organizations that communicate via the Internet, the protocols' running time is dominated by communication delays, while in LAN tests the contribution of these delays is strongly attenuated.

References

1. Aliasgari, M., Blanton, M., Zhang, Y., Steele, A.: Secure computation on floating point numbers. In: 20th Annual Network and Distributed System Security Symposium (NDSS 2013) (2013)
2. Aliasgari, M., Blanton, M., Bayatbabolghani, F.: Secure computation of hidden Markov models and secure floating-point arithmetic in the malicious model. Int. J. Inf. Secur. **16**(6), 577–601 (2017)
3. Aly, A., Smart, N.P.: Benchmarking privacy preserving scientific operations. In: Deng, R.H., Gauthier-Umaña, V., Ochoa, M., Yung, M. (eds.) ACNS 2019. LNCS, vol. 11464, pp. 509–529. Springer, Cham (2019). https://doi.org/10.1007/978-3-030-21568-2_25
4. Bogdanov, D., Kamm, L., Laur, S., Sokk, V.: Rmind: a tool for cryptographically secure statistical analysis. IEEE Trans. Dependable Secur. Comput. **15**(3), 481–495 (2018)
5. Bogdanov, D., Niitsoo, M., Toft, T., Willemson, J.: High-performance secure multiparty computation for data mining applications. Int. J. Inf. Secur. **11**(6), 403–418 (2012)
6. Catrina, O.: Round-efficient protocols for secure multiparty fixed-point arithmetic. In: 12th International Conference on Communications (COMM 2018), pp. 431–436. IEEE (2018)
7. Catrina, O.: Efficient secure floating-point arithmetic using Shamir secret sharing. In: 16th International Joint Conference on e-Business and Telecommunications: SECRYPT (Security and Cryptography), vol. 2, pp. 49–60. SciTePress (2019)
8. Catrina, O., de Hoogh, S.: Improved primitives for secure multiparty integer computation. In: Garay, J.A., De Prisco, R. (eds.) SCN 2010. LNCS, vol. 6280, pp. 182–199. Springer, Heidelberg (2010). https://doi.org/10.1007/978-3-642-15317-4_13
9. Catrina, O., de Hoogh, S.: Secure multiparty linear programming using fixed-point arithmetic. In: Gritzalis, D., Preneel, B., Theoharidou, M. (eds.) ESORICS 2010. LNCS, vol. 6345, pp. 134–150. Springer, Heidelberg (2010). https://doi.org/10.1007/978-3-642-15497-3_9
10. Catrina, O., Saxena, A.: Secure computation with fixed-point numbers. In: Sion, R. (ed.) FC 2010. LNCS, vol. 6052, pp. 35–50. Springer, Heidelberg (2010). https://doi.org/10.1007/978-3-642-14577-3_6
11. Cramer, R., Damgård, I., Ishai, Y.: Share conversion, pseudorandom secret-sharing and applications to secure computation. In: Kilian, J. (ed.) TCC 2005. LNCS, vol. 3378, pp. 342–362. Springer, Heidelberg (2005). https://doi.org/10.1007/978-3-540-30576-7_19
12. Cramer, R., Damgård, I., Nielsen, J.B.: Secure Multiparty Computation and Secret Sharing. Cambridge University Press, UK (2015)

13. Damgård, I., Thorbek, R.: Non-interactive proofs for integer multiplication. In: Naor, M. (ed.) EUROCRYPT 2007. LNCS, vol. 4515, pp. 412–429. Springer, Heidelberg (2007). https://doi.org/10.1007/978-3-540-72540-4_24

14. Damgård, I., Fitzi, M., Kiltz, E., Nielsen, J.B., Toft, T.: Unconditionally secure constant-rounds multi-party computation for equality, comparison, bits and exponentiation. In: Halevi, S., Rabin, T. (eds.) TCC 2006. LNCS, vol. 3876, pp. 285–304. Springer, Heidelberg (2006). https://doi.org/10.1007/11681878_15

15. Dimitrov, V., Kerik, L., Krips, T., Randmets, J., Willemson, J.: Alternative implementations of secure real numbers. In: 23rd ACM Conference on Computer and Communications Security (CCS 2016), pp. 553–564. ACM (2016)

16. Ercegovac, M.D., Lang, T.: Digital Arithmetic. Morgan Kaufmann, Burlington (2003)

17. Kamm, L., Willemson, J.: Secure floating point arithmetic and private satellite collision analysis. Int. J. Inf. Secur. 14(6), 531–548 (2015)

18. Markstein, P.: Software division and square root using Goldschmidt's algorithms. In: 6th Conference on Real Numbers and Computers, pp. 146–157 (2004)

19. Reistad, T., Toft, T.: Linear, constant-rounds bit-decomposition. In: Lee, D., Hong, S. (eds.) ICISC 2009. LNCS, vol. 5984, pp. 245–257. Springer, Heidelberg (2010). https://doi.org/10.1007/978-3-642-14423-3_17

Secure and Efficient Matrix Multiplication with MapReduce

Radu Ciucanu[1]([✉]), Matthieu Giraud[2], Pascal Lafourcade[2], and Lihua Ye[3]

[1] INSA Centre Val de Loire, Univ. Orléans, LIFO EA 4022, Bourges, France
radu.ciucanu@insa-cvl.fr
[2] Université Clermont Auvergne, LIMOS CNRS UMR 6158, Aubière, France
{matthieu.giraud,pascal.lafourcade}@uca.fr
[3] Harbin Institute of Technology, Harbin, China
16s003041@stu.hit.edu.cn

Abstract. MapReduce is one of the most popular distributed programming paradigms that allows processing big data sets in parallel on a cluster. MapReduce users often outsource data and computations to a public cloud, which yields inherent security concerns. In this paper, we consider the problem of matrix multiplication and one of the most efficient matrix multiplication algorithms: the Strassen-Winograd (SW) algorithm. Our first contribution is a distributed MapReduce algorithm based on SW. Then, we tackle the security concerns that occur when outsourcing matrix multiplication computation to a honest-but-curious cloud i.e., that executes tasks dutifully, but tries to learn as much information as possible. Our main contribution is a secure distributed MapReduce algorithm called S2M3 (**S**ecure **S**trassen-**W**inograd **M**atrix **M**ultiplication with **M**apReduce) that enjoys security guarantees such as: none of the cloud nodes can learn the input or the output data. We formally prove the security properties of S2M3 and we present an empirical evaluation devoted to show its efficiency.

Keywords: Cloud security · Privacy-preserving cloud computations · MapReduce · Matrix multiplication · Strassen-Winograd algorithm

1 Introduction

Matrix multiplication is a mathematical tool useful for solving various problems spanning over a plethora of domains e.g., statistical analysis, medicine, image processing, machine learning or web ranking. Indeed, Markov chains applications on genetics and sociology [6], or applications such that computation of shortest paths [28,32], convolutional neural network [21] deal with data processed as matrix multiplication. In such applications, the size of the matrices to be multiplied is often very large. The matrix multiplication is also the original purpose for which the Google implementation of MapReduce was created. Indeed, such multiplications are needed by Google in the computation of the

M. S. Obaidat (Ed.): ICETE 2019, CCIS 1247, pp. 132–156, 2020.
https://doi.org/10.1007/978-3-030-52686-3_6

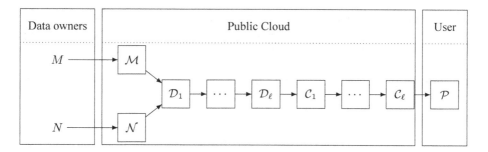

Fig. 1. Architecture of SW matrix multiplication with MapReduce.

PageRank algorithm [12]. Whereas a naive matrix multiplication algorithm has cubic complexity, many research efforts have been made to propose more efficient algorithms. One of the most efficient algorithms is Strassen-Winograd [25,29] (denoted as SW in the sequel), the first sub-cubic time algorithm, with an exponent $\log_2 7 \approx 2.81$. The best algorithm known to date [18] has an exponent ≈ 2.38. Although many of the sub-cubic algorithms are not necessarily suited for practical use as their hidden constant in the big-O notation is huge, the SW algorithm and its variants emerged as a class of matrix multiplication algorithms in widespread use.

In this paper, we tackle the problem of distributing the SW algorithm using the MapReduce paradigm and we address the inherent security concerns that occur when outsourcing data and computations to a public cloud. The outsourced data can be communicated over some network and processed on some machines where malicious cloud admins could learn and leak sensitive data.

Problem Statement. Two distinct data owners respectively hold compatible square matrices M and N of dimension $d \in \mathbb{N}^*$. A user (who does not know the matrices M and N) wants their product $P := MN$. Matrices M and N are sent to the distributed file system of some public cloud provider. We assume that the matrices M (resp. N) is initially spread over a set $\mathcal{M}$ (resp. $\mathcal{N}$) of nodes of the public cloud storing a chunk of M (resp. N), i.e., a set of elements of M (resp. N). The final result P is computed over sets of nodes $\mathcal{D}_1, \ldots, \mathcal{D}_\ell, \mathcal{C}_1, \ldots, \mathcal{C}_\ell$ before it is sent to the user's nodes $\mathcal{P}$, where ℓ depends on the dimension d. Moreover, we assume that data owners (resp. the user) cannot collude with the public cloud and the user (resp. the public cloud and data owners). We illustrate the architecture of SW matrix multiplication with MapReduce in Fig. 1.

We expect the following security properties:

1. The user cannot learn any information about input matrices M and N,
2. Cloud nodes cannot learn any information about matrices M, N, and P.

Related Work. Chapter 2 of [22] presents an introduction to the MapReduce paradigm. The security and privacy concerns of MapReduce have been summarized in a recent survey [13]. The state-of-the-art techniques for secure execution of MapReduce computations focus on problems such as word search [3], information retrieval [26], grouping and aggregation [7], equijoins [5,14], set intersection [9], and matrix multiplication [4]. The goal of these works is similar to ours i.e., execute MapReduce computations such that the public cloud cannot learn any information on the input or output data.

In this paper, we focus on matrix multiplication. Recently, [4] secured the two standard MapReduce algorithms for matrix multiplication using one and two MapReduce rounds cf. Chap. 2 of [22]. For each algorithm, they proposed two approaches: SP (*Secure-Private*) and CRSP (*Collision-Resistance Secure-Private*). The two approaches are based on the Paillier partially homomorphic cryptosystem [27]. Contrary to the CRSP approach, the SP approach assumes that cloud nodes do not collude. In this paper, we assume that all cloud nodes can collude, hence our secure protocol S2M3 can be considered as a CRSP approach. We show that MapReduce matrix multiplication can be done faster using the SW algorithm, compared to the standard MapReduce matrix multiplication for both no-secure and secure approaches.

Distributed matrix multiplication has been thoroughly investigated in the secure multi-party computation model (MPC) [1,15,16,30], whose goal is to allow different nodes to jointly compute a function over their private inputs without revealing them. The aforementioned works on secure distributed matrix multiplication have different assumptions compared to our MapReduce framework: (i) they assume that nodes contain entire vectors, whereas the division of the initial matrices in chunks as done in MapReduce does not have such assumptions, and (ii) in MapReduce, the functions specified by the user [12] are limited to *map* (process a key/value pair to generate a set of intermediate key/value pairs) and *reduce* (merge all intermediate values associated with the same intermediate key) while the MPC model relies on more complex functions than map and reduce. Moreover, generic MPC protocols [11,24] allow several nodes to securely evaluate any function such that matrix multiplication computation. Such protocols could be used to secure MapReduce. However, due to their generic nature, they are inefficient and require a lot of interactions between parties. Our goal is to design a secure and efficient MapReduce protocol based on the SW algorithm.

Summary of Contributions and Paper Organization. This paper is an extension of our previous paper [10], which is to the best of our knowledge the first one to propose a secure MapReduce protocol based on the SW algorithm. We next discuss the organization and contributions of this paper.

- In Sect. 2, we introduce preliminary notions: crypographic tools and the basic SW algorithm.
- In Sect. 3, we present our first contribution, that is a MapReduce version of the SW matrix multiplication algorithm. We call our protocol SM3 (**S**trassen-**W**inograd Matrix Multiplication with **M**apReduce).
- In Sect. 4, we present our secure protocol for SW matrix multiplication with MapReduce, which is the main contribution of the paper. Our secure protocol S2M3 (**S**ecure **S**trassen-Winograd **M**atrix **M**ultiplication with **M**apReduce)

relies on the MapReduce paradigm and on Paillier's public-key cryptosystem. The public cloud performs the multiplication on the encrypted data. At the end of the computation, the public cloud sends the result to the user that queried the matrix multiplication result. The user has just to decrypt the result to discover the matrix multiplication result. The public cloud cannot learn none of the input or output matrices.

– In Sect. 5, we present an experimental evaluation of our two MapReduce protocols (SM3 and S2M3) using Hadoop [17], the Apache MapReduce implementation.

– In Sect. 6, we formally prove, using a standard security model, that the S2M3 protocol satisfies the security properties from the problem statement, which hold even in the presence of collusions among the cloud's nodes.
  All theorems and lemmas from this paper are new with respect to the first version of our paper [10].

– In Sect. 7, we discuss conclusions and future work.

The main novel content of this paper w.r.t. [10] *consists of new non-trivial proofs, which significantly add more than 30% of new material (the volume of the paper actually increased from 8 to 25 pages). Moreover, as required in the instructions, we have enriched the paper structure, and avoided as much as possible the verbatim repetitions e.g., we have changed the title, abstract, introduction, as well as the presentation of the subset of material that is common to* [10]. *Moreover, among the figures in this paper, only the 2 from Sect. 5 are common to* [10].

2   Preliminaries

We present cryptographic tools in Sect. 2.1 and the SW algorithm in Sect. 2.2

2.1   Cryptographic Tools

Notations. We define some notations that we use throughout the paper.

$a\|b$	Concatenation of two strings a and b
$x \xleftarrow{\$} E$	Uniformly random choice of a value x from the set E
$\text{lcm}(a, b)$	Least common multiple of two integers a and b
$a := b + c$	Set the result of $b + c$ into a
$S^{a \times b}$	Matrix of a rows and b columns with elements in S
$A \times B$	Cartesian product between A and B
ε	Empty string

Negligible Function. A function $\mu : \mathbb{N} \to \mathbb{R}^+$ is called *negligible* if for every positive polynomial $p(\cdot)$ there exists $N_p \in \mathbb{N}$ such that for all integers $x > N_p$, we have $\mu(x) < 1/p(x)$.

Experiments. Security property of a cryptosystem can be proven using an *experiment* (or game). We call an experiment, an algorithm that proposes some *challenge* to an adversary (i.e., a probabilistic polynomial-time algorithm). The challenge can be considered as an algorithmic problem that the adversary tries to solve. If the adversary successfully resolves the challenge, we say that the adversary *wins the experiment*.

In order to have concrete adversary model, the adversary may have access to black-box algorithms (sometimes with some restrictions), called *oracles*. An oracle allows the adversary to learn some information that she cannot obtain by herself in order to solve the experiment. For instance, an oracle can be an algorithm that decrypts some ciphertexts using a key that the adversary does not know. We denote by $\mathcal{A}^{\mathsf{Oracle}}$ to mean that the adversary $\mathcal{A}$ has access to the oracle denoted Oracle.

When there is no such an adversary that wins the experiment with a non-negligible probability in polynomial-time, then we say that the cryptosystem is secure according to the considered property.

Computational Indistinguishability [23]. We first recall that a *distribution ensemble* is a sequence of random variables indexed by a countable set. In the context of secure computation, this sequence of random variables are indexed by $I \in \mathcal{I}$ where $\mathcal{I}$ is the set of all inputs of parties, and by the security parameter $\lambda \in \mathbb{N}$, i.e., $X_0 := \{X(I, \lambda)\}_{I \in \mathcal{I}, \lambda \in \mathbb{N}}$.

Let $X_0 := \{X(I, \lambda)\}_{I \in \mathcal{I}, \lambda \in \mathbb{N}}$ and $Y_0 := \{Y(I, \lambda)\}_{I \in \mathcal{I}, \lambda \in \mathbb{N}}$ be two distribution ensembles. We say that X_0 and Y_0 are *computationally indistinguishable* if for every probabilistic polynomial algorithm D outputting a single bit, there exists a negligible function $\mu(\cdot)$ such that for every $I \in \mathcal{I}$ and every $\lambda \in \mathbb{N}$, we have

$$\big| \Pr[D(X(I, \lambda)) = 1] - \Pr[D(Y(I, \lambda) = 1] \big| \leq \mu(\lambda) \, .$$

We call the algorithm D a *distinguisher*, and we denote by $X_0 \stackrel{c}{\equiv} Y_0$ two computationally indistinguishable distribution ensembles.

Simulation-Based Proofs. The security proofs from this paper follow the ideal/real simulation paradigm [20]. In other terms, proofs are based on the indistinguishability of two different distribution ensembles X^0 and X^1. However, in many cases it is infeasible to directly prove this indistinguishability. Instead, we use the *hybrid argument* consisting in the construction of *simulators* that generate a sequence of distributions ensembles, starting with X^0, and ending with X^1. Then, we prove that consecutive distribution ensembles are indistinguishable. The indistinguishability between X^0 and X^1 is therefore obtained by transitivity.

Secure Multiparty Computation. Some cryptographic protocols involve several participants, called *parties*, in order to jointly compute a function over their inputs while keeping those inputs private. This model is called *multiparty computation* [31]. Unlike traditional cryptosystems where the adversary is outside of the system and tries, for instance, to break the confidentiality or the integrity of communication, the adversary in this model controls one of the parties. We consider *semi-honest* (or *honest-but-curious*) adversaries [19]. Such an adversary controls one of the parties and follows the protocol specification exactly.

However, it may try to learn more information than allowed by looking at the transcript of message that it received and its internal state. A protocol that is secure in the presence of semi-honest adversaries does guarantee that there is no *inadvertent leakage* of information.

Intuitively, a multiparty protocol is secure if whatever can be computed by a party participating in the protocol can be computed based on its input and output *only*. This idea is formalized according to the simulation paradigm by requiring the existence of a *simulator* who generates the *view* of a party, i.e., all values received, computed, and sent by this party during an execution of the protocol. More formally, the view is defined as follows: Let $\lambda \in \mathbb{N}$ be a security parameter, and π be a n-party protocol. The view of the party P_i, for all $i \in [\![1, n]\!]$, during an execution of π on $I = (I_i)_{i \in [\![1, n]\!]}$ is denoted $\text{view}_{P_i}^{\pi}(I, \lambda)$ and equals (I_i, M_i, O_i), where I_i is the input of P_i, M_i represents messages sent by other parties and received by P_i, and O_i is the output of P_i computed from I_i and M_i during the protocol execution. We denote by $\text{view}_{P_i, P_j}^{\pi}(I, \lambda) = (\text{view}_{P_i}^{\pi}(I, \lambda), \text{view}_{P_j}^{\pi}(I, \lambda))$, with $i, j \in [\![1, n]\!]$, the joint view of a collusion between parties P_i and P_j.

Since the parties have input and output, the simulator must be given a party's input and output in order to generate its view. Thus, the security is formalized by saying that there exists a simulator that simulates a party's view in a protocol execution given its *input* and *output*. The formalization implies that a party cannot extract any information from her view during the protocol *execution* beyond what they can derive from their input and prescribed output.

We now formally define the security of a multiparty protocol with respect to static semi-honest adversaries [23]: Let π be a n-party protocol that computes the function $f = (f_i)_{i \in [\![1, n]\!]}$ for parties $(P_i)_{i \in [\![1, n]\!]}$ using inputs $I = (I_i)_{i \in [\![1, n]\!]} \in \mathcal{I}$ and security parameter $\lambda \in \mathbb{N}$. We say that π *securely computes* f *in the presence of static semi-honest adversaries* if there exists, for each party P_i with $i \in [\![1, n]\!]$, a probabilistic polynomial-time simulator $\mathcal{S}_i$ such that $\mathcal{S}_{P_i}(1^{\lambda}, I_i, f_i(I)) \overset{c}{\equiv} \text{view}_{P_i}^{\pi}(I, \lambda)$. We say that π is *secure against collusions* between parties P_i and P_j with $i, j \in [\![1, n]\!]$, if there exists probabilistic polynomial-time simulators $\mathcal{S}_{P_i, P_j}$ such that $\mathcal{S}_{P_i, P_j}((1^{\lambda}, I_i, f_i(I)), (1^{\lambda}, I_j, f_j(I))) \overset{c}{\equiv} \text{view}_{P_i, P_j}^{\pi}(I, \lambda)$.

Asymmetric Encryption. Let $\lambda \in \mathbb{N}$ be a security parameter. An *asymmetric encryption* scheme is a triple of polynomial-time algorithms $(\mathcal{G}, \mathcal{E}, \mathcal{D})$ such that

- $\mathcal{G}(1^{\lambda})$ is a probabilistic algorithm that takes as input the security parameter λ, and outputs a private key sk from the secret key space $\mathcal{K}_s$, a public key pk from the public key space $\mathcal{K}_p$, a plaintext space $\mathcal{M}$, and a ciphertext message $\mathcal{C}$.
- $\mathcal{E}(pk, m)$ is a deterministic or probabilistic algorithm that takes as input a public key $pk \in \mathcal{K}_p$ and a plaintext $m \in \mathcal{M}$, and outputs a ciphertext $c \in \mathcal{C}$.
- $\mathcal{D}(sk, c)$ is a deterministic algorithm that takes as input a secret key $sk \in \mathcal{K}_s$ and a ciphertext $c \in \mathcal{C}$, and outputs either a plaintext $m \in \mathcal{M}$ or a special reject value (distinct from all messages).

In the following, we only consider *correct* asymmetric encryption schemes, that is schemes such that, for any $\lambda \in \mathbb{N}$, we have

$$\Pr \left[(sk, pk, \mathcal{M}, \mathcal{C}) := \mathcal{G}(1^\lambda); m \xleftarrow{\$} \mathcal{M}; m' := \mathcal{D}(sk, m) \colon m = m' \right] = 1 .$$

Indistinguishability Under Chosen Plaintext Attack. The *indistinguishability under chosen plaintext attack* is a fundamental security property for asymmetric encryption schemes. Intuitively, this security notion implies that two different plaintexts can be distinguished by their respective ciphertext. In other terms, a ciphertext leaks no information about its corresponding plaintext.

Consider an adversary that chooses a couple of plaintexts (m_0, m_1), and that receives the encryption of one of the two plaintexts. If such an adversary is not able to guess the chosen message with a non-negligible probability, then the asymmetric encryption scheme achieves the indistinguishability security under chosen plaintext attack.

The basic definition of indistinguishability under chosen plaintext attack allows one adversary to submit a couple of plaintexts only one time. However, it is know that the indistinguishability security under chosen plaintext attack is equivalent to the indistinguishability security under *multiple chosen plaintexts* attack in a multi-user setting [2]. That means the adversary can receive several public keys and choose several couples of plaintexts (m_0, m_1). For each of these couples, the adversary receives the encryption of m_b for the different public keys, where the same $b \in \{0, 1\}$ is used each time.

More precisely, we use the Left-Or-Right definition [2]. Let $\Pi = (\mathcal{G}, \mathcal{E}, \mathcal{D})$ be an asymmetric encryption scheme, $\mathcal{A} \in \text{PPT}(\lambda)$, and $(\alpha, \beta) \in \mathbb{N}^2$. For all $i \in [\![1, \beta]\!]$, the oracle $\mathcal{E}(pk_i, (\text{LoR}_b(\cdot, \cdot), \alpha))$ takes as input a couple of plaintexts (m_0, m_1), and returns $\mathcal{E}(pk_i, m_b)$. Moreover, this oracle cannot be called more than α times.

We define the (α, β)-indistinguishability under chosen plaintext attack (IND-CPA) experiment, denoted $\text{Exp}_{\Pi, \mathcal{A}}^{\text{indcpa-}b_{\alpha, \beta}}$ for the adversary $\mathcal{A}$ against Π in Fig. 2.

Experiment: $\text{Exp}_{\Pi, \mathcal{A}}^{\text{indcpa-}b_{\alpha, \beta}}(\lambda)$

foreach $i \in [\![1, \beta]\!]$ **do**
  | $(sk_i, pk_i, \mathcal{M}_i, \mathcal{C}_i) := \mathcal{G}(\lambda)$
$b_* := \mathcal{A}^{\mathcal{E}(pk_1, (\text{LoR}_b(\cdot, \cdot), \alpha)), \dots, \mathcal{E}(pk_\beta, (\text{LoR}_b(\cdot, \cdot), \alpha))}(\lambda)$
return b_*

Fig. 2. IND-CPA experiment.

We define the advantage of the adversary $\mathcal{A}$ with respect to Π as follows

$$\text{Adv}_{\Pi, \mathcal{A}}^{\text{indcpa}_{\alpha, \beta}}(\lambda) := \left| \Pr \left[\text{Exp}_{\Pi, \mathcal{A}}^{\text{indcpa-}1_{\alpha, \beta}}(\lambda) = 1 \right] - \Pr \left[\text{Exp}_{\Pi, \mathcal{A}}^{\text{indcpa-}0_{\alpha, \beta}}(\lambda) = 1 \right] \right| .$$

Indistinguishability Under Multiple Chosen Plaintexts Attack [2]. Let $\lambda \in \mathbb{N}$ be a security parameter. An *asymmetric encryption scheme* Π achieves the (α, β)-indistinguishability security under multiple chosen plaintexts attack, if there exists a negligible function $\mu(\cdot)$ such that

$$\max_{\mathcal{A} \in \text{PPT}(\lambda)} \left\{ \text{Adv}_{\Pi, \mathcal{A}}^{\text{indcpa-}b_{\alpha, \beta}}(\lambda) \right\} \leq \mu(\lambda) .$$

In the sequel, we denote by $\text{Exp}_{\Pi, \mathcal{A}}^{\text{indcpa-}b}$ the IND-CPA experiment.

Paillier's Cryptosystem. Paillier's cryptosystem is an asymmetric encryption scheme. It is well known due to its homomorphic properties described next. Let $\lambda \in \mathbb{N}$ be a security parameter. The Paillier cryptosystem is an asymmetric encryption scheme defined by a triple of polynomial-time algorithms $(\mathcal{G}, \mathcal{E}, \mathcal{D})$ such that:

- $\mathcal{G}(1^\lambda)$ generates two prime numbers p and q according to the security parameter λ, sets $n := p \cdot q$ and $\Lambda := \text{lcm}(p - 1, q - 1)$, generates the group $(\mathbb{Z}_{n^2}^*, \cdot)$, randomly picks $g \in \mathbb{Z}_{n^2}^*$ such that $M := (L(g^\Lambda \mod n^2))^{-1} \mod n$ exists, with $L(x) := (x - 1)/n$. It sets $sk := (\Lambda, M)$, $pk := (n, g)$, $\mathcal{M} := \mathbb{Z}_n$, and $\mathcal{C} := \mathbb{Z}_{n^2}^*$. Finally, it outputs $((sk, pk), \mathcal{M}, \mathcal{C})$.
- $\mathcal{E}(pk, m)$ randomly picks $r \in \mathbb{Z}_n^*$, computes $c := g^m \cdot r^n \mod n^2$, and outputs c.
- $\mathcal{D}(sk, c)$ computes $m := L(c^\Lambda \mod n^2) \cdot M \mod n$, and outputs m.

Paillier's cryptosystem achieves the indistinguishability security against chosen plaintext attack under the DCR assumption [27].

Next, we present the homomorphic properties of Paillier's cryptosystem.

Homomorphic Addition of Plaintexts. Let m_1 and m_2 be two plaintexts in $\mathbb{Z}_n$. The product of the two associated ciphertexts with the public key $pk = (n, g)$, denoted $c_1 := \mathcal{E}(pk, m_1) = g^{m_1} \cdot r_1^n \mod n^2$ and $c_2 := \mathcal{E}(pk, m_2) = g^{m_2} \cdot r_2^n \mod n^2$, is the encryption of the sum of m_1 and m_2. Indeed, we have:

$$\begin{aligned}
\mathcal{E}(pk, m_1) \cdot \mathcal{E}(pk, m_2) &= c_1 \cdot c_2 \mod n^2 \\
&= (g^{m_1} \cdot r_1^n) \cdot (g^{m_2} \cdot r_2^n) \mod n^2 \\
&= (g^{m_1 + m_2} \cdot (r_1 \cdot r_2)^n) \mod n^2 \\
&= \mathcal{E}(pk, m_1 + m_2 \mod n) .
\end{aligned}$$

We also remark that $\mathcal{E}(pk, m_1) \cdot \mathcal{E}(pk, m_2)^{-1} = \mathcal{E}(pk, m_1 - m_2)$.

Specific Homomorphic Multiplication of Plaintexts. Let m_1 and m_2 be two plaintexts in $\mathbb{Z}_n$ and $c_1 \in \mathbb{Z}_{n^2}^*$ be the ciphertext of m_1 with the public key pk, i.e., $c_1 := \mathcal{E}(pk, m_1)$. With Paillier's cryptosystem, c_1 raised to the power of m_2 is the encryption of the product of the two plaintexts m_1 and m_2. Indeed, we have:

$$\mathcal{E}(pk, m_1)^{m_2} = c_1^{m_2} \mod n^2$$
$$= (g^{m_1} \cdot r_1^n)^{m_2} \mod n^2$$
$$= (g^{m_1 \cdot m_2} \cdot r_1^{n \cdot m_2}) \mod n^2$$
$$= \mathcal{E}(pk, m_1 \cdot m_2 \mod n) .$$

P_2	P_1
	$c_1 := \mathcal{E}(pk, m_1)$
	$c_2 := \mathcal{E}(pk, m_2)$
	$\delta_1, \delta_2 \xleftarrow{\$} \mathbb{Z}_n$
	$\alpha_1 := c_1 \cdot \mathcal{E}(pk, \delta_1)$
$\mathcal{D}(sk, \alpha_1) = m_1 + \delta_1 \mod n \xleftarrow{\alpha_1, \alpha_2}$	$\alpha_2 := c_2 \cdot \mathcal{E}(pk, \delta_2)$
$\mathcal{D}(sk, \alpha_2) = m_2 + \delta_2 \mod n$	
$c := \mathcal{E}(pk, (m_1 + \delta_1) \cdot (m_2 + \delta_2) \mod n) \xrightarrow{c}$	$\mathcal{E}(pk, m_1 \cdot m_2 \mod n)$

Fig. 3. Paillier interactive multiplicative homomorphic protocol [11].

Interactive Homomorphic Multiplication of Ciphertexts. Cramer et al. [11] show that a two-party protocol makes possible to perform multiplication over ciphertexts using additive homomorphic encryption schemes as Paillier's cryptosystem. More precisely, P_1 knows two ciphertexts $c_1, c_2 \in \mathbb{Z}_{n^2}^*$ of the plaintexts $m_1, m_2 \in \mathbb{Z}_n$ encrypted using the public key pk of P_2, she wants to obtain the ciphertext corresponding to $m_1 \cdot m_2$ without revealing to P_2 the plaintexts m_1 and m_2. In order to do that, P_1 has to interact with P_2 as described in Fig. 3. First, P_1 randomly picks $\delta_1, \delta_2 \in \mathbb{Z}_n$ and sends to Alice $\alpha_1 := c_1 \cdot \mathcal{E}(pk, \delta_1)$ and $\alpha_2 := c_2 \cdot \mathcal{E}(pk, \delta_2)$. By decrypting respectively α_1 and α_2, P_2 recovers respectively $m_1 + \delta_1 \mod n$ and $m_2 + \delta_2 \mod n$. She sends to P_1 $c := \mathcal{E}(pk, (m_1 + \delta_1) \cdot (m_2 + \delta_2) \mod n)$. Then, P_1 can deduce the value of $\mathcal{E}(pk, m_1 \cdot m_2 \mod n)$ by computing $c \cdot (\mathcal{E}(pk, \delta_1 \cdot \delta_2 \mod n) \cdot c_1^{\delta_1} \cdot c_2^{\delta_2})^{-1}$.

Indeed, $\mathcal{E}(pk, (m_1 + \delta_1) \cdot (m_2 + \delta_2) \mod n) = \mathcal{E}(pk, m_1 \cdot m_2 \mod n) \cdot \mathcal{E}(pk, m_1 \cdot \delta_2 \mod n) \cdot \mathcal{E}(pk, m_2 \cdot \delta_1 \mod n) \cdot \mathcal{E}(pk, \delta_1 \cdot \delta_2 \mod n)$.

2.2 Strassen-Winograd Algorithm

Let M and N two compatible matrices such that $M \in \mathbb{R}^{a \times b}$ and $N \in \mathbb{R}^{b \times c}$ with $(a, b, c) \in (\mathbb{N}^*)^3$. We denote by $m_{i,j}$ the element of the matrix M which is in the i-th row and the j-th column with $i \in [\![1, a]\!]$ and $j \in [\![1, b]\!]$. In the same way, we denote by $n_{j,k}$ the element of the matrix N which is in the j-th row and k-th column with $j \in [\![1, b]\!]$ and $k \in [\![1, c]\!]$. Moreover, we denote by P the product MN, and by $p_{i,k}$ the element of the matrix P which is in the i-th row and the k-th column with $i \in [\![1, a]\!]$ and $k \in [\![1, c]\!]$.

Strassen-Winograd Algorithm for 2-Power Size Matrices. The Strassen-Winograd matrix multiplication algorithm is denoted SW. It works with two square matrices of same dimension. We assume that $M, N \in \mathbb{R}^{d \times d}$ where $d := 2^k$ and $k \in \mathbb{N}^*$.

First, the SW algorithm splits matrices M and N into four quadrants of equal dimension such that

$$M := \begin{bmatrix} M_{11} & M_{12} \\ M_{21} & M_{22} \end{bmatrix}, \quad \text{and} \quad N := \begin{bmatrix} N_{11} & N_{12} \\ N_{21} & N_{22} \end{bmatrix}.$$

Using these 8 quadrants, SW performs the computation presented below.

– 8 additions

$$\begin{aligned}
S_1 &:= M_{21} + M_{22}, & T_1 &:= N_{12} - N_{11}, \\
S_2 &:= S_1 - M_{11}, & T_2 &:= N_{22} - T_1, \\
S_3 &:= M_{11} - M_{21}, & T_3 &:= N_{22} - N_{12}, \\
S_4 &:= M_{12} - S_2, & T_4 &:= T_2 - N_{21}.
\end{aligned}$$

– 7 recursive SW matrix multiplications

$$\begin{aligned}
R_1 &:= M_{11}N_{11}, & R_5 &:= S_1T_1, \\
R_2 &:= M_{12}N_{21}, & R_6 &:= S_2T_2, \\
R_3 &:= S_4N_{22}, & R_7 &:= S_3T_3. \\
R_4 &:= M_{22}T_4,
\end{aligned}$$

– 7 final additions

$$\begin{aligned}
P_1 &:= R_1 + R_2, & P_5 &:= P_4 + R_3, \\
P_2 &:= R_1 + R_6, & P_6 &:= P_3 - R_4, \\
P_3 &:= P_2 + R_7, & P_7 &:= P_3 + R_5. \\
P_4 &:= P_2 + R_5,
\end{aligned}$$

Then, the final result is $P := \begin{bmatrix} P_1 & P_5 \\ P_6 & P_7 \end{bmatrix}$.

This algorithm works only if the dimension of M and N is equal to a 2-power integer. However, two methods exist to use SW algorithm with any dimension.

3   Strassen-Winograd Matrix Multiplication with MapReduce

We present our MapReduce protocol that computes the multiplication of square matrices M and N using the Strassen-Winograd algorithm. It is denoted SM3, and assumes that matrices' dimension is a 2-power integer.

Each protocol is decomposed in two phases: (i) the *deconstruction* phase, and (ii) the *combination* phase. The aim of the deconstruction phase is to divide recursively M and N until the recursive Strassen-Winograd matrix multiplications have an order that is equal to 1. The aim of the combination phase is to combine all results of scalar multiplications to build $P := MN$. Each phase is composed of a Map function and of a Reduce function. Due to the recursive nature of the Strassen-Winograd algorithm, each phase is run several times depending on the protocol. At the last round of the combination phase of each protocol, the public cloud obtains $P := MN$ and sends it to the user.

3.1 Strassen-Winograd MapReduce Protocol

The Strassen-Winograd matrix multiplication protocol, denoted SM3, assumes that M and N are two matrices such that $M, N \in \mathbb{R}^{d \times d}$ and $\ell := \log_2(d) \in \mathbb{N}^*$.

Deconstruction Phase. We present the deconstruction phase of SM3. The Map function (resp. the Reduce function) of the deconstruction phase is presented in Fig. 4 (resp. Fig. 5).

Map function:

Input: $(key, value)$
// key: id of a chunk of M or N
// $value$: collection of $(i, j, m_{i,j})$ or $(k, l, n_{k,l})$
foreach $(i, j, m_{i,j}) \in value$ **do**
 | emit$_{\mathcal{M} \to \mathcal{D}_1}(0, (\mathtt{M}, i, j, m_{i,j}, d))$
foreach $(k, l, n_{k,l}) \in value$ **do**
 | emit$_{\mathcal{N} \to \mathcal{D}_1}(0, (\mathtt{N}, k, l, n_{k,l}, d))$

Fig. 4. Map function for the deconstruction phase of the SM3 protocol.

– *The Map Function.* It is run only during the first MapReduce round of the deconstruction phase by sets of nodes $\mathcal{M}$ and $\mathcal{N}$. It consists in rewriting each matrix element sent by data owners in the form of key-value pair such that they share the same key initialized to 0. Hence, when the set of nodes $\mathcal{M}$ receives chunks of M from the owner, the Map function creates for each matrix element $m_{i,j}$ the key-value pair $(0, (\mathtt{M}, i, j, m_{i,j}, d))$, where d is the dimension of M. Likewise, when the set of nodes $\mathcal{N}$ receives chunks of N from the owner, the Map function creates for each matrix element $n_{k,l}$ the key-value pair $(0, (\mathtt{N}, k, l, n_{k,l}, d))$. We stress that $\mathtt{M}$ and $\mathtt{N}$ in the values are the names of matrices, that can be encoded with a single bit, and not the matrices themselves. During other rounds of the deconstruction phase, the Map function is the identity function.
– *The Reduce Function.* It is executed by nodes $\mathcal{D}_s$, with $s \in [\![1, \ell]\!]$. Each key is associated to two matrices sent from previous nodes. When $s = 1$, matrices are M and N and are sent by nodes $\mathcal{M}$ and $\mathcal{N}$. When $s \in [\![2, \ell]\!]$, the two matrices correspond to a recursive matrix multiplication and are sent by $\mathcal{D}_{s-1}$. The Reduce function follows the Strassen-Winograd algorithm using these two matrices. Since the Strassen-Winograd algorithm needs to compute

---

Reduce function:

Input: $(key, values)$
// key: $t \in \{0, 7\}^\ell$
// values: collection of $(\mathtt{M}, i, j, m_{i,j}, \delta)$ or $(\mathtt{N}, k, l, n_{k,l}, \delta)$

```
// Build M and N from values
```
$M := (m_{i,j})_{(\mathtt{M},i,j,m_{i,j},\delta) \in values}$
$N := (n_{k,l})_{(\mathtt{N},k,l,n_{k,l},\delta) \in values}$

```
// Split M and N into four quadrants of equal dimension
```
$$\begin{bmatrix} M_{11} & M_{12} \\ M_{21} & M_{22} \end{bmatrix} := M \quad , \quad \begin{bmatrix} N_{11} & N_{12} \\ N_{21} & N_{22} \end{bmatrix} := N$$

```
// Build submatrices according to the Strassen-Winograd
algorithm
```
$S_1 := M_{21} + M_{22} \quad S_3 := M_{11} - M_{21} \quad T_1 := N_{12} - N_{11} \quad T_3 := N_{22} - N_{12}$
$S_2 := S_1 - M_{11} \quad\ S_4 := M_{12} - S_2 \quad\ T_2 := N_{22} - T_1 \quad\ T_4 := T_2 - N_{21}$

```
// Create a list L containing couple of matrices
```
$L := \big[[M_{11}, N_{11}], [M_{12}, N_{21}], [S_4, N_{22}], [M_{22}, T_4], [S_1, T_1], [S_2, T_2], [S_3, T_3]\big]$

if $\delta > 2$ **then**
$\quad \delta' := \delta/2$
$\quad \ell' := \log_2(d/\delta')$
$\quad$ **foreach** $u \in [\![1, 7]\!]$ **do**
$\qquad (m'_{v,w})_{v,w \in [\![1, \delta']\!]} := L[u][0]$
$\qquad (n'_{v,w})_{v,w \in [\![1, \delta']\!]} := L[u][1]$
$\qquad$ **foreach** $(v, w) \in [\![1, \delta']\!]^2$ **do**
$\qquad\quad \text{emit}_{\mathcal{D}_{\ell'-1} \to \mathcal{D}_{\ell'}}(t \| u, (\mathtt{M}, v, w, m'_{v,w}, \delta'))$
$\qquad\quad \text{emit}_{\mathcal{D}_{\ell'-1} \to \mathcal{D}_{\ell'}}(t \| u, (\mathtt{N}, v, w, n'_{v,w}, \delta'))$
else
$\quad$ **foreach** $u \in [\![1, 7]\!]$ **do**
$\qquad \text{emit}_{\mathcal{D}_\ell \to \mathcal{C}_1}(t, (u, 1, 1, L[u][0] \cdot L[u][1], 1))$

Fig. 5. Reduce function for the deconstruction phase of the SM3 protocol.

7 recursive matrix multiplications, the Reduce function produces key-value pairs for 7 different keys where each key is associated to a pair of submatrices to multiply. These key-value pairs are sent to the next nodes of the deconstruction phase $\mathcal{D}_{s+1}$. For the last round of the deconstruction phase, i.e., when $s = \ell$, matrix multiplications are degenerated into scalar multiplications. Hence, the Reduce function produces key-values pairs with the result of scalar multiplications and sends them to the set of nodes $\mathcal{C}_1$.

Combination Phase. We present the combination phase of SM3. In this phase, the Map function is just the identity function. The Reduce function of the combination phase is presented in Fig. 6.

Reduce function:

Input: $(key, values)$
// key: $t_0 \ldots t_e$ such that $e \in [\![0, \ell]\!]$ and $t_z \in [\![0, 7]\!]$ for $z \in [\![0, e]\!]$
// values: collection of $(u, i, j, r_{i,j}, \delta)$ such that $u \in [\![1, 7]\!]$ and $i, j \in [\![1, \delta]\!]$

// Build matrices R_u from values with $u \in [\![1, 7]\!]$
foreach $u \in [\![1, 7]\!]$ **do**
$\quad |\quad R_u := (r_{i,j})_{(u,i,j,r_{i,j},\delta) \in values}$

$P_1 := R_1 + R_2 \qquad P_3 := P_2 + R_7 \qquad P_5 := P_4 + R_3 \qquad P_7 := P_3 - R_5$
$P_2 := R_1 + R_6 \qquad P_4 := P_2 + R_5 \qquad P_6 := P_3 - R_4$

$(p_{v,w})_{v,w \in [\![1, 2 \cdot \delta]\!]} := \begin{bmatrix} P_1 & P_5 \\ P_6 & P_7 \end{bmatrix}$

if $\delta < d$ **then**
$\quad |\quad \delta' := 2 \cdot \delta$
$\quad |\quad \ell' := \log_2(\delta')$
$\quad |\quad$ **foreach** $(v, w) \in [\![1, 2 \cdot \delta']\!]^2$ **do**
$\quad |\quad\quad |\quad \mathrm{emit}_{\mathcal{D}_{\ell'} \to \mathcal{D}_{\ell'+1}}(t_0 \ldots t_{e-1}, (t_e, i, j, p_{v,w}, 2 \cdot \delta'))$
else
$\quad |\quad$ **foreach** $(v, w) \in [\![1, d]\!]^2$ **do**
$\quad |\quad\quad |\quad \mathrm{emit}_{\mathcal{D}_\ell \to \mathcal{P}}((v, w), p_{v,w})$

Fig. 6. Reduce function for the combination phase of the SM3 protocol.

- *The Map Function.* The Map function corresponds to the identity function.
- *The Reduce Function.* It is executed by each set of nodes $\mathcal{C}_s$ with $s \in [\![1, \ell]\!]$. For the first round of the combination phase, i.e., when $s = 1$, each key is associated to 7 values corresponding to the scalar multiplications sent by $\mathcal{D}_\ell$. The Reduce function follows the Strassen-Winograd algorithm and combines all these values to build matrices of dimension 2 that is sent to the next nodes $\mathcal{C}_2$. Other rounds of the combination phase work in the same way but in this case, each key is associated to 7 matrices of dimension δ and produces a matrix of dimension $2 \cdot \delta$. At the last round, i.e., $s = \ell$, the Reduce function produces key-value pairs corresponding to the final result $P = MN$ and send them to the user's set of nodes $\mathcal{P}$.

4 Secure Strassen-Winograd Matrix Multiplication with MapReduce

Protocol SM3 presented in the previous Section reveals both matrices, intermediate results, and the product of M by N to the public cloud. For instance, nodes $\mathcal{M}$ and $\mathcal{N}$ learn respectively M and N, while the last set of nodes of the combination phase learns $P := MN$. Below, we describe these protocols with a secure approach.

We assume that the MapReduce's user has a Paillier public key denoted pk which is available to the data owners and the public cloud. Since we use Paillier's cryptosystem, the matrix multiplication is computed modulo n, where n is the modulo of pk.

4.1 Preprocessing for Secure Strassen-Winograd Matrix Multiplication

In order to avoid the public cloud from learning the content of the two matrices and the result of their product, each data owner performs a preprocessing on its own matrix. This preprocessing is done in a way allowing the public cloud to perform the same computation, as in protocols presented in the previous Section, in a partially homomorphic way while privacy constraints are satisfied. To run the preprocessing, data owners use the Paillier public key pk of the MapReduce's user where $pk := (n, g)$, and n being the product of two prime numbers generated according to a security parameter λ, and $g \in \mathbb{Z}_{n^2}^*$.

The preprocessing is simple. It consists in the encryption of each element of the matrix owned by the data owner using the Paillier's cryptosystem with the public key pk of the MapReduce's user. At the end of the encryption, it outputs the corresponding encrypted matrix. In the following, we denote by a star an encrypted matrix, i.e., M^* is the encrypted matrix associated to M. Moreover, elements of M^* are denoted $m_{i,j}^*$ for $i, j \in [\![1, d]\!]$, where d is the dimension of the square matrix M.

4.2 Secure Approach

The secure approach for SM3 protocol is denoted S2M3. This protocol uses the Paillier's cryptosystem and its partial homomorphic properties to ensure privacy of elements of matrices and to allow the public cloud to compute the matrix multiplication.

In our secure approach, we assume that the MapReduce's user and the public cloud do not collude, i.e., the public cloud does not know the secret key sk of the MapReduce's user. Indeed, if that is the case then the public cloud is able to decrypt all ciphertexts, and then to learn the content of both matrices and the result of the matrix multiplication.

The three secure protocols are similar to protocols presented in the previous Section. Each protocol is also decomposed into the deconstruction phase and the combination phase. Moreover, secure approaches have the same number of rounds for each phase than their plain version.

For the sake of clarity, we define the two following functions used in secure approaches.

– Paillier.Add(pk, A, B). This function takes matrices $A := (\mathcal{E}(pk, a_{i,j}))_{i,j\in[\![1,d]\!]}$ and $B := (\mathcal{E}(pk, b_{i,j}))_{i,j\in[\![1,d]\!]}$ as input such that $A, B \in (\mathbb{Z}_{n^2}^*)^{d\times d}$. For each $(i, j) \in [\![1, d]\!]^2$, the function computes $c_{i,j} := \mathcal{E}(pk, a_{i,j}) \cdot \mathcal{E}(pk, b_{i,j})$ and outputs the encrypted matrix $C := (c_{i,j})_{i,j\in[\![1,d]\!]}$ that correspond to the encryption of the sum of A and B.

– Paillier.Sub(pk, A, B). This function takes matrices $A := (\mathcal{E}(pk, a_{i,j}))_{i,j \in [\![1,d]\!]}$
and $B := (\mathcal{E}(pk, b_{i,j}))_{i,j \in [\![1,d]\!]}$ as input such that $A, B \in (\mathbb{Z}_{n^2}^*)^{d \times d}$. For each
$(i, j) \in [\![1, d]\!]^2$, the function computes $c_{i,j} := \mathcal{E}(pk, a_{i,j}) \cdot \mathcal{E}(pk, b_{i,j})^{-1}$ and outputs the encrypted matrix $C := (c_{i,j})_{i,j \in [\![1,d]\!]}$ that correspond to the encryp-
tion of the subtraction of B to A.

Moreover, secure approaches use the Paillier interactive multiplicative homomorphic protocol denoted Paillier.Inter and presented in Fig. 3.

4.3   Secure Strassen-Winograd Matrix Multiplication Protocol

The secure Strassen-Winograd matrix multiplication protocol, denoted S2M3,
assumes that M and N are two matrices such that $M, N \in \mathbb{Z}_n^{d \times d}$ and $\ell :=
\log_2(d) \in \mathbb{N}^*$.

Deconstruction Phase. We present the deconstruction phase of S2M3. The
Map function is the same than for SM3 protocol presented in Fig. 4. The only
difference is that it operates on encrypted matrices M^* and N^* sent by data
owners after the preprocessing.

The Reduce function is presented in Fig. 7. Since it operates on encrypted
matrices, we use functions Paillier.Add and Paillier.Sub to add or subtract two
matrices. Moreover, it uses the Paillier interactive multiplicative homomorphic
protocol Paillier.Inter during the last round of the decomposition phase to the
encryption of the multiplication of two elements.

Combination Phase. As for SM3 protocol, the Map function of the combination phase is the identity function. The Reduce function of the combination
phase is presented in Fig. 8. The only difference compared to S2M3 protocol is
the use of Paillier.Add and Paillier.Sub functions for addition and subtraction of
encrypted matrices.

5   Experimental Results

We present the experimental results for our SM3 and S2M3 protocols, together
with extensions using dynamic padding and dynamic peeling methods allowing
square matrix multiplication of arbitrary dimension (see our technical report [8]
for pseudocode and proofs of these extensions).

5.1   Dataset and Settings

For each experiment, we generate two random square matrices and of order
d such that $240 \leq d \leq 450$ for no-secure protocols, and $90 \leq d \leq 300$ for
secure protocols. Elements of both matrices are in $[\![0, 10]\!]$. For each order d,
we perform matrix multiplication with protocols using static padding, dynamic
padding, and dynamic peeling methods. We also compare the results to the
standard matrix multiplication using one MapReduce round [22] and the secure

---

Reduce function:

Input: $(key, values)$
// key: $t \in \{0, 7\}^\ell$
// values: collection of $(\mathtt{M}, i, j, m_{i,j}^*, \delta)$ or $(\mathtt{N}, k, l, n_{k,l}^*, \delta)$

// Build M^* and N^* from values
$M^* := (m_{i,j}^*)_{(\mathtt{M},i,j,m_{i,j}^*,\delta) \in values}$
$N^* := (n_{k,l}^*)_{(\mathtt{N},k,l,n_{k,l}^*,\delta) \in values}$

// Split M^* and N^* into four quadrants of equal dimension
$\begin{bmatrix} M_{11}^* & M_{12}^* \\ M_{21}^* & M_{22}^* \end{bmatrix} := M^*$, $\begin{bmatrix} N_{11}^* & N_{12}^* \\ N_{21}^* & N_{22}^* \end{bmatrix} := N^*$

// Build submatrices according to the Strassen-Winograd
algorithm
$S_1 := \mathsf{Paillier.Add}(pk, M_{21}^*, M_{22}^*)$ $T_1 := \mathsf{Paillier.Sub}(pk, N_{12}^*, N_{11}^*)$
$S_2 := \mathsf{Paillier.Sub}(pk, S_1, M_{11}^*)$ $T_2 := \mathsf{Paillier.Sub}(pk, N_{22}^*, T_1)$
$S_3 := \mathsf{Paillier.Sub}(pk, M_{11}^*, M_{21}^*)$ $T_3 := \mathsf{Paillier.Sub}(pk, N_{22}^*, N_{12}^*)$
$S_4 := \mathsf{Paillier.Sub}(pk, M_{12}^*, S_2)$ $T_4 := \mathsf{Paillier.Sub}(pk, T_2, N_{21}^*)$

// Create a list L containing couple of matrices
$L := [[M_{11}^*, N_{11}^*], [M_{12}^*, N_{21}^*], [S_4, N_{22}^*], [M_{22}^*, T_4], [S_1, T_1], [S_2, T_2], [S_3, T_3]]$

if $\delta > 2$ **then**
    $\delta' := \delta/2$
    $\ell' := \log_2(d/\delta')$
    foreach $u \in [\![1,7]\!]$ **do**
        $(m_{v,w}')_{v,w \in [\![1,\delta']\!]} := L[u][0]$
        $(n_{v,w}')_{v,w \in [\![1,\delta']\!]} := L[u][1]$
        foreach $(v, w) \in [\![1,\delta']\!]^2$ **do**
            $\mathsf{emit}_{\mathcal{D}_{\ell'-1} \to \mathcal{D}_{\ell'}}(t \| u, (\mathtt{M}, v, w, m_{v,w}', \delta'))$
            $\mathsf{emit}_{\mathcal{D}_{\ell'-1} \to \mathcal{D}_{\ell'}}(t \| u, (\mathtt{N}, v, w, n_{v,w}', \delta'))$
else
    foreach $u \in [\![1,7]\!]$ **do**
        $\mathsf{emit}_{\mathcal{D}_\ell \to \mathcal{C}_1}(t, (u, 1, 1, \mathsf{Paillier.Inter}(L[u][0], L[u][1]), 1))$

Fig. 7. Reduce function for the deconstruction phase of the S2M3 protocol.

approach denoted CRSP-1R [4]. For each experiment, we stop the Strassen-Winograd recursive matrix multiplication when the dimension of matrices is less than 16. Then, we use the MM-1R protocol for the no-secure approach, and the CRSP-1R protocol for the secure approach. Our secure protocols are based on the Paillier's cryptosystem. We use Gaillier[1], a Go implementation of the Paillier's cryptosystem. Note that Gaillier is not an optimized implementation. Hence, we use it with a 64-bit RSA modulus as proof of concept.

---

[1] https://github.com/actuallyachraf/gomorph.

Reduce function:

Input: $(key, values)$
// key: $t_0 \cdots t_e$ such that $e \in [\![0, \ell]\!]$ and $t_z \in [\![0, 7]\!]$ for $z \in [\![0, e]\!]$
// values: collection of $(u, i, j, r_{i,j}^*, \delta)$ such that $u \in [\![1, 7]\!]$ and $i, j \in [\![1, \delta]\!]$

// Build matrices R_u from values with $u \in [\![1, 7]\!]$
foreach $u \in [\![1, 7]\!]$ **do**
$\quad | \quad R_u := (r_{i,j})_{(u,i,j,r_{i,j}^*,\delta) \in values}$

$P_1 := \mathsf{Paillier.Add}(pk, R_1, R_2) \qquad P_5 := \mathsf{Paillier.Add}(pk, P_4, R_3)$
$P_2 := \mathsf{Paillier.Add}(pk, R_1, R_6) \qquad P_6 := \mathsf{Paillier.Add}(pk, P_3, R_4)$
$P_3 := \mathsf{Paillier.Add}(pk, P_2, R_7) \qquad P_7 := \mathsf{Paillier.Sub}(pk, P_3, R_5)$
$P_4 := \mathsf{Paillier.Add}(pk, P_2, R_5)$

$(p_{v,w})_{v,w \in [\![1, 2 \cdot \delta]\!]} := \begin{bmatrix} P_1 & P_5 \\ P_6 & P_7 \end{bmatrix}$

if $\delta < d$ **then**
$\quad | \quad \delta' := 2 \cdot \delta$
$\quad | \quad \ell' := \log_2(\delta')$
$\quad | \quad$ **foreach** $(v, w) \in [\![1, 2 \cdot \delta']\!]^2$ **do**
$\quad | \quad \quad | \quad \mathsf{emit}_{\mathcal{D}_{\ell'} \to \mathcal{D}_{\ell'+1}}(t_0 \cdots t_{e-1}, (t_e, i, j, p_{v,w}, 2 \cdot \delta'))$
else
$\quad | \quad$ **foreach** $(v, w) \in [\![1, d]\!]^2$ **do**
$\quad | \quad \quad | \quad \mathsf{emit}_{\mathcal{D}_\ell \to \mathcal{P}}((v, w), p_{v,w})$

Fig. 8. Reduce function for the combination phase of the S2M3 protocol.

5.2 Results

In Fig. 9, we present CPU times for the no-secure SM3 protocols using the static padding method denoted SM3-sPad, the dynamic padding method denoted SM3-Pad, or the dynamic peeling method denoted SM3-Peel. Moreover, we compare them to the standard matrix multiplication using one MapReduce round [22], denoted MM-1R.

First we observe that without any security, our SM3-Pad and SM3-Peel protocols perform the matrix multiplication faster than the standard matrix multiplication for the largest dimensions. This trend can be seen when matrices' dimension is larger than 300. Moreover, we remark that our protocol SM3-sPad is more efficient than the state-of-the-art protocol MM-1R when matrices' dimension tend to a 2-power integer. Indeed, we note that SM3-sPad is faster than MM-1R when matrices' dimension is between 450 and $512 = 2^8$.

We show in Fig. 10, CPU times for secure protocols computing the SW matrix multiplication. We compare them to a state-of-the-art secure standard matrix multiplication protocol CRSP-1R using one MapReduce round [4].

Same observations than no-secure protocols can be done for secure protocols. Indeed, we also remark that our S2M3-Pad and S2M3-Peel protocols perform the matrix multiplication faster than our protocol CRSP-1R.

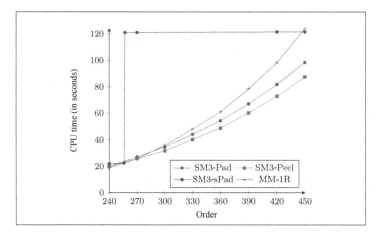

Fig. 9. CPU time vs order of matrices for the state-of-the-art MM-1R protocol using one MapReduce round [22] and for our SM3 protocols using static and dynamic padding methods, and dynamic peeling method.

Finally, for both no-secure and secure protocols, we remark that the protocol using the dynamic peeling method is always faster than the protocol using the dynamic padding method. As we have seen previously, the deconstruction phase and the combination phase use $\lceil \log_2(d) \rceil$ MapReduce rounds for the dynamic padding method, while they use $\lfloor \log_2(d) \rfloor$ MapReduce rounds for the dynamic peeling method, where d is matrices' dimension.

6 Security Proofs

We provide formal security proof for S2M3, S2M3-Pad, and S2M3-Peel protocols. We use the standard multiparty computations definition of security against semi-honest adversaries [23].

6.1 Security Proof for S2M3 Protocol

S2M3 protocol assumes that the public cloud's nodes may collude, hence in a security point of view, all sets of nodes are considered as a unique set of nodes when they collude.

We model S2M3 protocol with four parties P_M, P_N, P_C, and P_P using respective inputs $I := (I_M, I_N, I_C, I_P) \in \mathcal{I}$, and a function $g := (g_M, g_N, g_C, g_P)$ such that:

- P_M is the data owner of M. It has the input $I_M := (M, pk)$, where M is its private matrix and pk is the Paillier's public key of the MapReduce's user. P_M returns $g_M(I) := \bot$ because it does not learn anything.

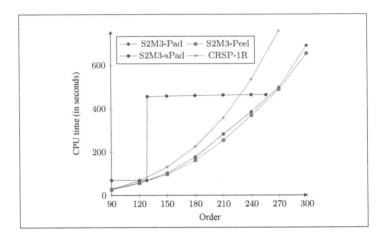

Fig. 10. CPU time vs order of matrices for the CRSP-1R protocol [4] and for our S2M3 protocols using static and dynamic padding methods, and dynamic peeling method.

- P_N is the data owner of N. It has the input $I_N := (N, pk)$, where N is its private matrix and pk is the Paillier's public key of the MapReduce's user. P_N returns $g_N(I) := \bot$ because it does not learn anything.
- P_C is the public cloud's nodes that represents the collusion between all sets of nodes of the deconstruction phase and of the combination phase. It has the input $I_C := (pk)$, where pk is the Paillier's public key of the user. P_C returns $g_C(I) := d \in \mathbb{N}^*$ because it learns matrices dimensions.
- $P_{\mathcal{P}}$ is the set of nodes $\mathcal{P}$ of the MapReduce's user. It has the input $I_{\mathcal{P}} := (pk, sk)$, where (pk, sk) is the Paillier's key pair of the MapReduce's user. $P_{\mathcal{P}}$ returns $g_{\mathcal{P}}(I) := P$ because the user obtains the result of the matrix multiplication at the end of the protocol.

Note that for the sake of clarity, we consider that P_C sends the product of the encrypted matrices to $P_{\mathcal{P}}$ instead of storing them in a database.

The security of S2M3 protocol is given in Theorem 1.

Theorem 1. *Assume Paillier's cryptosystem is IND-CPA, then S2M3 securely computes the matrix multiplication in the presence of semi-honest adversaries even if public cloud's nodes collude.*

The security proof for S2M3 protocol (Theorem 1) is decomposed in Lemma 1 for parties P_M and P_N, Lemma 2 for party P_C, and Lemma 3 for party $P_{\mathcal{P}}$.

Lemma 1. *There exists probabilistic polynomial-time simulators $\mathcal{S}_M^{\text{S2M3}}$ and $\mathcal{S}_N^{\text{S2M3}}$ such that:*

$$\left\{\mathcal{S}_M^{\text{S2M3}}(1^\lambda, I_M, g_M(I))\right\}_{I \in \mathcal{I}, \lambda \in \mathbb{N}} \overset{\text{c}}{\equiv} \left\{\text{view}_M^{\text{S2M3}}(I, \lambda)\right\}_{I \in \mathcal{I}, \lambda \in \mathbb{N}},$$

$$\left\{\mathcal{S}_N^{\text{S2M3}}(1^\lambda, I_N, g_N(I))\right\}_{I \in \mathcal{I}, \lambda \in \mathbb{N}} \overset{\text{c}}{\equiv} \left\{\text{view}_N^{\text{S2M3}}(I, \lambda)\right\}_{I \in \mathcal{I}, \lambda \in \mathbb{N}}.$$

Proof. The view of P_M contains M^* (the encryption of M) obtained from the preprocessing and that is sent to P_C. Simulator $\mathcal{S}_M^{\text{S2M3}}$ has input (M, pk). It encrypts each element of M using pk to build M^*. Hence, $\mathcal{S}_M^{\text{S2M3}}$ performs exactly the same computation as S2M3 protocol and describes exactly the same distribution as $\text{view}_M^{\text{S2M3}}(I, \lambda)$. Building the simulator $\mathcal{S}_N^{\text{S2M3}}$ in the same way, it describes exactly the same distribution as $\text{view}_N^{\text{S2M3}}(I, \lambda)$.

Lemma 2. *Assume Paillier's cryptosystem is IND-CPA, then there exists a probabilistic polynomial-time simulator $\mathcal{S}_C^{\text{S2M3}}$ such that:*

$$\left\{ \mathcal{S}_C^{\text{S2M3}}(1^\lambda, I_C, g_C(I)) \right\}_{I \in \mathcal{I}, \lambda \in \mathbb{N}} \stackrel{c}{\equiv} \left\{ \text{view}_C^{\text{S2M3}}(I, \lambda) \right\}_{I \in \mathcal{I}, \lambda \in \mathbb{N}}.$$

Function: SW-Deconstruction

SW-Deconstruction$(A, B, U, \text{view}, pk)$:

$$\begin{bmatrix} A_{11} & A_{12} \\ A_{21} & A_{22} \end{bmatrix} := A, \quad \begin{bmatrix} B_{11} & B_{12} \\ B_{21} & B_{22} \end{bmatrix} := B$$

$S_1 := \text{Paillier.Add}(pk, A_{21}, A_{22})$ $T_1 := \text{Paillier.Sub}(pk, B_{12}, B_{11})$
$S_2 := \text{Paillier.Sub}(pk, S_1, A_{11})$ $T_2 := \text{Paillier.Sub}(pk, B_{22}, T_1)$
$S_3 := \text{Paillier.Sub}(pk, A_{11}, A_{21})$ $T_3 := \text{Paillier.Sub}(pk, B_{22}, B_{12})$
$S_4 := \text{Paillier.Sub}(pk, A_{12}, S_2)$ $T_4 := \text{Paillier.Sub}(pk, T_2, B_{21})$

$L := \big[[A_{11}, B_{11}], [A_{12}, B_{21}], [S_4, B_{22}], [A_{22}, T_4], [S_1, T_1], [S_2, T_2], [S_3, T_3]\big]$

foreach $[A_0, B_0] \in L$ **do**
    if $dim(A_0) = dim(B_0) = 1$ **then**
      | $U := U \cup \{[A_0, B_0]\}$
    else
      $\text{view} := \text{view} \cup \{[A_0, B_0]\}$
      SW-Deconstruction$(A_0, B_0, U, \text{view}, pk)$

Fig. 11. Function SW-Deconstruction for simulator $\mathcal{S}_C^{\text{S2M3}}$ presented in Fig. 13.

Function: SW-Combination

SW-Combination$(R_1, \ldots, R_7, \text{view}, pk)$:
$P_1 := \text{Paillier.Add}(pk, R_1, R_2)$ $P_5 := \text{Paillier.Add}(pk, P_4, R_3)$
$P_2 := \text{Paillier.Add}(pk, R_1, R_6)$ $P_6 := \text{Paillier.Add}(pk, P_3, R_4)$
$P_3 := \text{Paillier.Add}(pk, P_2, R_7)$ $P_7 := \text{Paillier.Add}(pk, P_3, R_5)$
$P_4 := \text{Paillier.Add}(pk, P_2, R_5)$

$$P := \begin{bmatrix} P_1 & P_5 \\ P_6 & P_7 \end{bmatrix}$$

$\text{view} := \text{view} \cup \{P\}$
return (P, view)

Fig. 12. Function SW-Combination for simulator $\mathcal{S}_C^{\text{S2M3}}$ presented in Fig. 13.

Proof. We recall that $P_{\mathcal{C}}$ is the collusion of sets of nodes of the public cloud, i.e., $\mathcal{M}$, $\mathcal{N}$, $\mathcal{D}_i$ and $\mathcal{C}_i$ for $i \in [\![1, \ell]\!]$. $P_{\mathcal{C}}$ receives M^* and N^* from the data owners.

Simulator of $P_{\mathcal{C}}$ is given in Fig. 13. Function SW-Deconstruction presented in Fig. 11 simulates the public cloud's view during the deconstruction phase. The view contains all submatrices corresponding the recursive matrices multiplications. Moreover, the last set of nodes of the deconstruction phase $\mathcal{D}_\ell$ sends couples of ciphertexts (x_i, y_i), with $i \in [\![1, 7^\ell]\!]$, to $P_{\mathcal{P}}$ and receives all corresponding ciphertexts $R_i^{(\ell)}$ returned by $P_{\mathcal{P}}$ to compute multiplication on encrypted coefficients.

$\underline{\text{Simulator: } \mathcal{S}_{\mathcal{C}}^{\text{S2M3}}(1^\lambda, pk, d)}$

$U := \emptyset$
view $:= \emptyset$
foreach $(i, j) \in [\![1, d]\!]^2$ **do**
$\quad \mid (\alpha_{i,j}, \beta_{i,j}) \xleftarrow{\$} (\mathbb{Z}_n)^2$
$M^* := \left(\mathcal{E}(pk, \alpha_{i,j})\right)_{i,j\in[\![1,d]\!]}, \quad N^* := \left(\mathcal{E}(pk, \beta_{i,j})\right)_{i,j\in[\![1,d]\!]}$

SW-Deconstruction$(M^*, N^*, U, \text{view}, pk)$

foreach $i \in [\![1, 7^\ell]\!]$ **do**
$\quad \mid (r_i, s_i, t_i) \xleftarrow{\$} (\mathbb{Z}_n)^3$
$\quad \mid x_i := \mathcal{E}(pk, r_i)$
$\quad \mid y_i := \mathcal{E}(pk, s_i)$
$\quad \mid R_i^{(\ell)} := \mathcal{E}(pk, t_i)$
$\quad \mid$ view $:=$ view $\cup \{R_i^{(\ell)}\}$

foreach $k \in [\![\ell, 1]\!]$ **do**
$\quad \mid$ **foreach** $j \in [\![1, 7^{k-1}]\!]$ **do**
$\quad \mid \quad \mid (R_j^{(k-1)}, \text{view}') := $ SW-Combination$(R_{7 \cdot j-6}^{(k)}, \ldots, R_{7 \cdot j}^{(k)})$
$\quad \mid \quad \mid$ view $:=$ view $\cup$ view$'$
return view

Fig. 13. Simulator $\mathcal{S}_{\mathcal{C}}^{\text{S2M3}}$ for the proof of Lemma 2.

Function SW-Combination presented in Fig. 12 simulates the public cloud's view during one round of the combination phase. For each round, it combines submatrices according the SW algorithm.

Let $\lambda \in \mathbb{N}$ be a security parameter. Assume there exists a polynomial-time distinguisher D such that for all inputs $I \in \mathcal{I}$, we have:

$$\left| \Pr[D(\mathcal{S}_{\mathcal{C}}^{\text{S2M3}}(1^\lambda, I_{\mathcal{C}}, g_{\mathcal{C}}(I))) = 1] - \Pr[D(\text{view}_{\mathcal{C}}^{\text{S2M3}}(I)) = 1] \right| = \mu(\lambda), \quad (1)$$

where μ is a non-negligible function in λ. We show how to build a probabilistic polynomial-time adversary $\mathcal{A}$ such that $\mathcal{A}$ has a non-negligible advantage to win the IND-CPA experiment on the Paillier's cryptosystem. Then we conclude the proof by contraposition. Adversary $\mathcal{A}$ is presented in Fig. 14. At the end of its execution, $\mathcal{A}$ uses the distinguisher D to compute the bit b^* before returning it. First, we remark that:

$$\Pr\left[\mathsf{Exp}^{\mathrm{indcpa\text{-}0}}_{\mathrm{Paillier},\mathcal{A}}(\lambda) = 1\right] = \Pr\left[D(\mathrm{view}^{\mathrm{S2M3}}_{\mathcal{C}}(I,\lambda)) = 1\right]. \tag{2}$$

Indeed, when $b = 0$, the view that $\mathcal{A}$ uses as input for D is computed as in real S2M3 protocol. Then the probability that the experiment returns 1 is equal to the probability that the distinguisher returns 1 on inputs computed as in real protocol. On the other hand, we have:

$$\Pr\left[\mathsf{Exp}^{\mathrm{indcpa\text{-}1}}_{\mathrm{Paillier},\mathcal{A}}(\lambda) = 1\right] = \Pr\left[D(\mathcal{S}^{\mathrm{S2M3}}_{\mathcal{C}}(1^\lambda, I_{\mathcal{C}}, g_{\mathcal{C}}(I))) = 1\right]. \tag{3}$$

When $b = 1$, the view that $\mathcal{A}$ uses as input for D is computed as in the simulator $\mathcal{S}^{\mathrm{S2M3}}_{\mathcal{C}}$. Then the probability that the experiment returns 1 is equal to the probability that the distinguisher returns 1 on inputs computed as in the simulator $\mathcal{S}^{\mathrm{S2M3}}_{\mathcal{C}}$. Finally, we evaluate the probability that $\mathcal{A}$ wins the IND-CPA experiment:

$$\begin{aligned}
\mathsf{Adv}^{\mathrm{indcpa}}_{\mathrm{Paillier},\mathcal{A}}(\lambda) &= \left|\Pr\left[\mathsf{Exp}^{\mathrm{indcpa\text{-}1}}_{\mathrm{Paillier},\mathcal{A}}(\lambda) = 1\right] - \Pr\left[\mathsf{Exp}^{\mathrm{indcpa\text{-}0}}_{\mathrm{Paillier},\mathcal{A}}(\lambda) = 1\right]\right| \\
&= \left|\Pr\left[D(\mathcal{S}^{\mathrm{S2M3}}_{\mathcal{C}}(1^\lambda, I_{\mathcal{C}}, g_{\mathcal{C}})) = 1\right] - \Pr\left[D(\mathrm{view}^{\mathrm{S2M3}}_{\mathcal{C}}(I,\lambda)) = 1\right]\right| \\
&= \mu(\lambda),
\end{aligned}$$

which is non-negligible and concludes the proof by contradiction.

Adversary: $\mathcal{A}^{\mathcal{E}(pk,\mathsf{LoR}_b(\cdot,\cdot))}$

$U := \emptyset$
$\mathrm{view} := \emptyset$
foreach $i \in [\![1,d]\!]$ **do**
    foreach $j \in [\![1,d]\!]$ **do**
        $(m_{i,j}, n_{i,j}) \xleftarrow{\$} (\mathbb{Z}_n)^2$
        $(\alpha_{i,j}, \beta_{i,j}) \xleftarrow{\$} (\mathbb{Z}_n)^2$
$M^* := \left(\mathcal{E}(pk, \mathsf{LoR}_b(m_{i,j}, \alpha_{i,j}))\right)_{i,j \in [\![1,d]\!]}$
$N^* := \left(\mathcal{E}(pk, \mathsf{LoR}_b(n_{i,j}, \beta_{i,j}))\right)_{i,j \in [\![1,d]\!]}$
SW-Deconstruction$(M^*, N^*, U, \mathrm{view}, pk)$

foreach $i \in [\![1, 7^\ell]\!]$ **do**
    $(r_i, s_i, t_i) \xleftarrow{\$} (\mathbb{Z}_n)^3$
    $x_i := \mathcal{E}(pk, r_i)$
    $y_i := \mathcal{E}(pk, s_i)$
    $R_i^{(\ell)} := \mathcal{E}(pk, \mathsf{LoR}_b(U[i-1][0] \cdot U[i-1][1], t_i))$
    $\mathrm{view} := \mathrm{view} \cup \{R_i^{(\ell)}\}$

foreach $k \in [\![\ell, 1]\!]$ **do**
    foreach $j \in [\![1, 7^{k-1}]\!]$ **do**
        $(R_j^{(k-1)}, \mathrm{view}') := $ SW-Combination$(R^{(k)}_{7\cdot j - 6}, \ldots, R^{(k)}_{7\cdot j})$
        $\mathrm{view} := \mathrm{view} \cup \mathrm{view}'$
return view

Fig. 14. Adversary $\mathcal{A}^{\mathcal{E}(pk,\mathsf{LoR}_b(\cdot,\cdot))}$ for the proof of Lemma 2.

Lemma 3. *There exists a probabilistic polynomial-time simulator $\mathcal{S}_{\mathcal{P}}^{\text{S2M3}}$ such that:*

$$\left\{ \mathcal{S}_{\mathcal{P}}^{\text{S2M3}}(1^{\lambda}, I_{\mathcal{P}}, g_{\mathcal{P}}(I)) \right\}_{I \in \mathcal{I}, \lambda \in \mathbb{N}} \overset{\text{C}}{\equiv} \left\{ \text{view}_{\mathcal{P}}^{\text{S2M3}}(I, \lambda) \right\}_{I \in \mathcal{I}, \lambda \in \mathbb{N}}. \tag{4}$$

Proof. Simulator $\mathcal{S}_{\mathcal{P}}^{\text{S2M3}}$ is presented in Fig. 15. The view of $P_{\mathcal{P}}$ contains the couple of ciphertexts (x_i, y_i) sent by the set of nodes $\mathcal{D}_{\ell}$ during the deconstruction phase run by $P_{\mathcal{C}}$ and the answer z_i sent by $P_{\mathcal{P}}$ to $P_{\mathcal{C}}$ that contains the encryption of the multiplication of x_i and y_i, for $i \in [\![1, 7^{\ell}]\!]$. Since x_i and y_i are randomized by $P_{\mathcal{C}}$, there are indistinguishable to random ciphertexts in the $P_{\mathcal{P}}$ point of view. The view of $P_{\mathcal{P}}$ also contains $P^* := (\mathcal{E}(pk, p_{i,j}))_{i,j \in [\![1,d]\!]}$ that is sent by $P_{\mathcal{C}}$. Finally, $\mathcal{S}_{\mathcal{P}}^{\text{S2M3}}(1^{\lambda}, (pk, sk), P)$ describes exactly the same distribution as $\text{view}_{\mathcal{P}}^{\text{S2M3}}(I, \lambda)$, which concludes the proof.

Simulator: $\mathcal{S}_{\mathcal{P}}^{\text{S2M3}}(1^{\lambda}, (pk, sk), P)$

foreach $i \in [\![1, 7^{\ell}]\!]$ **do**
$\quad (r_i, s_i) \xleftarrow{\$} (\mathbb{Z}_n)^2$
$\quad x_i := \mathcal{E}(pk, r_i)$
$\quad y_i := \mathcal{E}(pk, s_i)$
$\quad z_i := \mathcal{E}(pk, r_i \cdot s_i)$
$P^* := (\mathcal{E}(pk, p_{i,j}))_{i,j \in [\![1,d]\!]}$
$\text{view} := \left(\{(x_i, y_i), z_i\}_{i \in [\![1, 7^{\ell}]\!]}, P^* \right)$
return view

Fig. 15. Simulator $\mathcal{S}_{\mathcal{P}}^{\text{S2M3}}$ for the proof of Lemma 3.

7 Conclusions and Future Work

We have presented SM3, a protocol to compute the Strassen-Winograd matrix multiplication using the MapReduce paradigm. Moreover, we also extend in our technical report [8] this protocol to SM3-Pad and SM3-Peel protocols using respectively the dynamic padding and the dynamic peeling methods allowing square matrix multiplication of arbitrary dimension. We have also presented a secure approach for these three protocols denoted S2M3, S2M3-Pad, and S2M3-Peel satisfying privacy guarantees such that the public cloud does not learn any information on input matrices and on the output matrix. To achieve our goal, we have relied on the well-known Paillier's cryptosystem and on its homomorphic properties. We have compared our three no-secure protocols (resp. secure protocols) with the state-of-the-art MapReduce matrix multiplication protocol of Leskovec et al. [22] (resp. with the CRSP protocol proposed by Bultel et al. [4]) and shown that our protocols are more efficient.

Looking forward to future work, we aim to investigate the matrix multiplication with privacy guarantees in different big data systems (e.g., Spark, Flink) whose users also tend to outsource data and computations as MapReduce.

References

1. Amirbekyan, A., Estivill-Castro, V.: A new efficient privacy-preserving scalar product protocol. In: Proceedings of the 6th Australasian Data Mining Conference (AusDM), pp. 209–214 (2007)
2. Bellare, M., Boldyreva, A., Micali, S.: Public-key encryption in a multi-user setting: security proofs and improvements. In: Proceedings of the International Conference on the Theory and Application of Cryptographic Techniques (EUROCRYPT), pp. 259–274 (2000)
3. Blass, E., Pietro, R.D., Molva, R., Önen, M.: PRISM - privacy-preserving search in MapReduce. In: Proceedings of the 12th International Symposium on Privacy Enhancing Technologies (PETS), pp. 180–200 (2012)
4. Bultel, X., Ciucanu, R., Giraud, M., Lafourcade, P.: Secure matrix multiplication with MapReduce. In: Proceedings of the 12th International Conference on Availability, Reliability and Security (ARES), pp. 11:1–11:10 (2017)
5. Bultel, X., Ciucanu, R., Giraud, M., Lafourcade, P., Ye, L.: Secure joins with MapReduce. In: Zincir-Heywood, N., Bonfante, G., Debbabi, M., Garcia-Alfaro, J. (eds.) FPS 2018. LNCS, vol. 11358, pp. 78–94. Springer, Cham (2019). https://doi.org/10.1007/978-3-030-18419-3_6
6. Chartrand, G.: Introductory Graph Theory. Dover Books on Mathematics. Dover Publications, New York (2012)
7. Ciucanu, R., Giraud, M., Lafourcade, P., Ye, L.: Secure grouping and aggregation with MapReduce. In: Proceedings of the 15th International Joint Conference on e-Business and Telecommunications, vol. 2: SECRYPT (International Conference on Security and Cryptography), pp. 514–521 (2018)
8. Ciucanu, R., Giraud, M., Lafourcade, P., Ye, L.: Secure and efficient matrix multiplication with MapReduce. Technical report (2019). https://sancy.iut-clermont.uca.fr/~lafourcade/PAPERS/PDF/technical-report-CGLY.pdf
9. Ciucanu, R., Giraud, M., Lafourcade, P., Ye, L.: Secure intersection with MapReduce. In: Proceedings of the 16th International Joint Conference on e-Business and Telecommunications, vol. 2: SECRYPT (International Conference on Security and Cryptography). pp. 236–243 (2019)
10. Ciucanu, R., Giraud, M., Lafourcade, P., Ye, L.: Secure strassen-winograd matrix multiplication with MapReduce. In: Proceedings of the 16th International Joint Conference on e-Business and Telecommunications, vol. 2: SECRYPT (International Conference on Security and Cryptography), pp. 220–227 (2019)
11. Cramer, R., Damgård, I., Nielsen, J.B.: Multiparty computation from threshold homomorphic encryption. In: Proceedings of the International Conference on the Theory and Application of Cryptographic Techniques (EUROCRYPT), pp. 280–299 (2001)
12. Dean, J., Ghemawat, S.: MapReduce: simplified data processing on large clusters. In: Proceedings of the 6th Symposium on Operating System Design and Implementation (OSDI), pp. 137–150 (2004)
13. Derbeko, P., Dolev, S., Gudes, E., Sharma, S.: Security and privacy aspects in mapreduce on clouds: a survey. Comput. Sci. Rev. **20**, 1–28 (2016)
14. Dolev, S., Li, Y., Sharma, S.: Private and secure secret shared MapReduce (Extended Abstract). In: Ranise, S., Swarup, V. (eds.) DBSec 2016. LNCS, vol. 9766, pp. 151–160. Springer, Cham (2016). https://doi.org/10.1007/978-3-319-41483-6_11

15. Du, W., Atallah, M.J.: Privacy-preserving cooperative statistical analysis. In: Proceedings of the 17th Annual Computer Security Applications Conference (ACSAC), pp. 102–110 (2001)
16. Dumas, J., Lafourcade, P., Orfila, J., Puys, M.: Dual protocols for private multi-party matrix multiplication and trust computations. Comput. Secur. **71**, 51–70 (2017)
17. Foundation, A.S.: Apache Hadoop (release 3.2.0) (2019). https://hadoop.apache.org/
18. Gall, F.L.: Powers of tensors and fast matrix multiplication. In: Proceedings of the International Symposium on Symbolic and Algebraic Computation (ISSAC), pp. 296–303 (2014)
19. Goldreich, O.: The Foundations of Cryptography - Basic Applications, vol. 2. Cambridge University Press, Cambridge (2001)
20. Goldreich, O., Micali, S., Wigderson, A.: How to play any mental game or a completeness theorem for protocols with honest majority. In: Proceedings of the 19th Annual ACM Symposium on Theory of Computing (STOC), pp. 218–229 (1987)
21. Krizhevsky, A., Sutskever, I., Hinton, G.E.: ImageNet classification with deep convolutional neural networks. Commun. ACM **60**(6), 84–90 (2017)
22. Leskovec, J., Rajaraman, A., Ullman, J.D.: Mining of Massive Datasets, 2nd edn. Cambridge University Press, Cambridge (2014)
23. Lindell, Y.: How to simulate it - a tutorial on the simulation proof technique. In: Tutorials on the Foundations of Cryptography, pp. 277–346 (2017)
24. Ma, Q., Deng, P.: Secure multi-party protocols for privacy preserving data mining. In: Proceedings of the 3rd International Conference on Wireless Algorithms, Systems, and Applications (WASA), pp. 526–537 (2008)
25. Macedo, H.D.: Gaussian elimination is not optimal. J. Logic. Algebraic Methods Program. **85**(5), 999–1010 (2016)
26. Mayberry, T., Blass, E., Chan, A.H.: PIRMAP: efficient private information retrieval for MapReduce. In: Proceedings of the 17th International Conference on Financial Cryptography and Data Security (FC), pp. 371–385 (2013)
27. Paillier, P.: Public-Key cryptosystems based on composite degree residuosity classes. In: Stern, J. (ed.) EUROCRYPT 1999. LNCS, vol. 1592, pp. 223–238. Springer, Heidelberg (1999). https://doi.org/10.1007/3-540-48910-X_16
28. Shoshan, A., Zwick, U.: All pairs shortest paths in undirected graphs with integer weights. In: Proceedings of the 40th Annual Symposium on Foundations of Computer Science (FOCS), pp. 605–615 (1999)
29. Strassen, V.: Gaussian elimination is not optimal. Numerische Mathematik **13**(4), 354–356 (1969)
30. Wang, I., Shen, C., Zhan, J., Hsu, T., Liau, C., Wang, D.: Toward empirical aspects of secure scalar product. IEEE Trans. Syst. Man Cybern. **39**(4), 440–447 (2009)
31. Yao, A.C.: Protocols for secure computations (Extended Abstract). In: Proceedings of the 23rd IEEE Annual Symposium on Foundations of Computer Science (FOCS), pp. 160–164 (1982)
32. Zwick, U.: All pairs shortest paths in weighted directed graphs exact and almost exact algorithms. In: Proceedings of the 39th Annual Symposium on Foundations of Computer Science (FOCS), pp. 310–319 (1998)

An Invisible Hybrid 3D Video Watermarking Robust Against Malicious Attacks

Dorra Dhaou[1]([✉]), Saoussen Ben Jabra[1,2], and Ezzeddine Zagrouba[1]

[1] Université de Tunis El Manar, Institut Supérieur d'Informatique, LR16ES06
Laboratoire de Recherche en Informatique, Modélisation et Traitement de
l'Information et de la Connaissance (LIMTIC), 2 Rue Abou Raihane Bayrouni,
2080 Ariana, Tunisia
dorradhaou@gmail.com, saoussen.bj@gmail.com
ezzeddine.zagrouba@uvt.tn
[2] Université de Sousse, École Nationale d'Ingénieurs de Sousse (ENISo), BP 264,
4023 Sousse Erriadh, Tunisia

Abstract. Digital watermarking is known as the most suitable solution to protect 3D videos. Hence, proposing a watermarking technique robust against malicious attacks and especially against collusion becomes a crucial challenge for many researchers. In fact, collusion is usually not considered in the assessment of anaglyph 3D video watermarking schemes. In this paper, an invisible and robust watermarking method dedicated to anaglyph 3D videos is proposed. It embeds a signature in the selected mosaics generated from different groups of frames forming the original video. The choice of the mosaic as an embedding target guarantees robustness against collusion which considered as the most dangerous attack for any video watermarking technique. First, several mosaic images are generated from every set of 25 frames of the original video and they are compared using a similarity measure. In order to obtain a high level of invisibility, the signature will not be embedded in all mosaics but only in the ones which are not similar. Second, the signature is inserted on each selected mosaic image using a hybrid embedding scheme based on the least significant bit and the discrete wavelet transform. Finally, all the marked frames are restored from the marked mosaic images and they are recombined to the unmarked ones to reconstruct the marked anaglyph video. To prove the robustness of the suggested method, different manipulations are applied to various anaglyph videos and several metrics are calculated. Obtained results confirm its robustness against the image processing attacks, the enhancement attacks, and the frame-based attacks, in addition to dangerous video attacks such as MPEG-4 and H264-AVC compression and collusion attacks.

Keywords: Collusion · Watermarking · Mosaic generation · Anaglyph video · Hybrid · Signature embedding · Invisibility · Robustness

© Springer Nature Switzerland AG 2020
M. S. Obaidat (Ed.): ICETE 2019, CCIS 1247, pp. 157–179, 2020.
https://doi.org/10.1007/978-3-030-52686-3_7

1   Introduction

The popularity of 3D videos increases day-to-day due to the evolution and the development of 3D technology and the rapid access to the internet. Hence, 3D videos are taken an enormous public attention compared to 2D videos. Actually, various display technologies are invented to perceive videos in 3D and they can be classified into 6 categories: Stereoscopy, auto-stereoscopy, multi-view auto-stereoscopy, holography, integral imaging, and volumetric displays. The first three displays are the most economical and simplest 3D technologies available recently [14]. In this paper, we are interested in the stereoscopy technology where a specified eye glasses are required to perceive in 3D, such as anaglyph glasses, polarized glasses, and active shutter glasses. In the polarized 3D system, the 3D perception is displayed using the polarisation of filters where the viewer need to use a pair of an expensive polarized filter glasses and others displays to separate the perceived scene to the appropriate left or right eye. While in the active shutter 3D system, the viewer need an alternate liquid crystal shutter glasses to make the stereo images represented alternately. This process permits to fuse the stereo images in the human mind to create a 3D effect. These glasses are very expensive, they are provided with an electronic device which make them heavy and the viewer feels uncomfortable when he wears them for a long time. In the anaglyph 3D system, two superimposed images illustrating the same scene seeing from two different angles; the right view in cyan and the left one in red are required to perceive a printed image in relief as well as a colored glasses provided with two filters of two complementary colors. This last technique is the simplest and cheapest way to perceive data in 3D. The study of the anaglyph 3D system has recently taken the attention of the researchers in various domains because it is not complicated and don't need any specific hardware, just a cyan-red glasses.

The 3D technology has developed and progressed rapidly nowadays. Hence, the accessibility of 3D videos contents became very easy thanks to the internet. Despite that, 3D videos cannot be shared without security and protection from any kind of attacks. Therefore, the digital watermarking is the most adequate technique to secure 3D videos Actually, 3D video watermarking scheme consists of two main process: the insertion of a selected signature in an original 3D video, and the extraction of the embedded signature from the marked 3D video. In the literature, Different 2D videos based watermarking approaches have been proposed [5,18]. However, the field is still not enough experienced for 3D videos due to the diversity of 3D displays and the complexity of 3D data. A little number of watermarking techniques dedicated to 3D anaglyph videos were proposed in recent years, and they did not satisfy the main watermarking requirements; the invisibility and the robustness, especially the robustness against the most dangerous attacks viz. the compression and the collusion attacks. The later consists of estimating and then removing the embedded signature in the marked video to obtain the original one. To resist this attack, several 2D video watermarking techniques were proposed. They are based either on the use of mosaic images (sprites) as a destination to embed the signature [3,4] or on a complex scheme which make very hard the extraction of the mark after collusion attack. In fact, the similar physical points in all frames forming the video should be marked similarly in order to withstand the collusion attack. For this reason, the best embedding destination is the mosaic image generated from the video.

In this paper, an invisible and robust watermarking approach dedicated to anaglyph 3D video is put forward. In fact, different mosaic images will be generated first from each group of 25 frames until the end of the whole video frames. Second, the generated mosaic images are compared to each other and the dissimilar mosaic images will be selected for the insertion of the mark. Next, a binary image is chosen as a signature and it will be inserted in each selected mosaic image, unlike the previous technique [13] where the authors insert the signature directly in all the mosaic images forming the original video even in the similar ones. A hybrid embedding scheme, which is based on the Least Significant Bit (LSB) and the Discrete Wavelet Transform (DWT) algorithms, is performed to insert the signature. Hence, a high level of invisibility of the suggested method will be obtained thanks to the insertion only in the mosaic images which are different since the similar ones are not used during the video reconstruction. In addition, the use of mosaic image as a destination to insert the signature will allows obtaining robustness against malicious manipulations like collusion and compression attacks. Comparatively to the previous work [13], the suggested method is evaluated using more data sets and it is validated by calculating other metrics such as the Peak Signal-to-Noise Ratio (PSNR), the Structural Similarity Index (SSIM), the Normalized Correlation (NC), the Normalized Hamming Distance (NHD), and the Bit Error Rate (BER) in order to prove the level of invisibility and robustness of the put forward approach. Furthermore, more related works about robust video watermarking techniques against collusion and anaglyph 3D image and 3D video watermarking approaches are introduced and discussed in this work.

The remainder of this paper is organized as follows: Sect. 2 deals with a state of the art about the collusion attack and the existing video watermarking schemes robust against it, the existing anaglyph 3D images watermarking approaches, and the related works for anaglyph 3D video watermarking methods. Sect. 3 explains the proposed anaglyph 3D video watermarking method which is based on mosaic images as an embedding target using a hybrid domain. Sect. 4 evaluates the suggested approach using the obtained experimental results. Sect. 5 depicts a comparison of the proposed scheme with the existing ones. The final section recapitulates the whole paper and gives some perspectives for future researches.

2   Related Works

2.1   Robust Video Watermarking Techniques Against Collusion

As well as geometric attacks, frame-based attacks and temporal attacks, the collusion is treated as a very important video attack in video watermarking. The collusion is a very dangerous attack which allow obtaining an unmarked video without knowing the watermarking algorithm. The attacker need just to have many different copies of the marked video to estimate and remove the embedded mark in the video. There are two fundamental types of collusion attacks:

1. Collusion type 1 (Fig. 1): The attacker obtains a set of different marked videos which are marked using the same signature. To approximate the embedded signature, the attacker averages all the marked videos. If all of them have the same mark, then the used averaging method allows to obtain the corresponding mark. Afterward, to get the unmarked videos, the obtained signature will be extracted from the marked ones.

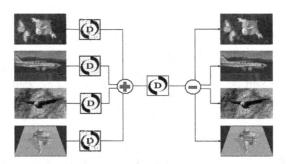

Fig. 1. Type 1 of collusion attack (different videos marked with the same mark.)

2. Collusion type 2 (Fig. 2): The attacker receives first a group of samples of the same video marked with various signatures. Second, he tries to pick up the identical corresponding video frames. Then, the different video scenes are separated from each other and the signatures are mixed together by calculating the average of all the adjacent frames in order to decide the unmarked frames. Finally, the attacker combines all the obtained unmarked frames to generate an unmarked video. If the consecutive video frames are sufficiently different, then the second type will be achieved successfully.

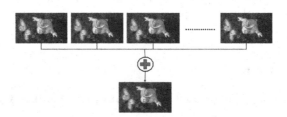

Fig. 2. Type 2 of collusion attack(the same video marked with different marks.)

The collusion is an important and considerable attack in video watermarking. For this reason, the number of video watermarking techniques which can resist collusion attack increases more and more [4,11]. In fact, the researchers proposed two solutions to resist collusion attack either by using a scheme which is based on the insertion in the mosaic images or by using a complex embedding scheme which makes hard the extraction of the signature. Actually, a mosaic image, called also a sprite, is a panoramic illustration enclosing all the data information incorporated into the video sequence. Three fundamental phases are necessary to generate the mosaic image [33]. The first phase is the detection of all the points of interest existing in all the frames forming the video sequence. The second phase consists first of matching the extracted feature points from different images to retrieve similar feature points, then removing the predicted mismatch using the random sample consensus which is used to filter the false matched points between two images, and finally aligning either two continuous frames or the frame and the valid mosaic image by applying the suitable transformation. In the third phase, the average filtering is used to integrate the image in order to obtain the mosaic image by determining the analogous part of the transformed image and joining it to the previous mosaic image.

According to the first solution, a video watermarking technique which is robust against collusion, frame dropping and MPEG4 compression was proposed in [21]. this scheme is based on a Spread Spectrum (SS) algorithm and a spatial insertion domain, where the signature was inserted in the mosaic image generated from all the frames forming the video sequence. [4] proposed a blind video watermarking scheme based on a dynamic multi-sprite generation algorithm to protect the video copyright where the signature was embedded in the different generated sprites using the Middle Significant Bit (MIDSB) technique. This method is robust against collusion attack as well as usual and temporal attacks and have a reduced complexity. In [3], to resist collusion attack, the mark was inserted in the sprites generated from each set of frames forming the original video, using the LSB algorithm. Another video watermarking technique which resist collusion attack in addition to noise and MPEG4 Compression attacks was put forward in [20]. The signature was inserted in the chosen regions of moved objects of the mosaic image obtained from the original video. To protect the video from malicious manipulations, the authors in [20] have used three frequency domains based algorithms: DWT, SVD, and Discrete Cosine Transform (DCT). To protect videos from collusion attack and other video manipulations, authors in [19] suggested a video watermarking method based on the detection of the feature regions from the whole video using a crowdsourcing technique. The signature was embedded in the obtained mosaic image using a multi-frequency insertion domain.

Corresponding to the second solution, a robust and blind video watermarking technique is proposed in [6], where the mark was embedded in the coefficients obtained after the DWT decomposition of each video frame. This scheme needs a low processing time and it is robust against collusion, common video attacks and combined ones. To protect videos from collusion attack, authors in [15] proposed a DWT and a Group Search Optimization algorithm based video watermarking. The mark was embedded in some selected frames using the GSO algorithm after applying the DWT decomposition to optimize the selected positions. [1] proposed a video watermarking technique which is adequate for copyright protection and authentication applications. This scheme was based on bit plane slicing method and hybrid insertion algorithm using the contourlet transform, the DWT, and the Singular Value Decomposition (SVD). It resist image processing attacks, temporal attacks and collusion attack. A robust real time video watermarking scheme based on the krawtchouk moments and the DCT was put forwarded in [5] where the mark was embedded in the selected DCT coefficients of the matrix of the Krawtchouk moments obtained from the luminance component. The marked frames were obtained from marked moments to generate the marked video. Indeed, the authors in [5] are interested on the first type of collusion attack where the same mark is inserted into different video frames. This technique make difficult the extraction of mark. It is robust against geometric and temporal attacks in addition to collusion attack. A frame by frame video watermarking algorithm was presented in [22]. Indeed, different marks were embedded in each frame forming the cover video using a Block Truncation Coding, DWT and SVD methods. This technique makes difficult the estimation of mark and enhances both invisibility and robustness against usual attacks as well as collusion attacks. An other blind video watermarking method based on the DCT and the Complex Zernike Moments (CZM) is presented in [17]. It withstand rotation and collusion attacks. In fact, a binary mark was inserted in each luminance channel of all the frames forming the video sequence using the CZM in order to make the scheme robust against video frames based attacks and against rotation. In addition, to resist collusion attack, the authors used a pseudo random number generator and a permutation vector to diversify the embedding blocks.

Some complex 3D data watermarking schemes have been proposed in order to withstand collusion attacks. The authors in [16] were proposed a 3D mesh watermarking scheme based on the mesh spectral analysis and the anti-collusion fingerprint code. Another 3D watermarking technique resist collusion attacks was suggested [25]. It was invariant to the view synthesis process utilized in the depth image based rendering algorithm, where the chosen signature was inserted in the coefficients of the 3rd level of 2D dual-tree complex wavelet transform of the main view image. This technique resist noise, synthesis view attacks, compression in addition to collusion attacks.

2.2   Anaglyph 3D Image Watermarking

Recently, various watermarking techniques are proposed in the literature to protect anaglyph 3D images. They can be classified using two criteria: the selected insertion domain and the chosen channel to embed the signature [12].

Actually, most of the authors were chosen almost the frequency domain and the right as an embedding target. The mark can be inserted into the coefficients bits recovered either after applying DWT [7, 32], DCT [23], or Fractional Fourier Transform (FrFT) [31]. Moreover, the mark can be inserted either into blue, red image [26] or into all blue, red and depth images composing the anaglyph image [28, 32]. In fact, A blind watermarking technique was proposed in [24] to secure 3D anaglyph images which is based on the jacket matrix and the 3D-DWT. The jacket matrix was applied on the middle-level sub-band blocks of the anaglyph image. Then, the signature was added to the diagonal elements of these blocks because they are less delicate to the signature manipulation. This method prove a good invisibility level and a good robustness against various attacks. The authors in [26] were proposed an anaglyph image watermarking method based on DWT, where the chosen signature was embedded just in the cyan image. This scheme prove a significant level of invisibility, and an insufficiency of robustness against attacks. Likewise, the authors in [31] were chosen to embed the signature only in the cyan image of the anaglyph image but, using the 2D-FrFT domain. The PSNR value calculated between marked and original anaglyph image was about 27 dB which present a low level of invisibility. While, the signature was inserted in all the images forming the anaglyph 3D images (red, cyan and depth image) using the wavelet decomposition in [28, 32]. The two proposed algorithms were robust against various attacks and were showed a high level of invisibility. Another DWT based anaglyph watermarking technique was suggested in [7] which contains two phases. During the training phase, the Genetic Algorithm was applied to optimize the coefficient bits of LH and HL bands, and then the Back Propagation Neural Network was performed to train them. During the testing step, the Advanced Encryption Standard technique was developed to embed the binary signature. This approach was compared with other previous works and the experimental results validate the performance of this scheme. The writers in [8] were proposed a watermarking scheme to protect the copyrights of anaglyph images. In fact, the signature was encrypted first using the Arnold transformation and then, it was embedded, using the principal component analysis, in the selected sub-bands of the transformed anaglyph image using the non sub-sampled contourlet transform. This scheme was shown a high invisibility level and a good robustness against different manipulations. In [23], the DCT frequency domain was chosen as an embedding target by applying the Quantization of Index Modulation (QIM). Indeed, the DCT was applied to the mark and the luminance Y channel of the original image, where the signature was inserted using the QIM. The evaluation was shown an acceptable level of invisibility, where the PSNR value was about 41 dB, and robustness against noises and JPEG compression. Another two invisible and robust watermarking schemes based on DCT were suggested in order to secure the anaglyph 3D images [30]. In the first scheme, the authors were tried to embed the signature in the coefficients obtained with DCT using the Spread Spectrum algorithm. In the second one, the adaptive Dither Modulation (DM) technique with Watson's improved perception model was applied, where the mark was inserted just into the middle frequency coefficients of the DCT. The two proposed schemes has presented an acceptable level of invisibility and a good robustness against different kind of attacks.

As a comparison, the existing works based on DWT domain and the blue image as an embedding destination, provide the highest invisibility level and the best robustness against different kind of attacks, compared with the works based on DCT and FrFT domains [12].

2.3 Anaglyph 3D Video Watermarking

A few number of existing works are proposed until now to secure anaglyph 3D videos. As a matter of fact, a blind DWT based anaglyph video watermarking was proposed in 2013 [29], where the signature is inserted in the blue images of all the video frames. The authors choose the blue images as an embedding target because the change in the blue color is slightly observed by the human visual system. Therefore, a lack of robustness may be caused if the attackers target only blue images and then the embedded signature will be easily lost. In 2015, the writers were tried to enhance the proposed method by embedding the signature, using the DWT, in all the blue images forming the frames where a scene change is detected [27]. However, this algorithm can provoke a fragile watermarking scheme if an anglyph 3D video contains just one or few number of scenes. Another anaglyph 3D video watermarking scheme based on Group of Pictures (GOP) and the DWT was suggested in [9]. Indeed, the authors have divided first the original video into a set of GOPs, second, they have divided each GOP into three images types (I, B and R) to embed the given binary mark. Finally, they have recombined all the marked GOPs to obtain the marked anaglyph 3D video. In fact, the cyan and red images are both marked in B and R images, respectively. While the cyan, red and depth images are all marked in I images. Hence, if an attacker tries to extract the signature inserted in B images, then, the signature still found in I and R images. This technique affords a high visual quality level and a good robustness against usual manipulations, compression and frame based attacks. In [10], an anaglyph 3D video watermarking algorithm which resist MPEG-4 and H264-AVC video compression was suggested. It is based on the use of two signatures and on a hybrid embedding algorithm using both a spatial and frequency domains: LSB, DWT, and DCT. Indeed, the first mark is embedded in both cyan and red images obtained from each frame forming the video using a DCT and LSB based algorithms, respectively. The second mark is inserted in the Low frequency bands of the obtained anaglyph frame after applying the first embedding. To obtain the marked anaglyph frames, the inverse of DWT was applied.

Most of the previous existing techniques resist usual image processing attacks, geometric attacks and compression but they cannot resist collusion attack which is considered as the most dangerous video manipulation. In 2019, an anaglyph 3D video watermarking approach based on multi-sprite generation is proposed in [11]. It is robust against collusion attack thanks to the use of multi-sprites generated from each set of 25 frames as an insertion target. In addition, multi-sprites allow a good reconstruction quality compared with a single sprite generated from the whole of video. In fact, the chosen mark is embedded in the high frequency and the low frequency sub-bands of each generated sprite using the DWT based technique and the middle significant bit (MIDSB) algorithm, respectively. This scheme provides an acceptable visual quality level compared with [9,10] due to the application of the inverse sprite generation during the marked video reconstruction.

3   Proposed Robust Watermarking Method

The study of the existing anaglyph 3D video watermarking schemes demonstrate a significant invisibility level and good robustness against many attacks. On the other hand, most of them ignore malicious attacks such as MPEG compression and mainly collusion attacks. The main object in this paper is to take into consideration the robustness against malicious attacks. Hence, the use of mosaic images as a target of the signature insertion in the proposed anaglyph 3D video watermarking method is necessary. As a matter of fact, all the frames of a video sequence can be depicted in a single mosaic image. However, several obstacles can be caused like the long processing time in the mosaic generation and the degradation effect after the reconstruction of the mosaic image. In other words, if a video sequence contains many frames, then the size of the generated mosaic image will be too large, the time generation will be augmented, and the video quality will be altered. Hence, the generation of multiple mosaic images from a video sequence can be performed as a solution for the previous problems. Indeed, it consists of dividing the video sequence into many groups of frames, instead of using the whole video, and generating a mosaic image for each of them, similarly to a single mosaic image. This process requires the use of different parameters to determine the required frame number to generate the mosaic image [2].

To retrieve a good solution robust against collusion attack and reduce the problems of the generation of a single mosaic image from the whole video, a robust anaglyph 3D video-based watermarking scheme is put forward in this paper. It is based on the use of multiple mosaic images and a hybrid insertion domain as an insertion destination. In fact, the original anaglyph video will be first divided into many sub-sequences per a second containing each 25 frames and a mosaic image will be generated for each sub-sequence. The generation method based on SURF descriptor proposed in [4] will be used to generate different mosaic images. It consists in updating the mosaic image using just the most recent obtained mosaic image and the valid received frame. This method [4] will be used thanks to its decreased time processing and lowered information quantity required during the treatment of the mosaic images. Second, a comparison between each two successive mosaic images is performed where each mosaic image will be compared with its previous one. If the two compared mosaic images are identical so one of them will be selected to embed the chosen signature into it and the other one will not be used and it will not be required during the reconstruction of the final marked anaglyph 3D video which that the inverse mosaic image generation will not be applied to the unmarked mosaic images. Actually, for the first second, the mosaic image will be generated and the mark will be automatically embedded into it. Next, another mosaic image will be generated from the second set of 25 frames and then compared with the first one. If they are similar, the mark will not be inserted in the second mosaic. If they are different, the mark should be inserted in the second mosaic image. After that, another mosaic image will be generated from the next second and will be compared to the previous one. If they are not resembling, the chosen mark will be inserted into the generated mosaic image otherwise it will not be embedded. This process will be continued until the end of the frames forming the anaglyph 3D video. Therefore, the mark will not be inserted in all the generated mosaic images from each 25 frames. It will be embedded only in the mosaic image which are not similar to each other. Besides, to compare each two successive mosaic images, the PSNR is calculated between a mosaic image and its previous one. If the calculated PSNR value is higher than the threshold 50 dB, then the two compared mosaic images are identical and the mark will be embedded in one of them. In this process, the determined threshold is used as a secret key to select in which mosaic image the mark will be inserted. Hence, the security of the proposed scheme, which is defined as the ability to withstand unauthorized mark removal, insertion or detection manipulations, will be enhanced since the attacker cannot easily locate the position of the inserted signature. After the selection of the signature locations, both the DWT and LSB based algorithms are used to embed the signature in all the mosaic images which are different to each other. Finally, these marked mosaic images will be divided into marked sub-sequence frames. Then, the marked frames will be recombined with the unmarked ones and they will be all used to reconstruct the marked anaglyph video. Indeed, Multiple mosaic images are selected because of their higher reconstruction quality compared with a unique mosaic image, the selection of only the mosaic images, which are not similar to embed the signature, enhances the invisibility of the proposed approach because if a number of mosaic images is not marked then the application of the inverse mosaic generation is not necessary for them during the marked video reconstruction. Furthermore, the hybrid domain is chosen because it ameliorates both the visual quality of the marked video and the robustness against malicious manipulations.

The general outline of the suggested method is depicted in Fig. 3. It comprises different steps: Generating a mosaic image from each 25 frames per second, comparing each obtained successive mosaics using the PSNR as a similarity measure, embedding the selected signature in all the mosaics which are not similar, restoring the marked frames from the marked mosaics, and finally recombining the unmarked frames to the marked one to reconstruct the final marked anaglyph video.

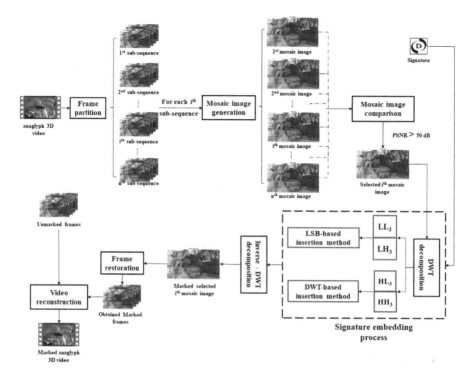

Fig. 3. The general outline of the proposed scheme.

3.1 Proposed Embedding and Detection Algorithms

The first main step in a watermarking scheme is the insertion of an invisible signature in the corresponding media and the second step is the extraction of this embedded signature.

To embed the chosen signature in the anaglyph 3D video, different steps are applied after the generation of the mosaic images and the selection of those which are different to each other. In fact, firstly, regarding the size of each selected generated mosaic image, the signature is spread. Next, the 3rd level of wavelet transform is applied to both the spread mark and the selected mosaic image, where high and low frequency sub-bands coefficients are obtained. Then, the insertion step is going through a hybrid domain: spacial and frequency domains. In fact, the coefficients of the high-frequency (HH_3 and HL_3) of the spread mark are joined to those of the each selected mosaic image in order to have the marked ones as in Eq. 1.

$$Marked_{HH} = HH_{frame} + \alpha * HH_{mark}$$
$$Marked_{HL} = HL_{frame} + \alpha * HL_{mark}$$
$$(1)$$

Secondly, an LSB based insertion algorithm is performed where the first bit of the spread mark are inserted in the least significant bits of each low frequency coefficients (LL_3 and LH_3) of each selected mosaic image pixels because they enclose the whole of the image information. Indeed, the insertion in the low frequency conceive a scheme which resist different compression attacks and the visual quality of the marked mosaic image does not be altered when the first bit is modified. Third, the inverse of wavelet transform is applied to the marked high and low frequency coefficient to generate the different marked mosaic images. Finally, the marked frames are reconstructed from all the marked mosaic images and they are joined with the rest unmarked frames to create the final marked anaglyph 3D video.

Concerning the detection step, the generated mosaic images from the original anaglyph 3D video are required in order to validate the existence of the signature in the designated anaglyph 3D video and remove it. As a matter of fact, the inverse of the embedding method is performed to extract the embedded mark. Firstly, the marked anaglyph 3D video is decomposed into different mosaic images generated from each 25 marked frames. Then, each two successive mosaic images are compared to each other using the PSNR and those, which are not identical, are selected to extract the embedded mark. Next, the 3rd level of wavelet transform is applied on each selected marked mosaic image. Secondly, the coefficients of the low frequency LL_3 and LH_3 of every mosaic image are selected and the least significant bits are taken out to find the embedded bits of the spread signature. Besides, the high frequency coefficients HH_3 and HL_3 of each marked mosaic images are subtracted from those of the original ones. Then, the I-DWT is performed to retrieve the embedded spread mark. The final step consists of dividing the spread signature into many signatures and selecting among them the signature corresponding the most to the inserted mark.

4   Experimental Results

The MATLAB platform version 8.6 is used to implement the put forward approach on a PC qualified by an Intel Core i7-7500U CPU and 8 GB of memory. The assessment of this scheme is based mainly by two criteria: invisibility and robustness. To demonstrate the effectiveness of the proposed approach, various tests are performed on a set of original anaglyph 3D videos. In fact, these videos have a number of various properties such as the texture of background, the movement in the different schemes, the resolution and the number of frames in the video. The different selected video's properties are illustrated in Table 1. The selected signature to be embedded in the different anaglyph 3D videos is a binary image with 32×32 of size.

4.1   Invisibility

The invisibility means that the mark embedded in any video cannot be observed by the human eye and don't alter the visual quality of the video. After embedding the mark in different anaglyph 3D video tests, no significant degradation between original (Fig. 4.a) and marked (Fig. 4.b) anaglyph video is perceived.

Table 1. Properties of the video tests.

Videos	Properties			
	Resolution	Frame-number	Movement	Background-Texture
Video 1	1280 × 720	650	Slow	Textured
Video 2	1280 × 720	1050	Rapid	Textured
Video 3	640 × 320	875	Slow	Uniform
Video 4	1280 × 720	750	Rapid	Textured
Video 5	1280 × 720	4500	Medium	Textured
Video 6	480 × 360	250	Slow	Uniform
Video 7	480 × 360	300	Slow	Textured
Video 8	1280 × 720	900	Medium	Uniform
Video 9	640 × 320	400	Medium	Uniform
Video 10	480 × 360	725	Slow	Textured
Video 11	1280 × 720	950	Rapid	Textured
Video 12	1280 × 720	575	Medium	Textured

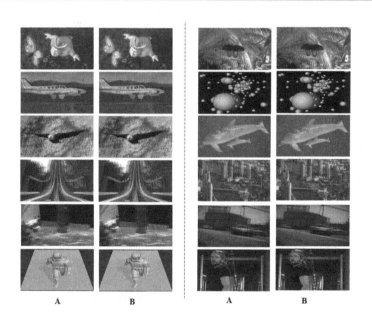

Fig. 4. a- Original frames. b- Marked frames.

To prove quantitatively the high level of the invisibility of the proposed app-roach, the average of the PSNR (Mean-PSNR) values and the average of the SSIM (Mean-SSIM) are calculated between original and marked anaglyph 3D videos. In fact, a PSNR value is calculated for each frame forming the original and the marked video sequence.

Suppose that a video contains p frames of size (M×N), the Mean-PSNR is calculated between the pth original I_p and marked video frame $\hat{I}_p$ as follows:

$$(Mean - PSNR)_{dB} = \frac{1}{p} \sum_{p=1}^{p} PSNR_p \tag{2}$$

$$(PSNR_p)_{dB} = 10.\log_{10}(\frac{max_{I_p}^2}{MSE_p}) \tag{3}$$

Where max_{I_p} is the maximum pixel value of the original frame I_p, and MSE_p is the mean squared error calculated between original and marked frames (4).

$$(MSE_p)_{dB} = \frac{1}{M \times N} \sum_{i=1}^{M} \sum_{i=1}^{N} [I_p(i,j) - \hat{I}_p(i,j)]^2 \tag{4}$$

Usually, the higher the Mean-PSNR value, the better quality of the marked video. In other words, a high level of invisibility is obtained with an average PSNR value superior to 40 dB. The obtained Mean-PSNR values for anaglyph 3D video tests are illustrated in Fig. 5. They show that the proposed watermarking method provides a high invisibility rate with the selected mark where the minimum Mean-PSNR value is about 58 dB and its maximum is about 70 dB.

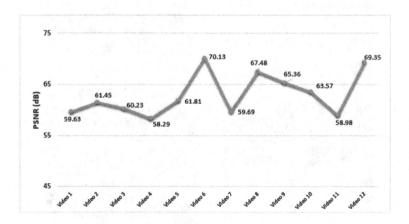

Fig. 5. The Mean-PSNR values obtained for different anaglyph 3D video tests.

To measure the similarity between original and marked video, the Mean-SSIM is calculated (Fig. 6). It is defined as in Eq. 5, where the input is the original video frames and the marked ones and the output is an integer value: close to 1 for better quality of marked video and close to 0 for lower quality.

$$Mean - SSIM = \frac{1}{p} \sum_{p=1}^{p} SSIM(I_p, \hat{I}_p) \tag{5}$$

$$SSIM(I_p, \hat{I}_p) = \frac{(2\mu_{I_p}\mu_{\hat{I}_p} + C_1)(2\sigma_{I_p\hat{I}_p} + C_2)}{(\mu_{I_p}^2 + \mu_{\hat{I}_p}^2 + C_1)(\sigma_{I_p}^2 + \sigma_{\hat{I}_p}^2 + C_2)} \quad (6)$$

Where:

- μ_{I_p} and $\mu_{\hat{I}_p}$ are the mean intensity values for original and marked p^{th} frame, respectively.
- $\sigma_{I_p\hat{I}_p}$ represents the covariance of the original and marked p^{th} frame.
- σ_{I_p} and $\sigma_{\hat{I}_p}$ denote the variances and deviations of the original and marked p^{th} frame, respectively.
- C_1 and C_2 are two constants used to maintain stability. They are defined as:

$$C_1 = (K_1 L)^2 \quad and \quad C_2 = (K_2 L)^2 \quad (7)$$

Where L is the dynamic range of the video frames, $K_1 < 1$ and $K_2 < 1$

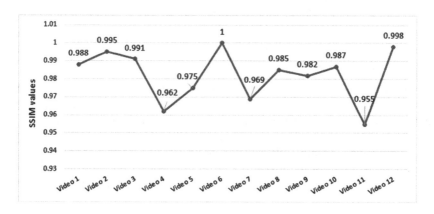

Fig. 6. The Mean-SSIM values obtained for different anaglyph 3D video tests.

4.2 Robustness

In order to evaluate the robustness of the proposed technique, various usual and malicious attacks are applied on the different anaglyph 3D video tests. To quantify the visual quality of the extracted mark after applying the attacks,in other words, the robustness of the proposed watermarking method, the NC, the BER, and the NHD are calculated between original and extracted mark. The acceptable value for these metrics is between 0 and 1. Indeed, the NC is used to predict the similarity between the original mark and the extracted one from the marked anaglyph 3D video as defined in the following equation:

$$NC = \frac{\sum_{i=1}^{M}\sum_{j=1}^{N} W(i,j).\hat{W}(i,j)}{\sum_{i=1}^{M}\sum_{j=1}^{N}[W(i,j)]^2} \quad (8)$$

Where, W and $\hat{W}$ are the pixel values of the original and extracted mark, respectively. And, $M \times N$ is the size of the mark.

If there is a correlation between the original mark and the extracted one, the maximum NC value will be close to 1, which confirm the robustness of the watermarking algorithm and if there is a large difference, it converges to 0.

The BER is used to calculate the degree of dissimilarity (the error rate) between the extracted mark and the original one as in Eq. 9. Contrary to the NC, the smaller BER value, the better robustness of the proposed technique. It is close to 0 if there is a similarity between extracted and original mark and it converges to 1 otherwise.

$$BER = number\ of\ error\ bits/number\ of\ total\ bits \qquad (9)$$

The NHD is defined as in Eq. 10. It is used as a similarity degree calculated between original W and extracted mark $\hat{W}$, which have N as its length, to decide the robustness of the proposed approach. In fact, the better robustness result is represented by the smaller hamming distance.

$$NHD = \frac{1}{N} \sum_{i=1}^{N} W(i) \bigoplus \hat{W}(i) \qquad (10)$$

Actually, a robust video watermarking technique should resist almost three types of attacks which are the normal image processing attacks include the geometric attacks, the temporal synchronization attacks such as frame based attacks and frame rate conversion, and the dangerous attacks such as MPEG compression and collusion. Initially, different image processing attacks are applied on all the test videos. First, some geometric attacks, such as rotation using variable angles (20°, 50° and 90°), scaling (reduction of 10% and 40% and enlargement

Table 2. The average of NHD, BER, and NC values for different video tests after geometric attacks.

Attacks		NHD	BER	NC
Rotation	20°	0	0	1
	50°	0.01	0.001	0.998
	90°	0.04	0.003	0.996
Translation	-	0.03	0.002	0.997
Resizing	-	0.05	0.003	0.995
Scaling	Reduction 10%	0	0	1
	Reduction 40%	0.03	0.002	0.997
	Enlargement 200%	0.08	0.006	0.983
Cropping	5%	0	0	1
	35%	0.08	0.005	0.988
	50%	0.1	0.006	0.972

of 200%), cropping and resizing. After applying these geometric attacks on the different frames forming the video tests, an NC values between 0.97 and 1, a BER values between 0 and 0.006, and an NHD values between 0 and 0.08, are obtained. These results are illustrated in Table 2, which guarantee the robustness of the suggested scheme against geometric attacks, because the DWT is invariant to them and the mark is repeated in the sprite of each sub-sequence video.

Second, different noises are applied to the marked anaglyph videos to validate the robustness of the proposed method against them, viz. the salt & pepper with density of 0.1, the Gaussian with variance of 0.01, the Speckle with variance of 0.04, and the Poisson noise. The average of obtained NC, BER, and NHD measures are depicted in Table 3, which confirm the possibility of extracting the mark after the applied noises. Then, several enhancement based attacks are tested. In fact, two types of filtering are applied on the marked sequences in order to highlight or remove certain frames features, like the median, and the Gaussian filters. The BER, the NHD, and the NC measures were almost about 0.006, 0.085, and 0.98, respectively. Thanks to the invariance of the used wavelet transform, the suggested technique is robust against filtering attacks. Afterwards, the contrast adjustment and the histogram equalization are performed as an enhancement based attacks, to enhance the contrast of the marked video sequences. The signature still readable and it can be extracted where the average of NC, NHD, and BER values are about 1, 0, and 0, respectively. In addition, a blurring method is applied as an attack on the marked video where a low-pass filter is used with a Gaussian variance equal to 5. The detection of the signature is done successfully where the NC, NHD, and BER values are close to 0.99, 0.03 and 0.001, respectively for almost anaglyph video tests.

Table 3. The average of NHD, BER, and NC values for different video tests after noise and enhancement based attacks.

Attacks		NHD	BER	NC
Noise	Salt and Pepper d = 0.1	0.01	0.002	0.996
	Gaussian V = 0.01	0.02	0.002	0.997
	Poisson	0.05	0.004	0.992
	Speckle V = 0.04	0.07	0.003	0.994
Filtering	Median	0.09	0.006	0.983
	Gaussian	0.08	0.006	0.985
Contrast adjust.	-	0	0	1
Histogram equal.	-	0	0	1
Blurring	-	0.03	0.001	0.997

Secondly, some temporal synchronization attacks are performed by testing several frame based attacks and frame rate conversion on the marked anaglyph

3D videos tests. In fact, the frame dropping, the frame swapping, and the frame duplication attacks are applied in order to remove the embedded signature in the marked anaglyph 3D videos tests. Since all the different generated mosaic images contain their own signature, the detection of the signature still possible after duplicating several frames in the same marked video, or removing some of them, or changing the order of a number of marked frames. The obtained average of NC, NHD, and BER values confirm the robustness of the proposed approach after these frames based attacks where they are about 0.99, 0.01 and 0.001, respectively. After that, the frame rate conversion attack is applied where the frame rate is changed from 30 fps to 10 fps. The signature detection is achieved due to the use of the mosaic images as an embedding target where the mark is located in all the mosaic images, which are not similar, containing in the marked video. Table 4 represents the average of the obtained results for all the video tests.

Table 4. The average of NHD, BER, and NC values for different video tests after frame-based attacks.

Attacks	NHD	BER	NC
Frame duplication	0	0	1
Frame dropping	0	0	1
Frame swapping	0.02	0.001	0.999
Frame rate conversion 15 fps	0.05	0.002	0.995

Finally, the suggested technique is evaluated against dangerous attacks such as H264-AVC and MPEG-4 compression with a varying bit rate (from 2 Mbps to 512 kbps). The compression is realized under the mediacoder application[1], which is suitable for transcoding different video. The acquired results prove the robustness of the put forward method against compression thanks to the use of multi-sprites as a target of mark insertion. In fact, the obtained average of NC value is about 0.99, the corresponding average NHD value is close to 0.01, and the average of BER value is equal to 0.002, approximately. Moreover, the collusion attack, which is known as the most dangerous manipulation in video watermarking techniques, is evaluated. Indeed, it estimates the inserted signature and then removes it from the marked video without degrading its visual quality. During the experimentations, the first and second type of collusion attack are tested and the proposed approach resists them. The results of NHD, BER, and NC values are illustrated in the following table and they confirm the robustness of the suggested scheme against collusion attack due to the use of multi-sprites which represents similarly the same physical points of each frame forming the video. The Table 5 represents the average of the NC, NHD and BER values obtained after applying the compression attacks and the two types of collusion attack on the marked anaglyph video tests.

---

[1] http://www.mediacoderhq.com.

Table 5. Obtained results after compression and collusion attacks for different test videos.

Attacks		NHD	BER	NC
Compression	MPEG-4	0.02	0.003	0.995
	H264-AVC	0.01	0.001	0.999
Collusion	Type-1	0	0.001	1
	Type-2	0.01	0.002	0.997

5   Comparative Study

In order to justify the performance of the proposed approach, a comparative study between the proposed method and the existing watermarking techniques dedicated to anaglyph 3D videos [9–11,13,27,29] is performed.

Based on the invisibility criteria, the PSNR value measured for the proposed scheme and the existing works confirms the high level of invisibility of the suggested approach compared with some existing approaches. In fact, these values of PSNR are represented in Fig. 7, where the PSNR value of the put forward technique is close to 70 dB. Compared to a previous published work [13], the proposed approach has a higher visual quality level due to the insertion of the mark only in the generated mosaics which are not similar first and secondly because the similar mosaics are not used during the marked video reconstruction. In other words, The invisibility degradation shown in [13] is due to the use of all the marked mosaics in the reconstruction of the marked video which provoke a loss of some information.

Based on the robustness criteria, the comparative study, summarized in Table 6, confirms the robustness of the proposed scheme against almost of manipulations such as the image processing based attacks, enhancement based attacks, frame based attacks, and malicious attacks. In fact, the proposed method is robust

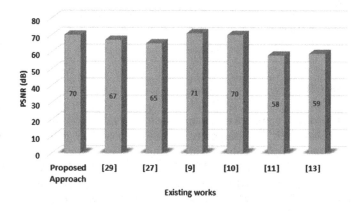

Fig. 7. Invisibility comparison based on the PSNR measurements.

against different geometric attacks, different additional noises, several enhancement attacks such as filtering, blurring, contrast adjustment, and histogram equalization, various frame based attacks viz., frame insertion, swapping, dropping and frame rate changing, and malicious attacks such as MPEG-4 and H264-AVC compression and collusion attacks. Whereas, most of the existing techniques are not robust against the different frame based attacks and malicious attacks. Indeed, all of the existing works are not robust against the frame rate conversion attacks. [9,10,27,29] cannot resist the collusion attacks compared with [11,13] and the proposed technique which are robust against collusion. In addition, only [10] and the suggested scheme resist the H264-AVC compression, the translation, and the frame insertion attacks. Only [27,29] are not robust against MPEG-4 compression, frame dropping and swapping, scaling, resizing, and speckle and poisson noises attacks.

Table 6. Comparison of the robustness of existing anaglyph 3D video watermarking against several attacks.

Different attacks		Proposed approach	[29]	[27]	[9]	[10]	[11]	[13]
Geometric Attacks	Rotation	✓	✓	-	✓	✓	✓	✓
	Translation	✓	-	-	✓	-	-	-
	Cropping	✓	✓	✓	✓	✓	✓	✓
	Resizing	✓	-	-	✓	✓	✓	✓
	Scaling	✓	-	-	✓	✓	✓	✓
Noise	Salt and Pepper	✓	✓	✓	✓	✓	✓	✓
	Gaussian	✓	✓	✓	✓	✓	✓	✓
	Speckle	✓	-	-	✓	✓	✓	✓
	Poisson	✓	-	-	✓	✓	✓	✓
Enhancement attacks	Filtering	✓	✓	✓	✓	✓	✓	✓
	Contrast adjust.	✓	✓	✓	✓	✓	✓	✓
	Histogram equal.	✓	✓	✓	✓	✓	✓	✓
	Blurring	✓	✓	✓	✓	✓	✓	✓
Frame-based attacks	Frame insertion	✓	-	-	-	✓	-	-
	Frame swapping	✓	-	-	✓	✓	✓	✓
	Frame dropping	✓	-	-	✓	✓	✓	✓
	Frame rate conversion	✓	-	-	-	-	-	-
Malicious Attacks	MPEG-4 comp.	✓	-	-	✓	✓	✓	✓
	H264-AVC comp.	✓	-	-	-	✓	-	-
	Collusion	✓	-	-	-	-	✓	✓

6   Conclusions

An efficient and robust watermarking approach dedicated to anaglyph 3D video is discussed in this paper. The suggested method is based on generating multiple mosaic images from the anaglyph 3D video, which presents an adequate and suitable embedding destination for both 2D and 3D videos. To improve and enlarge the invisibility level of the proposed method and enhance its robustness against various manipulations, different mosaic images are generated from each 25 frames and compared using a similarity measure. Then, a signature was inserted only in the mosaics which are not identical, using a spatial and frequency domain by applying an LSB and a DWT based insertion algorithms where both the high and low frequency sub-bands, obtained after the wavelets decomposition, are selected to embed the signature. The LSB technique was applied on the LL and LH sub-bands and the DWT based technique was applied to the HH and HL sub-bands. The selection of multiples mosaic images as a destination of the signature insertion gives more robustness against dangerous attacks mostly against collusion attack and a higher visual quality of the marked video after the reconstruction process compared with a unique mosaic image created from the whole video sequence. In addition, the use of a significant threshold as a secret key to select the different mosaic images to embed the mark maximises the security level of the proposed technique. Moreover, the invisibility level and the robustness degree against different image processing attacks are enhanced due to the use of the DWT and the LSB based watermarking techniques.

Various Experimentations were realized on different anaglyph 3D test videos and they confirm the robustness of the suggested technique against the applied attacks viz. different image processing attacks, some enhancement attacks, and several frame-based attacks, as well as dangerous video attacks such as MPEG-4 and H264-AVC compression and collusion attack where the obtained average of NC value was up to 0.8, the average of NHD value and BER value, as well as dangerous video attacks such as MPEG-4 and H264-AVC compression and collusion attack where the obtained average of NC value was up to 0.8, the average of NHD value and BER value were under 0.04 and 0.006, respectively. Furthermore, the average of PSNR and SSIM values calculated between original and marked videos proves the good visual quality rate of the put forward scheme. Additionally, the proposed technique was compared with the existing watermarking approaches dedicated to anaglyph 3D videos. This comparative study confirms that the suggested technique has an acceptable performance rate in terms of invisibility and the best one in terms of robustness. Finally, the proposed method can be more ameliorated and by changing the algorithm of the insertion step and upgrading the process of mosaic images generation.

References

1. Agilandeeswari, L., Ganesan, K.: A robust color video watermarking scheme based on hybrid embedding techniques. Multimedia Tools Appl. **75**(14), 8745–8780 (2015). https://doi.org/10.1007/s11042-015-2789-9
2. Barhoumi, W., Bakkay, M.C., Zagrouba, E.: An online approach for multi-sprite generation based on camera parameters estimation. Signal Image Video Process. **7**(5), 843–853 (2011). https://doi.org/10.1007/s11760-011-0273-1
3. Bayoudh, I., Ben Jabra, S., Zagrouba, E.: On line video watermarking-a new robust approach of video watermarking based on dynamic multi-sprites generation, In: VISAPP. pp. 158–165 (2015)
4. Bayoudh, I., Ben Jabra, S., Zagrouba, E.: Online multi-sprites based video watermarking robust to collusion and transcoding attacks for emerging applications. Multimedia Tools Appl. **77**(11), 14361–14379 (2017). https://doi.org/10.1007/s11042-017-5033-y

5. Bayoudh, I., Ben Jabra, S., Zagrouba, E.: A robust video watermarking for real-time application. In: International Conference on Advanced Concepts for Intelligent Vision Systems, pp. 493–504 (2017)
6. Cruz-Ramos, C., Reyes-Reyes, R., Nakano-Miyatake, M., Pérez-Meana, H.: A blind video watermarking scheme robust to frame attacks combined with mpeg2 compression. J. Appl. Res. Technol. **8**(3), 323–337 (2010)
7. Devi, H.S., Singh, K.M.: A robust and optimized 3d red-cyan anaglyph blind image watermarking in the DWT domain. Contemporary Eng. Sci. **9**, 1575–1589 (2016). https://doi.org/10.12988/ces.2016.69156
8. Devi, H.S., Singh, K.M.: A novel, efficient, robust, and blind imperceptible 3d anaglyph image watermarking. Arabian J. Sci. Eng. **42**(8), 3521–3533 (2017)
9. Dhaou, D., Ben Jabra, S., Zagrouba, E.: An efficient group of pictures decomposition based watermarking for anaglyph 3d video. In: the 13th International Joint Conference on Computer Vision, Imaging and Computer Graphics Theory and Applications (VISIGRAPP 2018, VISAPP), pp. 501–510 (2018)
10. Dhaou, D., Ben Jabra, S., Zagrouba, E.: An efficient anaglyph 3d video watermarking approach based on hybrid insertion. In: Vento, M., Percannella, G. (eds.) International Conference on Computer Analysis of Images and Patterns, pp. 96–107. Springer, Cham (2019). https://doi.org/10.1007/978-3-030-29891-3_9
11. Dhaou, D., Jabra, S.B., Zagrouba, E.: A multi-sprite based anaglyph 3d video watermarking approach robust against collusion. 3D Research **10**(2), 21 (2019)
12. Dhaou, D., Ben Jabra, S., Zagrouba, E.: A review on anaglyph 3d image and video watermarking. 3D Research **10**(2), 13 (2019)
13. Dhaou, D., Ben Jabra, S., Zagrouba, E.: A robust anaglyph 3d video watermarking based on multi-sprite generation, pp. 260–267 (2019)
14. Farid, M.S.: Introduction to 3DTV and 3D-Cinema, pp. 1–26 (2015)
15. Gupta, G., Gupta, V.K., Chandra, M.: An efficient video watermarking based security model. Microsystem Technol. **24**(6), 2539–2548 (2017). https://doi.org/10.1007/s00542-017-3689-x
16. Hou, J.U., Yu, I.J., Lee, H.K.: Collusion attack resilient 3d mesh watermarking based on anti-collusion fingerprint code. Appl. Sci. **8**(7), 1040 (2018)
17. Karmakar, A., Phadikar, A., Phadikar, B.S., Maity, G.K.: A blind video watermarking scheme resistant to rotation and collusion attacks. J. King Saud University-Comput. Inf. Sci. **28**(2), 199–210 (2016)
18. Kerbiche, A., Ben Jabra, S., Zagrouba, E., Charvillat, V.: Robust video watermarking approach based on crowdsourcing and hybrid insertion. In: International Conference on Digital Image Computing: Techniques and Applications (DICTA), pp. 1–8 (2017)
19. Kerbiche, A., Jabra, S.B., Zagrouba, E., Charvillat, V.: A robust video watermarking based on feature regions and crowdsourcing. Multimedia Tools Appl. **77**(20), 26769–26791 (2018). https://doi.org/10.1007/s11042-018-5888-6
20. Kerbiche, A., Jabra, S.B., Zagrouba, E.: A robust video watermarking based on image mosacing and multi-frequential embedding. In: 8th International IEEE Conference on Intelligent Computer Communication and Processing, pp. 159–166 (2012)
21. Koubaa, M., Elarbi, M., Amar, C.B., Nicolas, H.: Collusion, mpeg4 compression and frame dropping resistant video watermarking. Multimedia Tools Appl. **56**(2), 281–301 (2012)
22. Manaf, A.A., Boroujerdizade, A., Mousavi, S.M.: Collusion-resistant digital video watermarking for copyright protection application. Int. J. Appl. Eng. Res. **11**(5), 3484–3495 (2016)

23. Munoz-Ramirez, D.O., Reyes-Reyes, R., Ponomaryov, V., Cruz-Ramos, C.: Invisible digital color watermarking technique in anaglyph 3d images. In: 12th International Conference on Electrical Engineering, Computing Science and Automatic Control (CCE), pp. 1–6 (2015)

24. Prathap, I., Anitha, R.: Robust and blind watermarking scheme for three dimensional anaglyph images. Comput. Electric. Eng. **40**(1), 51–58 (2014). https://doi.org/10.1016/j.compeleceng.2013.11.005

25. Rana, S., Sur, A.: View invariant dibr-3d image watermarking using DT-CWT. Multimedia Tools Appl. **78**(12), 16665–16693 (2019)

26. Ruchika, P., Parth, B.: Robust watermarking for anaglyph 3d images using DWT techniques. Int. J. Eng. Technical Res. (IJETR) **3**(6), 55–58 (2015)

27. Salih, J.W., Abid, S.H., Hasan, T.M.: Imperceptible 3d video watermarking technique based on scene change detection. Int. J. Adv. Sci. Technol. **82**, 11–22 (2015). https://doi.org/10.14257/ijast.2015.82.02

28. Sanjay, R.Z., Ravindra, B.R.: A robust DWT watermarking for 3d images. Int. J. Emerging Trends Technol. (IJETT) **2**(1), 210–214 (2015)

29. Waleed, J., Jun, H.D., Hameed, S., Hatem, H., Majeed, R.: Integral algorithm to embed imperceptible watermark into anaglyph 3d video. Int. J. Adv. Comput. Technol. **5**(13), 163 (2013)

30. Wang, C., Han, F., Zhuang, X.: Robust digital watermarking scheme of anaglyphic 3d for RGB color images. Int. J. Image Process. (IJIP) **9**(3), 156 (2015)

31. Rakesh, Y., Krishna, D.R.: Digital watermarked anaglyph 3d images using FRFT. Int. J. Comput. Trends Technol. (IJCTT) **41**(2), 77–80 (2016). https://doi.org/10.14445/22312803/IJCTT-V41P113

32. Zadokar, S.R., Raskar, V.B., Shinde, S.V.: A digital watermarking for anaglyph 3d images. In: International Conference on Advances in Computing, Communications and Informatics (ICACCI), pp. 483–488 (2013)

33. Zeng, L., Zhang, S., Zhang, J., Zhang, Y.: Dynamic image mosaic via sift and dynamic programming. Mach. Vis. Appl. **25**(5), 1271–1282 (2014)

Copyright Protection Method for Vector Map Data

Yuliya Vybornova[1]([⊠]) [iD] and Vladislav Sergeev[1,2]

[1] Samara National Research University, Samara, Russia
vybornovamail@gmail.com, vserg@geosamara.ru
[2] Image Processing Systems Institute of RAS – Branch of the FSRC "Crystallography
and Photonics" RAS, Samara, Russia

Abstract. In this paper, we propose a copyright protection method for vector
cartographic data, mostly used in geographic information systems. The method is
based on the following key ideas: firstly, the watermark image is embedded into
the vector map by cyclically shifting the vertex list of each polygonal object, and
secondly, the watermark image is used as a secondary carrier for the watermark,
presented in the form of a bit sequence. A new sequence detection algorithm providing high robustness against map cropping is proposed. The experimental study
on the information capacity of the watermark image is performed. The experimental study on the method robustness against vector data transformations is
performed. It is shown that the proposed method is robust against all possible
transformations of the vector map and, thus, completely suits for copyright protection. The quality analysis of the proposed method is performed. It is shown
that the obtained method for vector map data protection satisfies all the necessary
requirements for watermarking methods, thereby demonstrating a clear advantage
over the known ones.

Keywords: Geographic information systems · Vector map · Copyright
protection · Digital watermarking · Raster image · Discrete fourier transform ·
Pseudorandom sequences

1 Introduction

The use of vector cartographic data in any field is impossible without their transmission through open channels, which allows the adversary to implement such well-known
threats as forgery and unauthorized distribution. This fact makes it necessary to verify the
integrity and authenticity of cartographic data, as well as to provide copyright protection
for such data.

The existing methods [1] for vector data protection are based on watermarking mostly
performed by introducing slight (in terms of map accuracy) distortions into data: values
of vertex coordinates, polyline/polygon angles, local statistical characteristics of the map
objects, etc.

The watermark, generally represented as a bit sequence of a given length, either
directly specifies such distortions (in case when watermarking is performed in the spatial

© Springer Nature Switzerland AG 2020
M. S. Obaidat (Ed.): ICETE 2019, CCIS 1247, pp. 180–202, 2020.
https://doi.org/10.1007/978-3-030-52686-3_8

domain), or is embedded into the discrete spectral decomposition (Fourier, Cosine, or Wavelet transform) coefficients of vertex coordinates or object features (in case when watermarking is performed in the frequency domain).

These methods, depending on the level of watermark resistance to distortions, are aimed at solving various problems of vector data protection. Robust watermarking methods are designed for solving the problem of copyright protection (protection against unauthorized distribution). Methods for protection against modifications are implemented on the basis of semi-fragile and fragile watermarks, which are used to ensure data authenticity and integrity respectively.

The quality of the watermarking method is characterized by the following criteria:

1) accuracy of carrier data (relative similarity between the original vector map and a carrier map containing a watermark);
2) watermark robustness (resistance of the embedded information to attacks and carrier transformations);
3) information capacity (number of watermark bits that can potentially be embedded);
4) computational complexity (the time required to implement the watermark embedding and extraction);
5) security of watermark location (unpredictability of the watermark position on the vector map).

Existing methods are classified depending on the used approaches:

1) *Zero watermarking.* According to this approach (used, for example, in [2, 3]), to form a watermark the key characteristics of the carrier are used, that is, those characteristics by which a digital map can be unambiguously identified. In this case, the obtained watermark is not embedded into the protected data but stored as a reference: at the verification stage, the watermark is formed again, and then is compared with the reference one.
2) *Adaptive watermarking.* Similarly to zero watermarking approach, the watermark is formed in accordance with some local characteristics of the carrier data. However, this approach does not imply a separate watermark storage: the constructed watermark is embedded into the protected data according to some known watermarking strategy. For example, such an approach is used in [4–7].
3) *Classic watermarking.* Here, in contrast to the adaptive approach, the watermark does not depend on local characteristics of the carrier and can be represented by an arbitrary digital signal of a predetermined form (e.g., a bit string or a raster image). This approach is used, for example, in [8–12].
4) *Multiple watermarking.* This approach (used, for example, [13]) implies the embedding of several watermarks differing in robustness to simultaneously solve various tasks of vector data protection, such as copyright protection, authentication and integrity verification.
5) *Reversible/Lossless watermarking.* This approach (used, for example, in [14–17]), provides the opportunity to restore the coordinate values after watermark extraction, thereby preserving the accuracy of the carrier map. This approach is obviously

suitable only for secure transmission and not suitable for storage, since after restoring the original data, the embedded watermark will be completely deleted.

The above-mentioned watermarking approaches predetermine the disadvantages of known methods:

1. Despite the fact that all conversions are performed with a given accuracy and almost invisible to the legitimate user, the issue of data accuracy after the embedding procedure is a key problem in the field of digital map protection, since the introduction of even small errors can significantly affect the physical meaning of carrier map objects (for example, changing the boundaries of the real estate even by a few meters is unacceptable).
2. As a rule, they do not provide robustness against such map transformations as cropping, vertex addition and removal, or object addition and removal.
3. During embedding and extraction procedures, a set of map objects must be strictly ordered. Since the location of objects on the map is quite random, there is a need to store some extra identifiers for objects or watermark positions.

The embedding approach to vector map protection, we proposed earlier in [18], can form the basis for a whole group of methods, focused on specific tasks, such as copyright, authenticity and integrity protection of map data, as well as localization of unauthorized changes introduced into a vector map.

In this paper, we propose a further investigation of the method [18] in the direction of solving the copyright protection problem using robust watermarking.

The paper [18] is devoted mainly to a theoretical description of the watermark image construction and a deep study on the information capacity of the method based on the simplest algorithm for detecting amplitude peaks.

In this paper, we increase the method robustness against transformations by introducing a new detector of watermark sequences, and also compare it with the previous one by the criterion of information capacity. Unlike the experiments conducted in [18], the new experiments are carried out not on the one map, but on a set of maps differing in size, which provide the opportunity to choose the method parameters more rationally depending on the map size and the selected detector. Also in this paper, not only the information capacity of the method is experimentally investigated, but also the robustness and computational complexity of the resulting method. It is shown that the resulting method can be used to solve the problem of copyright protection.

Section 2 briefly describes the ideas of our new approach to vector data watermarking. Section 3 describes an algorithm for watermarking a vector map using a raster image, as well as an algorithm for image extraction. Sections 4 and 5 contain an algorithm for construction of a noise-like watermark image serving as a secondary carrier for the bit sequence and an algorithm for extraction of such a sequence, respectively. Sections 6, 7 and 8 present the results of the experimental studies of the proposed watermarking method according to various quality criteria.

2 Brief Description of Proposed Watermarking Approach

1. As a carrier for watermark embedding, we use a set of polygonal objects. All polygons are closed, each of them is defined by a list of its vertex coordinates, numbered sequentially. Any polygon vertex can be selected as the first element in the vertex list: the only requirement here is that the vertex order should remain unchanged. Thus, the first idea of the method is that the digital watermark is embedded into data by cyclically shifting the list of vertices of each polygon without changing the value of their coordinates, that is, without any distortion of the vector map.

2. The second idea of the method is to use a raster image superimposed on a selected fragment of the vector map as a watermark. Certainly, the vector map does not provide an opportunity to place raster data, but its objects (in our case, polygons) can be mapped to the image in such a way as to geometrically coincide with some pixels. The set of pixels, corresponding to polygons, forms an irregular grid, and thus the entire image can be approximately restored by using one of the existing interpolation methods [19].

3. The described two ideas imply that raster image itself is used as a robust watermark providing copyright protection for a digital map. So, the third idea, complementing the first two, is to use a watermark image as a secondary carrier for another watermark, represented in the form of a bit sequence. This allows to automate the map authentication procedure, since the watermark sequence can itself carry all the necessary identifying information and its analysis does not require the comparison with the original watermark.

4. In order to ensure robustness of the embedded bit sequence against image interpolation errors, addition or removal of map objects, geometrical transformations and cropping of the map, and etc., each bit embedded into the carrier image should not correspond to a separate point (pixel) or a local area on the image plane. Therefore, the fourth idea consists in embedding of a bit sequence into the spatial-frequency domain of the carrier image by extending watermark bits on the entire image plane "holographically" [20], i.e. by representing each bit in the form of a two-dimensional harmonic function of the corresponding spatial frequency.

3 Watermark Embedding and Extraction

The algorithm for embedding in vector data is performed according to the following steps.

1) A map fragment large enough and saturated with polygons is selected.
2) A noise-like watermark image is superimposed on the selected fragment. For this, the coordinates of the bounding box $x_{min}, y_{min}, x_{max}, y_{max}$ are determined, and for each i-th object of the vector map, a mapping of the following form is calculated:

$$x_i, y_i \rightarrow n_1, n_2 : n_1 = \frac{x_i - x_{min}}{step_X}, \quad n_2 = \frac{y_{max} - y_i}{step_Y},$$

$$step_X = \frac{x_{max} - x_{min}}{N}, step_Y = \frac{y_{max} - y_{min}}{N}.$$

3) Then, for each polygon, the following procedure is performed:

    a) the most significant bit of the introduced binary number is embedded by setting the direction of the vertex traversal: clockwise or counterclockwise, depending on the bit value. This step is optional, but its implementation can significantly increase the method robustness against vertex reordering attacks.

    b) coordinates of the polygon centroid are determined x_{ci}, y_{ci};

    c) the watermark image pixel, corresponding to the center of gravity, is selected. Its value is rounded to a b-bit binary number, depending on the number of vertices. If the polygon consists of at least 2^{b-1} vertices, b bits of the pixel value can be embedded with no errors;

    d) b^2 equidistant rays are drawn from the gravity center and marked with a b-bit binary numbers;

    e) for each polygon vertex, the angular distance, which values vary in the range of $[0, 359°]$, is calculated relative to the ray directed northwards;

    f) the vertex with angular distance closest to the ray marked with embedded value is assigned first in the list of vertices by cyclic shift operation.

Figure 1 shows an example of embedding into a polygon with four vertices. In this case, it is possible to embed only three bits of information with no errors: two bits by cyclic shift and one bit by setting vertex traversal).

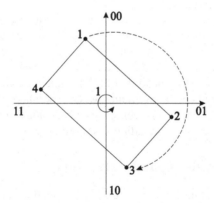

Fig. 1. Embedding of three bits into a polygonal object.

The extraction of the watermark image from the vector map is performed as follows:

1) a blank raster image with a sufficiently small grid cells is superimposed on the map;
2) all the polygon objects of the map are selected;
3) the most significant bit is determined according to the vertex traversal (if this step was not omitted when embedding);
4) for each polygon the center of gravity is calculated, and the relative location of the first vertex is determined;

5) the watermark pixel corresponding to the polygon centroid is assigned a value of *b*-bit binary number calculated according to the rotation angle of the first vertex;

6) the undetermined pixel values are calculated by using the nearest neighbor method based on a triangulated irregular network [19];

Figure 2 demonstrates the extraction of three bits from a polygon.

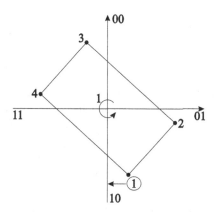

Fig. 2. Extraction of three bits from a polygonal object

A detailed study of embedding and extraction algorithms is given in [21].

4 Watermark Image Construction

Let $\mathbf{S} = \{s_1 s_2 \dots s_l\}$, $1 \leq l \leq L$ be a binary watermark sequence of length L. We propose to form a two-dimensional spatial spectrum $F_c(\omega_1, \omega_2)$ of an image represented as $2(L + 2)$ two-dimensional unit impulses located in the spectral domain on two rings of different radii: r и $r + \Delta r$, as illustrated in Fig. 3 for one half-plane of the two-dimensional spectrum (because the image is real the second half-plane displays the spectrum symmetrically about the center). In Fig. 3, unit impulses are indicated with black circles. All but two impulses are located with equal step (angle) starting from the spectrum origin on a ring of smaller or larger radius, depending on the value of the corresponding bit of the watermark sequence. Two impulses located on both rings at the same (e.g. zero) angle indicate the beginning of the sequence.

By applying the two-dimensional inverse Fourier transform to the spectrum, we get the two-dimensional image function itself. In practice, when working with a digital image instead of a continuous spectrum, it is necessary to use a discrete Fourier transform (DFT), taking into account the well-known features of such a conversion: integer arguments in the spatial and spectral domain, periodicity of functions in two dimensions, possible overlap effects, etc. Thus, in order to form a noise-like watermark image of size $N_1 \times N_2$ pixels it is necessary to arrange the impulses on two rings in the two-dimensional discrete spectral domain as described above, and then apply the inverse DFT.

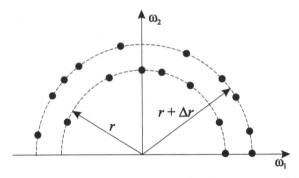

Fig. 3. Embedding of a binary sequence into image spectrum [18].

It should be noted that due to the spectrum discreteness, the coordinates of unit samples should be rounded to integer values and, therefore, may overlap when arranging on the rings. Thus, the DFT dimensions and the radii r, $(r + \Delta r)$ must be sufficiently large, so that rounding errors could not affect the watermark extraction.

As the last step of constructing the carrier image, the values of its pixels can be normalized to a standard range, for example, $[0, 255]$:

$$f_{255}(n_1, n_2) = 255 \frac{f(n_1, n_2) - \min\limits_{n_1, n_2} f(n_1, n_2)}{\max\limits_{n_1, n_2} f(n_1, n_2) - \min\limits_{n_1, n_2} f(n_1, n_2)}.$$

An example of the resulting noise-like image with embedded watermark sequence corresponding to spectrum in Fig. 3 is shown in Fig. 4.

Fig. 4. Example of noise-like image carrying the watermark sequence ($N_1 = N_2 = 512$, $r = 8$, $\Delta r = 4$, $L = 15$, $\mathbf{S} = \{101101001011101\}$) [18].

To ensure the unpredictability of the embedded watermark, we propose to form real and imaginary parts of the complex spectrum with random values of impulses:

$$\mathrm{Re}F(u_l, v_l) = \cos(rand(90));$$

$$\mathrm{Im}F(u_l, v_l) = \sin(rand(90)).$$

Here, $u_l = (r + s_l \Delta r) \times \cos \frac{\pi l}{L+1}$, $v_l = (r + s_l \Delta r) \times \sin \frac{\pi l}{L+1}$, $1 \leq l \leq L + 1$, $rand(90)$ – pseudo-random number with values varying in the range of [0,90]. To provide the opportunity to reimplement the watermark generation procedure, a deterministic algorithm for producing random values is required. In this regard, an alternative implementation of the Password-Based Key Derivation Function based on the use of cryptographically secure Blum-Blum-Shub pseudo-random sequence generator is proposed [22].

5 Watermark Sequence Extraction

The extraction of a sequence from an image approximately (with interpolation) reconstructed from a vector map consists of the following obvious steps:

1) calculation of a two-dimensional discrete spectrum of the image (using DFT);
2) detection of spectral components with a large amplitude (impulses) and determination of their coordinates;
3) detection of the fact of watermark presence, i.e. the fact that the impulses are located on two concentric rings in the spectral plane; estimation of the radii of these rings;
4) search of the sequence beginning key, i.e. a pair of impulses located at the same angle to the spectrum origin;
5) reading of the watermark sequence bits clockwise or counterclockwise starting from the sequence beginning key.

To detect spectral components of a large amplitude, we developed two algorithms: a detector based on threshold processing (hereinafter referred to as a threshold-based detector) and a detector based on local filtering (hereinafter referred to as a filter-based detector).

To find large spectral impulses using a threshold-based detector, a simple rule is used:

$$|F(k_1, k_2)| > \frac{1}{2} \max_{n_1, n_2} |F(n_1, n_2)|,$$
$$(n_1, n_2) \neq (0, 0)$$

where $F(n_1, n_2)$ is the image DFT, n_1, n_2 are the integer arguments of the discrete spectrum ($0 \leq n_1 \leq N_1 - 1$, $0 \leq n_2 \leq N_2 - 1$).

The minimum values of the radii reliably ensuring the efficiency of the proposed detector are established experimentally and can be approximately described by the formula: $r \geq 0,36 L$.

The minimum acceptable distance between the rings, necessary for a reliable sequence extraction is $\Delta r = 4$.

It should be noted that when using this detector, the correct localization of amplitude peaks is impossible if a noise-like watermark is cropped. That is why we propose an additional algorithm that allows to detect amplitude peaks in the spectrum of a cropped image.

To find large spectral impulses using a filter-based detector, a local window of size 3×3 is used. First, local maxima of the DFT module are selected:

$$|F(k_1, k_2)| = 0, \ \ if \ \ |F(k_1, k_2)| < \max_{m_1, m_2} |F(k_1 + m_1, k_2 + m_2)|, m_1, m_2 = \overline{0, 2}.$$

Next, the largest $2 \times (L + 2)$ elements are selected from the remaining.

The minimum values of the radii reliably ensuring the efficiency of the proposed detector are established experimentally and can be approximately described by the formula: $r \geq 0, 83 L$.

The minimum acceptable distance between the rings, necessary for a reliable sequence extraction is $\Delta r = 8$.

6 Study on Information Capacity

In the paper [18] to investigate the potential use of a noise-like image embedded into the vector map as a secondary container for the watermark presented in the form of a bit sequence, we conducted computational experiments using a threshold-based detector. In this paper, we repeat the error modeling experiment (experiment 1) but for the filter-based detector and compare the results with previously obtained. We also expand the experiment with real data (experiment 2) by increasing the data set and present the results for both detectors.

To form test samples of noise-like images, binary sequences were produced using a pseudo-random number generator as equally probable and independent. For each combination of parameters, we generated 100 noise-like images.

The only difference between the performance requirements for the two detectors consists in the parameters of minimum radii, as shown in Sect. 5. In both experiments, these requirements were taken into account when forming test samples of noise-like images.

6.1 Experiment 1

Obviously, the main errors occurred during the reconstruction of watermark image carried by a vector map and, consequently, during the bit sequence extraction, are caused by the following:

- the image is extracted from the map as a set of spaced pixels corresponding to the polygonal map objects;
- extracted pixels are quantized due to the fact that only few binary digits can be embedded into each polygon.

To evaluate the effect of these distortions on the watermark sequence, we conducted the following computational experiment. K pixels of the generated noise-like image are selected randomly (independently and equally likely for each coordinate). Each pixel is quantized to a b-bit binary number (i.e. into 2^b levels). Next, the image is interpolated and attempt to extract the watermark sequence is performed.

As an indicator of the watermark sequence integrity, we considered the experimentally estimated probability of its correct extraction, p, depending on the number of reference pixels K. Estimation of the extraction probability is calculated for each sample of 100 images. The variable values are: radius r, bit depth (i.e. number of bits per pixel b), and sequence length L.

The results of this experiment for the threshold-based detector are given in [18]. Figure 5 shows the results obtained for the filter-based detector. The dependence of the extraction probability on the number of polygons with variable values of bit depth is presented for the following cases: a) $L = 10$, $r = 10$, b) $L = 50$, $r = 60$, c) $L = 100$, $r = 116$.

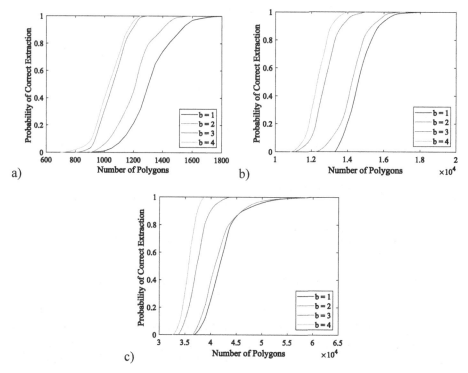

Fig. 5. Dependence of the extraction probability on the number of polygons with variable values of bit depth b for a) $L = 10$, $r = 10$; b) $L = 50$, $r = 60$; c) $L = 100$, $r = 116$.

Some obvious conclusions follow from the presented results, which are also true for a threshold-based detector, as shown in [18].

The more objects on the map (pixels corresponding to polygons), the higher the probability of correct extraction. At the same time, the longer the watermark sequence, the higher the requirements for the number of objects needed for its extraction.

The quality of the extraction increases with an increase in the bit depth of the pixels corresponding to the map objects. It also looks natural, since an increase in the bit depth reduces the pixel quantization noise and, consequently, the total error of the carrier image reconstruction decreases. However, when setting the bit depth value higher than $b = 3$, we see almost no effect of improving the quality. Moreover, in practical applications it is difficult to implement persistent high bit depth due to the fact that on the real map simple polygons (mostly, quadrangles) dominate: therefore, no more than three-digit binary numbers can be embedded: two digits by setting the first vertex in the polygon vertex list, and one of digit - by altering the direction of vertex traversal.

For a fixed length of the bit sequence, the extraction quality is higher, the smaller the r, i.e. the lower the frequency of the carrier image. On the other hand, the minimum possible value of this parameter is limited by the discreteness of the two-dimensional image spectrum, namely, its ring into which a sequence of length L is embedded.

Figure 6 shows the dependence of the watermark image capacity $b \times L$ on the number of polygons for a fixed values of the achievable probability p for both impulse detectors.

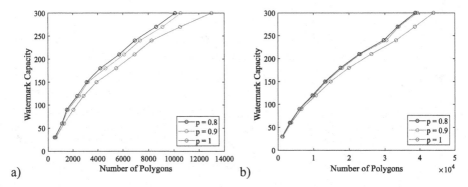

a)   b)

Fig. 6. Dependence of carrier image capacity on the number of polygons for various values of achievable probability: a) threshold-based detector; b) filter-based detector.

The main difference between the two detectors is the number of polygons, required for the correct extraction: to ensure the efficiency of the filter-based detector, we need several times more polygonal objects than for the threshold-based one. This is explained by the fact that in the case of a detector based on local filtering, the minimum radii of the rings used to form a noise-like image are several times larger, and therefore the frequency of such images is higher, and so the number of reference points required for correct interpolation.

This experiment allows to draw conclusions on the rational choice of optimal parameters for reliable extraction of watermark sequence depending on the selected detector and the number of polygons on the vector map.

6.2   Experiment 2

In the previous experiment, the map watermarking procedure is simulated, but the embedding into real data is not performed. To confirm the performance of the proposed method for real vector cartographic data, we have conducted a second experiment using a fragments of the real urban development map ranging in size from 1,000 to 100,000 objects.

The sizes of watermark images depending on the size of the vector map are shown in Table 1.

Table 1. Minimum sizes of the watermark images.

Map size, polygons	Watermark size, pixels
1000–30000	512×512
30000–80000	1024×1024
80000–100000	2048×2048

In addition to confirmation of the method applicability on real data, this experiment is aimed at the qualitative assessment of the effect arising from errors introduced by such data regarding the model case presented in the previous experiment.

When modeling data from experiment 1, interpolation is performed on uniformly scattered points, and quantization is carried out strictly at a given level. Thus, in experiment 2 we investigate the probabilities of the correct extraction from noise-like images of three types at once that is, we consider three different cases demonstrating the influence of errors introduced by the proposed method:

1) The ideal case (model data from experiment 1). Interpolation is performed using a mask with evenly scattered points superimposed on noise-like images quantized at a given level.
2) Interpolation is performed on an irregular grid of pixels extracted from a map (Fig. 7) superimposed on noise-like images quantized at a given level. This data allow us to trace how the unevenness of the grid affects the result of interpolation and the result of extraction in general.
3) Data extracted from the map. This data allow us to trace how the unevenness of the number of polygon vertices affects the result of extraction.

Embedding of a b-bit number into a polygon can be performed with no errors, if the polygon consists of at least 2^{b-1} vertices. For example, to embed a 3-bit number, we should take a polygon of 4 vertices. Such polygons are most likely for maps representing buildings. Embedding of 5 bits requires 16 vertices, which is unlikely for the type of vector maps considered in this paper. Therefore, in general, for urban development maps if $b > 3$, the behavior of the watermarking method may be random to some extent, i.e. depending on the particular map and particular watermark image. In this regard, in further experiments, when modeling the watermarking method, we consider only the case $b = 3$.

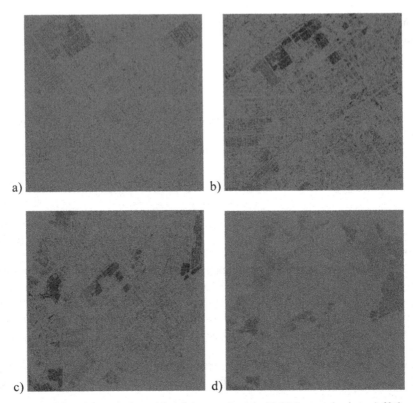

Fig. 7. Non-uniform interpolation grid: a) 5 thousand points; b) 20 thousand points; c) 60 thousand points; d) 100 thousand points.

To calculate the probabilities of correct extraction, the experiment was performed on samples of 100 random watermark images produced for each $L = \overline{10, 100}$ (the radii of the spectral rings are chosen to be minimal).

First, we present the results obtained for threshold-based detector. The dependence of the extraction probability on the number of polygons P for various values of the sequence length are shown in Fig. 8.

The findings of experiment 1 tell us that the quality of extraction is higher, the greater the number of polygons on the map. On the real data, this statement remains true only for certain map sizes, which is also true for the case of interpolation on irregular grid. This is caused by the fact that the selected map fragments of size $P \geq 60000$ are not rectangular, so the corresponding masks of irregular grids (Fig. 8). The absence of reference points at the edges obviously affects the interpolation quality. Thus, when embedding it is necessary to take this fact into account and select map fragments in such a way as to make it possible to construct Delaunay triangulation over the entire bounding box.

The larger L, the greater the drop in quality. For $L \geq 90$ watermark sequence cannot be retrieved correctly in case of embedding into real cartographic data.

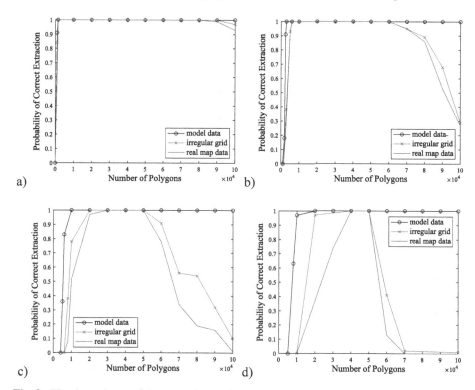

Fig. 8. The dependence of the extraction probability on the number of polygons for threshold-based detector: a) $L = 10$; b) $L = 30$; c) $L = 60$; d) $L = 80$.

Next, we present the results obtained for filter-based detector. The dependence of the extraction probability on the number of polygons P for various values of the sequence length are shown in Fig. 9.

Previously, when investigating threshold-based detector, we concluded that the extraction quality noticeably decreases for any L in cases where the map fragments are not enough saturated with polygons. In this current case, for $L \leq 30$ the watermark sequences are extracted correctly even for the large values of P.

For $L < 40$ the method errors do not affect the extraction quality. In other cases, the quality of extraction decreases not only because the watermark pixel values are rounded depending on the number of polygon vertices, but also because of the interpolation grid irregularity. The maximum length of sequence that can be correctly extracted from real map data is $L = 60$.

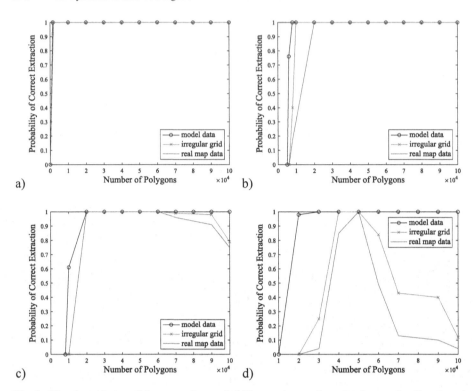

Fig. 9. The dependence of the extraction probability on the number of polygons for filter-based detector: a) $L = 10$; b) $L = 30$; c) $L = 40$; d) $L = 60$.

7 Study on Robustness Against Transformations

Despite the fact that according to the results of two experiments, the threshold-based detector demonstrates increased information capacity, this algorithm cannot be used as part of the method for copyright protection of vector map data, since, as noted earlier, it is not robust to cropping, but also not sufficiently resistant to errors occurred during interpolation on an irregular grid. However, this detector can be used in tasks where high information capacity plays a more important role than robustness against attacks, for example, in the task of vector map authentication.

In this regard, we have constructed the resulting copyright protection method on the basis of the filter-based detector. In this Section, we present a study on robustness of the obtained method.

The translation and scaling operations do not affect the embedded image, since the positions of the polygon centroids and the map bounding box are transformed by the same amount.

The invariance of mapping a raster image on a vector map with respect to these transformations can be proofed as follows.

1) *Translation.* Let the vector map be shifted by the Δx value along the OX axis and by the Δy value along the OY axis.

Then the coordinates of all polygon centroids are also shifted, so for the i-th object the coordinates are calculated as $x_{ci} + \Delta x$, $y_{ci} + \Delta y$. Similarly, the coordinates of the bounding box are calculated as $x_{\min} + \Delta x$, $y_{\min} + \Delta y$, $x_{\max} + \Delta x$, $y_{\max} + \Delta y$.

As a result, the mapping of a raster image on a vector map is:

$$\frac{x_i + \Delta x - (x_{\min} + \Delta x)}{step_X} = \frac{x_i - x_{\min}}{step_X}, \frac{y_{\max} + \Delta y - (y_i + \Delta y)}{step_Y} = \frac{y_{\max} - y_i}{step_Y},$$

that coincides with the original.

2) *Scaling.* Let the vector map be scaled by k_{sc} times. Then the coordinates of all polygon centroids are changed by the same factor, so for the i-th object the coordinates are $k_{sc} \cdot x_{ci}$, $k_{sc} \cdot y_{ci}$. Similarly, the coordinates of the bounding box are calculated as $k_{sc} \cdot x_{\min}$, $k_{sc} \cdot y_{\min}$, $k_{sc} \cdot x_{\max}$, $k_{sc} \cdot y_{\max}$.

As a result, the mapping of a raster image on a vector map is:

$$\frac{k_{sc} \cdot x_i - k_{sc} \cdot x_{\min}}{k_{sc} \cdot step_X} = \frac{x_i - x_{\min}}{step_X}, \frac{k_{sc} \cdot y_{\max} - k_{sc} \cdot y_i}{k_{sc} \cdot step_Y} = \frac{y_{\max} - y_i}{step_Y},$$

that coincides with the original.

To study the method robustness against all the other transformations, the experiments are constructed as follows. In a vector map of a given size, 100 noise-like watermarks are embedded successively. The length of the binary sequence carried by each watermark is $L = 10$. After this, the watermarked map is attacked using conversions of various degrees, and the watermark is extracted from the modified map. We consider the method robust to attack (conversion) if the watermark sequence is extracted without errors in 100 cases out of 100.

3) *Rotation.* Table 2 presents the dependence of the robustness against rotation on the size of the vector map.

Table 2. Dependence of the maximum acceptable rotation angle on the size of the map.

Map size, polygons	2000	3000	4000	6000	8000	10000	20000	50000	10000
Rotation angle, °	0	5	5	15	20	20	25	25	25

The method is robust to rotation if the map size $P \geq 3000$. The maximum acceptable angle of map rotation reaches $25°$ for the maps of size $P \geq 20000$.

4) *Cropping.* Figure 10a shows the dependence of the maximum acceptable coefficient $k_{cr} = \frac{N_{cr}}{N}$ on the map size for the case of arbitrary cropping.

Figure 10b shows the dependence of the maximum acceptable coefficient k_{cr} on the map size for the case of centered cropping.

It can be seen from the figures that for maps of size $P \leq 50000$ the method robustness does not depend on the type of cropping. However, in the case of arbitrary cropping the maximum allowable cropping factor decreases for large maps.

This is explained by the fact that, as already noted in the previous section, these map fragments are non-rectangular. Therefore, when arbitrary cropping, a fragment with

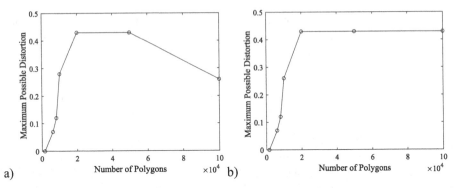

a)   b)

Fig. 10. Dependence of the maximum allowable fraction of cropping on the size of the map: a) arbitrary cropping; b) centered cropping.

empty areas can be selected. It is worth noting that for maps of sizes $20000 \leq P \leq 50000$, regardless of the cropping type, the coefficient k_{cr} reaches 43%.

5) *Object addition.* Figure 11 shows the dependence of the maximum acceptable coefficient $k_{add} = \frac{P_{add}}{P}$ on the map size P.

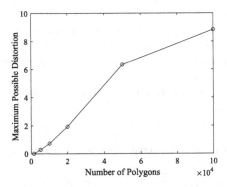

Fig. 11. Dependence of the maximum acceptable share of added objects on the size of the map.

It can be seen from the figure that the coefficient k_{add} increases rapidly along with the map size: for the map of size $P = 2000$ the coefficient $k_{add} = 0,05$. For a map of size $P = 20000$ the coefficient $k_{add} = 1,93$. Obviously, in a semantic sense such a number of non-meaningful objects depreciates the vector map, which means that the proposed method is robust against object addition.

6) *Object deletion.* Figure 12 shows the dependence of the maximum acceptable coefficient $k_{del} = \frac{P_{del}}{P}$ on the map size P. For small maps $P \leq 20000$ the coefficient grows rapidly: for example, for $P = 3000$ the coefficient $k_{del} = 0,29$. It is obvious that in most cases, removing such a fraction of objects is enough to depreciate the map. Thus, according to the results of the experiment, the proposed method is robust against object deletion.

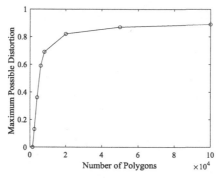

Fig. 12. Dependence of the maximum acceptable share of deleted objects on the size of the map.

7) *Vertex addition.* The vertex addition procedure is performed as follows. A random polygon of a vector map is selected. Then a random polygon edge, described as (x_1, y_1), (x_2, y_2), $x_1 \leq x_2$, is selected. After that a random point (x_{edge}, y_{edge}), $x_{edge} = x_1 + x_{shift}$, $y_{edge} = k_{edge} \cdot x_{edge} + b_{edge}$ is selected on the edge. Here, $x_{shift} = $

$$random\,(0, x_2 - x_1),\ k_{edge} = \begin{cases} \frac{(y_2 - y_1)}{(x_2 - x_1)}, & x_2 \neq x_1 \\ 0, & else \end{cases},\ b_{edge} = y_2 - k_{edge} \cdot x_2.$$

As a result, the coordinates of the new vertex are calculated: $(x_{edge}, y_{edge} + y_{shift})$, $y_{shift} = random\,(0, \frac{y_2 - y_1}{100})$.

As a result of the experiment, it was found that vertex addition does not affect the correctness of the watermark extraction: the sequence is extracted properly even for $k_{vertadd} = \frac{V_{add}}{V} = 10000$, where V is a total number of vertices of all the polygons on the map. This is explained by two facts: first, the most significant bit of the watermark is embedded by changing the vertex traversal order, which does not depend on the number of polygon vertices. Secondly, even if a new vertex is assigned the first in the polygon vertex list, the distance between the new and old first vertices is too small to change the values of the watermark bits that are encoded by the location of the first vertex.

8) *Vertex deletion.* The vertex deletion procedure is performed as follows. A random polygon consisting of six or more vertices is selected on the vector map. After this, a random polygon vertex is selected and deleted.

Table 3 presents the dependence of the maximum acceptable coefficient $k_{vertdel} = \frac{V_{del}}{V}$ on the map size.

Table 3. Dependence of the maximum acceptable fraction of deleted vertices on the size of the map.

Map size, polygons	2000	2500	3000	4000	8000	10000	20000	50000	10000
$k_{vertdel}$	0	0.2	0.2	*max*	*max*	*max*	*max*	*max*	*max*

The table shows that for the map size $P \geq 4000$ the coefficient $k_{vertdel}$ reaches its maximum value. The maximum coefficient $k_{vertdel}$ is calculated on the basis of the total number of vertices that can potentially be removed from the map: in this experiment, it we assume that a random vertex can be deleted from an object only if the number of vertices of this object is $V_{pol} \geq 6$.

9) *Vertex reordering.* In this experiment, the method is implemented in two modes: "changing the vertex traversal order" and "without changing the vertex traversal order".

According to the results we can conclude that in the "changing the vertex traversal order" mode, the method is robust to random cyclic shift of the polygon vertex lists, but is not robust to the random alteration vertex traversal order, since the traversal order encodes the most significant bits of the watermark image. In the "without changing the vertex traversal order" mode the proposed method demonstrates the resistance to the vertex traversal order alteration, but do not resist the cyclic shift of the polygon vertex lists, since in this case the first vertices encode the bits of the watermark image.

Obviously, in order to achieve simultaneous robustness against both types of vertex reordering attacks, it is necessary to embed into each polygon two watermarks at once: one significant bit of the watermark image by changing the vertex traversal order, several significant bits (including the first) by cyclically shifting the polygon vertex list.

8   Study on Quality of Proposed Method

This Section provides an analysis of the proposed copyright protection method for all quality criteria.

1) *Accuracy of carrier data.* Obviously, the distortions introduced by the proposed watermarking method do not affect the coordinate information of the map (but only affect the order of the vertices), therefore, the watermarked map completely coincides with the original.

2) *Information Capacity.* As shown in Sect. 6, the watermark capacity depends on the detector of amplitude peaks, as well as on the number of map objects: the more objects on the map, the more watermark bits can carry the noise-like image.

3) *Watermark Robustness.* The proposed copyright protection method for vector map data is robust against all possible map transformations. Resistance parameters increase with the number of vector objects on the map. Table 4 shows the results of the study on robustness depending on vector map size for each type of conversion. Plus denotes invariance to transformation. ($V_{max} = maxV_{del}$ is the maximum number of vertices on the map that can be deleted).

4) *Watermark Location Security.* This quality criterion means the unpredictability of the embedded watermark values. In order to ensure that this requirement is met, at the stage of the complex spectrum synthesis, the impulses are assigned random values produced using the Pass-word-Based Key Derivation Function algorithm based on the cryptographically robust Blum-Blum-Shub pseudo-random sequence generator. Thus, for each sequence of length L we can form $90^{2(L+1)}$ (90^{L+1} – for the real part of the complex spectrum, and the same number for the imaginary part) different watermarks. It should be noted that, the total number of brute-force combinations to guess the watermark sequence is 2^L.

Table 4. Results of the study on robustness.

Number of polygons P, thousands	2	3	4	6	8	10	20	50	100
Translation	+	+	+	+	+	+	+	+	+
Scaling	+	+	+	+	+	+	+	+	+
Rotation	0°	5°	5°	15°	20°	20°	25°	25°	25°
Cropping	3%	5%	5%	7%	12%	26%	43%	43%	43%
Obj. Addition	$0,05 \cdot P$	$0.15 \cdot P$	$0,21 \cdot P$	$0,5 \cdot P$	$0,61 \cdot P$	$0,72 \cdot P$	$1,93 \cdot P$	$6,34 \cdot P$	$8,83 \cdot P$
Obj. Deletion	$0,05 \cdot P$	$0.29 \cdot P$	$0,36 \cdot P$	$0,59 \cdot P$	$0,69 \cdot P$	$0,71 \cdot P$	$0,82 \cdot P$	$0,87 \cdot P$	$0,89 \cdot P$
Vert. Addition	+	+	+	+	+	+	+	+	+
Vert. Deletion	0	$0.2 \cdot V$	V_{max}	V_{max}	V_{max}	V_{max}	V_{max}	V_{max}	V_{max}
Reordering	+	+	+	+	+	+	+	+	+

5) *Computational Complexity.* The experimental study on the computational complexity evaluation was conducted on a personal computer, which characteristics are shown in Table 5.

Table 5. Experiment conditions.

Hardware/Software type	Parameters
CPU	IntelCore i5-2400 CPU @ 3.10 GHz 3.10 GHz
RAM	16 GB
Operating system	Windows 7 Professional (64-bit)

Table 6 presents the average time of a noise-like image construction.

Table 6. Average time of a noise-like image construction.

Size, pixels	512×512	1024×1024	2048×2048
Time, seconds	0.059	0.344	1.536

Table 7 presents the average time needed to embed the watermark image into the map.

Table 7. Average time of the map watermarking.

Size, polygons	2500	5000	10000	20000	50000	100000
Time, seconds	0.413	0.421	0.470	0.574	1.754	6.653

Table 8 presents the average time needed to extract the watermark image from the map.

Table 8. Average time of the image extraction.

Size, polygons	2500	5000	10000	20000	50000	100000
Time, seconds	0.069	0.080	0.091	0.115	0.380	1.657

Table 9 presents the average time needed to extract the watermark sequence from the noise-like image.

Table 9. Average time of the watermark sequence extraction.

Size, pixels	512×512	1024×1024	2048×2048
Time, seconds	0.611	3.589	20.079

The above study of computational complexity shows that the operating time of each module depends on the size of the map: to ensure the efficient operation, it is advisable to divide large maps into smaller fragments.

9 Conclusions

In this paper, we propose a copyright protection method for vector cartographic data. The method is based on the following key ideas: firstly, the watermark image is embedded into the vector map by cyclically shifting the vertex list of each polygonal object, and secondly, the watermark image is used as a secondary carrier for the watermark, presented in the form of a bit sequence.

The vector map watermarking algorithm is described, as well as the algorithm for extraction of the image from the map. The algorithm for construction of a noise-like watermark image serving as a secondary carrier for the bit sequence and an algorithm for extraction of such a sequence are given. The new sequence detection algorithm providing high robustness against map cropping is proposed.

An experimental study on the information capacity of the carrier image is conducted. The results allow to obtain conclusions regarding the rational choice of parameters for reliable extraction of the binary watermark sequence depending on the number of polygons of the vector map and selected detector.

The experimental study on the method robustness against vector data transformations is performed. It is shown that the proposed method is robust against all possible transformations of the vector map and, thus, completely suits for copyright protection.

The quality analysis of the proposed method is performed. It is shown that the resulting method for vector map data protection satisfies all the necessary requirements for watermarking methods, thereby demonstrating a clear advantage over the known ones.

Acknowledgements. The reported study was funded by RFBR (Russian Foundation for Basic Research): project № 19-29-09045, project № 19-07-00474, project № 19-07-00138, project № 20-37-70053.

References

1. Abubahia, A., Cocea, M.: Advancements in GIS map copyright protection schemes – a critical review. Multimedia Tools Appl. **76**(10), 12205–12231 (2017). https://doi.org/10.1007/s11 042-016-3441-z
2. Peng, Y., Yue, M.: A zero-watermarking scheme for vector map based on feature vertex distance ratio. J. Electr. Comput. Eng. **2015**, 1–6 (2015)
3. Li, A., Lin, B.-X., Chen, Y.: Study on copyright authentication of GIS vector data based on Zero-watermarking. Int. Arch. Photogram. Remote Sens. Spatial Inf. Sci. **37**(B4), 1783–1786 (2008)
4. Ren, N., Wang, Q., Zhu, C.: Selective authentication algorithm based on semi-fragile watermarking for vector geographical data. In: 22nd International Conference on Geoinformatics, pp. 1–6 (2014)
5. Da, Q., Sun, J., Zhang, L., Kou, L., Wang, W., Han, Q., Zhou, R.: A novel hybrid information security scheme for 2D vector map. Mob. Networks Appl. **23**, 1–9 (2018)
6. Wang, N., Bian, J., Zhang, H.: RST invariant fragile watermarking for 2D vector map authentication. Int. J. Multimedia Ubiquitous Eng. **10**(4), 155–172 (2015)
7. Kim, J.: Robust vector digital watermarking using angles and a random table. Adv. Inf. Sci. Serv. Sci. **2**(4), 1–13 (2010)
8. Lee, S.H., Kwon, K.R.: Vector watermarking scheme for GIS vector map management. Multimedia Tools Appl. **63**(3), 757–790 (2013). https://doi.org/10.1007/s11042-011-0894-y
9. Peng, Z., Yue, M., Wu, X., Peng, Y.: Blind watermarking scheme for polylines in vector geo-spatial data. Multimedia Tools Appl. **74**, 11721–11739 (2015)
10. Wang, Y., Yang, C., Zhu, C.: A multiple watermarking algorithm for vector geographic data based on coordinate mapping and domain subdivision. Multimedia Tools Appl. **77**(15), 19261–19279 (2017). https://doi.org/10.1007/s11042-017-5358-6
11. Ohbuchi, R., Ueda, H., Endoh, S.: Robust watermarking of vector digital maps. In: Proceedings of IEEE International Conference on Multimedia and Expo, pp. 577–580 (2002)
12. Voigt, M., Busch, C.: Watermarking 2D-vector data for geographical information systems. In: Proceedings of the SPIE, Security and Watermarking of Multimedia Content, vol. 4675, pp. 621–628 (2002)
13. Peng, Y., Lan, H., Yue, M., Xue, Y.: Multipurpose watermarking for vector map protection and authentication. Multimedia Tools Appl. **77**(1), 1–21 (2017)

14. Peng, F.A, Yan, Z.J., Long, M.: Reversible watermarking for 2D vector map based on triple differences expansion and reversible contrast mapping. In: International Conference on Security, Privacy and Anonymity in Computation, Communication and Storage, pp. 147–158 (2017)

15. Wang, N., Zhao, X., Xie, C.: RST invariant reversible watermarking for 2D vector map. Int. J. Multimedia Ubiquitous Eng. **11**(2), 265–276 (2016)

16. Cao, L., Li, X.: Iterative embedding-based reversible watermarking for 2D-vector maps. In: Proceedings of 17th IEEE International Conference on Image Processing (ICIP), pp. 3685–3688 (2010)

17. Wang, N., Men, C.: Reversible watermarking for 2-D vector map authentication with localization. Comput. Aided Des. J. **44**(4), 230–330 (2012)

18. Vybornova, Y., Sergeev, V.: Method for vector map protection based on using of a watermark image as a secondary carrier. In: Proceedings of the 16th International Joint Conference on e-Business and Telecommunications, ICETE 2019, SECRYPT. 2019, vol. 2, pp. 284–293 (2019)

19. Vybornova, Y.D.: Application of spatial interpolation methods for restoration of partially defined images. In: CEUR Workshop Proceedings, vol. 2210, pp. 89–95 (2018)

20. Glumov, N.I., Mitekin, V.A.: The new blockwise algorithm for large-scale images robust watermarking. Comput. Opt. **35**(3), 368–372 (2010)

21. Vybornova, Y.D., Sergeev, V.V.: A new watermarking method for vector map data. In: Proceedings of SPIE, Eleventh International Conference on Machine Vision (ICMV 2018), vol. 11041, no. 11, pp. 1–8 (2019)

22. Vybornova, Y.D.: Password-based key derivation function as one of Blum-Blum-Shub pseudo-random generator applications. Procedia Eng. **201**, 428–435 (2017)

Dynamic Taint Tracking Simulation

Fabian Berner$^{(\boxtimes)}$, René Mayrhofer, and Johannes Sametinger

LIT Secure and Correct Systems Lab, Johannes Kepler University Linz, Linz, Austria
{fabian.berner,rene.mayrhofer,johannes.sametinger}@jku.at

Abstract. Detection of unauthorized disclosure of sensitive data is still an open problem. Taint tracking is one effective approach to detect information disclosure attacks. In this paper, we give an overview of dynamic taint tracking systems for Android. First, we discuss systems and identify their shortcomings. The contribution of this paper is to present a novel solution for these shortcomings. For that purpose, we have developed a simulation concept and a prototype implementation. Special features are the possibility to record simulations and play them back automatically. By comparing the original simulation with a repeated simulation a changed security level can be detected.

Keywords: Android · Information disclosure · Taint analysis · Taint tracking simulation

1 Introduction

Mobile devices like smartphones, tablets, and smartwatches have become ubiquitous in recent years. Since the amount of sensitive data stored on mobile devices has increased, they have become worthwhile targets for attackers. Attacks can pursue a direct purpose like *espionage*, *spamming*, or provide *targeted advertising*. Stolen information can also be used by cyber-criminals for other attacks like *social engineering*, *spoofing*, *phishing*, or other *frauds*. In particular, the danger of frauds has increased recently because of commercial and payment services are now also available on our mobile devices.

An overview of Android security systems can be found, for example, in [23,25,30]. These ones as well as other similar studies do not focus on dynamic taint analysis but rather discuss various security system approaches for Android. Most papers dealing with novel taint tracking systems also distinguish their specific system from other ones, e.g., [24,31].

Dynamic taint tracking systems can be used to detect app-based information disclosure attacks by monitoring information flows between a data source and data sink. In a previous paper [3], we have focused on the evaluation of dynamic taint tracking systems, identifying shortcomings and revealing possible future work. This article is an extended version of [3]. Now, our focus is on a simulation concept for the detection of information disclosure. In the first part of this paper, we again give an overview of existing systems, evaluate them and identify their shortcomings. In the second part, we will present the concept of a novel dynamic taint tracking system that tries to mitigate identified shortcomings by using simulation and, thus, changing the analysis paradigm.

© Springer Nature Switzerland AG 2020
M. S. Obaidat (Ed.): ICETE 2019, CCIS 1247, pp. 203–227, 2020.
https://doi.org/10.1007/978-3-030-52686-3_9

2   Taint Tracking

Information Disclosure means "unauthorized disclosure" of "sensitive data" [20]. To detect *information disclosure* attacks, we focus on *dynamic* taint tracking techniques (or taint analysis). In dynamic analysis systems, the object of investigation is executed and monitored, whereas a static analysis system analyzes the source code without execution. In general, both techniques are appropriate to detect information disclosure attacks. The main advantage of dynamic analysis is that apps can be tested in the same system, configuration, and the same libraries as on the target system. Therefore, it is possible to detect attacks that need certain prerequisites. A *colluding apps* attack for example can only start its malicious function if all colluding apps are installed. In [34], *Zheng et al.* discuss the problems of static analysis in the context of apps written in Java. In particular, they see the missing ability to analyze *dynamically bound* code (e.g., with *reflection* or *generics*) as a major problem of static analysis approaches. *Wei et al.* argue in [26] that static analysis of Android apps is particularly challenging because the control flow of Android apps is event-based and therefore unpredictable. *Xia et al.* add that some of the code paths identified in static analysis "could never happen in real execution" [29]. Other big challenges are *code obfuscation* and *code encryption*. Encrypted or obfuscated code cannot be analyzed by a static analysis system. For attackers, these are easy ways to hide a malicious code. Compared to static analysis, dynamic analysis appears to be more promising to detect information disclosure attacks so far. The main disadvantage of dynamic analysis is that only the executed program paths are analyzed. This leads to problems especially in short analysis processes with low path coverage. Nevertheless, it has to be mentioned that hybrid analysis, i.e., a combination of static and dynamic analysis, can boost the quality of security analysis, e.g., see [10, 15]. Typically, static analysis is performed as an upstream analysis and the results are used as input for dynamic analysis. On the basis of this upstream analysis, the dynamic analysis can be used to run through specific execution paths of the program in a more targeted manner and thus potentially find more security gaps.

Taint Tracking is a data flow analysis technique by marking specific data with a *taint tag* or *taint* for short. The taint itself is transparent for programs that use this data. Therefore, it can be imagined as a watermark. Tainted data originates from a *taint source* and leaves the system in a *taint sink*. Typically, taint source and the taint sink are system library methods. Taint tracking means monitoring the data flow between taint source and taint sink. To evaluate the usage of the tainted data, the *taint propagation* logic monitors the program flow and detects whether the tainted data is processed or copied. If tainted data is copied, the copy is also marked with the same taint as the original data. Taint tags are stored in a taint tag storage. *Overtainting* describes the case when insensitive data is tainted and monitored. Overtainted data flowing to a taint sink leads to *false positives*. *Undertainting* describes the opposite, when sensitive data is not marked by the taint tracking. Undertainting can lead to *false negatives*.

Different dynamic taint tracking systems exist for Android. Most of them are based on *Taintdroid*, while other approaches are Minemu, TaintART or TaintMan. *Taintdroid* is used to date by default as a standard for taint tracking in Android, and it has been extended by other academic security systems. Taintdroid was implemented for the Dalvik Virtual Machine (VM) but has not been ported to the newer Android Runtime

(ART). *TaintART* [24] is an unofficial successor of Taintdroid and is based on Android's ART. The authors released an implementation as an open source on Github[1]. *Minemu* is a taint tracking system integrated in an emulator [5]. Its latest version was published in 2011 and is therefore outdated. TaintMan [31] is also an unofficial successor of Taintdroid, but not yet publicly available at the time of publication. It can be executed on the Dalvik VM as well as in ART. Subsequently, we will focus on Taintdroid and TaintART only.

2.1 Taintdroid

Taintdroid is the best known taint tracking system for Android. It was published in 2010 by *William Enck et al.*, [7] who developed it within the scope of his PhD thesis under the title *Analysis Techniques for Mobile Operating System Security* [9]. An enhancement to the Taintdroid concept was published in 2014 [8].

Taintdroid has been used by many security systems for Android, mostly in academia because of its advanced development and its availability as open source. In the design of any dynamic security analysis system, developers have to decide between performance and storage requirements. Generally speaking, it is possible to reduce the performance overhead of a security analysis system by using more storage capacity and vice versa. Taintdroid's tracking approach is optimized to minimize performance and storage overhead by limiting the amount of different kinds of data sources. The majority of taint tracking systems uses a *shadow memory* or *taint map*. These are both being specific data structures that contain taint information [9, p. 58].

In Taintdroid, the *taint tag storage* is called *virtual taint map*. To store taints in the virtual taint map, Taintdroid uses a 32-bit vector for each data type provided by Dalvik (*method local variable, method arguments, class static fields, class instance fields* and *arrays* [9]). Each of the 32 bits stands for a specific taint tag type and thereby for a defined set of sensitive data. Taintdroid is therefore limited to 32 types of trackable data.

Taintdroid is often cited in the context of taint tracking and some of its limitations are discussed in different publications.

The detection of malicious code can be prevented while Taintdroid's security analysis is running, i.e., by *sandbox detection* and by *evasion techniques*. Sandbox detection includes several techniques to detect whether execution is monitored by a security analysis system. Evasion techniques prevent detection, for example, by awaiting the end of security analysis. Attacks can also use weaknesses of Taintdroid's taint propagation mechanism. Such attacks are discussed by *Sarwar et al.* in [19]. Finally, covert channels can bypass the official Inter Process Communication (IPC) mechanisms and therefore cannot be tracked by Taintdroid.

A variety of security systems is based on Taintdroid. Systems that detect information disclosure attacks and help to protect sensitive data on Android devices. Two example systems are *MOSES* and *TreeDroid*. More examples are given in [3]. *MOSES*, short for *MOde-of-uses SEparation in Smartphones*, presented by *Russello et al.*, [17,33] provides app isolation (*soft virtualization*) by policies that can be modified at runtime.

---

[1] Online: https://github.com/mssun/taintart-art. Last downloaded: 30.12.2019.

MOSES is a program that places apps and the respective sensitive data in isolated profiles, e.g., *work, private* and *default* [11]. MOSES uses Taintdroid taint propagation mechanism to monitor information flows between different profiles. *TreeDroid* by *Dam et al.* is another policy-based security system that uses Taintdroid's data flow tracking technique [6]. TreeDroid generates tree automata for a given app and provides fine-grained policy enforcement at runtime.

2.2   TaintART

TaintART by *Sun, Wei and Lui* was published in late 2016 [24]. Since the Dalvik VM, which Taintdroid is based on, was replaced by ART in Android 5.0 (released in November 2014), Taintdroid has become outdated. The prototypical implementation was done for Android 6.0 [24], which uses ART as runtime environment for apps. The *TaintART compiler* integrates the taint logic into the compiled application. At runtime, *TaintART runtime* executes the compiled native code and tracks tainted data. TaintART distinguishes between four levels of information disclosure, from low to high security needs [24].

To speed up taint tracking, TaintART uses a CPU register as the fastest storage on a computer for taint tag storage. The prototypical implementation is built on a 32-bit ARM processor as target architecture and can therefore save 32 taint tags. To avoid the limitation of registers, TaintART is also able to temporarily store additional taint tags in the device's memory.

TaintART provides three taint propagation logic methods: (1) *basic taint propagation*, (2) *taint propagation via methods calls*, and (3) *propagation between apps through Binder IPC*. For the basic taint propagation, the ART compiler generates a Control Flow Graph (CFG), which is used by the TaintART compiler to instrument the source code for variable-level taint tracking. In case a method is called, TaintART uses an invocation taint propagation to track tainted data in method parameters. The third part is a message-level propagation for Android's Binder IPC.

Compared with Taintdroid, the advantage of TaintART is its compatibility with ART which is the new runtime environment in Android. Therefore, TaintART is an interesting alternative to Taintdroid: on the one hand, it is partly similar to Taintdroid and, on the other hand, it improves the concept of taint tracking. Compared to Taintdroid, one of the improvements is the possible integration of *NDroid* (c.f. [14]) for analyzing native code. To the best of the authors' knowledge, there is no specific attack vector published yet that targets TaintART. Similar to Taintdroid, TaintART's analysis can also be circumvented by collaborating applications that use covert channels to bypass TaintART's analysis mechanism.

2.3   Shortcomings

A description of existing dynamic taint tracking systems and a detailed comparison is given in [3]. Subsequently, we describe shortcomings that these systems share.

Detection Rates. No security system is able to detect all possible information disclosure attacks. This is in the nature of things, but it proves that analysis at runtime on a mobile device with real sensitive data is problematic. Every false-negative on a real mobile device that stores real sensitive data leads to a real information disclosure, which is irreversible. On real mobile devices, it is also problematic to execute an upstream analysis before executing the app because it slows down the start of the app. Another point is the analysis of apps that use native code functions or libraries. Most of the evaluated security systems are not able to analyze native code.

Limited System Resources. Security analysis at runtime on a mobile device costs valuable resources. Especially the energy consumption is one of the major concerns for mobile devices. Even if devices become more powerful, we may not forget that Android penetrates also into other areas. *Android Wear* powered devices like smart watches are just one example. This shortcoming becomes evident only on security systems running on the mobile device directly.

User Interface Complexity. A runtime security analysis either has to be fully automated or the user has to react manually to identify potential security risks. Without expert knowledge in computer security, however, the average user may react incorrectly to the security systems warning. Another – maybe worse – reaction to messages of the security system could be deactivation of the detection mechanism in case the user is overwhelmed by the amount and complexity of security warnings.

Analysis Abstraction Level. Most of the security systems use a fully automated high level analysis or a manual low level analysis. A good balance between these two analysis approaches is rare. Especially the lack of customizability of the data collection mechanisms and security analysis is the major disadvantage of most existing systems.

Detection of Collaborating Apps. Taint tracking systems can be used to detect information flows between apps. However, they are only able to analyze information flows that use overt channels like IPC.

Security Analysis Rerun. Because of the short release cycles of Android apps as well as of Android itself, an automated rerun of security analysis and a subsequent comparison of analysis results seem to be an important function of a security system. In order to fully exhaust the potential of analysis reruns, *degrees of freedom* as well as *variations* should be considered. Variation arises through even minimal divergences in automatic security analysis reruns. Degrees of freedom instead are desirable because they enable the user to repeat a security analysis run with slightly different variables, if necessary. Such variables can, for example, be a newer version of an app or a new version of a mobile device Operating System (OS).

Granularity of Reaction. Most systems adopt the *all-or-nothing* principle. It means that possible reactions are not fine-grained enough. An example is *AppFence* that disconnects all internet connections as soon as a possible information disclosure is detected [18]. In this case, it would actually be sufficient to interrupt only the connection through which the information has been leaked.

Suspicion-based Analysis. This shortcoming is closely connected with restrictions due to the predetermined analysis abstraction level. A fully automated analysis or a manual analysis system are not appropriate to analyze an application for a specific suspicion. A security analysis approach is needed that can be used to analyze the behavior of an app to confirm or rule out the suspicion.

Summary. Table 1 shows the mapping between shortcomings and taint tracking systems. Stars (*) indicate a shortcoming for a specific system. Dashes (-) are used when a shortcoming has not been proved to be true.

Table 1. Summary of shortcomings [3].

	Detection rates	Limited system resources	User Interface complexity	Analysis abstraction level	Detection of collaborating apps	Security analysis rerun	Suspicion-based analysis
TaintDroid [7]	*	*	*	*	*	*	*
TaintART [24]	*	*	*	*	*	*	*
TaintMan [31]	*	*	*	*	*	*	*
Andrubis [27]	*	-	-	*	*	*	*
AppFence [18]	*	*	*	*	*	*	*
AppsPlayground [16]	*	-	-	*	*	*	*
DroidBox [13]	*	*	*	*	*	*	*
Graa et al. [10]	*	*	*	*	*	*	*
Mobile Sandbox [21]	*	-	-	*	*	*	*
MOSES Droid [33]	*	*	*	*	*	*	*
Ndroid [14]	*	-	-	*	-	*	*
TreeDroid [6]	*	-	-	*	*	*	*
QuantDroid [12]	*	*	*	*	*	*	*
vetDroid [32]	*	-	-	*	*	*	*
YAASE [18]	*	*	*	*	*	*	*

Legend: shortcoming * ... exists ; - ... does not exist

To address some of the above shortcomings, we propose a changed security analysis concept that is based on dynamic taint tracking: instead of a live analysis we propose an upstream analysis approach, which is executed by a security expert before the app is used in a productive way. The analysis is executed in a virtual environment, which allows an extended analysis data collection mechanism. Existing systems, that are executed on real mobile devices are limited by performance reasons. Since the virtual device is not used in a productive way, it is possible to use fake data instead of real sensitive data. Thereby the analysis puts no real sensitive data on risk. To extend the system's architecture, the system needs to be built on an extendable and open architecture.

3   Simulation Concept for Information Disclosure Detection

In order to overcome the shortcomings of existing systems, we have developed the concept as well as a prototypical implementation of a simulation environment to evaluate security concerning the disclosure of information. The system is named *Simulacron* after the novel "Simulacron3" by Daniel Francis Galouye, in which an entire city is simulated, but the inhabitants are not aware of the simulation.

As general conditions, we have considered the following boundaries as important for our simulation environment:

– *Locally executed code:* sandbox-based security systems are only able to monitor and analyze local executed code.
– *Unmanipulated apps:* the properties and configuration of apps should not be modified by code injection.
– *Analysis of collaborating apps:* a distributed attack vector over two or more apps that are running on the same device can be monitored and analyzed.
– *Dynamic analysis:* as discussed above, a dynamic analysis approach seems to be better suitable then static analysis. Static analysis is disregarded.
– *Bytecode:* besides the code execution in a runtime environment, apps can also be (partly) written in native code. Based on an existing dynamic taint tracking system, our approach focuses on detecting security issues in code that runs in a runtime environment.

On the other side, there are also boundaries of detectable mobile device threats:

– *Information disclosure attacks:* the focus lies on information disclosure attacks on mobile devices. Other kinds of attacks could also be detected, but these are beyond the scope of this research.
– *Application level:* the security analysis focuses on the detection of application-level information disclosure attacks (e.g. colluding applications; covert channels; confused deputy). Information disclosure attacks on OS or library-level are not considered.
– *Local attacks:* attacks from outside the mobile device are not considered (e.g. exploitation of an app; remote code execution).

Other system boundaries are apps that use sandbox detection and evasion techniques. Especially the prototypical implementation, which is based on the Android Emulator, is very easy to detect (e.g., [28]). The threat of sandbox detection by malicious apps and the attended evasion attacks is disregarded in this concept and its prototypical implementation.

The general idea is to analyze apps before their use and to make them available in a Secure Meta Market (SMM) (e.g., [1]) within a company or organization. Simulation enables test automation and automatic test replays (hereafter: simulation replays), keeping test efforts for security officers or administrators as low as possible. First ideas of our simulation concept have been presented in [2–4].

The target group for Simulacron are, for example, administrators, a company's security representative or external security service providers like pen testers.

Figure 1 depicts an architecture overview of Simulacron. The basis is a VM running a virtual Android instance enhanced by an existing taint tracking system. The virtual OS executes the applications we want to analyze. The taint-tracker is used to monitor the information flows between the applications and libraries on the virtual device.

One or more applications can be executed on the virtual OS. The applications usually communicate with the OS and the outside world via functions of the system library.

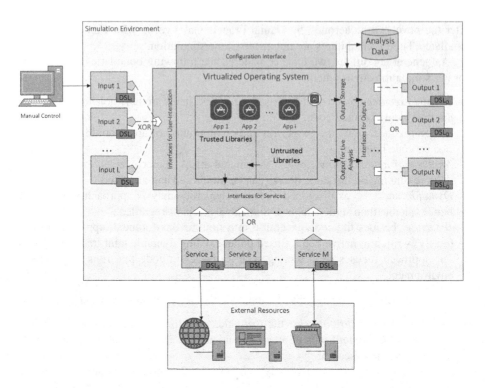

Fig. 1. Simulation environment [2].

We assume a trustworthy system image that exclusively provides unmanipulated system functions. In Fig. 1, the system functions of the operating system are counted as trusted libraries. 3rd party libraries that are not trustworthy are called untrusted libraries. Untrusted libraries represent a danger for the security analysis with Simulacron, because for example possible information disclosures within the library code may not be detected by the used taint-tracker.

We consider three different plugin types for adapting the simulation environment: *Input plugins* can be used to simulate any user interaction. The user interaction can be done either by manual operation or by input generators like fuzzing tools. *Service plugins* can be used to simulate other mobile devices or other services. Other parts can either be fully simulated or be connected to the simulation environment via a stub service. The purpose of service plugins is to monitor communication with other devices. By simulating other devices, a security analysis does neither endanger the security of real devices, nor of any sensitive data and enables the detection of attack vectors that are distributed over several devices.

The security analysis itself, i.e., the evaluation of collected analysis data, can be implemented via *output plugins*. The analysis can be done either in parallel to the simulation execution (*live*) or after the simulation (*post-mortem*). Signature-based analysis methods are particularly suitable because mainly causal relationships and certain data patterns have to be identified during security analysis. Signatures are attack patterns that are searched for in the analysis data using pattern matching. With different output plugins, different analysis methods can be integrated into the simulation environment, depending on the attack types for which the apps to be analyzed are to be examined. The communication between the described components is asynchronous. This means that a system component sends a message to another component without waiting for a response (*fire-and-forget* principle). Various data sources such as the virtual OS and its system library, the VM hypervisor as well as the input and service plugins are used to collect analysis data. The program logic processes the incoming analysis data, merges them and forwards them to the configured output plugins. The security analysis is performed either live or post-mortem. In a security analysis at runtime, the analysis data is sent directly to the used output plug-ins. If the security analysis should be performed after the simulation, the analysis data must be stored temporarily.

Information disclosure attacks cannot only be detected directly in the data sink where they leave the boundaries of the simulated device. Knowledge about application-internal processing of sensitive data can also be used, for example, to identify a kind of steganography, i.e. hiding sensitive data in other transmitted data, or coding of the data. Encrypted communication is another way of undetected disclosure of sensitive data, because simple monitoring at data sinks can be bypassed. In the simulation environment, the system library functions offered by the OS for encrypting data have to be extended in order to capture data to be encrypted before encryption actually takes place.

Sensitive data should not be processed within the simulation environment. Therefore, *fake data* such as contact data, SMS or changed GPS coordinates can be generated and uploaded to the virtual device. The generated fake data can also be used for security analysis by searching for them in the analysis data, from which a flow of information can be inferred. The collected analysis data is sent to the output plugins and processed. The concept of our simulation environment does not provide for automatic reactions that prevent an information flow. Due to the generated fake data, no sensitive data is endangered during a simulation. Consequently, no automated reactions are necessary.

3.1 Simulation Process

A new simulation (hereafter *original simulation*) or a replay of an existing simulation (hereafter *replayed simulation*) can be started by configuring the simulation environment and plugins. The plugin selection and configuration depend on the goals of the analysis. The kind of user interaction for a new simulation can be defined by selecting the input plugin. For simulation replays, the user interaction is replayed automatically based on the recorded user interaction (*touch events*) and *system events* from the original simulation (Fig. 2).

The selection of service plugins also allows different monitored communication partners for the simulation. However, the variation of service plugins for replayed simulations only makes sense when the variation of the simulated communication partners does not lead to an erroneous termination of the simulation. The output plugins for new simulations as well as for replayed simulations can be defined in advance of the security analysis. The analysis data is collected during the simulation itself.

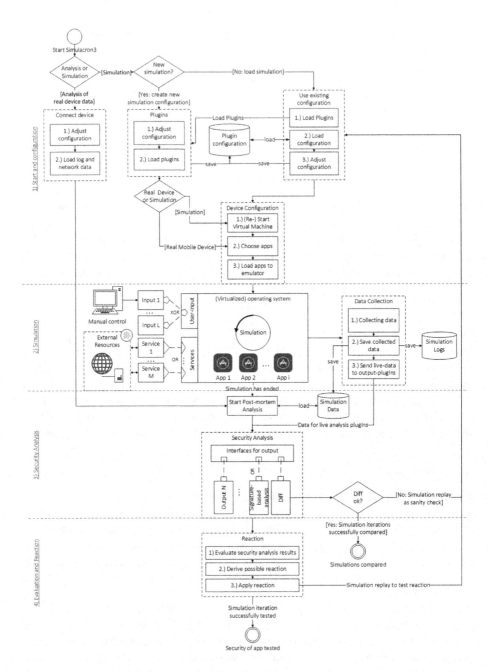

Fig. 2. Simulation process.

Parallel to the simulation, the system and touch events from the virtual OS are recorded for later simulation replay. Depending on the selected output plugin, the security analysis is performed either in parallel or at the end of the simulation. The architectural overview in Fig. 1 is adapted to reflect the process flow in the simulation process. The model gives an overview of how a user can use the Simulacron simulation environment. A preset standard configuration can either be used for the first security analysis or adapted to the specific needs, for example, if the user has a specific suspicion. In the following simulation runs, configuration can be adapted to the user's needs.

We can divide the simulation process into four main steps:

Step 1: *Start and Configuration*. The first step includes *start* and *configuration* of the simulation environment. Simulacron can be started either to execute a simulation run or to analyze the collected data of a real mobile device. To evaluate the analysis data of a real mobile device, the device has to be connected to Simulacron via USB or Wireless Local Area Network (WLAN). After the device has been connected, the analysis can be configured and the analysis data is loaded to Simulacron as well as the sniffed network traffic. Process step 2 ("Simulation") is skipped in this case because we want to analyze the data that has already been collected.

If Simulacron is started in a simulation mode, the user has to decide whether to load an existing configuration to replay a simulation or to create a new configuration. To use an existing configuration, Simulacron loads the needed plugins and the simulation configuration and installs the needed applications. After the simulation environment has been prepared for the simulation replay, the VM is started. In case the VM is already running, it has to be restarted to adopt the simulation configurations related to the VM or to the virtual OS. To start a new simulation, the user has to configure the VM and to decide which plugins should be loaded. To configure the VM, the user has to configure the virtual hardware, the OS ant its version, as well as the Apps to be installed.

Instead of a VM-based simulation, a real mobile device can be connected and configured as we will discuss later. Further steps remain the same; the difference is, however, that no restart of the real mobile device is needed because real mobile devices do not feature different OS-versions or configurations.

Step 2: *Simulation*. After initialization and configuration of the simulation environment, the actual simulation process can be started: the installed app can be started and, if necessary, preconfigured (e.g. a proxy server an app has to use).

Depending on the chosen input- and service-plugins, simulation is executed automatically, half-automated or manually. During the simulation, Simulacron collects simulation data which consist of *analysis data* and *simulation logs*. The analysis data is stored for a post-mortem analysis or is redirected to a live-analysis output-plugin. The *simulation log* contains user input and system events that are needed for replaying the simulations.

Due to the complexity of network communication, the replay of the recorded network data is not part of the Simulacron concept. The resulting prone to error network communication (e.g. occurring encrypted connections, or digital certificates to verify the authenticity and integrity) of replayed network traffic, could affect the simulation replay in a negative way.

If live analysis is executed parallel to simulation, the user gets the results displayed after the simulation or live during the simulation. Indeed, this is an implementation detail of the respective output-plugs; however, we can assume that in most cases the results are displayed live.

Step 3: *Security Analysis*. Step 3 includes the actual security analysis: the analysis data collected in the second step is evaluated. In case of a live analysis approach, this step is executed parallel to the simulation. If post-mortem analysis is done, this step is started after the simulation has ended or, in case of a real mobile device, after the analysis data has been loaded.

Since mobile devices are dynamic systems that change over time, the security level of an app can change, too. Therefore, Simulacron offers the possibility to compare two simulation runs to identify changed behavior of the app that needs security level adjustment. At the downstream decision branch, the user can decide whether the results of the simulation run require another simulation run or not, especially if the findings of two simulation runs differ strongly. In case deviations occur after a configuration change, a *sanity check* can be used to test whether the simulation record and replay function have worked correctly. For a sanity check, the original configuration has to be stored in order to replay the simulation as close to the original as possible. If the results of the sanity check are identical with the results of the original simulation, we can assume that the simulation record and replay function have worked correctly. Otherwise, the simulation replay has to be called into question.

Step 4: *Evaluation and Reaction*. The concept of Simulacron does not support automated reactions because it does not make sense to react to threats in a simulation environment. Nonetheless, in further development of Simulacron or of the output-plugins, an automated derive and recommendations to the user for action could be offered as an interesting new feature.

Step 4 includes manual reactions by the user. These reactions can be tested by an automated simulation rerun after the reaction has taken place (e.g. restricted access to resources or repealed permissions). Another simulation rerun with the original configuration as a sanity check can eliminate the possibility of an incorrect simulation rerun wherefore the original findings do not occur in the replayed simulation.

The following reactions are suitable for most cases: The app can be released over a dedicated SMM when no unauthorized disclosure of sensitive data is detected. In case an unauthorized disclosure of sensitive data is detected, the app will either be rejected or provided in a dedicated SMM with additional security requirements. These security requirements could prescribe for example the usage of policy enforcement systems to impede the malicious function.

Automatic Preliminary Analysis. Hybrid analysis is a well-known research field. According to the previous discussed system boundaries, Simulacron focuses only on the dynamic analysis. In order to discuss the possibility to expand static analysis for later developments, we need to describe how it can be integrated as an upstream analysis. The idea of a static upstream analysis is not new and is implemented in many systems presented, for example, in [10]. By combining static and dynamic analysis, the limitations of both approaches can be mitigated. In particular, bypassing of a dynamic analysis by sandbox detection and evasion techniques can be countered by the upstream analysis.

Another huge advantage of hybrid analysis is that the dynamic analysis can be implemented in a more efficient way. Without an upstream analysis, the dynamic analysis is more or less a black-box analysis, without any knowledge of the internal functionality and data processing. With an upstream analysis, the dynamic analysis of an application can be supported, for example, by preliminary selection of execution paths that deserve special attention. Such execution paths can be identified by the analysis of unusual code segments like loops that call thread sleeps, which may indicate a delayed execution of a malfunction.

The integration of a static upstream analysis particularly effects the first step of Simulacron analysis process. The static app analysis hooks between the device configurations, after the apps to be analyzed have been chosen by the user. The analysis is executed automatically based on the predefined static analysis rules. After the analysis has been executed, the results are saved and provided to Simulacron input- and output-plugins.

Customized input plugins can process the results of the preliminary analysis as input for the automated generation of user inputs to enter critical execution paths. The static analysis results can be used by the Simulacron user to select proper output plugins as well as an input for the executed security analysis. The results are also a valuable input for the comparison of two simulation runs (*diff*-function).

The proposed integration of the upstream analysis in Simulacron is just one possible way. The actual implementation could also intervene at other points in the process. Such an upstream analysis is assumed to be given and therefore is not implemented in the prototype of Simulacron.

3.2 Analysis Data Collection

The existing taint tracking systems have several limitations [3,4]. By shifting from a dynamic taint tracking system that is executed on a real mobile device to a simulation environment, the analysis data collection can be extended: firstly, in a simulation environment we can collect analysis data at more trace points, and, secondly, data collection and security analysis are not restricted by resource limitations. The idea in Simulacron – as well as in some other sandbox-based security systems – is to collect analysis data at different trace points and perform security analysis either live (parallel to the simulation run) or post-mortem (after the simulation run). The purpose of the different trace points is to obtain statistically independent analysis data and thus increase the reliability of the security analysis. For both live and post-mortem analysis, the analysis data has to be stored. For a live analysis, the analysis data has only to be buffered until the security analysis is ready for the next analysis data. In contrast, for a post-mortem analysis, the analysis data has to be stored until the simulation run has stopped and the security analysis is executed.

The technical challenge is – ideally – to monitor *all* ingoing and outgoing communication connections as well as IPC/Inter Component Communication (ICC) connections of the app to be analyzed. The monitoring of all communication connections is impeded by general limitations of data collection: especially encryption, unknown coding and proprietary communication protocols make a proper data collection nearly impossible. This also explains why it is not sufficient to monitor the outgoing network connections in order to detect information disclosure attacks. Needless to say, not every information flow is necessarily an unauthorized disclosure of sensitive data. In dynamic security analysis systems that run on a mobile device, the user has to distinguish between legitimate and illegitimate data flows. However, such analysis requires deep knowledge of data restrictions and protocols and is therefore often restricted to domain experts. An advantage of Simulacron's simulation environment concept is that one can either keep in mind when a legitimate information flow operation is executed or decide to avoid legitimate information flows and define all findings as an attack.

Every security analysis is based on collected analysis data. For a black-box-like app analysis, one can roughly distinguish between the following analysis data sources: the *app* itself, the *runtime environment* or *OS*, or *external sources*. Besides both internal analysis data sources discussed above, external sources can also be used to generate analysis data. For example, network data can be analyzed to detect running attacks. Examples would be the analysis whether sensitive data is sent in the payload of the data packets or whether connections to suspicious servers are opened. Every analysis data source can be used separately or combined with other sources to detect unauthorized disclosure of sensitive data. Most of security systems discussed in [3] focus on one of the described analysis data sources.

For device internal information flow tracking, dynamic taint tracking seems to be a proper solution. As discussed in [3], in the existing taint tracking systems there is a lack of comprising communication monitoring of the mobile device with external services and devices. There are three technology classes to connect a mobile device to services and other devices: *Cellular networks*, WLAN and Personal Area Network (PAN). All three technologies are possible information sinks, where information could leave the mobile device.

Besides the information sinks also the information sources are important analysis data sources, too, that can help to detect possible information disclosure attacks. The existing dynamic taint tracking approaches already monitor the defined library functions as *taint sources*. Here, it is necessary to check which data sources are already being monitored and where there is still room for improvement. *Enck et al.* distinguish in the dynamic taint tracking system *Taintdroid* between the following *taint sources* [8]:

- *Low-bandwidth-sensors:* sensor sources with only a small data throughput (e.g. GPS, acceleration sensor…)
- *High-bandwidth-sensors:* sensor sources with a high data throughput (microphone, camera…)
- *Information databases:* OS and app databases (e.g. address book, SMS-list, SSID …)

- *Device identifiers:* unique identifiers of the mobile device or user (e.g. IMEI, IMSI, SIM, ICCID...)

As described above, Taintdroid is limited to 32 different taint sources, which seems limiited to comprehensive analsis. Android Application Programming Interface (API) already distinguish between 17 different types of low-bandwidth-sensors[2]. Another important point of criticism is that Taintdroid is limited to one device. Sensors of PAN devices (e.g. a *smart watch* or an *activity tracker*) are not discussed in Taintdroid related papers. However, exactly the devices connected this way constantly generate highly personal and therefore sensitive data like health data, communication and position data.

For all four connection technologies and input sources, the analysis data can be collected at several trace points in the simulation environment. Information disclosure over cellular networks, LAN and PAN can be collected at different trace points: at system library-level, at *OS-level* ant at *hypervisor-level*. In Simulacron, analysis data is collected on all three levels, even if the boundaries between OS- and hypervisor-levels become blurred due to the close connection of Android, the Android emulator and the Android Debug Bridge (ADB).

The consolidation of analysis data is done in Simulacron by copy and forwarding the collected data using the *Logcat* logging system.

Network communication seems to be the most likely way for an unauthorised disclosure of sensitive data: data over cell network services are either very limited in data volume (e.g. Short Message Service (SMS)) or complex to use (e.g. disclosure over telephone connection). A disclosure attack over PAN technologies needs additional devices in the send and receive area of the attacked device.

Summarizing, Simulacron uses the following techniques to collect analysis data mainly at four trace points:

- *Taint tracking:* for monitoring information flows in apps, between apps as well as between apps and libraries.
- *Libraries:* information flows to a system library as well as selected 3rd-party library functions are monitored. In system libraries, all communication functions that could be used to send sensitive information and functions to receive information from PAN devices are instrumented with a code. Redirection of data flows is rejected in favor of a code instrumentation that copies and collects leaked data. As an assumption, we define the virtual OS as well as its system libraries as secure. That means that for the Simulacron concept attacks against the OS as well as malfunctions are not considered. Neither is the instrumentation of 3rd-party libraries part of this concept. Of course, other libraries can also be instrumented to copy and collect analysis data and thus be available for the Simulacron security analysis. Therefore, Fig. 1 uses the terms *trusted libraries* and *untrusted libraries* instead of *system libraries* and *3rd-party libraries*. Depending on the taint tracking approach, it is unclear how possible sensitive data is processed in untrusted libraries, which can be referred to as 3rd-party libraries that are not instrumented to collect analysis data. We suggest generating warnings, when apps call untrusted library functions. These warnings can be

---

[2] Online: https://developer.android.com/guide/topics/sensors/sensors_overview.html, last downloaded 30.11.2019.

processed in the security analysis and thus flow into the security evaluation of the app.

- *Network monitoring:* network traffic in Simulacron is either monitored at hypervisor- or at the OS-level, so information flows between two or more simulated devices can also be monitored. Service plugins are another type of network monitoring components, as described above.
- *User input and system events:* to replay simulations, the user input (e.g. in Android: *touch events*) and system events are collected.

3.3 Security Analysis

A signature-based analysis approach is the most promising method when finding disclosed information in collected analysis data. Anomaly-based detection, instead, is suitable for detecting anomalies indicating possible malicious functionality. Most of the analysis data is in plain text and therefore easy to analyze by signature-based analysis.

Findings are indivisible, i.e., one finding refers to one information disclosure. Conversely, one information disclosure can be indicated by one or more findings. The simulation environment cannot distinguish between findings caused by legitimate or by illegitimate operations. *Legal* means that an operation, in which information leaves the secure context, is knowingly executed by the user. An *illegitimate* operation is either unknowingly executed by the user or based on an attack or malicious application. Illegitimate operations lead to unwanted information disclosure of sensitive data. We may not confuse the indivisibility of findings with *single-step attacks* and *multi-step attacks*. Single-step attacks can be detected based on one entry of the analysis data. Multi-step attacks can only be detected by analyzing two or more analysis data entries. Findings provide a logical unit and are therefore described as indivisible.

Regular Expressions are an example for an easy-to-implement post-mortem approach for signature-based analysis. An example implementation of live analysis are off-the-shelf Complex Event Processing (CEP) systems. We propose the use of signature-based post-mortem analysis based on regular expressions, because they are fast, easy to use, and reliable. Data cannot be analyzed if it is encrypted, obfuscated or coded in some way. Alternative signature-based analysis techniques can be found for example in [22].

3.4 Recording Simulations

Our main idea is to collect as much input and output data as possible. Android distinguishes between touch and system events. *Touch events* comprise all user inputs and *system events* summarize all OS events such as incoming calls. To replay a simulation run, the recorded simulation data is processed to derive appropriate touch and system events that we can initiate. To later replay a simulation run, we first need to collect information about the system and its configuration including all the installed software. During the original simulation, any system and touch events have to be recorded with time-stamps. Some communication data that cannot be analyzed by other analysis techniques can be collected at a library level, e.g., encrypted network connections. We adjust encryption methods provided by system libraries to log any encrypted data. Even if taint tracking data, recorded network data and analysis data collected at service plugins are not replayed, they have to be recorded for later comparison of simulation runs. The security analysis results of a simulation run are valuable for a later simulation run comparison and therefore have to be collected, too. The collected analysis can be stored in files for a later replay.

3.5 Replaying Simulations

The ability to replay simulations helps users to repeat recurring activities faster. The idea is that the security analysis process does not have to be repeated manually, which would be time consuming and error-prone. Instead, we record the original simulation run and replay the simulation by repeating the system and touch events automatically. Simulations can be replayed in a automated or half-automated way in case the simulation is initiated by the user. For an automated simulation replay, it is possible to run the complete simulation environment as a cloud service. For full-automation, the simulation has to be started and executed without any manual user interaction. *Variation* as well as *degrees of freedom* pertain to the deviation of simulation replays. The difference between these two kinds of deviation is that variation describes an *unwanted* deviation of the simulation replay while degrees of freedom describe *wanted* derivations.

The question is how exactly a simulation can be replayed. Even if computers work strictly deterministic, there might be influence that is difficult to predict – especially in modern event-driven architectures. Accordingly, a simulation replay will vary in each replay. The purpose is to minimize the influence of variation on the simulation run and to avoid side-effects as far as possible. Beside the unwanted deviation that comes with variation, there are also degrees of freedom that can derivate a replayed simulation. Possible degrees of freedom define which wanted deviations are possible during a simulation replay.

The usefulness of most degrees of freedom is self explanatory: they are useful since the release cycles of the apps and mobile OS are very fast. By changing the app privileges and comparing the results of the original simulation and the replayed simulation run, possible reactions to mitigate the harm of malicious apps can be tested.

By changing the simulation configuration (more apps, less apps or other apps installed), the simulation user can analyze if the malicious function depends on whether certain other apps are installed. Of course, this function can only be used to confirm or refute a certain suspect. By using this degree of freedom, two or more apps (from the same manufacturer), can be tested for the attack vector family *colluding apps*. The degrees of freedom and the possibility of automated simulation replays result in a much more comprehensive security evaluation than with on-device security analysis, where only those attacks can be detected that are possible due to the respective system configuration. In addition, attacks can be reproduced in order to analyse them more precisely and find suitable countermeasures.

3.6 Comparing Simulations

To compare simulations, we have to define under which conditions two or more simulation runs are considered equal. As discussed before, different degrees of freedom as well as variation can affect simulation replays. Thereby, the comparison also becomes more complex. To evaluate the equivalence of two or more simulation runs, the comparison should ideally detect causal relationships between incoming user input or rather system events, and the occurrence of information disclosure attacks. An example for a causal relationship would be when the user clicks a button and executes malicious code which contains an information disclosure attack. We use different analysis data sources collected in different processes and threads. However, data collection can be more difficult because of scheduling and switching between the analysis data collection processes. Therefore, the detection of causal relationships between events and information disclosure attacks is impeded (Fig. 3).

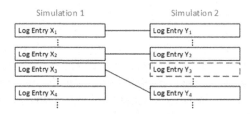

Fig. 3. Simulation comparison.

We imagine a graphical simulation comparison tool in which the user can decide on the comparability of two or more simulation runs. The idea is to represent simulation log entries, findings etc. in a diagram which can be visually analyzed by the user. For example, we can add supportive markings like coloring log entries and connection lines between equivalent nodes. Comparable nodes can be for example equal touch or system events, as well as equivalent findings in the analysis data.

To support the user who wishes to compare different simulation runs, the comparison tool needs a feature to show and hide information the user does not need. Especially the amount of simulation log entries needs to be reduced, which can be done, by hiding corresponding entries from both compared simulation runs. Additionally, manual hiding of simulation log entries by marking entries could support the user to reduce the amount of simulation log entries to review. Even if findings occur at the same simulation sequence indicating the same information disclosure, the user cannot be sure that both findings lead back to the same attack or vulnerability. This happens due to the fact that we focus on black-box analysis of unknown applications. By evaluating taint tracking data, the finding can be backtracked to the code where it is initiated. Thereby, the findings become more comparable and the equality can be ascertained.

3.7 Connecting Real Mobile Devices

There are a few scenarios which show that it would be advantageous to execute the applications on a real mobile device instead of a virtual device:

- *Data collection tuned with the real situation:* No matter how carefully the test cases are developed, they differ from the app usage in real life. Therefore, it could be useful to collect analysis data directly on a real mobile device and to analyze it later. This way the collected data is much closer to the real-world app usage.
- *Unreproducible test cases:* some test cases are difficult to reproduce in a simulation environment. This can happen when the circumstances leading to a security issue are unclear or when the simulation environment differs in its behavior from a real mobile device.
- *Avoid sandbox detection and evasion:* Simulacron as a sandbox-based security analysis approach can be detected by malware using sandbox detection and evasion techniques. Although we do not address sandbox detection and evasion for the VM-based simulation concept in Simulacron, as defined in the system boundaries, it has to be mentioned that a *bare-metal* approach may solve possible sandbox detection and evasion attacks.

As in the Simulacron simulation environment, an adapted Android with integrated taint tracker and adapted system libraries must be installed on the real mobile device.

As the first design decision for connecting real mobile devices to Simulacron, we have to choose an appropriate communication technology. Ideally, the same communication technology can be used to connect an emulator, a VM-based device or a real mobile device: a real mobile device can be connected to Simulacron via USB or WLAN. Both technologies are also often used for debugging an app that is executed on a real mobile device.

To connect a real mobile device to Simulacron, some components have to be adapted. This applies in particular to the mobile device connection as well as to the output plugins.

For connecting real mobile devices, there are two different connection modes: Either the real mobile device is permanently connected to Simulacron (*connection mode*) or the device is only connected to Simulacron when a simulation has been executed and the analysis data should be evaluated (*storage mode*).

All input-, service- and output-plugins are part of the Simulacron simulation environment and therefore only available when the real mobile device is connected to Simulacron. While most plugins could be used in the connection mode, only the post-mortem security analysis output-plugins are available for storage mode.

There are also limitations in the simulation replay capabilities. Theoretically, simulation replays are also possible on a real mobile device as long as it is connected to Simulacron. However, a real mobile device is exposed to detrimental environmental influences that can disturb or impede an orderly simulation replay. An example for such an influence could be a system interrupted by an incoming call. If the device is protected against such environmental influences, a proper simulation rerun can also be executed on a real mobile device.

3.8 Sanity Checks

After a simulation replay, it is often unclear whether the simulation is replayed in a correct way and is thus comparable with the original simulation run. This can be due to variation and other deviations in the system configuration. A changed simulation run can be due to a failed simulation record or replay. Therefore, it makes sense to validate the simulation replay mechanism by what we call a *sanity check*. A sanity check can be useful to test the replay mechanism after a deriving simulation replay as well as when the simulation replay seems to be executed correctly. The procedure for sanity checks is as follows:

1. Simulation replay with the same configuration and software versions as in the original simulation run, which means replay of simulation without using any degree of freedom.
2. Recording of the simulation run.
3. Comparison of the findings and event order of both simulation runs.

The comparison of the findings in both simulation runs is not sufficient to test whether both simulations runs are equal. Even with the same findings, simulations can differ. For example, two totally different simulations may lead to the same findings, or simulation runs may differ in a simulation interval without findings, or findings may simply not be detected in both simulation runs.

If different findings for both simulation runs are found, one may not conclude that the simulation record and replay mechanism have failed. This can also be caused by a deviation outside the simulation context, for example, when a used web service is not available in one simulation run. Another possible drawback of sanity checks is that the influence of variation cannot determined and can thus distort the results of the sanity checks. All these possible problems have to be kept in mind during the sanity checks. Even if the results of sanity checks are in these exceptional cases no guarantee for the correct record and replay of simulation runs, they can be used in most cases to check whether the simulation was recorded and replayed correctly or not.

4   Implementation Aspects

The prototype is developed as a Java application, which uses the Android Emulator for virtualization. Both parts communicate with each other via the public interfaces of the Android Emulator. The overall architecture of our simulation system has been depicted in Fig. 1.

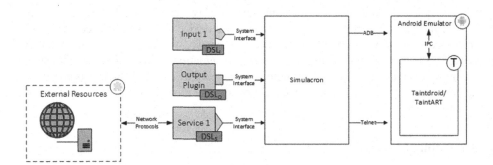

Fig. 4. Simulacron communication.

Figure 4 shows a more communication centric view on the prototypical implementation of Simulacron.

The choice of the virtualization solution fell on the Android Emulator because of its wide distribution and open source approach. The Android Software Development Kit (SDK) also provides various tools that facilitate communication with the Android Emulator, but also provide additional functionality.

The orchestration of the simulations, the generation of system and touch events, the collection and processing of the analysis data, as well as the security analysis is done by Simulacron and its plugins. The prototype is developed as a Java application and the communication between both system parts takes place via the ADB and the telnet server provided by the Android Emulator.

For the dynamic taint analysis, two existing taint-trackers for Android are used. This is Taintdroid on the one hand and TaintArt on the other. In the current state of the prototypical implementation, the integration of Taintdroid is complete and the integration of TaintArt is under development.

The collection of the analysis data takes place at different places in the Simulacron overall system as already described. For the collection and consolidation of the analysis data, different logging systems are used, which are read by Simulacron. Data from the virtualized device is forwarded to Simulacron via Logcat and the ADB. Log4J is used for logging in Simulacron and the Simulacron plugins. The analysis data from all logging sources is consolidated and processed by Simulacron to provide to prepare them for the security analysis.

5   Discussion and Evaluation

Our simulation system attempts to mitigate the shortcomings described above by changing the analysis paradigm of dynamic taint analysis. The shortcomings *detection rate* and *limited system resources* are mutually dependent in the case of existing systems. We approach the two shortcomings together by moving the performance intensive security analysis from the mobile device to a computer. This means that on the one hand the security analysis is not limited to the resources of the mobile device and on the other hand the limited system resources are available for apps. For example, these resources include computing power and memory, as well as battery power. By shifting the performance overhead to a computer, not only resources that would have been needed on the mobile device are made available. In addition, the security analysis can be improved by adding additional analysis data. This additional analysis data can be collected both on the virtual mobile device and from beyond the device context. Since the applications are executed on the virtual device as on a real device, the advantages of dynamic analysis are also retained: An example is the parallel execution of several applications to detect attack vectors like *colluding applications*, *confused deputy* and *covert channels*. The *Detection of Collaborating Applications* was also an identified shortcoming of some of the existing taint tracking systems. Thus, we also take the shortcoming *Detection of collaborating apps* into consideration. With previous taint tracking systems, the user has to make security-relevant decisions at run-time, which we have already discussed as shortcoming *User Interface complexity*. If, on the other hand, the analysis is carried out upstream - as in the proposed system - the security analysis can be carried out by an expert.

We can increase the abstraction level by the plugin-based architecture of our simulation environment, which can be extended by additional analysis data sources in combination with different security analysis approaches. In this way, different low-level and high-level approaches are possible. Either to minimize the analysis effort for the user witch fully automated high-level security analysis systems or manually executed analysis approaches. Low-level analysis has on the one hand a higher effort for the user, but on the other hand, has other advantages like the ability to analyze specific parts – say system calls – of an application. Also, a good balance between these two approaches can mitigate various disadvantages of one of both extremes. The inability of existing taint tracking systems to rerun security analyzes is a major limitation. The automated test rerun is a key feature if our concept that is linked to other useful features like *degrees of freedom*, the partial rerun of simulations or the simulation speedup to save resources. Our architecture also allows an automated simulation replay in a cloud service. For suspicion-based analysis, the data collection phase needs to be manually controlled by the user. Therefore, analysis systems which run in parallel are neither appropriate. In order to prevent misunderstandings: the inappropriate ability of automatic analysis systems to perform suspicion-based analysis should not be confused with automated replays, as discussed before. Automated replays can also be used in a suspicion-based analysis, for example to test a suspicious function of an app under different conditions.

A prototype implementation of the Simulacron concept is currently under development. The taint tracker is based on Taintdroid and TaintART. In first, promising attempts, for example, the *ScubDroid* anti TaintDroid attacks[3] could be detected, which are not detectable by the used taint tracker. It is also already possible to replay basic simulations. A detailed evaluation will be done and published after completion of the prototype.

The source code of the prototype is expected to be published after completion in summer 2020.

6   Conclusion

To detect information disclosure attacks, taint tracking seems to be a promising approach. At the time of this writing, neither the source code of TaintART nor that of TaintMan has been released, Taintdroid and its unofficial successors remain the main available taint tracking approaches for analyzing Android apps. Some of the discussed systems seem to be outdated; however, since every system has its specific purpose, we believe it is necessary to review the research done on the topic and different approaches for improving taint tracking. The evolved shortcomings show that there is a need for further research and new security systems.

Based on the shortcoming, we then have introduced our simulation approach that had been implemented as a prototype and aims at mitigating several of the shortcoming discussed before. We cannot completely solve all of the shortcomings shown above, but we have provided a valuable addition to other security systems. All discussed shortcomings are important, particularly the replay of security analysis runs with the ability to compare the security analysis results are an important feature for future taint tracking and other security systems. For all security systems that follow a scanner approach,

---

[3] Online: http://gsbabil.github.io/AntiTaintDroid/, downloaded 30.12.2019.

the possibility of automated security analysis reruns with result comparison seems the only appropriate way given the amount of apps used, the short release cycles of apps and mobile device OS as well as the heterogeneity of mobile computing caused by the amount of mobile device manufactures, mobile device OS and versions.

References

1. Armando, A., Costa, G., Verderame, L., Merlo, A.: Securing the bring your own device paradigm. Computer **47**(6), 48–56 (2014)
2. Berner, F.: Simulacron: Eine Simulationsumgebung zur automatischen Testwiederholung und Erkennung von Informationsabflüssen in Android-Applikationen. In: IT-Sicherheit als Voraussetzung für eine erfolgreiche Digitalisierung; [Tagungsband ... 16. Deutschen IT-Sicherheitskongress, 21.–23. Mai 2019], pp. 167–177 (2019)
3. Berner, F., Sametinger, J.: Dynamic taint-tracking: Directions for future research. In: SECRYPT 2019 - Proceedings of the International Conference on Security and Cryptography, pp. 85–94. Scitepress Digital Library, Prague (2019)
4. Berner, F., Sametinger, J.: Information disclosure detection in cyber-physical systems. In: Anderst-Kotsis, G., et al. (eds.) DEXA 2019. CCIS, vol. 1062, pp. 85–94. Springer, Cham (2019). https://doi.org/10.1007/978-3-030-27684-3_12
5. Bosman, E., Slowinska, A., Bos, H.: Minemu: the world's fastest taint tracker. In: Sommer, R., Balzarotti, D., Maier, G. (eds.) RAID 2011. LNCS, vol. 6961, pp. 1–20. Springer, Heidelberg (2011). https://doi.org/10.1007/978-3-642-23644-0_1
6. Dam, M., Le Guernic, G., Lundblad, A.: Treedroid: a tree automaton based approach to enforcing data processing policies. In: Proceeding CCS 2012 Proceedings of the 2012 ACM Conference on Computer and Communications Security, p. 894 (2012)
7. Enck, W., et al.: Taintdroid: an information-flow tracking system for realtime privacy monitoring on smartphones. In: Proceeding OSDI 2010 Proceedings of the 9th USENIX Conference on Operating Systems Design and Implementation (2010)
8. Enck, W., et al.: Taintdroid: an information-flow tracking system for realtime privacy monitoring on smartphones. ACM Trans. Comput. Syst. **32**(2), 1–29 (2014)
9. Enck, W.H.: Analysis Techniques for Mobile Operating System Security. Ph.D. thesis, Pennsylvania State University, May 2011
10. Graa, M., Cuppens-Boulahia, N., Cuppens, F., Cavalli, A.: Detection of illegal control flow in android system: protecting private data used by smartphone apps. In: Cuppens, F., Garcia-Alfaro, J., Zincir Heywood, N., Fong, P.W.L. (eds.) FPS 2014. LNCS, vol. 8930, pp. 337–346. Springer, Cham (2015). https://doi.org/10.1007/978-3-319-17040-4_22
11. Hornyack, P., Han, S., Jung, J., Schechter, S., Wetherall, D.: These aren't the droids you're looking for: retrofitting android to protect data from imperious applications. In: Chen, Y., Danezis, G., Shmatikov, V. (eds.) Proceedings of the 18th ACM Conference on Computer and Communications Security, p. 639 (2011)
12. Mollus, K., Westhoff, D., Markmann, T.: Curtailing privilege escalation attacks over asynchronous channels on android. In: 14th International Conference on Innovations for Community Services (I4CS), pp. 87–94 (2014)
13. QEMU Project: Networking (2017). https://wiki.qemu.org/Documentation/Networking
14. Qian, C., Luo, X., Shao, Y., Chan, A.T.: On tracking information flows through JNI in android applications. In: 2014 44th Annual IEEE/IFIP International Conference on Dependable Systems and Networks (DSN), pp. 180–191. IEEE (2014)

15. Rasthofer, S., Arzt, S., Miltenberger, M., Bodden, E.: Harvesting runtime values in android applications that feature anti-analysis techniques. In: Capkun, S. (ed.) Proceedings 2016 Network and Distributed System Security Symposium. Internet Society, 21–24 February 2016

16. Rastogi, V., Chen, Y., Enck, W.: Appsplayground: automatic security analysis of smartphone applications. In: Bertino, E., Sandhu, R., Bauer, L., Park, J. (eds.) Proceedings of the Third ACM Conference on Data and Application Security and Privacy, p. 209 (2013)

17. Russello, G., Conti, M., Crispo, B., Fernandes, E.: Moses: supporting operation modes on smartphones. In: Proceedings of the 17th ACM symposium on Access Control Models and Technologies - SACMAT 2012, p. 3. ACM Press (2012)

18. Russello, G., Crispo, B., Fernandes, E., Zhauniarovich, Y.: YAASE: yet another android security extension. In: 2011 IEEE Third International Conference on Privacy, Security, Risk and Trust (PASSAT)/2011 IEEE Third International Conference on Social Computing (SocialCom), pp. 1033–1040 (2011)

19. Sarwar, G., Mehani, O., Boreli, R., Kaafar, M.A.: On the effectiveness of dynamic taint analysis for protecting against private information leaks on android-based devices. In: Samarati, P. (ed.) SECRYPT 2013, 10th International Conference on Security and Cryptography. SciTePress (2013). http://www.nicta.com.au/pub?id=6865

20. Shirey, R.: Rfc 4949: Internet security glossary, version 2 (2007). https://tools.ietf.org/html/rfc4949

21. Spreitzenbarth, M., Schreck, T., Echtler, F., Arp, D., Hoffmann, J.: Mobile-Sandbox: combining static and dynamic analysis with machine-learning techniques. Int. J. Inf. Secur. **14**(2), 141–153 (2014). https://doi.org/10.1007/s10207-014-0250-0

22. Stallings, W., Brown, L., Bauer, M., Howard, M.: Computer Security: Principles and Practice. Always Learning, 2nd edn. Pearson, Boston (2012)

23. Sufatrio, Tan, D.J.J., Chua, T.W., Thing, V.L.L.: Securing android: a survey, taxonomy, and challenges. ACM Comput. Surv. **47**(4), 1–45 (2015)

24. Sun, M., Wei, T., Lui, J.C.: TaintART: a practical multi-level information-flow tracking system for android runtime. In: Katzenbeisser, S., Weippl, E. (eds.) Proceedings of the 2016 ACM SIGSAC Conference on Computer and Communications Security, pp. 331–342. ACM (2016)

25. Tam, K., Feizollah, A., Anuar, N.B., Salleh, R., Cavallaro, L.: The evolution of android malware and android analysis techniques. ACM Comput. Surv. **49**(4), 1–41 (2017)

26. Wei, F., Roy, S., Ou, X., Robby: Amandroid: a precise and general inter-component data flow analysis framework for security vetting of android apps. In: Ahn, G.J. (ed.) Proceedings of the 21st ACM Conference on Computer and Communications Security, pp. 1329–1341. ACM (2014)

27. Weichselbaum, L., Neugschwandter, M., Lindorfer, M., Fratantonio, Y., van der Veen, V., Platzer, C.: Andrubis: Android malware under the magnifying glass. Technical rep. TR-ISECLAB-0414-001, S. 1-10. Vienna University of Technology (2014)

28. Weisenmüller, H., Berner, F., Kaspar, F.: Sandbox-detection-angriffe gegen den android emulator: Aktuelle berichte aus forschung und lehre der fakultät informatik. Informatik Journal **2017/18**(7), 135–145 (2017)

29. Xia, M., Gong, L., Lyu, Y., Qi, Z., Liu, X.: Effective real-time android application auditing. In: 2015 IEEE Symposium on Security and Privacy (SP), pp. 899–914. IEEE (2015)

30. Xu, M., et al.: Toward engineering a secure android ecosystem. ACM Comput. Surv. **49**(2), 1–47 (2016)

31. You, W., Liang, B., Shi, W., Wang, P., Zhang, X.: TaintMan: an ART-compatible dynamic taint analysis framework on unmodified and non-rooted android devices. IEEE Trans. Dependable Secure Comput. **17**(1) (2017)

32. Zhang, Y., et al.: Vetting undesirable behaviors in android apps with permission use analysis. In: Sadeghi, A.R., Gligor, V., Yung, M. (eds.) The 2013 ACM SIGSAC Conference, pp. 611–622 (2013)
33. Zhauniarovich, Y., Russello, G., Conti, M., Crispo, B., Fernandes, E.: Moses: supporting and enforcing security profiles on smartphones. IEEE Trans. Dependable Secure Comput. **11**(3), 211–223 (2014)
34. Zheng, M., Sun, M., Lui, J.C.: DroidTrace: a ptrace based android dynamic analysis system with forward execution capability. In: 2014 International Wireless Communications and Mobile Computing Conference (IWCMC), pp. 128–133 (2014)

Signal Processing and Multimedia Applications

A Note Event-Based Decomposition of Polyphonic Recordings Applied to Single-channel Audio Source Separation

Alejandro Delgado Castro[1]($\boxtimes$) (ID) and John E. Szymanski[2] (ID)

[1] University of Costa Rica, San Pedro, San José, Costa Rica
alejandro.delgadocastro@ucr.ac.cr
[2] University of York, Heslington, UK
john.szymanski@york.ac.uk

Abstract. In this work, a novel decomposition method for single-channel polyphonic recordings is presented and applied to the separation of harmonic or nearly-harmonic sources from within an audio mixture. The proposed method is based on the iterative estimation and extraction of note events, where each event is defined as a section of audio containing largely harmonic energy identified as coming from a single sound source. In every iteration, the pitch trajectory of the predominant note event is automatically selected from an array of fundamental frequency estimates and used to guide the separation of the event's spectral content, using two different methods: time-frequency masking and time-domain subtraction. A residual signal is then generated and used as the input mixture for the next iteration. This iterative stage continues until a predefined maximum number of iterations is reached. After convergence, all detected note events are clustered into individual sources by exploiting end-user interaction. Performance evaluation is carried out on a set of test recordings, containing excerpts of real music performances with different levels of polyphony, and the obtained results are compared with those generated with an alternative semi-automatic algorithm.

Keywords: Audio source separation · Iterative multipitch estimation · Note events in polyphonic music · Separation of overlapping partials

1 Introduction

This work concentrates on the decomposition of a single-channel audio mixture into a number of note events, which can be clustered to form individual audio sources. Each note event is characterised by a continuous pitch trajectory, and

Sponsored by the University of Costa Rica (UCR) and the Costa Rican Ministry of Science, Technology and Telecommunications.

can be seen as a harmonic sound representing either a single musical note or a group of consecutive notes, potentially coming from the same source.

Note events are automatically estimated from the original audio mixture following an iterative approach. In every iteration, the pitch trajectory of the predominant note event is selected from a set of fundamental frequency estimates and used to separate its spectral content from the mixed spectrogram. The extraction of the predominant note event generates a residual, which is used as the input signal in the next iteration. This process repeats until a predefined maximum number of iterations is reached. When the iterative stage is complete, the proposed separation system considers end-user interaction as a way to cluster all detected note events into individual sources. A simplified block diagram of the proposed solution is shown in Fig. 1.

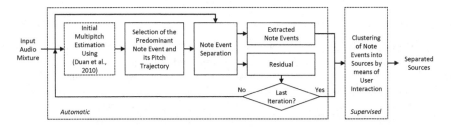

Fig. 1. Block diagram of the proposed system showing its two main stages: the automatic decomposition of the audio mixture into note events, and their clustering into individual sources [9].

Once the estimated pitch trajectory of the predominant note event is known, the separation process consists of detecting a set of relevant spectral peaks in every frame of the input spectrogram, and partitioning their energy between the predominant note event and the residual. This process is particularly critical for those peaks where the selected note event overlaps with other simultaneous sources, where additional processing is required to achieve a proper separation.

The rest of the paper is organised as follows. Section 2 defines the audio source separation problem and provides a brief review of previously presented solutions. Section 3 describes the proposed decomposition strategy for audio signals, in which note events are detected and extracted from within the input mixture. Section 4 addresses the clustering of note events into separated sources, while performance evaluation is presented and discussed in Sect. 5. Finally, Sect. 6 summarises our conclusions from this work.

2   Problem Definition and Related Work

Audio source separation is the signal processing task which consists of recovering the original constitutive sounds, called sources, of an observed mixture, which can be either single-channel (monaural) or multi-channel (stereo, surround sound, etc.). Monaural and stereophonic recordings are still very common within the audio industry, where the sources are usually considered to be the individual sounds coming from different musical instruments or voices [23].

An ideal audio source separation system should be able to take a polyphonic input signal and perform an optimal characterisation of the underlying sources, in order to partition the energy of the mixture into a number of output channels, each one associated with an individual source. In this case, all the energy of the mixture should be allocated within the extracted sources so that the original mixture can be perfectly reconstructed by adding them together.

Real systems, on the other hand, exhibit several limitations that do not allow a complete characterisation of the underlying sources, leading to incomplete separation results where the estimated sources are no longer fully disjoint. Moreover, a residual channel has to be generated to allocate unresolved energy of the mixture that could not be allocated to any of the estimated sources.

The way in which the output signals are estimated and separated will depend on the core structure of the algorithm, its assumptions, and the information or features that are used to characterise the sources. Some approaches estimate a set of output channels in just one pass, while other methods are designed to be iterative, i.e. one source is estimated and separated at a time.

Model-based source separation algorithms have been designed upon well-established signal processing techniques, such as computational auditory scene analysis [3,10,20,21], independent component analysis [1,2,8,20,24,28], independent subspace analysis [6,31], and non-negative matrix factorisation [4,13, 17,26]. The estimated sources are then extracted using other approaches, such as sinusoidal modelling and time-frequency masking.

One of the key issues in the separation of pitched signals relates to the disentangling of overlapping harmonics, which are very common given the wide use of the twelve-tone equal temperament scale in tonal music [36]. Regardless of the separation approach, the goal is to estimate the parameters (amplitudes, centre frequencies and phase angles) of the underlying frequency components that coincide in any observed overlapping partial. Depending on the number of frequency components and their degree of overlap, achieving a proper separation represents an ill-posed problem.

When overlapping harmonics are explicitly handled, methods usually rely on the availability of pitch trajectories for the underlying sources, which are normally detected first, in order to identify overlapping regions by considering a proximity criterion. Then, overlapping harmonics are resolved by sinusoidal modelling [27], spectral filtering [14], common amplitude similarity [22], matching pursuit [32], amplitude and phase reconstruction [29], or harmonic bandwidth companding [36].

More recently, data-driven solutions have focused on identifying the best way to separate the underlying components of a mixture by previously observing and learning from a large number of examples within a training database. The reliability of these systems depends on the size of their training database and the relevance of the audio examples included, which have to be correctly labelled before starting with the training stage. The strength of this alternative is that it does not depend on a set of explicit rules, since the system is able to learn its own way to achieve the best separation of the underlying sources.

Current limitations of data-driven approaches include long development stages and lack of generality due to limited training data. Machine learning techniques used in source separation include deep neural networks [15, 18, 19, 33] and convolutional neural networks [5, 7, 25], while gradient descent and back-propagation are among the most popular strategies used for training purposes [30].

3   Note-Event Based Decomposition

Music is very rich and non-stationary. Different playing styles transmit emotions and stimulate the audience in many different ways. However, this inherent complexity usually creates some difficulties for source separation algorithms. For example, the masking of weaker notes by louder ones, instruments playing in harmonic relation, or musical effects such as vibrato and tremolo.

To cope with some of these complexities, an iterative model-based separation approach is proposed, in which the underlying sources are obtained by clustering short sections of audio, hereafter referred to as note events. Each note event is defined as a section of audio containing largely harmonic energy, identified as coming from a single sound source, and characterised by a continuous pitch trajectory. The proposed semi-supervised separation system does not require any previous training stage and can be applied to any polyphonic mixture containing harmonic or nearly-harmonic sources.

This section describes the first stage of the proposed separation process, in which note events are iteratively detected and extracted from within the input mixture. In every iteration, an array of fundamental frequency estimates is generated and used to select the pitch trajectory of the predominant note event in the mixture. The spectral content associated with the predominant note event is then extracted using two different methods, namely, time-frequency masking and time-domain subtraction. A residual signal is also generated and used as the input mixture for the next iteration. This decomposition process stops when a predefined maximum number of iterations is reached.

The strategy used in this work to detect the predominant note event in every iteration is fully described in Sect. 3.1, while the extraction of its spectral content is addressed in Sect. 3.2.

3.1   Pitch Trajectory of the Predominant Note Event

In every iteration, the Short-Time Fourier Transform (STFT) of the input signal is taken, using 46.4 ms Hanning-windowed frames with no zero-padding. During the detection of the predominant pitch trajectory in the mixture, 50% overlap between adjacent frames is used. Then, the multipitch estimator by Duan et al. [11] is used to generate a set of fundamental frequencies associated with the current input mixture. The result is an initial array of pitch estimates that can be expressed as follows.

$$\mathbf{P} = \begin{pmatrix} p_{1,1} & p_{1,2} & \cdots & p_{1,L} \\ p_{2,1} & p_{2,2} & \cdots & p_{2,L} \\ \vdots & \vdots & \ddots & \vdots \\ p_{J,1} & p_{J,2} & \cdots & p_{J,L} \end{pmatrix} \tag{1}$$

where J is the number of levels and L is the total number of frames in the input spectrogram. The number of frames L is controlled by the duration of the input signal, the frame size and the hop size. The number of levels J, or the number of rows in array $\mathbf{P}$, is controlled by Duan's multipitch estimator itself and it varies depending on the complexity of the input signal.

For each fundamental frequency estimate in $\mathbf{P}$, a salience measure is computed based on the spectral magnitude summation of their first Γ partial amplitudes, as defined by (2).

$$s_{(j,m)} = \sum_{\gamma=1}^{\Gamma} |\mathbf{X}(\gamma p_{(j,m)}, m)| \tag{2}$$

where $s_{(j,m)}$ is the salience of the j-th pitch candidate in the m-th frame, with fundamental frequency $p_{(j,m)}$, and $\mathbf{X}(p, m)$ is the complex spectrogram of the current input signal. The result is matrix $\mathbf{S}$, shown in (3), that contains the salience measures for all pitch candidates in $\mathbf{P}$.

$$\mathbf{S} = \begin{pmatrix} s_{1,1} & s_{1,2} & \cdots & s_{1,L} \\ s_{2,1} & s_{2,2} & \cdots & s_{2,L} \\ \vdots & \vdots & \ddots & \vdots \\ s_{J,1} & s_{J,2} & \cdots & s_{J,L} \end{pmatrix} \tag{3}$$

Note events are detected by finding continuous segments of pitch estimates, across all levels of $\mathbf{P}$, for which the change in fundamental frequency between adjacent frames is not higher than one semitone. At the same time, the total salience and duration of each detected note event are computed. Considering the τ-th detected note event, which exists in level $j = j_\tau$, between frames m_a and m_b, its total salience $\mathcal{S}(\tau)$ and duration $\mathcal{D}(\tau)$ are defined as:

$$\mathcal{S}(\tau) = \sum_{m=m_a}^{m_b} s_{(j_\tau, m)} \tag{4}$$

$$\mathcal{D}(\tau) = m_b - m_a \tag{5}$$

If the total number of note events detected in a single iteration is denoted as T, their total salience and duration are normalised according to the following relations.

$$\hat{\mathcal{S}}(\tau) = \frac{\mathcal{S}(\tau)}{\sum_{i=1}^{T} \mathcal{S}(i)} \tag{6}$$

$$\hat{\mathcal{D}}(\tau) = \frac{\mathcal{D}(\tau)}{\sum_{i=1}^{T} \mathcal{D}(i)} \tag{7}$$

which means that the total salience and duration of all detected note events in the current iteration add to 1. Then, the predominance of the τ-th note event is defined as follows.

$$\mathcal{PD}_\tau = \hat{\mathcal{S}}(\tau) + \eta\hat{\mathcal{D}}(\tau) \tag{8}$$

where η is a parameter of the system, usually in the range from 0 to 1, that controls the influence of the duration on the selection of the predominant event. If $\eta = 0$, the decision is entirely based on total salience, while any $0 < \eta \le 1$ could be used to encourage the selection of long but relatively weak note events as the predominant one. After extensive experimentation, the value $\eta = 0.5$ has been found to be effective and will be used in the rest of this work.

Each detected note event is expanded to encompass potential missallocated estimates in adjacent frames. For instance, if the τ-th note event is considered (defined in between frames m_a and m_b at level j_τ), which starts with estimate $p_{(j_\tau, m_a)}$, the expansion will first try to find a similar estimate in frame $m_a - 1$. If the difference between estimates $p_{(j_\rho, m_a-1)}$ and $p_{(j_\tau, m_a)}$ is less than a semitone and the change in salience does not indicate a transition to a different note event, then the trajectory of the note event is expanded using estimate $p_{(j_\rho, m_a-1)}$ while the starting frame is updated by taking $m_a = m_a - 1$. The expansion continues at both ends of the pitch trajectory until a clear note transition or onset/termination is detected. The predominance of each note event is updated every time its pitch trajectory is expanded with a new pitch estimate.

Among the detected and expanded note events, the one with the greatest predominance is selected as the strongest and most significant note event, and consequently it will be chosen for extraction in the current iteration.

To illustrate the selection of the predominant note event, an example is presented in Fig. 2, for an input mixture consisting of violin and flute. The notes D♯4 and B4 are played by the violin, while the flute plays a G4, as shown in Fig. 2(a-b). During the first iteration of the system, an array of raw pitch estimates ($\mathbf{P}$) is generated with Duan's algorithm [11]. This initial set of estimates is presented in Fig. 2(c), from which the contours of the real notes can be distinguished. However, these real contours are formed with estimates from different levels of $\mathbf{P}$, whilst a very significant number of outliers are also present, making it very difficult to recognise the total number of notes present and their relative volumes. To overcome this problem, the proposed strategy constructs a set of 18 note events from the raw estimates in $\mathbf{P}$, which are shown in Fig. 2(d). Each of these events is now associated with a single continuous pitch trajectory, allowing a finer analysis of the input mixture and its components.

Duplicated note events are likely to occur after expanding continuous segments in different levels of $\mathbf{P}$, as shown in Fig. 2(d), where two numbers appear under the contours of each real note. This particular feature of the algorithm does not represent a problem, since duplicates are almost identical in length and they group the same set of pitch estimates. Hence, extracting one of the duplicates is usually equivalent to the extraction of both.

3.2 Separation of Spectral Content

The spectral content of the predominant note event is separated frame by frame. Each fundamental frequency estimate in the predominant pitch trajectory, is used to characterise the harmonic structure that has to be identified and extracted in every frame of input spectrogram. The separation strategy consists of identifying a set of spectral peaks closest to each harmonic frequency, and estimating their corresponding parameters (amplitudes, centre frequencies and phase angles). This information is then used to extract the predominant note event from within the input mixture using one of the two methods proposed, namely, time-frequency masking and time-domain subtraction.

For the sake of reducing the distortion introduced by the separation stage, the spectral content of the predominant note event is extracted from an input spectrogram with higher overlap between adjacent frames, produced by using a hop size of 87.5%. The pitch trajectory of the predominant note event is then linearly interpolated in order to cope with the higher number of frames. The following sections describe the stages of the separation process.

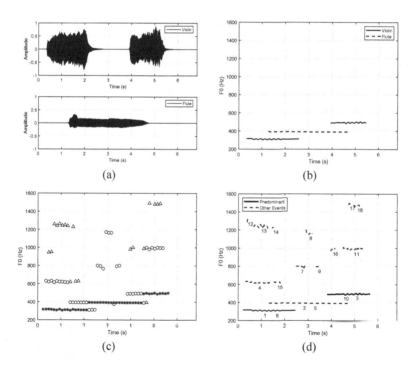

Fig. 2. Selection of the first predominant note event in a mixture of violin and flute. The violin plays the notes D♯4 and B4 while the flute plays a G4. (a) Original unmixed sources. (b) Ground-truth pitch trajectories. (c) Raw pitch estimates during the first iteration. Markers are used to identify estimates in the same level. (d) Predominant note event and other detected events during the first iteration.

Peak-Picking Strategy. The first task in the separation process is to detect spectral peaks in each time frame of the mixed spectrogram that are likely to have been produced by harmonic partials of the predominant note event, whilst ideally minimising the number of detected peaks produced by other sources, noise or artifacts of the time-frequency representation.

The pitch trajectory $\mathcal{P}_T(m)$ of the predominant note event is known and it contains the fundamental frequencies of the harmonic structure that has to be separated. In every frame, the peak-picking method computes the ideal centre frequencies of each harmonic partial associated with the corresponding fundamental frequency in each frame, and identifies the most significant spectral peaks closest to those harmonic frequencies. The peak-picking method receives the mixed complex spectrogram $\mathbf{X}$, the pitch trajectory $\mathcal{P}_T(m)$, the maximum number of harmonic partials to consider H_q, and returns an array $\mathbf{C}$, with dimensions $H \times M$, where H is the number of harmonic partials detected in every frame, and M is the number of significant frames in the pitch trajectory, containing the index of the central frequency bin of each selected spectral peak. Details of the proposed method are presented in Algorithm 1.

Algorithm 1: Peak-Picking Algorithm.

1: **function** PEAK-PICKING
   Input: Mixed Spectrogram $\mathbf{X}_{(K \times M)}$, Pitch Trajectory $\{\mathcal{P}_T\}_{(1 \times M)}$, Sampling Frequency f_s, Maximum Number of Harmonics to Extract H_q.
   Output: Array of Centre Frequency Bins of Selected Spectral Peaks $\mathbf{C}_{(H \times M)}$
2:     $m_a \leftarrow \arg[\mathcal{P}_T(\text{first})]$ ▷ Frame index of the first pitch estimate
3:     $m_b \leftarrow \arg[\mathcal{P}_T(\text{last})]$ ▷ Frame index of the last pitch estimate
4:     **for** $m = m_a$ to m_b **do**
5:         $f_0 \leftarrow \mathcal{P}_T(m)$ ▷ Current pitch estimate
6:         $h \leftarrow 1$ ▷ Harmonic counter
7:         $f_h \leftarrow f_0$ ▷ Harmonic frequency
8:         **while** $(h \leq H_q)$ AND $(f_h < \frac{f_s}{2})$ **do**
9:             $k \leftarrow \left\lfloor \frac{2 f_h K}{f_s} \right\rceil$ ▷ Closest frequency bin to f_h
10:            **if** k is a local minimum **then**   ▷ Local minimum condition
11:                $k \leftarrow$ Adjacent bin closest to f_h
12:            **end if**
13:            **for** $j = 1$ to 3 **do**   ▷ Centre bin refinement
14:                $k \leftarrow \underset{\tau \in [k-1:k+1]}{\text{argmax}} |\mathbf{X}(\tau, m)|$
15:            **end for**
16:            $\mathbf{C}(h, m) \leftarrow k$ ▷ Storing centre bin of h-th peak in frame m
17:            $h \leftarrow h + 1$ ▷ Updating harmonic counter
18:            $f_h \leftarrow h f_0$ ▷ Updating harmonic frequency
19:        **end while**
20:    **end for**
21:    **return** $\mathbf{C}$ ▷ Centre bins of spectral peaks
22: **end function**

The refinement of the centre bin position of every spectral peak (lines 10 to 15 in Algorithm 1) consists of two stages. First, the algorithm checks whether the initial centre bin position, which is obtained from the ideal centre frequency of the corresponding harmonic partial, is a local minimum or not (line 10). If it is a local minimum, the centre bin position is moved to the adjacent frequency bin that is closer to the ideal harmonic frequency, in order to reduce the risk of misleadingly tracking a different partial during the second stage of the refinement. Secondly, a series of three further refinements are conducted on the centre bin position with the aim of finding the local maximum in the vicinity of the initial centre bin position (line 13). Here, each relevant partial is assumed to be the result of convolving a pure sinusoidal component with a Hanning window. Hence, most of its energy concentrates around five frequency bins, namely, the middle one (closest to the frequency of the sinusoidal component) and two bins on each side of the central one.

This refinement strategy is designed to provide a cautious level of flexibility to the assumption of harmonicity, in order to cope with inharmonic instruments and with artifacts of the STFT. Although the algorithm starts looking at the ideal centre frequencies of the harmonic partials, their corresponding spectral peaks are assumed to be centred within a maximum deviation of 3 frequency bins from those ideal positions. Other alternatives such as measuring the degree of inharmonicity of the selected harmonic structure proved unreliable, in particular for low-pitched note events or in those cases where the polyphony of the input mixture is higher than 2.

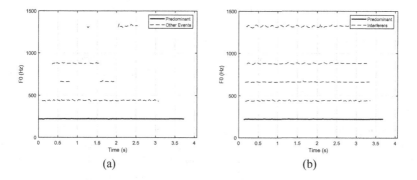

(a)   (b)

Fig. 3. Analysis of a mixture consisting of two violin notes: A3 and A4. (a) Predominant note event selection from a set of eight candidates. (b) Predominant note event at 220 Hz and four interfering events: one real at 440 Hz and three spurious at 660 Hz, 880 Hz and 1320 Hz.

An additional advantage of the refinement process is related to the proposed separation strategy of overlapping harmonics, where the position of the highest spectral peak in the vicinity of the ideal harmonic frequency is required to estimate the boundaries of the overlapping range and to initialise a dual-peak model for shared partials. Further details of the dual-peak model are provided in the following section.

Detection of Overlapping Partials. In this work, the detection of over-lapping partials takes place during the separation of each spectral peak associated with the predominant note event, using a combination of peak shape-based and proximity-based criteria. Selected spectral peaks are classified as fully-overlapping or semi-overlapping partials, where peaks in the first category are identified first by computing their proximity to the closest interfering event, which might indicate the presence of another spectral component associated with a note event in harmonic relationship coming from a different source.

After selecting the pitch trajectory of the predominant note event, all other note event candidates become potential interfering events. Their pitch contours are expanded by tracking their fundamental partials across the whole duration of the predominant note event, using the higher-rate magnitude spectrogram. As an example, a mixture of two violin notes (A3 and A4) is considered, where the note A3 is selected as the predominant one, as shown in Fig. 3(a). The other six candidates detected are used to construct the interfering events presented in Fig. 3(b). Some of these interferers are associated with real notes coming from a simultaneous source, such as the note A4, while others are spurious events introduced by the baseline multipitch estimator.

In every frame, all harmonic frequencies associated with the predominant and interfering events are computed up to the Nyquist frequency. Then, a set of spectral peaks associated with the predominant note event is identified according to Algorithm 1. If the distance between any of these spectral peaks and any interfering frequency is greater than 30 Hz, then the corresponding peak is classified as a semi-overlapping partial. Otherwise, the peak is assumed to be a fully-overlapping partial. Different separation methods are proposed to handle over-lapping partials depending on whether these are classified as semi-overlapping or fully-overlapping partials.

Semi-overlapping Partials. Spectral peaks associated with semi-overlapping partials are decomposed into a number of frequency components, using Parsons' method [27], which exploits the additive nature of overlapping harmonics. In Parsons' algorithm, a pure sinusoidal component is first generated using the estimated parameters of the shared peak, and then convolved with the window function to generate an equivalent single-component spectral peak, referred to here as the dominant component. Then, the shared peak is isolated from the original spectrum and the dominant component is subtracted from it in order to reveal potential overlapping components. If a significant peak appears in the resulting difference vector, it is treated as a secondary component associated with the potential contribution of another source, and its parameters are also estimated. Separation of the shared peak is then achieved by taking the component closest to the ideal centre frequency of the desired harmonic partial. Any uncovered peaks with magnitude more than 20 dB below the principal component are rejected as either spurious or inaudible.

Parsons' method was conceived in the context of separation of vocalic speech of two competing talkers, and it was not applied to polyphonic music, where the number of concurrent sources is typically higher. But its simplicity makes it suitable for the separation of semi-overlapping partials within the proposed framework, given that the ideal centre frequencies of the desired harmonic partials can be easily computed from the pitch trajectory, and the iterative nature of the system in which only one note event is extracted at a time. However, Parsons' method is used here under the assumption that the shared peak is the result of two underlying components, one of which corresponds to the target partial. But, instead of this being a limitation, Parsons' method is considered as a way to separate the desired partial from a more complex spectral structure.

Fully-Overlapping Partials. These are overlapping partials in which the underlying components are very close. The distance between their centre frequencies is usually less than a frequency bin, and a complete separation of the original components cannot be obtained. The proposed strategy does not attempt an exact separation, but focuses on extracting some percentage of the total energy in the shared partial, so that the remainder can be detected as part of a different note event in later iterations.

In this case, only the dominant component can be estimated. Then, an incomplete separation of the overlapping partial is achieved by extracting an attenuated version of its dominant component, in which the absolute magnitude is reduced according to the preservation rates assigned to its interfering events.

A preservation rate (α) is assigned to each interfering event, ranging from zero up to an arbitrary maximum A_{max}. If there is sufficient evidence that an interferer is an error (it does not associate with a real note), zero preservation rate is assigned and all the energy of the selected partials is removed. If there is uncertainty, a non-zero preservation rate is assigned and some energy of the shared partials is left in the residual, so it can be potentially detected as contributing to a different note event in later iterations. The preservation rate depends on:

- The level of correlation between the pitch-scaled trajectories of the predominant note event and the interferer.
- The total salience associated with the interferer.
- The presence of multiple harmonically-related interferers.

If the n th harmonic partial of the predominant note event collides with frequency components from K interfering events, with preservation rates denoted as $\alpha_1, \alpha_2, \ldots, \alpha_K$, then the dominant component is attenuated by multiplying its absolute magnitude by the following gain.

$$G_n = 1 - \sum_{k=1}^{K} \alpha_k \tag{9}$$

The second term in Eq. 9 cannot be greater than $2A_{max}$ to avoid leaving excessive energy in the residual. This attenuated component is the one taken as the target partial during the extraction of the note event.

3.3   Note Event Extraction

In the previous section, a set of spectral peaks in every frame was carefully analysed, classified and separated according to their shapes and proximity to potentially interfering components. The result is the estimated magnitude spectrogram of the separated predominant note event, with centre frequency bins for all selected harmonic partials in every frame indicated in array **C**. The next stage consists of extracting the spectral energy associated with the predominant note event from the input mixture. For this purpose, two different methods are presented and discussed in the upcoming sections.

Time-Frequency Masking. This method consists of fitting a non-binary time-frequency mask to extract the energy of all selected harmonic partials associated with the predominant note event in every frame. This mask is constructed for every harmonic partial, using a dual-peak model as a reference. Considering the h-th harmonic partial in the m-th frame, centred at frequency bin k^h, the boundaries of the spectral peak have to be determined based on its shape, and on the assumption that the energy within a stationary sinusoidal partial spans over a maximum of five frequency bins with centre at bin k^h (convolution of the original component with a Hanning window). Hence, the boundaries of the h-th harmonic partial are defined as follows.

$$k^h_{min} = k^h - 2 \tag{10}$$

$$k^h_{max} = k^h + 2 \tag{11}$$

If the original spectral peak $|\mathbf{X}(k^h_{min} : k^h_{max}, m)|$ has been decomposed into its dominant and secondary components, denoted here as $F_D(k)$ and $F_S(k)$, respectively, then the dual-peak model is used to generate an isolated approximation of the original spectral peak, hereafter referred to as the observed peak $O_T(k)$, defined by the following equation.

$$O_T(k) = \begin{cases} F_D(k) + F_S(k) & \text{if } |f_d - f_s| > 30\,\text{Hz} & (12a) \\ |\mathbf{X}(k, m)| & \text{if } |f_d - f_s| < 30\,\text{Hz} & (12b) \end{cases}$$

where f_d and f_s are the centre frequencies of the dominant and secondary components, respectively. Since the shape of the frequency component to be extracted is known from the previous separation stage, the notation $F_T(k)$ is used to indicate the estimated component of the spectral peak closest to the ideal centre frequency of the h-th harmonic partial, which can be either $F_D(k)$ or $F_S(k)$.

Then, the section of the time-frequency mask associated with the h-th harmonic partial in frame m is computed as follows.

$$\mathbf{M}_E(k_{min}^h : k_{max}^h, m) = \frac{F_T(k_{min}^h : k_{max}^h)}{O_T(k_{min}^h : k_{max}^h)} \tag{13}$$

where $\mathbf{M}_E(k, m)$ is the m-th frame of the time-frequency mask used to extract the predominant note event. When spectral peaks are well-spaced, the dual-peak approximation is very similar in shape to the observed spectral peak. But, when peaks are very close to each other, the dual-peak model provides a better fit of the time-frequency mask, in particular near the partial boundaries, and reduces the risk of errors by forcing the mask to be always within the range from 0 to 1.

Since the shape of every spectral peak is affected by the phase interaction with other components, significant changes in shape are expected to happen when moving from one frame to the next one, making the processing of some frames harder than it is for others. For this reason, the algorithm is expected to produce erroneous mask shapes for some harmonic partials in some particular frames, which tend to occur in bursts of no more than two or three consecutive frames for one particular partial. However, these problems can be significantly reduced if the final time-frequency mask is median-filtered using a short window. In this work, a median filter of length 5 has been selected and applied to smooth out some of the errors. The estimation of the time-frequency mask used for extraction, is summarised in Algorithm 2.

In order to separate the predominant note event from within the mixture, the input magnitude spectrogram $\mathbf{X}(k, m)$ is multiplied by the extraction mask $\mathbf{M}_E(k, m)$, and the result is converted back to the time domain by means of the Inverse Short-Time Fourier Transform (ISTFT), where the phase information is taken directly from the input mixture, as stated in the following equation.

$$\mathsf{Ne}_v(t) = \text{ISTFT}\{|\mathbf{X}(k, m)| \cdot \mathbf{M}_E(k, m), \angle\mathbf{X}(k, m)\} \tag{14}$$

where $\mathsf{Ne}_v(t)$ is the time-domain signal associated with the predominant note event detected in the v-th iteration of the system, which is kept in memory during the rest of the iterative stage, along with other note events extracted in previous iterations. The residual energy of the input mixture that is not assigned to the current note event is also separated with a different time-frequency mask, which can be obtained from the current extraction mask as follows.

$$\mathbf{M}_R(k, m) = 1 - \mathbf{M}_E(k, m) \tag{15}$$

After extracting the predominant note event, the residual signal in the v-th iteration, denoted as $\mathsf{Re}_v(t)$, is computed as in Eq. 16.

$$\mathsf{Re}_v(t) = \text{ISTFT}\{|\mathbf{X}(k, m)| \cdot \mathbf{M}_R(k, m), \angle\mathbf{X}(k, m)\} \tag{16}$$

Within the proposed iterative framework, the residual signal is used as the input for the next iteration, from which a new predominant note event might be detected and extracted. As stated before, this cycle continues until a predefined maximum number of iterations is reached.

Algorithm 2: Time-Frequency Masking Algorithm.

1: **function** TIME-FREQUENCY MASKING

    Input: Mixed Spectrogram $\mathbf{X}_{(K \times M)}$, Centre Frequency Bins of Selected Peaks $\mathbf{C}_{(H \times M)}$, Pitch Trajectory $\{\mathcal{P}_T\}_{(1 \times M)}$, Maximum Number of Harmonics to Extract H_q, Preservation Rates $A_{(H \times M)}$, and Sampling Frequency f_s.

    Output: Time-Frequency Extraction Mask $\{\mathbf{M}_E\}_{(K \times M)}$

2:    $\mathbf{M}_E \leftarrow \text{zeros}(K, M)$ ▷ Initializing extraction mask

3:    $[m_a, m_b] \leftarrow \text{Find-Limits}(\mathcal{P}_T)$ ▷ Start and end of pitch trajectory

4:    **for** $m = m_a$ **to** m_b **do**

5:        $f_0 \leftarrow \mathcal{P}_T(m)$ ▷ Current pitch estimate

6:        $h \leftarrow 1$ ▷ Harmonic counter

7:        $f_h \leftarrow f_0$ ▷ Harmonic frequency

8:        **while** $(h \leq H_q)$ **AND** $(f_h < \frac{f_s}{2})$ **do**

9:            $c_b \leftarrow \mathbf{C}(h, m)$ ▷ Centre bin of selected peak

10:        $[F_D(:), F_S(:), Dis] \leftarrow \text{Parsons-Method}(|\mathbf{X}(c_b, m)|)$ ▷ Decomposition

11:        **if** $Dis < 30$ Hz **then**   ▷ Peak classification

12:            $F_T(:) \leftarrow A(h, m) \times F_D(:)$ ▷ Fully-Overlapping

13:            $O_T(:) \leftarrow \mathbf{X}(:, m)$

14:        **else**

15:            $F_T(:) \leftarrow \text{Find-Closest}([F_D(:), F_S(:)], f_h)$ ▷ Semi-Overlapping

16:            $O_T(:) \leftarrow F_D(:) + F_S(:)$

17:        **end if**

18:        $c_b \leftarrow \text{Peak-Position}(F_T(:))$ ▷ Updating centre bin

19:        $[k_{min}^h, k_{max}^h] \leftarrow [c_b - 2, c_b + 2]$ ▷ Current peak limits

20:        $\mathbf{M}_E(k_{min}^h : k_{max}^h, m) \leftarrow \frac{F_T(k_{min}^h : k_{max}^h)}{O_T(k_{min}^h : k_{max}^h)}$ ▷ Extraction mask

21:        $h \leftarrow h + 1$

22:        $f_h \leftarrow h \times f_0$

23:        **end while**

24:    **end for**

25:    $\mathbf{M}_E \leftarrow \text{Median-Filtering}(\mathbf{M}_E, [m_a : m_b], 5)$ ▷ Smoothing extraction mask

26:    **return** $\mathbf{M}_E$ ▷ Extraction mask

27: **end function**

Time-Domain Subtraction. The extraction method presented in the previous section is particularly effective when harmonic partials are well spaced. However, if the average fundamental frequency of the predominant note event is low (usually below 200 Hz), the distance between centre frequencies of its harmonic partials is so small that any other component associated with a different source might produce complex shared peaks, as a result of more than two heavily overlapping partials. Finding the limits of these complex peaks is difficult and the extraction mask cannot always be obtained accurately.

When the shape of the extraction mask is inadequate for a particular harmonic partial, the extracted peak might show significant distortion that could affect the overall quality of the reconstructed event. The method presented in this section, which is based on time-domain subtraction, replaces the extraction mask with a different approach, in which the separated magnitude spectrogram of the predominant note event is estimated directly from individual synthetic partials, chosen just after decomposing each selected peak with Parsons' method.

The outcome of the process is a magnitude spectrogram that can be converted back to the time domain in order to recover the separated note event, while the residual is generated by subtracting this note event from the input mixture in the time domain. The main advantage of the process is that each component in the separated spectrogram should preserve its Hanning-windowed shape throughout the whole separation process, reducing the levels of distortion in the separated signals, independently of the frequency distance to other nearby components.

This alternative approach is very similar to the one discussed in the previous section, where every selected peak in array $\mathbf{C}$ is decomposed into its dominant and secondary components, following Parsons' method. Depending on the distance between their centre frequencies, a decision is made about whether to handle them as a set of semi-overlapping or fully-overlapping partials. If the peak is due to a group of semi-overlapping partials, the component closest to the ideal harmonic frequency is chosen as the target partial, otherwise an attenuated version of the dominant component is selected. However, instead of using the target partial to construct an extraction mask, it is directly incorporated as an element of the separated magnitude spectrogram of the predominant note event, denoted as $|\mathbf{Y}(k, m)|$, which avoids having to compute suitable boundaries for the observed shared peak. Algorithm 3 summarises this alternative method.

A time-domain signal $\mathsf{Ne}_v(t)$, corresponding to the predominant note event in the v-th iteration, is obtained by inverse transforming the separated magnitude spectrogram $|\mathbf{Y}(k, m)|$ using the phase information of the input mixture, as presented in Eq. 17.

$$\mathsf{Ne}_v(t) = \mathrm{ISTFT}\{|\mathbf{Y}(k, m)|, \angle\mathbf{X}(k, m)\} \tag{17}$$

The residual signal in the v-th iteration is obtained by subtracting the estimated predominant note event $\mathsf{Ne}_v(t)$ from the current input mixture $x_v(t)$, as defined in Eq. 18.

$$\mathsf{Re}_v(t) = x_v(t) - \mathsf{Ne}_v(t) \tag{18}$$

As the phase spectrum of the mixture is used to reconstruct the separated note event, a risk of producing a distorted waveform in the time domain always exists. However, it is believed that the quality of the reconstruction depends more on the accuracy of the centre frequencies and magnitudes of the separated harmonic partials than on the phase spectrum. Hence, any deviation of the phase information should not be critical if the accuracy of the estimated centre frequencies and magnitudes is acceptable. As in the previous section, the residual signal is used as the input mixture in the next iteration.

Algorithm 3: Time-Domain Subtraction Algorithm.

1: **function** TIME-DOMAIN SUBTRACTION

Input: Mixed Spectrogram $\mathbf{X}_{(K \times M)}$, Centre Frequency Bins of Selected Peaks $\mathbf{C}_{(H \times M)}$, Pitch Trajectory $\{\mathcal{P}_T\}_{(1 \times M)}$, Maximum Number of Harmonics to Extract H_q, Preservation Rates $A_{(H \times M)}$, and Sampling Frequency f_s.

Output: Separated Magnitude Spectrogram of Note Event $|\mathbf{Y}|_{(K \times M)}$

2: $\mathbf{Y} \leftarrow \text{zeros}(K, M)$ ▷ Initializing output spectrogram

3: $[m_a, m_b] \leftarrow \text{Find-Limits}(\mathcal{P}_T)$ ▷ Start and end of pitch trajectory

4: **for** $m = m_a$ to m_b **do**

5:    $f_0 \leftarrow \mathcal{P}_T(m)$ ▷ Current pitch estimate

6:    $h \leftarrow 1$ ▷ Harmonic counter

7:    $f_h \leftarrow f_0$ ▷ Harmonic frequency

8:    **while** $(h \leq H_q)$ AND $(f_h < \frac{f_s}{2})$ **do**

9:      $c_b \leftarrow \mathbf{C}(h, m)$ ▷ Centre bin of selected peak

10:     $[F_D(:), F_S(:), Dis] \leftarrow \text{Parsons-Method}(|\mathbf{X}(c_b, m)|)$ ▷ Decomposition

11:     **if** $Dis < 30$ Hz **then**   ▷ Peak classification

12:       $F_T(:) \leftarrow A(h, m) \times F_D(:)$ ▷ Fully-Overlapping

13:     **else**

14:       $F_T(:) \leftarrow \text{Find-Closest}([F_D(:), F_S(:)], f_h)$ ▷ Semi-Overlapping

15:     **end if**

16:     $|\mathbf{Y}(:, m)| \leftarrow |\mathbf{Y}(:, m)| + F_T(:)$ ▷ Updating output spectrogram

17:     $h \leftarrow h + 1$

18:     $f_h \leftarrow h \times f_0$

19:    **end while**

20: **end for**

21: **return** $\mathbf{Y}$ ▷ Separated spectrogram of note event

22: **end function**

---

4   Clustering of Note Events

When the iterative stage is complete, the energy contained in the original mixture is largely allocated within a set of note events. End-user interaction can now be used to cluster these note events into individual sources, using their pitch trajectories to decide the best way to group them. Listening to each separated note event can also provide further guidance during the clustering process. Instrument identification methods could be used at this stage to remove the need for user interaction, but these algorithms are not the emphasis of this work.

Using an example mixture of viola and clarinet, where the viola plays a single note (A4) and the clarinet plays four notes (D♯5, G5, A♯5, D♯6), the final set of estimated pitch trajectories is presented in Fig. 4(a), and their corresponding extracted note events, obtained in this case by means of time-domain subtraction, are shown in Fig. 4(b).

Note events 2, 3, 4 and 5 can now be grouped by the end-user to form the separated clarinet track, while note event 1 is used to form the separated viola track. Figure 5 shows a comparison between the original and estimated sources.

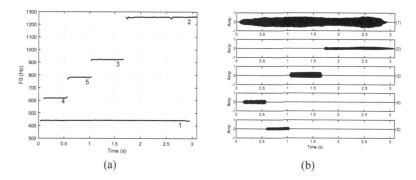

Fig. 4. Clustering of estimated note events from a mixture of viola and clarinet. (a) Estimated pitch trajectories of note events. (b) Extracted note events: (1) Viola A4, (2) Clarinet D♯6, (3) Clarinet A♯5, (4) Clarinet D♯5, and (5) Clarinet G5. The extraction order is shown with numbers [9].

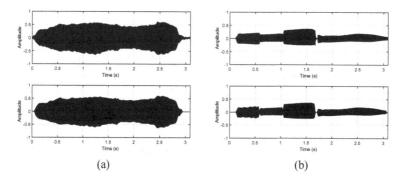

Fig. 5. Comparison between the original and estimated sources from a mixture of viola and clarinet [9]. (Top) Original source, (Bottom) Estimated source.

5   Performance Evaluation

5.1   Database

Test recordings were obtained from excerpts of the Bach10 database [11]. This dataset involves four pitched instruments, namely, violin, clarinet, tenor saxophone and bassoon. Additionally, a percussive source consisting of a synthesised sequence of snare drums and cymbals is also considered. These recordings are arranged in four groups according to their polyphony levels and the pitches of the musical notes present, as described in Table 1. The original sources and mixtures used in this experiment are available online[1].

---

[1] https://doi.org/10.5281/zenodo.3468471.

Table 1. Characteristics of the selected test recordings.

Group	Details
1	12 mixtures with polyphony 2 involving violin and clarinet, with fundamental frequencies in the range from 225 Hz to 750 Hz. A total of 254 musical notes are present
2	12 mixtures with polyphony 3 involving violin, clarinet and tenor saxophone, with fundamental frequencies in the range from 175 Hz to 750 Hz. A total of 386 musical notes are present, including harmonically-related notes
3	12 mixtures with polyphony 3 involving violin, clarinet and percussion, with fundamental frequencies in the range from 225 Hz to 750 Hz. A total of 254 musical notes are present, as well as several hundred percussive events
4	12 mixtures with polyphony 4 involving violin, clarinet, saxophone and bassoon, with fundamental frequencies in the range from 86 Hz to 750 Hz. A total of 546 musical notes are present, including harmonically-related notes

5.2 Methodology

In this work, separation performance is measured in accordance with the evaluation method presented in [34], which delivers the overall source-to-distortion ratio (SDR), source-to-interference ratio (SIR), and source-to-artifact ratio (SAR).

In every mixture, performance measures are calculated using the BSS-Eval toolbox [16], then averaged across the estimated sources, and finally reported in decibels (dB). For comparison, Oracle separation results are also calculated for each case using the BSS-Oracle toolbox [35]. Oracle results are, theoretically, the highest achievable separation results that can be obtained using time-frequency masking-based methods, but can only be obtained when the reference sources are available, serving as an upper bound in performance evaluation [12].

Note events are automatically detected in every test recording, using the strategy presented in Sect. 3, while their extraction from within the mixture is conducted using both variations of the proposed method, namely, Time-Frequency Masking (IES-TFM) and Time-Domain Subtraction (IES-TDS). The clustering of note events is conducted by the end-user, as described in the previous section. The proposed algorithms are applied considering the following parameters: frame size of 2048, 50% and 87.5% overlap rates, no zero-padding, Hanning window, $\Gamma = 5$, $A_{max} = 0.25$, $H_q = 30$. Based on the average number of real notes present in every test mixture, the iterative stage of the proposed algorithm is set to converge after extracting 45 note events, in order to detect as many real events as possible.

Results are then compared with a similar semi-supervised approach, known as Interactive Sound Source Separation Editor (ISSE) [4], where the end-user is required to provide annotations in order to constrain, regularise, or otherwise inform the algorithm. These annotations are introduced by highlighting relevant sections of the input spectrogram, while the separation of the sources is obtained by using an implementation of the Nonnegative Matrix Factorisation (NMF) algorithm.

5.3   Results and Discussion

Figure 6 shows the separation performance of the systems for the test mixtures in Group 1, where IES-TFM and IES-TDS exhibit a slightly higher overall separation quality than ISSE, in terms of SDR. While the proposed algorithms deliver separated sources with significantly less interference among them, ISSE introduces less artifacts in the separated tracks. This behaviour might be related to the initialisation of ISSE, which depends entirely on the annotations provided and where harmonicity is not an assumption. Even when these annotations provide the localisation of the fundamental partial of every note, the algorithm struggles to identify some of their overtones and delivers in some cases an incomplete separation of the notes.

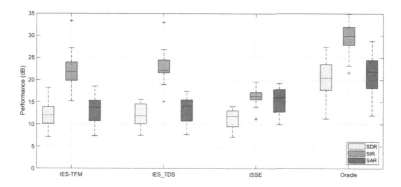

Fig. 6. Separation performance on 12 test mixtures with polyphony 2 in Group 1 (two harmonic sources). Two variations of the proposed system (IES-TFM and IES-TDS) are compared with a similar separation process (ISSE) and with the Oracle estimates (Oracle).

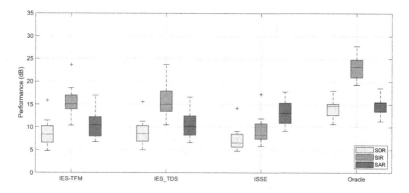

Fig. 7. Separation performance on 12 test mixtures with polyphony 3 in Group 2 (three harmonic sources). Two variations of the proposed system (IES-TFM and IES-TDS) are compared with a similar separation process (ISSE) and with the Oracle estimates (Oracle).

The incorporation of a third harmonic source within the test mixtures in Group 2 results in a reduction of the separation quality, as can be observed in Fig. 7. A higher number of simultaneous sources means additional difficulties in providing good annotations for the sources, reducing the overall performance of ISSE, but it also means additional problems during the separation of overlapping harmonics, which affects the separation quality of the proposed systems. However, the higher number of note events in the mixture and the proximity of their frequency components are causing a greater reduction in the separation performance on ISSE, compared with Fig. 6.

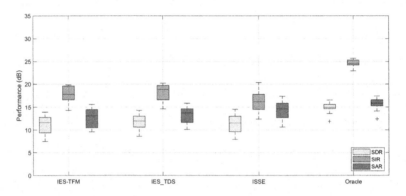

Fig. 8. Separation performance on 12 test mixtures with polyphony 3 in Group 3 (two harmonic and one percussive sources). Two variations of the proposed system (IES-TFM and IES-TDS) are compared with a similar separation process (ISSE) and with the Oracle estimates (Oracle).

Harmonically-related notes, which are present in some of the mixtures in Group 2, introduce an additional challenge for both algorithms and affect their separation performances. The IES systems are able to detect the pitch trajectories of many harmonically-related notes, however, an accurate separation of the original note events is not possible, since the amplitudes of their harmonic partials cannot be correctly estimated from the mixed spectrogram. Similarly, the ISSE system also has problems interpreting overlaps between the provided annotations, associated with different sources, and therefore tends to allocate most of the shared energy to only one of the sources.

Results in Fig. 8 correspond to the separation of the underlying sources from within the test mixtures in Group 3. Considering that the proposed methods are designed to detect harmonic content, the percussive output is consequently contained in a residual signal together with other non-harmonic content. In the case of ISSE, the percussion is instead extracted first by exploiting additional user-provided annotations of solo percussive regions of the spectrogram. In this case, the algorithms show similar separation quality, with the IES variations still showing slightly less interference in the separated sources, while the ISSE approach introduces slightly less artifacts. In this specific experiment, the percussive source does not affect the detection of note events within the IES automatic framework but, more generally, similar percussive effects might impact on the detection of musical notes with a fundamental frequency below 200 Hz.

Separation performances associated with the test mixtures in Group 4 are presented in Fig. 9. In this case, four sources are playing simultaneously in every mixture and the range of fundamental frequencies has been expanded to include low-pitched notes (86 Hz to 200 Hz), which represent a significant challenge for each algorithm due to the very short spacing between their harmonics and the increased likelihood of observing overlapping partials.

Figure 9 shows a significant reduction in separation quality delivered by each of the methods due to the increased polyphony of the mixtures. Although the ISSE still seems to generate less artifacts, the separated sources also exhibit higher levels of interference, suggesting that the annotations are not providing enough information to completely characterise each individual source. This problem is partially solved in the IES variations by assuming that the underlying sources are harmonic, which provides a simple but effective way to identify their frequency components based on the knowledge of their fundamental frequencies. The proposed dual-peak model provides a sharper separation of semi-overlapping harmonics, which also reduces interference among the separated sources. Problems associated with the separation of harmonically-related notes is another important factor that contributes to lowering the separation quality of all three methods investigated. When harmonically-related note events are detected by the proposed algorithms, their spectral content is arbitrarily partitioned using the strategy described in Sect. 3.2, which does not constitute a true separation of the real note events. Similarly, the ISSE method also struggles to identify harmonically-related notes and the information provided by the annotations is

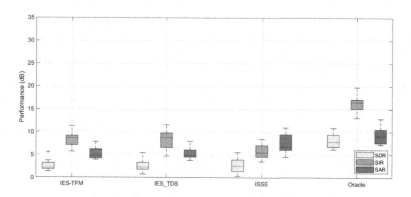

Fig. 9. Separation performance on 12 test mixtures with polyphony 4 in Group 4 (four harmonic sources). Two variations of the proposed system (IES-TFM and IES-TDS) are compared with a similar separation process (ISSE) and with the Oracle estimates (Oracle).

not enough to identify the actual characteristics of the underlying musical notes and their separation is also incomplete.

In general, an important advantage of IES over ISSE is that it allows end-user interaction during the final stage of the process (clustering of note events), which seems to be more effective than using it at the beginning of the separation, as in the case of the ISSE process. From the user perspective, listening to separated events and grouping them into individual sources is far easier than recognising harmonic structures and estimating frequencies from within the spectrogram of a complicated audio mixture.

6   Conclusions

The proposed separation framework is based on an automatic decomposition of the input recording into note events, followed by a clustering stage in which end-user interaction is used. This has proven to be effective for a variety of audio mixtures containing elaborate melodies in which harmonic or nearly-harmonic instruments are involved. From the end-user point of view, it has been observed that grouping separated note events to form individual sources is easier and more effective than recognising different harmonic structures within the spectrograms of highly complicated audio mixtures. However, additional user tests are required to fully support this statement.

To identify the harmonic partials of a given fundamental frequency, a peak-picking strategy has been proposed, which tolerates small deviations in frequency due to inharmonicity of the instrument or musical effects such as vibrato. However, there is always a risk of detecting an incorrect set of spectral peaks when the interaction between simultaneous notes is too large. In this case, a possibility is to incorporate additional information within the peak-picking algorithm, such as an estimation of the inharmonicity coefficient or the expected spectral envelope, in order to improve the way in which the next harmonic frequency is iteratively predicted in every frame, and hence, reduce the probability of misleadingly detecting an incorrect spectral peak.

Results from experiments have displayed very good separation performance for audio mixtures with polyphonies 2 and 3, in which the level of interference is usually low and the artifacts introduced by the process do not affect the overall audio quality of the separated sources.

Significant emphasis has been put on the separation of harmonic or nearly-harmonic sources from within polyphonic input recordings. However, this does not represent a restriction on the type of audio sources that can be processed by the algorithm, and mixtures containing harmonic instruments and percussion have also been studied. Due to the nature of the proposed solution, percussive events cannot be directly extracted from within the input mixture; rather, they tend to appear in the final residual signal that is obtained after the extraction of all harmonic sources.

Nevertheless, the presence of percussive sounds may complicate the detection of pitch trajectories, in particular, for low-pitched notes whose partials are heavily distorted by the low-frequency energy associated with percussive sources. Other extracted note events may also contain audible levels of interference caused by the incorrect extraction of additional energy at high frequencies associated with percussive events.

Slightly better separation results have been obtained by using time-domain subtraction as the way to extract note events from the input mixture, providing important evidence of the benefits associated with this softer extraction process, which is particularly useful when there is not enough information to characterise all the underlying components of the mixture.

Further work will be conducted with the aim of allowing the separation of multiple predominant note events in the same iteration, in order to increase the efficiency of the system and reduce computation times. Work will also concentrate on improving the separation of low-pitched musical notes. Different approaches to automate the clustering of note events into sources will be explored as a way to deliver a fully-automated source separation system that could be compared with other unsupervised algorithms based on machine learning.

References

1. Abdallah, S., Plumbley, M.D.: If the independent components of natural images are edges, what are the independent components of natural sounds? In: Proceedings of the International Conference on Independent Component Analysis and Blind Signal Separation, pp. 534–539 (2001)
2. Barry, D., Coyle, E., FitzGerald, D., Lawlor, R.: Single-channel source separation using short-time independent component analysis. In: Proceedings of the 119th AES Convention, pp. 1–6 (2005)
3. Brown, G.J., Cooke, M.: Computational auditory scene analysis. Comput. Speech Lang. **8**(4), 297–336 (1994)
4. Bryan, N.J., Mysore, G.J.: Interactive refinement of supervised and semi-supervised sound source separation estimates. In: Proceedings of the 38th IEEE International Conference on Acoustics, Speech and Signal Processing, pp. 883–887 (2013)
5. Cakir, E., Parascandolo, G., Heittola, T., Huttunen, H., Virtanen, T.: Convolutional recurrent neural networks for polyphonic sound event detection. IEEE/ACM Trans. Audio Speech Lang. Process. **25**(6), 1291–1303 (2017)
6. Casey, M.A., Westner, A.: Separation of mixed audio sources by independent subspace analysis. In: Proceedings of the International Computer Music Conference, pp. 154–161 (2000)
7. Chandna, P., Miron, M., Janer, J., Gómez, E.: Monoaural audio source separation using deep convolutional neural networks. In: Tichavský, P., Babaie-Zadeh, M., Michel, O.J.J., Thirion-Moreau, N. (eds.) LVA/ICA 2017. LNCS, vol. 10169, pp. 258–266. Springer, Cham (2017). https://doi.org/10.1007/978-3-319-53547-0_25
8. Davies, M., James, C.J.: Source separation using single-channel ICA. Sig. Process. **87**(8), 1819–1832 (2007)
9. Delgado Castro, A., Szymanski, J.: Semi-supervised audio source separation based on the iterative estimation and extraction of note events. In: Proceedings of the 16th International Conference on Signal Processing and Multimedia Applications, pp. 273–279 (2019)

10. Drake, L.A., Rutledge, J.C., Zhang, J., Katsaggelos, A.: A computational auditory scene analysis-enhanced beamforming approach for sound source separation. EURASIP J. Adv. Signal Process., 1–17 (2009)
11. Duan, Z., Pardo, B., Zhang, C.: Multiple fundamental frequency estimation by modeling spectral peaks and non-peak regions. IEEE Trans. Audio Speech Lang. Process. 18(8), 2121–2133 (2010)
12. Duan, Z., Zhang, Y., Zhang, C., Shi, Z.: Unsupervised single-channel music source separation by average harmonic structure modeling. IEEE Trans. Audio Speech Lang. Process. 16(4), 766–778 (2008)
13. Duong, N., Ozerov, A., Chevallier, L., Sirot, J.: An interactive audio source separation framework based on non-negative matrix factorization. In: Proceedings of the 39th IEEE International Conference on Acoustics, Speech and Signal Processing, pp. 1567–1571. IEEE, May 2014
14. Every, M.R., Szymanski, J.E.: Separation of synchronous pitched notes by spectral filtering of harmonics. IEEE Trans. Audio Speech Lang. Process. 14(5), 1845–1856 (2006)
15. Fan, Z.C., Jang, J.S.R., Lu, C.L.: Singing voice separation and pitch extraction from monaural polyphonic audio music via DNN and adaptive pitch tracking. In: Proceedings of the 2nd IEEE International Conference on Multimedia Big Data, pp. 178–185 (2016)
16. Févotte, C., Gribonval, R., Vincent, E.: BSS EVAL toolbox user guide. Technical report 1706, Institut de Recherche en Informatique et Systèmes Aléatoires (2005)
17. FitzGerald, D., Cranitch, M., Coyle, E.: Extended nonnegative tensor factorisation models for musical sound source separation. Comput. Intell. Neurosci. (2) (2008)
18. Grais, E.M., Roma, G., Simpson, A., Plumbley, M.D.: Two-stage single-channel audio source separation using deep neural networks. IEEE/ACM Trans. Audio Speech Lang. Process. 25(9), 1469–1479 (2017)
19. Grais, E.M., Sen, M.U., Erdogan, H.: Deep neural networks for single-channel source separation. In: Proceedings of the 39th IEEE International Conference on Acoustics, Speech and Signal Processing, pp. 3734–3738. IEEE (2014)
20. Jang, G.J., Lee, T.W., Oh, Y.H.: Single-channel signal separation using time-domain basis functions. IEEE Signal Process. Lett. 10(6), 168–171 (2003)
21. Li, P., Guan, Y., Xu, B., Liu, W.: Monaural speech separation based on computational auditory scene analysis and objective quality assessment of speech. IEEE Trans. Audio Speech Lang. Process. 14(6), 2014–2023 (2006)
22. Li, Y., Woodruff, J., Wang, D.: Monaural musical sound separation based on pitch and common amplitude modulation. IEEE Trans. Audio Speech Lang. Process. 17(7), 1361–1371 (2009)
23. Liutkus, A., Durrieu, J.L., Daudet, L., Richard, G.: An overview of informed audio source separation. In: Proceedings of the International Workshop on Image Analysis for Multimedia Interactive Services, pp. 3–6 (2013)
24. Mika, D., Kleczkowski, P.: ICA-based single channel audio separation: new bases and measures of distance. Arch. Acoust. 36(2), 311–331 (2011)
25. Miron, M., Janer, J., Gómez, E.: Monaural score-informed source separation for classical music using convolutional neural networks. In: Proceedings of the 18th International Conference on Music Information Retrieval, pp. 55–62 (2017)
26. Ochiai, E., Fujisawa, T., Ikehara, M.: Vocal separation by constrained non-negative matrix factorization. In: Processing of the APSIPA Annual Summit and Conference, pp. 480–483 (2015)
27. Parsons, T.W.: Separation of speech from interfering speech by means of harmonic selection. J. Acoust. Soc. Am. 60(1976), 911 (1976)

28. Pedersen, M.S., Wang, D., Larsen, J., Kjems, U.: Overcomplete blind source separation by combining ICA and binary time-frequency masking. In: Proceedings of the IEEE Workshop on Machine Learning for Signal Processing, pp. 15–20 (2005)
29. Ponce de León Vázquez, J., Beltrán Blázquez, J.R.: Blind separation of overlapping partials in harmonic musical notes using amplitude and phase reconstruction. EURASIP J. Adv. Signal Process. (223), 1–16 (2012)
30. Rafii, Z., Liutkus, A., Stoter, F.R., Mimilakis, S.I., FitzGerald, D., Pardo, B.: An overview of lead and accompaniment separation in music. IEEE/ACM Trans. Audio Speech Lang. Process. **26**(8), 1307–1335 (2018)
31. Taghia, J., Doostari, M.A.: Subband-based single-channel source separation of instantaneous audio mixtures. World Appl. Sci. J. **6**(6), 784–792 (2009)
32. Tjoa, S.K., Liu, K.J.R.: Factorization of overlapping harmonic sounds using approximate matching pursuit. In: Proceedings of the 12th International Conference on Music Information Retrieval, pp. 257–262 (2011)
33. Uhlich, S., Giron, F., Mitsufuji, Y.: Deep neural network-based instrument extraction from music. In: Proceedings of the 15th IEEE International Conference on Acoustics, Speech and Signal Processing, pp. 2135–2139 (2015)
34. Vincent, E., Gribonval, R., Févotte, C.: Performance measurement in blind audio source separation. IEEE Trans. Audio Speech Lang. Process. **14**(4), 1462–1469 (2006)
35. Vincent, E., Gribonval, R., Plumbley, M.D.: Oracle estimators for the benchmarking of source separation algorithms. Signal Process. **87**(8), 1933–1950 (2007)
36. Zivanovic, M.: Harmonic bandwidth companding for separation of overlapping harmonics in pitched signals. IEEE/ACM Trans. Audio Speech Lang. Process. **23**(5), 898–908 (2015)

Automatic Sleep Scoring Toolbox and Its Application in Sleep Apnea

Rui Yan[1,2]([⊠]), Fan Li[2], Xiaoyu Wang[2], Tapani Ristaniemi[1], and Fengyu Cong[1,2]

[1] Faculty of Information Technology, University of Jyväskylä, 40014 Jyväskylä, Finland
ruiyanmodel@foxmail.com
[2] School of Biomedical Engineering, Faculty of Electronic Information and Electrical
Engineering, Dalian University of Technology, Dalian 116024, China

Abstract. Sleep scoring is a fundamental but time-consuming process in any sleep laboratory. Automatic sleep scoring is crucial and urgent to help address the increasing unmet needs for sleep research. Therefore, this paper aims to develop an automatic sleep scoring toolbox with the capability of multi-signal processing. The toolbox allows the user to choose signal types and the number of target classes. In addition, a user-friendly interface is provided to display sleep structures and related sleep parameters. The proposed approach employs several automatic processes including signal preprocessing, feature extraction and classification in order to save labor costs without compromising accuracy. For the phase of feature extraction, a huge number of features are considered including statistical characters, frequency characters, time-frequency characters, fractal characters, entropy characters and nonlinear characters. Their contribution to distinguishing between different sleep stages are compared in this article. The classifier we used for sleep stages discrimination is the random forest algorithm. The performance of the proposed approach is tested on the patients with sleep apnea by assessing accuracy, sensitivity and precision. The model achieves an accuracy of 82% to 86% for patients with varying degrees of sleep-disordered breathing, which indicates that sleep-disordered breathing does not significantly affect the performance of the proposed model. The proposed automatic scoring toolbox would alleviate the burden of the physicians, speed up sleep scoring, and expedite sleep research.

Keywords: Polysomnography · Multi-modality analysis · MATLAB toolbox · Automatic sleep scoring · Sleep-disordered breathing

1 Introduction

Sleep covers almost one-third of human lifespan. Adequate and high-quality sleep is vital to our physical and mental well-being [1]. However, and likely because of our ephemeral lifestyle in modern society, sleep disorder complaints increase dramatically among people. One of the most common sleep disorders seen in sleep medicine centers is sleep apnea, which is characterized by repetitive cessations of the respiratory flow during sleep [2]. These nocturnal respiratory disturbances can induce sleep-EEG changes, which promotes sleep fragmentation and an increase of arousals [3]. Studies

© Springer Nature Switzerland AG 2020
M. S. Obaidat (Ed.): ICETE 2019, CCIS 1247, pp. 256–275, 2020.
https://doi.org/10.1007/978-3-030-52686-3_11

have found that the distortion of sleep signals aggravates the burden of sleep scoring [4], especially reducing inter-scorer agreement. Clinically, the gold standard of diagnosis of sleep apnea is overnight polysomnography (PSG) (sleep study), which is carried out in a specialized hospital-based sleep laboratory. Polysomnography records simultaneously tens of sleep signals including electroencephalograms (EEG), electromyograms (EMG), electrooculogram (EOG), electrocardiogram (ECG), pulse oximetry, airflow, respiratory effort etc. Generally, according to the rules of Rechtschaffen & Kales (R&K) [5] and the most recently updated American Academy of Sleep Medicine rules (AASM) [6], these PSG recordings are scored manually by at least one registered sleep technologist (RST) to obtain the sequence of sleep stages and related sleep parameters.

The R&K rules divide sleep into five distinct stages: non-rapid eye movement (NREM) stages 1, 2, 3 and 4 and rapid eye movement stage (stage R), while the most recently developed standard AASM merges stages 3 and 4 into N3 due to their prevalent low-frequency oscillations. Generally, sleep experts divide sleep recordings into 30-s intervals called one epoch and classify each epoch based on its amplitude and frequency characteristics, as described in Table 1. The process of assigning a sleep stage to every epoch of polysomnographic recordings is called sleep scoring. Sleep scoring is a very important step in sleep research and clinical interpretation of polysomnography. However, the process of sleep scoring is labor-intensive, as studies have revealed that the annotation of 8-h recording requires approximately 2–4 h [7]. Following the development of computerized methods, interests have been initiated to score automatically polysomnographic recordings, allowing the expert to avoid spending too much time on this time-consuming work. Nevertheless, it is a challenging problem because of the nonstationary nature of EEG signals and the complexity of sleep phenomena.

Numerous attempts have been made to automate sleep scoring [8, 9]. These methods were usually composed of two main components: feature generation or extraction and classification. For the phase of feature extraction, various signal processing techniques were explored such as wavelet transform [10, 11], empirical mode decomposition [12, 13], Hilbert-Huang transform [14, 15], Fourier transform [16] and short-time Fourier transform (STFT) [9, 17]. Then, diverse features, such as statistic features, frequency features and nonlinear features, were extracted from the transformed or decomposed signals of EEG, EOG and/or EMG [18, 19]. For classification, support vector machine (SVM) [20], random forest [19], K-nearest neighbor classifier [21], Naive Bayes [22], artificial neural network [23] etc. have been employed in literatures. In these studies, the agreement between automatic methods and human experts ranged from 80% to 90% [15, 23].

Besides traditional approaches, Liang and his colleagues [24] integrated multiscale entropy and autoregressive models for single-channel EEG achieving good performance. Another recent attempt proposed by Dimitriadis et al. [22] calculated the cross-frequency coupling of predefined frequency pairs, which demonstrated the effectiveness of phase-to-amplitude coupling and amplitude-to-amplitude coupling for the automatic classification of sleep stages. In addition, some studies based on waveform detection have emerged, the most famous of which was deep learning methods [25]. CNNs were especially promising because they can learn complex patterns and 'look' at the data in a similar way as a 'real brain' although working with raw data required a huge amount of training data and computational resources [26].

In previous studies, ECG signals, as a substitute for standard techniques for determining sleep stages, were mainly used in portable sleep monitoring systems [27, 28]. Some studies proposed that sleep scoring with ECG is less complex but equally accurate when compared to PSG analysis [8]. Krakovská and Mezeiová [29] found the ECG feature named zero-crossing rate performed well in automatic sleep scoring, but was still inferior to those from the signals of EEG, EOG and EMG. Yan et al. [19] revealed that ECG features were useful for differentiating stage R and W from other stages. Moreover, evidence from sleep physiology also suggested that the autonomous nervous system was regulated in totally different ways during wakefulness, slow-wave sleep and REM sleep [30]. Heart rate (HR) and arterial blood pressure decreased during non-REM sleep, while increased significantly during REM sleep, due to the modulations in sympathetic and parasympathetic activity [31]. Analysis of heart-rate variations enabled us to track the transition from wakefulness to sleep. Therefore, the author believed that ECG had promising prospects in automatic sleep scoring.

In our previous study [32], we proposed an automatic sleep scoring toolbox with the capability of multi-signal processing. Following automatic signal processing and analysis, the proposed toolbox achieved an average accuracy of 85.76% for 100 healthy subjects. Moreover, a user-friendly interface was provided to display sleep structures and related sleep parameters. Given the complexity of clinical conditions, the present article aims to extend the toolbox to patients with sleep apnea. More specifically, this work extends our preliminary work [32] in four aspects. First, the proposed toolbox covers multiple target domains so users can choose the number of target categories according to their needs. Second, more non-statistical features are considered to effectively track the variance of signals. Third, our previous study [32] performed feature evaluations based on a single experiment. The random-forest classifier accepts the number of features selected at random for each decision split, and therefore, it is necessary to perform 100 repeated experiments to obtain reliable results. Fourth, we investigate the influence of sleep-disordered breathing on classification. Healthy subjects and patients are diverging in their sleep structures, and therefore, it is important to examine whether these dissimilarities give rise to any difference in classification performance. To evaluate the performance of the proposed toolbox, various parameters such as accuracy, sensitivity and precision, will be considered in the following article.

The article is organized as follows: Sect. 2 gives an overview of the proposed toolbox. Experimental data and methodology are described in Sect. 3. Section 4 demonstrates the performance of proposed toolbox and the model transferability between patients with different degrees of sleep apnea. Section 5 provides discussions of the results and limitations of this study. Finally, conclusions are given in Sect. 6.

Table 1. The characteristics of adult sleep records during each sleep stage [6].

Sleep stage	Description
Stage W	a) The EEG will show mixed beta and alpha activities as the eyes open and close, and predominantly alpha activity (8–13 Hz) when the eyes remain closed b) The EOG channels will show eye blinking, reading eye movements or rapid eye movements c) Submental EMG is relatively high tone
Stage N1	a) The EEG pattern is characterized by low amplitude, predominantly 4–7 Hz activity (theta wave). Vertex sharp waves with duration <0.5 s may occur in stage N1 b) The EOG often shows slow eye movements in stage N1 c) The EMG amplitude is variable but often lower than in stage W
Stage N2	a) The EEG is characterized by predominant theta activity and occasional quick bursts of faster activity. Sleep spindles (commonly 12–14 Hz) and K complexes may appear here b) The EOG usually shows no eye movement activity c) The chin EMG shows variable amplitude, but it is usually lower than in stage W, and maybe as low as in stage R sleep
Stage N3	a) The EEG activity is marked by high-amplitude slow waves b) Eye movements are not typically seen during stage N3 sleep c) The chin EMG is of variable amplitude, often lower than in stage N2 sleep and sometimes as low as in stage R sleep
Stage R	a) It is characterized by relatively low-amplitude, mixed-frequency EEG activity without K complexes or sleep spindles. Sawtooth waves (2–6 Hz, sharply contoured triangular) are strongly supportive of the presence of stage R sleep b) Rapid eye movements are characteristic of stage R sleep c) The chin EMG usually shows the lowest level of the entire recording

2 System Overview

The toolbox proposed in this article aims to accelerate the process of sleep scoring, alleviating the burden of physicians. With this consideration in mind, we design a user-friendly operation interface, as shown in Fig. 1, in order to facilitate operations and visualize analysis results. The interface consists of a training module, an offline prediction module, an online prediction module, several parameter panels and visualization panels. The following lines briefly describe the operation of the toolbox and the functions of the main modules. To run the proposed toolbox, a MATLAB environment was required which can be found at this link https://www.mathworks.com/.

If you have enough training data and want to train your model, the training module can help you. It should be mentioned that the user needs to select the signal type (multiple choice), the target number of stages (single selection) and the power frequency noise (a number). The software then automatically performs signal pre-processing, feature

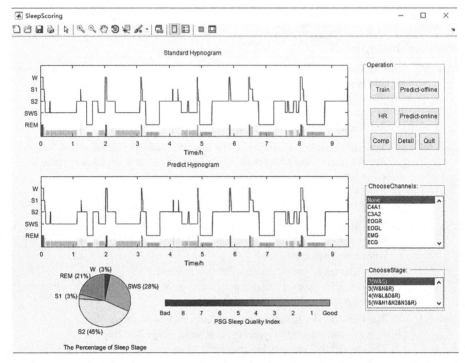

Fig. 1. The interface of sleep scoring toolbox.

extraction and classifier training. The trained model would be stored in a folder named "Current Results" in the current working directory.

If you want to evaluate the sleep structure for new sleep recordings, the prediction module can help you whether or not you have a trained model. This module automatically checks if the user has a trained model (searches for a folder named "Current Results"). If no model is found in the folder, it would allow the user to specify a folder or load a predefined model. Once the model is determined, the module will automatically process the test data based on model parameters. Finally, the application interface displays the predicted sleep structure, related sleep parameters and the estimated sleep quality index. If a hypnogram (e.g., labels scored by RST) is available for the test data, the interface would display both hypnogram and predicted labels together. The disagreement between hypnogram and predicted labels would be highlighted by pressing a button named "Comp". Clicking the "Detail" button would pop up a new panel to display related sleep parameters. A button named "HR" is used to analyze the variance of heartbeat during sleep.

The online prediction module is similar to the offline prediction process except for the real-time updating results. This module can be connected to a sleep monitoring device to perform real-time analysis of sleep signals and real-time visualization sleep structures. The real-time update sleep signal will be saved in the memory as a TXT file.

3 Materials and Methods

3.1 Experiment Data

The all-night sleep recordings are provided by the Sleep Heart Health Study (SHHS) database, of which only the first round (SHHS-1) is selected in this study. The Sleep Heart Health Study (SHHS) is a multi-center cohort study held during 1995-1998 to investigate whether sleep-disordered breathing is associated with a higher risk of various cardiovascular diseases. In that study, 6441 individuals aged 40 years or older were recruited to undergo an overnight PSG and physical examination. Full details of SHHS study designs can be found in Quan et al.'s study [33].

Subjects employed in the present study did not use beta-blockers, alpha-blockers, inhibitors, and did not suffer documented hypertension, heart disease, or history of stroke. Patients with or without sleep-disordered breathing were randomly selected from the SHHS1 dataset. Table 2 summarized the characteristics of the employed subjects.

Each record was scored by an experienced research assistant or sleep technologist according to the R&K rules. Sleep recordings were segmented into 30-s per epoch and labelled as wakefulness (W), non-rapid eye movement stage (NREM, containing N1, N2, N3 and N4) and rapid eye movement stage (R). According to the recently updated AASM standards, NREM stages 3 and 4 were merged into N3 in the present article.

Table 2. Subject characteristics.

Category	Number	Age	AHI range	AHI	Epoch
Normal breathing	100	46.86 (4.22)	AHI < 5	2.11 (1.46)	97,514
Mild sleep apnea	30	48.50 (4.37)	$5 \leq$ AHI < 15	8.95 (2.62)	28,995
Moderate sleep apnea	30	48.53 (3.57)	$15 \leq$ AHI < 30	22.08 (4.83)	28,953
Severe sleep apnea	30	48.07 (4.86)	AHI $\geq$ 30	41.38 (10.34)	28,713

3.2 Signal Pre-processing

For the predefined model and the following experiments, four modalities of polysomnography (PSG) signals were analyzed: two EEG channels (C4-A1 and C3-A2, following the 10–20 international electrode placement system), two electrooculography (EOG) channels (ROC and LOC), one submental electromyography (EMG) channel and one electrocardiography (ECG) channel. All of the aforementioned signals were fully included in the evaluation process without discarding any recorded segments, thereby to have a near-clinical situation.

In order to remove noise and artefacts, a notch filter, a high-pass filter with a cut-off frequency of 0.3 Hz and a low-pass filter with a cut-off frequency of 30 Hz were applied to the signals of EEG, EOG and ECG. In terms of EMG, a notch filter, a high-pass filter with a cut-off frequency of 10 Hz and a low-pass filter with a cut-off frequency of

75 Hz were performed. If the sampling frequency is less than twice the cutoff frequency, the corresponding filtering process would be skipped. Overnight night recordings were smoothed by their mean value $\pm 5 \times$standard deviation to remove outliers. In order to eliminate individual differences, sleep signals were normalized to $[-100, 100]$. All signals were divided into 30-s epochs, each epoch corresponding to a single sleep stage. Signal interruption due to electrode fall-off or amplifier failure can be identified by judging the standard deviation of epochs. If $std(x_{epoch}) < 0.01$, the epoch was judged as an interruption and was eliminated.

3.3 Feature Extraction

This study considers a variety of conventional and neoteric characteristics serving as distinctive markers for various psycho-physiological states. They are summarized in Table 3. Some of the parameters are introduced in the following, and the others can be found in our previous studies [19, 32].

In order to reduce the influence of extreme values, percentiles, instead of the maximum and minimum values, are used to measure the signals' amplitude. Besides, variance, skewness, kurtosis etc. are calculated which have proven to be good indicators of the amplitude distribution [11].

The calculation of all spectral measures is based on the short time Fourier transform (STFT). The signal epoch is separated by a 3 s hamming moving window with 2 s overlap. Each partition is zero-padded to 5 times the length of sampling points, then a Fourier transform is calculated. The final spectal density is achieved by averaging spectral densities of the twenty-nine partitions.

Given the important role of rhythm waves and sleep events, the relative spectral power and spectral entropy are computed in the corresponding sub-frequency bands. Table 4 lists the EEG rhythm wave and sleep events together with their frequency ranges. Power ratios are computed based on the relative spectral power of rhythm waves and sleep events. The following power ratios are computed: delta/theta, delta/alpha, delta/beta, theta/alpha, theta/beta, alpha/beta, alpha/(theta + delta), delta/(theta + alpha) and theta/(beta + delta).

Nonlinear features are good methods to quantify the complexity of time series. Some nonlinear measures are described as follows.

The second difference of raw signal is defined as,

$$D = 1/(N-2) \sum\nolimits_{n=1}^{N-2} |x(n+2) - x(n)| \tag{1}$$

where N is the length of time series $x(n)$.

The fourth power of raw data,

$$P = log_{10} \sum\nolimits_{n=1}^{N} x(n)^4 \tag{2}$$

Entropy is a concept addressing irregularity or predictability. The greater entropy is often associated with more randomness and less system order. Recently, several different estimators of entropy have been introduced to quantify the oscillation of time series. In this paper, spectral entropy, Shannon entropy, Tsallis entropy ($q = 2$) and Renyi entropy ($\alpha = 2$) [34] are considered. Their corresponding definitions are listed below.

Spectral entropy,

$$SpE = \frac{1}{\ln(N)} \sum_{f=f_{min}}^{30Hz} P(f) * ln(P(f)) \tag{3}$$

where N is the length of the time series, $P(f)$ indicating the power spectral power, and f_{min} is set as 0.3 Hz in terms of the signals of EEG, EOG and ECG, and 10 Hz of EMG.

Shannon entropy,

$$ShnE = -\sum_{n=1}^{N} p_i ln(p_i) \tag{4}$$

where $p_i = n_i/N$ is the histogram distribution of the time series x, N the length of the signal x, and n_i is the number of samples within the ith bin.

Tsallis entropy,

$$TslE = \frac{1}{1-q} \left(1 - \sum_{n=1}^{N} p_n^q \right) \tag{5}$$

where q is entropic index.

Renyi entropy [15],

$$RyiE = \frac{1}{1-\alpha} log_2 \left(\sum_{n=1}^{N} p_n^{\alpha} \right) \tag{6}$$

where α is the Renyi's entropy order.

3.4 Feature Normalization

After all of the features extracted, post-processing is performed, which helps reduce the influence of signal noise. The outlier of each feature is defined as the element that is more than three standard deviations from the mean. All outliers would be replaced by their nearest non-outlier value.

In order to balance numerical ranges and reduce the impact of variability between-subjects or within-subjects, each feature vector of individuals is separately normalized to [0, 1] by the following formula,

$$\bar{p}_{i,j} = \left[p_{i,j} - min(p_j) \right] / \left[max(p_j) - min(p_j) \right] \tag{7}$$

where p_j denotes an independent feature vector from an individual, and $p_{i,j}$ is an element in the jth feature vector.

Table 3. Parameter list.

Type	Feature name
Statistical measures	The 5th, 25th, 75th, 95th percentile (Pre5, Pre25, Pre75, Pre95), Variance (V), Root mean square (Rms), Skewness (S), Kurtosis (K), Hjorth parameters (HA, HM, HC), Zero-Crossing (ZC)
Spectral measures	Power spectral density (PSD), Mean value of PSD (mPSD), Median value of PSD (mdPSD), Power ratio (PR), Relative spectral power (P), Mean of instantaneous frequency(Ifq), Mean frequency (mF), Median frequency (mdF), Brain rate (BR), Spectral centroid (Sc), Spectral width (Sw), Spectral asymmetry (Sa), Spectral flatness (Sk), Spectrum flatness (Sf), Spectral slope (Ss), Spectral decrease (Sd), Spectral edge frequency at 90% and 50% (edge90, edge50), Difference of spectral edges (Edge_D)
Nonlinear measures	Mean Teager energy (MTE), Mean energy (E), Mean curve length (CL), the second differences (SecD), The 4th Power (P4)
Fractal measures	Petrosian fractal dimension (PFD)
Entropy measures	Spectral entropy (spE), Shannon entropy (dnE), Renyi entropy (ryE), Tsallis entropy (tsE), Log energy entropy (lgE)
Mutual measures	Coherence (Ch), Coefficient (Cf)

Table 4. Rhythm waves and events of sleep EEGs.

Name	Frequency band
Slow wave activity	0.5–2.0 Hz
Delta	0–3.99 Hz
Theta	4–7.99 Hz
Alpha	8–13 Hz
Beta	13–30 Hz
Sawtooth waves	2–6 Hz
Sleep spindles	12–14 Hz
K complex	0.5–1.5 Hz

3.5 Classification

In order to capture the characters of sleep stages and to predict new instances, the present article employs a random forest (RF) classifier because it is relatively parameter-free, robust to outliers, fast to train and resistant to overfitting [35]. This study designs a classifier with 200 trees, where each tree is created using a randomly selected set of m features ($m = \sqrt{M}$, where M is the total number of features.). These features will be used to design decision nodes of each tree. Those decision nodes divide test samples into specific categories, and the final classification results are achieved by the most votes in the forest. Moreover, the RF classifier is able to store the out-of-bag information for each node, which provides an estimation of the importance of each feature. The classifier is trained using 10-fold cross-validation. The test set is completely independent, so the test set consists of data that the model has never seen before.

3.6 Result Correction

Studies have found that sleep transitions are not a random process. However, traditional classifiers can only give their decisions based on information of the current stage, but can't remember the context. The objective of this phase is to utilize the strengths of the hidden Markov model to complement the weaknesses of conventional classifiers. Firstly, hidden Markov model (HMM) is trained using the classification results of validation dataset. The HMM parameters, namely transition matrix, emission matrix and initial matrix, are described as follows. Concerning the initial matrix, all states have equal probabilities to be the initial state.

The transition matrix $A = \{a_{ij}\}$ stores the probability of stage s_j following stage s_i. a_{ij} can be calculated by the following formula,

$$a_{ij} = \frac{\sum S_i \to S_j}{\sum_{t=1}^{N} s_t = S_i} \tag{8}$$

where s_t denotes sleep stage of each epoch, N the number of epochs, and $S_i, S_j \in \{W, R, N1, N2, N3\}$.

The emission matrix [36] is calculated from the confusion matrix $C = \{c_{ij}\}$ where c_{ij} represents the probability of classifying stage S_i as stage S_j.

$$a_{ij} = \frac{N_{s_i \to s_j}}{N_{s_i}} \tag{9}$$

where N_{s_i} denotes the total number of stage S_i, $N_{s_i \to s_j}$ the number of stage S_i classified to stage S_j, and $S_i, S_j \in \{W, R, N1, N2, N3\}$.

After determining the HMM model, the Viterbi algorithm [37] is used to find the most likely sequence of states through the trellis. The correction algorithm takes a sequence of observations (classifier output) as input and returns a sequence of states as output (correct stages). The correction process refer to the observations prior to and posterior to the current epoch, which makes the corrected stages avoid unreasonable stages transitions. More specifically, the stage transition $[W, R, N2]$ would be corrected to $[W, N1, N2]$. The study by Liang et al. [38] illustrated some unreasonable transitions. Experiments have proved that these unreasonable transitions can be corrected by the proposed method.

3.7 PSG Sleep Quality Index

In order to provide an objective estimation of sleep quality, the toolbox proposes a sleep quality index which is built according to items of the Pittsburgh Sleep Quality Index

(PSQI). PSQI is a standard self-report questionnaire for assessing sleep quality during the previous month [39]. The self-report questionnaire is relatively subjective and can be easily exaggerated or minimized by the person completing it. Therefore, the toolbox calculates various sleep parameters (Table 2 in reference [32]) from the predicted sleep structure. Afterwards, statistical scoring is performed based on these sleep parameters. The score is then normalized into a range of [0, 9] that is PSG sleep quality index. The PSG index is displayed in the bar in the lower-right corner of the interface. Detailed sleep parameters can be obtained by pressing the button "Detail".

4   Performance Assessment

To demonstrate the generalizability of the proposed toolbox, the proposed model was tested on subjects with normal, mild, moderate and severe sleep-disordered breathing. Model performance was evaluated by accuracy, sensitivity and precision. Accuracy indicated the fraction of correct detections. Sensitivity represented the proportion of positive epochs that are correctly identified. Precision is the proportion of epochs predicted as belonging to the positive class to epochs that actually belong to the positive class. Their definitions [11] were listed below.

$$Acc = \frac{TP + TN}{TP + FN + FP + TN}(\%) \tag{10}$$

$$Sen = \frac{TP}{TP + FN}(\%) \tag{11}$$

$$Pre = \frac{TP}{TP + FP}(\%) \tag{12}$$

where TP, TN, FP and FN respectively denote true positives, true negatives, false positives and false negatives.

4.1   Influence of Signal Types

In order to explore the relationship between signal types and classification accuracy, we performed a greedy search on signal fusions for two to six sleep stages. The results were shown in Fig. 2 where the column denoted the mean accuracy of 100 normal sleep-breathing subjects and the bars represented the standard deviation. Four target domains were highlighted in different colors in Fig. 2. For each target domain, twelve signal fusions were considered and displayed along X-axis where signals' name was abbreviated with its middle letter.

As can be seen from Fig. 2, with the enrichment of signal types, the mean value of accuracy increased, and the uncertainty decreased to some extent. More specifically, Fig. 2 indicated that the required signal types increased with the fineness of sleep scoring. If sleep recordings were classified into two stages, namely wakefulness (W) and sleep (S), all considered signal fusions gave satisfactory results. As the number of sleep stages increased, the number of required signals increased accordingly if a satisfactory accuracy was desired.

From the perspective of signal types, the signal fusions containing EEG signals showed better classification accuracy, indicating that EEG signals played a vital role in sleep scoring. The discriminative information provided by ECG and EMG channels was inferior to that from EEG and EOG signals. Nevertheless, the richness of signal modalities contributed to the increasing accuracy of sleep stages classification, but up to a certain point.

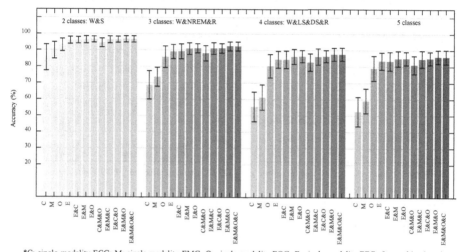

*C: single-modality ECG; M: single-modality EMG; O: single-modality EOG; E: single-modality EEG; &: combination signals; 2 classes: wakefulness and sleep (W&S); 3 classes: wakefulness, non-rapid eye movement sleep and rapid eye movement sleep (W&NREM&REM); 4 classes: wakefulness, light sleep (containing N1 and N2), deep sleep (N3) and rapid eye movement sleep (W&LS&DS &REM); 5 classes: W, N1, N2, N3 and R

Fig. 2. The classification accuracy for different signal fusions and target class.

4.2 Feature Evaluation

To further elucidate the features' contribution to automatic sleep scoring, the importance of features, measured by their contribution to distinguishing each pair of sleep stages, were derived from the random forest classifier. Given random-forest classifier randomly selected a subset of features for each decision split, and therefore, we performed 100 repeated tests for each experiment. The final importance of each feature was the average of 100 tests. The top 15 features was highlighted in Fig. 3, where features were sorted in descending order of discriminative ability.

Figure 3 indicated that the optimal feature subset was a fusion of statistical measures (e.g. Percentiles, Hjorth parameters, Zero-Crossing), spectral measures (e.g. spectral edge, power spectral density), entropy measures (e.g. spectral entropy), fractal measures (e.g. Petrosian fractal dimension) and nonlinear measures (e.g. mean curve length, The 4th Power). Varied features captured signals from multiple aspects, thereby improving accuracy.

Sleep stages	N3-N2	N3-N1	N3-R	N3-W	N2-N1	N2-R	N2-W	N1-R	N1-W	R-W
Top1	E.K	E.lgE	E.lgE	E.ZC	E.Sf	M.lgE	E.P-St	M.lgE	E.P-St	M.lgE
Top2	E.lgE	E.Sf	E.per75	E.PFD	E.PFD	M.per25	E.spE-St	M.per25	E.spE-St	M.K
Top3	E.per75	E.per75	E.K	E.ifq	E.P-K	Cf	E.PFD	M.per75	E. θ/β	M.per25
Top4	O.ifq	E.K	Cf	O.P4	E.ryE	E.spE-sp	E.ZC	M.per5	E. θ (α+β)	M.per75
Top5	O.mdF	E.ZC	E.PFD	E.Sf	E.spE-K	M.per5	E.ifq	M.SecD	E.ifq	M.per5
Top6	E.Sf	E.spE-K	E.Sf	O.ryE	E.P4	O.spE-α	O.P4	M.K	O.P4	E.P-St
Top7	O.K	E.ifq	E.per25	E.θ/β	O.PFD	E.P-sp	E.θ/(α+β)	Ch	E. θ/α	M.CL
Top8	E.PFD	E.P-K	E.spE-K	E.spE-β	Ch	M.per75	O.ryE	M.CL	O.spE-δ	E.spE-St
Top9	E.Sw	E.spE-β	E.Rms	M.per25	E.δ/θ	O.P-α	E.P-δ	M.mdPSD	E.P-δ	E. θ/(α+β)
Top10	Cf	E.PFD	E.per95	E.Sw	E.Rms	M.K	E. δ/α	M.per95	O.SecD	M.SecD
Top11	O.ZC	E.per25	E.P-β	M.P4	Cf	E.spE-K	E. δ/(α+β)	O.spE-α	O.ryE	E. θ/α
Top12	E.per25	E.HM	E.spE-β	M.per5	M.P4	E.ryE	Ch	M.ryE	E.ZC	M.per95
Top13	O.edge50	E.per95	E.spE-St	M.per95	E.per95	Cf	E.spE-δ	M.Sw	E. δ/(α+β)	E.PFD
Top14	E.SecD	E.per5	E.ryE	E.K	E.lgE	Ch	O.S	O.P-α	E.P-K	E. θ/β
Top15	E.spE-θ	E.Sw	E.P-δ	E.HM	E.spE-θ	E.PFD	Ch	M.Sk	O.S	Ch

(left margin label: Top 15 features)

*EEG features (colour: yellow); EOG features (colour: green); EMG features ((colour: red)); ECG features (colour: blue); Mutual information (color: gray).

*-K: K-complex; -sp: sleep spindle; -St: Sawthooth;

Fig. 3. Selected features for distinguishing specific pair of sleep stages.

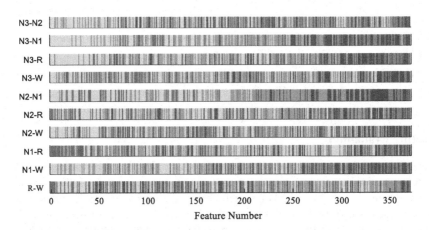

*EEG features (colour: yellow); EOG features (colour: green); EMG features ((colour: red)); ECG features (colour: blue); Mutual information (color: gray). Decreasing importance from left to right.

Fig. 4. Feature distributions for distinguishing each pair of sleep stages.

Figure 4 listed the distribution of feature importance in distinguishing each pair of sleep stages. As can be seen from the Fig. 4, the features from EEG contributed to the recognition of most stages. EMG features were good at distinguishing stage R and wakefulness, partly because of the apparent change of EMG amplitude in stage R and stage W. ECG features were inferior to those from the signals of EEG, EOG and EMG, which is consistent with the previous studies [29]. Nevertheless, the ECG features showed their contribution in distinguishing stage N3, R and W.

4.3 Performance on Transfer Learning

Table 5 presented the confusion matrix of classification results. Except for stage N1, all other stages were correctly classified with a precision of 80% or more. Stage N1 was considered as a transient state between wakefulness and "real" sleep, so it usually contained information of two or three sleep stages. As a result, the scoring of N was quite obscure, even for sleep scoring experts [29].

The model's generalizability was assessed by patients with mild, moderate, and severe sleep-disordered breathing. It was worth noting that the model was trained on 100 subjects with normal sleep-breathing. Therefore, all patients with sleep-disordered breathing consisted of information that the model had never seen before. Table 6, 7 and 8 displayed the confusion matrix of test subjects. As can be seen from tables, the model performed slightly better in normal and mild apnea cases than in moderate and severe cases. Nevertheless, even for patients with severe sleep-disordered breathing, the proposed model could provide per-epoch sensitivity and precision comparable to state of the art, indicating that the proposed model had good transferability between healthy populations and patients.

Table 5. Confusion matrix for AHI < 5 subjects.

		Technologists' score stage					Pre.
	Stage	W	R	N1	N2	N3	
Proposed	W	18370	134	716	504	23	93.0%
	R	589	15817	504	1727	0	84.9%
	N1	274	98	750	382	0	49.9%
	N2	1177	906	1044	38035	2726	86.7%
	N3	11	2	0	2202	11523	83.9%
Sen.		90.0%	93.3%	24.9%	88.8%	80.7%	
Acc.							86.65%

Table 6. Confusion matrix for 5 < AHI < 15 subjects.

		Technologists' score stage					Pre.
	Stage	W	R	N1	N2	N3	
Proposed	W	5849	70	328	155	13	91.2%
	R	119	4261	163	315	0	87.7%
	N1	122	32	303	161	0	49.0%
	N2	325	459	333	11110	930	84.4%
	N3	3	0	0	501	3443	87.2%
Sen.		91.1%	88.4%	26.9%	90.8%	78.5%	
Acc.							86.1%

Table 7. Confusion matrix for 15 < AHI < 30 subjects.

		Technologists' score stage					Pre.
	Stage	W	R	N1	N2	N3	
Proposed	W	5290	169	411	469	13	83.3%
	R	133	4089	135	286	0	88.1%
	N1	87	175	273	295	0	32.9%
	N2	498	460	367	11268	1000	82.9%
	N3	23	2	0	654	2856	80.8%
Sen.		87.7%	83.5%	23.0%	86.9%	73.8%	
Acc.							82.1%

Table 8. Confusion matrix for AHI > 30 subjects.

		Technologists' score stage					Pre.
	Stage	W	R	N1	N2	N3	
Proposed	W	5735	177	352	440	3	85.5%
	R	266	3490	129	226	0	84.9%
	N1	122	172	247	165	0	35.0%
	N2	735	582	406	11439	678	82.7%
	N3	30	0	1	727	2591	77.4%
Sen.		83.2%	79.0%	21.8%	88.0%	79.2%	
Acc.							81.9%

5   Discussion

Burgeoning public interest in sleep health had provided a strong impetus for the study of automatic sleep scoring. To the best of our knowledge, limited toolbox or software was available for automatic sleep scoring, although there were many theoretical studies in this field. In previous studies, some portable devices were developed based on ECG and respiration. For example, Hermawan et al. [28] developed a real-time monitoring device that classified sleep into 2 stages (wakefulness and sleep) with an average precision of 0.941. Recently, some deep-learning-based scoring tools sprouted out, such as SLEEPNET [40] and SeqSleepNet [41]. The classification accuracy of these deep-learning-based tools was not less than 0.85 with the support of tremendous training data and highly configured computer (like GPU or server). Compared with previous studies, the proposed toolbox provided comparable or better precision and greater freedom. Even for the subjects with severe sleep-disordered breathing, the model performance met or exceeded the accepted benchmark of $Acc = 80\%$ between trained human scorers [42]. In addition, the proposed toolbox evaluated all epochs, including severely contaminated or distorted epochs, thereby to have a near-clinical condition.

The MATLAB-based toolbox allowed users to select the available signal types and the number of target classes. Based on our aforementioned analysis, it was worth adding multi-modality sensors, if a satisfactory accuracy was desired. This conclusion was consistent with previous research that claimed features from multi-modality signals were beneficial to the improvement of scoring accuracy [9], but up to a certain point. Compared to our previous results [32], the importance of features from 100 repeated tests was slightly different from the results from a single experiment. One possible explanation was that the random forest randomly selected features for decision splits. Besides that, it can also be attributed to changes of features. In the present article, we refined the frequency bands of EEG signals and calculated more non-statistical features for EEG rhythm waves and sleep events in the present paper, thereby making the contribution of EEG signals even more prominent. Unfortunately, after 100 repeated tests, we did not find an ECG feature in the first 15 features, although some ECG features performed well in several tests. That may be attributed to the characteristics of the classifier. The random forest classifier tended to select features containing many distinct values over those containing few distinct values [43]. Compared to changes of EEG and EMG signals during sleep, changes of heart rate seems to be slow and gradual. Nevertheless, we found that the ECG features performed relatively well in distinguishing stage N3, R and W, as shown in Fig. 4.

From the perspective of applications, the proposed toolbox would be helpful for researchers, especially the newcomers in this field, to accelerate their understanding of sleep structures. It can also be used in clinic to expedite the annotation of PSG records, thereby alleviating the burden of the physicians. The online prediction module provides the potential to automatically control sleep tasks by combining the toolbox with sleep experiments.

Even though our results are encouraging, our model still has several limitations. One of them is that the performance of proposed toolbox is affected by the data property. Since our model learns from the training data, it might not perform well if the test data and training data have different properties. For example, a scoring model trained by healthy subjects may not perform well on patients. In that case, the model might need to be re-trained or fine-tuned if a good precision is desired.

Another complaint about the proposed algorithm might be worse N1 precision. A possible cause is the obscure character of stage N1. From the neurophysiological standpoint, N1 is a transition phase between wakefulness and sleep, which contains information of two or three sleep stages. The recognition of stage N1 is also an enormous challenge for other published models, even for sleep scoring experts [7]. Another reason affecting the precision of stage N1 might be unbalanced instances. It is caused by the natural asymmetric distribution of sleep stages. In this article, we did not consider any sample-balance strategy, such as resampling, since according to our study, the improved precision of stage N1 comes at the expense of other stages. We believe that preserving the natural sleep structure best represents how the model would perform in a production setting.

The proposed model performs slightly better in normal and mild apnea cases than moderate and severe cases. This can trace back to different pathological manifestations of patients with normal breathing and patients with severe apnea. Studies have shown that patients with severe sleep apnea suffer from sleep fragmentation and an increase of arousals, which pose a challenge to sleep scoring. Other physiological changes in sleep apnea can't be excluded. Some studies found significant changes in EEG spectral power as disease progression [44]. Other studies have shown that patients with severe obstructive apnea had higher activity level in the sympathetic nervous system [45], which modulate the activity of brain and cardiopulmonary system. In addition to pathological factors, another explanation for the model's poor performance in severe apnea cases is model-mismatch. The author believes that the model accuracy can be further improved by training with sufficient data on severe apnea cases.

6 Conclusions

This study proposed an automatic sleep scoring toolbox with the capability of multi-signal processing. It allowed users to choose the signal type and target domain according to their needs. Sleep recordings can be automatically analyzed in batches or individually. In addition, different signals' fusions and a huge number of characteristics were investigated in present studies to highlight their contribution to automatic sleep scoring. The performance of the proposed model has been tested on patients with varying degrees of sleep apnea. The patient-specific accuracy ranged from 82% to 86%, indicating good generalizability of the proposed model. Compared with manual scoring, the proposed automatic scoring toolbox was cost-effective, which would alleviate the burden of the physicians, speed up sleep scoring and expedite sleep research.

Acknowledgements. The authors would like to thank the SHHS for providing the polysomnographic data. This work was supported by the scholarships from China Scholarship Council (Nos. 201606060227).

References

1. Strine, T.W., Chapman, D.P.: Associations of frequent sleep insufficiency with health-related quality of life and health behaviors. Sleep Med. **6**, 23–27 (2005). https://doi.org/10.1016/j.sleep.2004.06.003
2. Pagel, J.F., Pandi-Perumal, S.R.: Primary Care Sleep Medicine: A Practical Guide. Springer, Heidelberg (2014)
3. Nano, M.-M., Long, X., Werth, J., Aarts, R.M., Heusdens, R.: Sleep apnea detection using time-delayed heart rate variability. In: 2015 Annual International Conference of the IEEE Engineering in Medicine and Biology Society, pp. 7679–7682 (2015). https://doi.org/10.1109/EMBC.2015.7320171
4. Schluter, T., Conrad, S.: An approach for automatic sleep stage scoring and apnea-hypopnea detection. In: 2010 IEEE 10th International Conference on Data Mining (ICDM), pp. 230–241. IEEE (2010)
5. Rechtschaffen, A., Kales, A.: A Manual of Standardized Terminology, Techniques and Scoring System for Sleep Stages of Human Subjects. US Natl. Inst. Heal, Washington DC (1968)
6. Berry, R.B., et al.: Rules for scoring respiratory events in sleep: update of the 2007 AASM manual for the scoring of sleep and associated events. J. Clin. Sleep Med. **8**, 597–619 (2012). https://doi.org/10.5664/jcsm.2172
7. Hassan, A.R., Bhuiyan, M.I.H.: A decision support system for automatic sleep staging from EEG signals using tunable Q-factor wavelet transform and spectral features. J. Neurosci. Methods **271**, 107–118 (2016). https://doi.org/10.1016/j.jneumeth.2016.07.012
8. Faust, O., Razaghi, H., Barika, R., Ciaccio, E.J., Acharya, U.R.: A review of automated sleep stage scoring based on physiological signals for the new millennia. Comput. Methods Programs Biomed. **176**, 81–91 (2019). https://doi.org/10.1016/j.cmpb.2019.04.032
9. Boostani, R., Karimzadeh, F., Nami, M.: A comparative review on sleep stage classification methods in patients and healthy individuals. Comput. Methods Programs Biomed. **140**, 77–91 (2017). https://doi.org/10.1016/j.cmpb.2016.12.004
10. Khalighi, S., Sousa, T., Pires, G., Nunes, U.: Automatic sleep staging: a computer assisted approach for optimal combination of features and polysomnographic channels. Expert Syst. Appl. **40**, 7046–7059 (2013). https://doi.org/10.1016/j.eswa.2013.06.023
11. Şen, B., Peker, M., Çavuşoğlu, A., Çelebi, F.V.: A comparative study on classification of sleep stage based on EEG signals using feature selection and classification algorithms. J. Med. Syst. **38**, 18 (2014). https://doi.org/10.1007/s10916-014-0018-0
12. Hassan, A.R., Bhuiyan, M.I.H.: Computer-aided sleep staging using complete ensemble empirical mode decomposition with adaptive noise and bootstrap aggregating. Biomed. Signal Process. Control **24**, 1–10 (2016). https://doi.org/10.1016/j.bspc.2015.09.002
13. Hassan, A.R., Hassan Bhuiyan, M.I.: Automatic sleep scoring using statistical features in the EMD domain and ensemble methods. Biocybern. Biomed. Eng. **36**, 248–255 (2016). https://doi.org/10.1016/j.bbe.2015.11.001
14. Li, Y., Yingle, F., Gu, L., Qinye, T.: Sleep stage classification based on EEG hilbert-huang transform. In: 2009 4th IEEE Conference Industrial Electronics and Applications ICIEA 2009, pp. 3676–3681 (2009). https://doi.org/10.1109/ICIEA.2009.5138842
15. Fraiwan, L., Lweesy, K., Khasawneh, N., Wenz, H., Dickhaus, H.: Automated sleep stage identification system based on time-frequency analysis of a single EEG channel and random forest classifier. Comput. Methods Programs Biomed. **108**, 10–19 (2012). https://doi.org/10.1016/j.cmpb.2011.11.005
16. Otzenberger, H., Simon, C., Gronfier, C., Brandenberger, G.: Temporal relationship between dynamic heart rate variability and electroencephalographic activity during sleep in man. Neurosci. Lett. **229**, 173–176 (1997). https://doi.org/10.1016/S0304-3940(97)00448-5

17. Álvarez-Estévez, D., Fernández-Pastoriza, J.M., Hernández-Pereira, E., Moret-Bonillo, V.: A method for the automatic analysis of the sleep macrostructure in continuum. Expert Syst. Appl. **40**, 1796–1803 (2013). https://doi.org/10.1016/j.eswa.2012.09.022

18. Šušmáková, K., Krakovská, A.: Discrimination ability of individual measures used in sleep stages classification. Artif. Intell. Med. **44**, 261–277 (2008). https://doi.org/10.1016/j.artmed.2008.07.005

19. Yan, R., et al.: Multi-modality of polysomnography signals' fusion for automatic sleep scoring. Biomed. Signal Process. Control **49**, 14–23 (2018). https://doi.org/10.1016/j.bspc.2018.10.001

20. Seifpour, S., Niknazar, H., Mikaeili, M., Nasrabadi, A.M.: A new automatic sleep staging system based on statistical behavior of local extrema using single channel EEG signal. Expert Syst. Appl. **104**, 277–293 (2018). https://doi.org/10.1016/j.eswa.2018.03.020

21. Gharbali, A.A., Najdi, S., Fonseca, J.M.: Investigating the contribution of distance-based features to automatic sleep stage classification. Comput. Biol. Med. **96**, 8–23 (2018). https://doi.org/10.1016/j.compbiomed.2018.03.001

22. Dimitriadis, S.I., Salis, C., Linden, D.: A novel, fast and efficient single-sensor automatic sleep-stage classification based on complementary cross-frequency coupling estimates. Clin. Neurophysiol. **129**, 815–828 (2018). https://doi.org/10.1101/160655

23. Özşen, S.: Classification of sleep stages using class-dependent sequential feature selection and artificial neural network. Neural Comput. Appl. **23**, 1239–1250 (2013). https://doi.org/10.1007/s00521-012-1065-4

24. Liang, S.F., Kuo, C.E., Hu, Y.H., Pan, Y.H., Wang, Y.H.: Automatic stage scoring of single-channel sleep EEG by using multiscale entropy and autoregressive models. IEEE Trans. Instrum. Meas. **61**, 1649–1657 (2012). https://doi.org/10.1109/TIM.2012.2187242

25. Chambon, S., Thorey, V., Arnal, P.J., Mignot, E., Gramfort, A.: DOSED: a deep learning approach to detect multiple sleep micro-events in EEG signal. In: 2018 IEEE 28th International Workshop on Machine Learning Signal Processing, pp. 1–6 (2018)

26. Malafeev, A., et al.: automatic human sleep stage scoring using deep neural networks. Front. Neurosci. **12**, 1–15 (2018). https://doi.org/10.3389/fnins.2018.00781

27. Ebrahimi, F., Setarehdan, S.K., Nazeran, H.: Automatic sleep staging by simultaneous analysis of ECG and respiratory signals in long epochs. Biomed. Signal Process. Control **18**, 69–79 (2015). https://doi.org/10.1016/j.bspc.2014.12.003

28. Hermawan, I., Alvissalim, M.S., Tawakal, M.I., Jatmiko, W.: An integrated sleep stage classification device based on electrocardiograph signal. In: 2012 International Conference on Advanced Computer Science and Information Systems, pp. 37–41 (2012)

29. Krakovská, A., Mezeiová, K.: Automatic sleep scoring: a search for an optimal combination of measures. Artif. Intell. Med. **53**, 25–33 (2011). https://doi.org/10.1016/j.artmed.2011.06.004

30. Roebuck, A., et al.: A review of signals used in sleep analysis. Physiol. Meas. **35**, 1–57 (2014). https://doi.org/10.1088/0967-3334/35/1/R1

31. Trinder, J., et al.: Autonomic activity during human sleep as a function of time and sleep stage. J. Sleep Res. **10**, 253–264 (2001). https://doi.org/10.1046/j.1365-2869.2001.00263.x

32. Yan, R., Li, F., Wang, X., Ristaniemi, T., Cong, F.: An automatic sleep scoring toolbox: multi-modality of polysomnography signals' processing. In: Proceedings of the 16th International Joint Conference on E-Business Telecommunication, vol. 1, pp. 307–315 (2019). https://doi.org/10.5220/0007925503010309

33. Quan, S.F., et al.: The sleep heart health study: design, rationale, and methods. Sleep **20**, 1077–1085 (1997). https://doi.org/10.1093/sleep/20.12.1077

34. Khalighi, S., Sousa, T., Santos, J.M., Nunes, U.: ISRUC-sleep: a comprehensive public dataset for sleep researchers. Comput. Methods Programs Biomed. **124**, 180–192 (2016). https://doi.org/10.1016/j.cmpb.2015.10.013

35. Cooray, N., Andreotti, F., Lo, C., Symmonds, M., Hu, M.T.M., De Vos, M.: Automating the detection of rem sleep behaviour disorder. In: Proceedings of the Annual International Conference on IEEE Engineering Medicine and Biology Society EMBS, pp. 1460–1463, July 2018. https://doi.org/10.1109/EMBC.2018.8512539

36. Esmael, B., Arnaout, A., Fruhwirth, R.K., Thonhauser, G.: Improving time series classification using Hidden Markov Models. In: Proceedings of the 2012 12th International Conference on Hybrid Intelligent Systems HIS 2012, pp. 502–507 (2012). https://doi.org/10.1109/HIS.2012.6421385

37. Hagenauer, J., Germany, W.: A viterbi algorithm with soft-decision outputs and its applications In: The Soft-Output Symbol- by-Symbol MAP and Viter-. Compute, pp. 1680–1686 (1989)

38. Liang, S.F., Kuo, C.E., Hu, Y.H., Cheng, Y.S.: A rule-based automatic sleep staging method. J. Neurosci. Methods **205**, 169–176 (2012). https://doi.org/10.1016/j.jneumeth.2011.12.022

39. Sohn Il, S., Kim, D.H., Lee, M.Y., Cho, Y.W.: The reliability and validity of the Korean version of the Pittsburgh sleep quality index. Sleep Breath. **16**, 803–812 (2012). https://doi.org/10.1007/s11325-011-0579-9

40. Biswal, S., et al.: SLEEPNET: automated sleep staging system via deep learning. arXiv Prepr. arXiv1803.01710 (2017)

41. Phan, H., Andreotti, F., Cooray, N., Chen, O.Y., De Vos, M.: SeqSleepNet: end-to-end hierarchical recurrent neural network for sequence-to-sequence automatic sleep staging. IEEE Trans. Neural Syst. Rehabil. Eng. **27**, 400–410 (2019). https://doi.org/10.1109/TNSRE.2019.2896659

42. Zhang, L., Fabbri, D., Upender, R., Kent, D.: Automated sleep stage scoring of the sleep heart health study using deep neural networks. Sleep, 1–10 (2019). https://doi.org/10.1093/sleep/zsz159

43. Loh, W.Y., Shin, Y.S.: Split selection methods for classification trees. Stat. Sin. **7**, 815–840 (1997)

44. Rahman, M.J., Mahajan, R., Morshed, B.I.: Exacerbation in obstructive sleep apnea: early detection and monitoring using a single channel EEG with quadratic discriminant analysis. In: International IEEE/EMBS Conference on Neural Engineering NER, pp. 85–88, March 2019. https://doi.org/10.1109/NER.2019.8717054

45. Van Steenkiste, T., Groenendaal, W., Deschrijver, D., Dhaene, T.: Automated sleep apnea detection in raw respiratory signals using long short-term memory neural networks. IEEE J. Biomed. Heal. Inform. **23**, 2354–2364 (2018). https://doi.org/10.1109/JBHI.2018.2886064

Author Index

Printed in the United States
By Bookmasters